SEEKING SAFETY WITH THE SUNNAH

GREGORY HEARY

Everyone seeks safety in both the worldly life and the afterlife in every aspect in totality. The only way to achieve such comprehensive security is through the prophetic sunnah of your era, which in our modern time is that of the final prophet Muhammad bin Abdullah; as Muslims recognize. Yet despite Muslim recognition and lipservice to this valuable life raft needed to stay safe with in the tumultuous seas we travel on during our trip to our eternal homes in either paradise or hellfire, many Muslims fail to actually practice what we know the prophet(s) preached. We will claim to be Sunni and the more sincere and pious will claim to be Salafi with noble intentions but actions that fall far short of the mark we strive to shoot for. Others in the past have practically excelled beyond our highest aspirations because of many reasons. The chief reason due to this failure on our part being exactly how desperate we are in seeking safety. For someone who doesn't know how to swim, they fear drowning to such an extent that they not only will avoid the deep end of a pool, sea, lake or ocean but take extreme precaution and don't even like to get wet or go near potential swimming spots. This is because wetness at a swimming spot can lead to eventual drowning. So, for us today drowning in sins with perpetual wetness, even for those wise and strong enough to be blessed to swim to a certain extent in the ocean of sinful chaos called planet earth, we are totally in the dangerous deep end without much hope of long-term survival for our faith from a religious perspective. Unless Allah mercifully blesses us to get desperate humility so we take our precautionary security measures to the extent that care-free risky people call us crazy due to our safety concerns. Truly our intentions should be not to get wet from sins rather than just avoid drowning. Rather this is what Allah commands of believers and his special friends. You are not balanced well with one foot in the deep end of the devilish ocean and another in the desert sand around the Kaba. Just like an amphibious fish out of water, humans have a limit to our potential spiritual survival rate when we go near to sinful satanic footsteps that lead to the devil's throne above the water. Any second we spend in our lifetime flirting with danger is dangerous and a moment we will regret regarding our lifespan for which we will be brought to account for on the Day of Judgement. There are no free moments of time where God will not judge us for what we did. Everyone is accountable at all times of the day, except those with prophetic exceptions such as the prepubescent child, the insane and the sleeper. But even the sleeper can get rewarded for sleeping or punished depending on their circumstances. And the insane can be rewarded or punished as well depending on their circumstances prior to insanity. Whereas the child who has not reached puberty or the age of discernment while mercifully given more leeway regarding their life at that time still can earn rewards for what they are doing with their life. Likewise regarding the child, if they misspend their time in childhood they can still suffer for the rest of their life due to the corruption of their childhood development setting them back so much they never catch up to their peers from a faith based point of view. So, in reality there are no seconds of life that should be free from safety seeking no matter what stage of life you are in. Anyone alive who is relaxed regarding their spirituality is riskily foolish and ignorant of their reality and lowly position with their Creator. The one who feels safe spiritually is in the most danger of all. Truly the sinner who knows they a big-time trouble maker is better than the sin-free who thinks they are safe. This is because one attitude leads to seeking safety while the latter attitude leads to eventual surprise damnation. The prophets taught us to strive continuously until we die without cessation of effort. So everyone alive today has a lot of religious work left to do. Anyone relying on their good past has despaired of attaining a good future due to presently being distracted. Likewise anyone wailing over their bad past is better than the previously mentioned for such wailing is better than being distracted by imagined goodness yet still falls into the category of lost focus thereby impacting their future in a manner less than what is best. The best position most likely to result in safety is to do your best every second of your life. But what does that mean to do your best every moment in striving to attain safety? Well if you feared something in this life that threatened you with danger what would you do? You would stressfully be filled with adrenaline and act with hyper-focus until you escaped to safety and the moment of danger passed because your very life depends on it. Well, our afterlife depends on several exams we are taking and have yet to take. Thus we should be in stress mode constantly filled with spiritual adrenaline until we get to the only place of safety, paradise. Anyone less stressed than this is not blessed with the recipe for success in both lives.

If you think you are happy now, how is that possible when you don't know if you will go to heaven or hell? And if you are sad now, how is that possible if you don't know if you will go to heaven or hell? And even if you were one of the few blessed to receive authentic information from a prophet personally announcing you of your future place in paradise, then still how can you be happy when you don't know what Allah will say to you regarding all your errors? Consider even if you do eventually go to paradise and achieve security for eternity, the sins you did will have been done. Even if Allah mercifully forgives you, the fact remains that you will have always done something that Allah forbade you from doing. So how can you even enjoy yourself in paradise while cognizant of that? Nobody is perfect and it is destined that all of us err but still how can a friend of God who professes love be satisfied with any amount of crime on their permanent record even if they aren't imprisoned in the blazing hellfire? Aren't you ashamed to have a criminal record in the divine court that necessitates you begging for mercy and being granted clemency? What if Allah decides you did one sin too many to qualify for paradise? It is a sad affair indeed when other species like angels are sinless and they record our deeds, and animals act on instinct without being blameworthy on the same planet we play on. Truly humanity is heedless except those whom Allah blesses to seek safety with the Sunnah strictly as if their salvation actually depends upon it, which it does.

Certainly strictness and desperation are two qualities required for seeking salvation. In reality the desperate person is the one most strict in seeking the pleasure of their Creator in order to obtain a drink from the fountain Allah gives each prophet in the afterlife for their followers to drink from so they never go thirsty again. Are you sincere in striving to quench your thirst eternally?

If so then you must be quick to fast from sinfulness and potential sins.

The Quran was not revealed in order to cause distress but this book that I'm writing is for that purpose. Because some of us need spiritual stress in order to focus. While with the majority of medical cases shock therapy and cauterization is disliked, there are rare breeds of beings that benefit from such harsh healthcare. So to establish motivation that liberates turning cyclical sinners into faith-filled winners this treatise is designed to treat those with such characteristics. Some wild animals can be domesticated with treats and others require toughness in their training process. As such I advise myself first because I need my harsh reminders personally the most. Besides advice to oneself is more likely to impact its target audience. If I improve as a result of this book reminding me with beneficial motivation that stirs my soul then my goal is achieved. Because for you to benefit from my words while I fail to do so would put me at a great loss despite perhaps having a positive influence. Gaining influence is an extreme tragedy if you fail to correctly influence your own daily life.

Simply put, if you are not hard on yourself then who will be? Who cares more about you going to paradise and avoiding hellfire than you do? It's not going to physically harm anybody if you burn in hell. So truthfully nobody cares to fix your life up. So stop acting like a child! Become maturely responsible and act stingy with sinfulness exposure as a shrewd accountant for the betterment of your afterlife. Committing sins decreases your faith. Why then would you voluntarily choose to decrease your faith by sinning? You may never recover from such a fall. So never risk a part of your faith that you may never get back through years of struggle, if you are even given years to try to make amends for it. The similitude the Scholars give is that a person is like the perpetual climber of a ladder on their way to paradise. If you stop climbing the ladder to your Lord and go down via the lowly devilish deeds then how will you ever catch up to the other person who consistently kept climbing? Even if you obey Allah again as well as you did before you will never attain the companionship of the contemporary pious climbers you were formerly competing with. Unless you climb faster than you did before. Therefore if you ever sin, you have to play catchup and work harder than you were working before just to get back to where you would've been had you taken it easy on the road to paradise without sinning. Thus you have two options to paradise, the easier sin-free path or the path where you constantly work harder and harder and harder getting more and more pious everytime you sin. But then in such a case is it likely for a sinner to always get better than they were before the sin? When did sinning become a way to become pious? The opposite is usually the case in that the sinful gets slower in climbing towards paradise because their past ruins their piety potential even if they get forgiven. For if you were so pious that you were going to get increasingly more and more pious then wouldn't you do so without sinning in the first place? Why weren't you trying your best before you made a mess and forced yourself into a position where you have to increase your spiritual progress speed merely to attain the spot you were scheduled to be at before you sinned? Time is not a luxury we can waste on sinfulness. So don't fool yourself into the path of downgrades. Do your best now so you don't have to do a better job tomorrow to get into the spot you could have today. It could take more than a week to recover from a single second of sin committed in a weak moment, and even if you do recover you will be weaker in the future as a result. Wounds hurt warriors. We are in a spiritual warzone as long as we are alive. So how many hits can you afford to take before you get knocked out? I don't want any more crimes on my record to ask my Lord forgiveness for. Truly it is a virtue to beg Allah alone for forgiveness and it pleases him to supplicate for purification. But aren't you ashamed to have your main spiritual virtue being constant apologies? It's great to always apologize as fast as possible even if you do so often due to errors. Yet don't you have dignity of character? Why is it every time you sincerely beg Allah with tears it is because you messed up big-time? Aren't you ashamed enough so that you are never ashamed in such a state again? Aren't you prominent enough and blessed enough that you are going to keep your promise not to return to sin? Instead of your piety being in that you constantly promise not to repeat sins you allegedly repent from, wouldn't you want to be the person that says "I repented sincerely years ago and never did that sin again." Rather than the one who says, "Sorry Allah, I did it again even though I said I would never do it again." Aren't you tired of the cycle and the recycling of your repentance speeches? Let's say Allah forgave you as generous as Allah is and as undeserving as you are. What benefit did you gain? You would have a life of crime that you don't get punished for much. What reward can you expect for that? Do criminals get praise and glory after release from prison on parole for good behavior? Or is it those who never did crimes to get incarcerated that are more advantageous in their ranking? Blessed forgiveness for your sins is different than getting blessed rewards for doing good. The two cannot be compared and the distance between them is like night and day. Do you prefer living in the darkness of disobedience or the light of unquestioned total loyalty to Allah? Wouldn't you prefer to be someone who Allah knows their voice for asking for blessings instead of the one Allah only knows for their frequent pleas for forgiveness? Realistically you have two options. You could be someone who the Judge constantly reads reports of your crimes in the news. Or you could be someone who the Judge constantly reads reports of your good deeds in the news that angels bring. Which do you want to be?

Islam is a religion and lifestyle that closes the doors to all evils and potential evils. This is because prevention from sickness is a better cure than medicine is once diseased by the dangers of sin. Thus we have to Quarantine ourselves from sin and exposure to sin as if we were living through a global pandemic cautious about contagion as if our life depended on it. Because our salvation in the afterlife does in fact depend on it. The world is like a fire. Fire does have some benefit to it if used correctly but it's a whole lot more dangerous than it is beneficial. So for the sake of God be careful! For the sake of God can you stop doing crimes! How? Well we already know the questions and the correct answers on the test of life we are taking, along with what to prepare for in the grave, because the Merciful Almighty Judge told us through revelation and prophets exactly how to succeed guaranteed. So does that finally motivate you to learn to read and understand Arabic? Or are you content in getting the translated version of Allah's speech and translations of the rules for life? Would you ever want to take an exam in any other important course relying on foreign language translations other students studying for the same test made based on the notes they got from the teachers? Or would you care enough to learn what the teachers (prophets) actually taught word for word? While it's possible to pass with strict adherence to translated course material, isn't it a lot wiser to align your linguistic abilities with the divine speech itself? Allah sent an Arabic book and you believe it but you didn't care enough to learn to read it verbatim? Did you ever ask forgiveness for that too? Or are you acting like a foreigner trying to graduate from all the difficult advanced university classes while never bothering to learn the language the textbooks are in? How can the person who can't read the textbook as it is do as well on the test as the person who can? It's possible but unlikely, especially when even Arabs make mistakes and they have better access to the prophetic religion than non-Arabs. The point is if you spent the time you were sinning on learning Arabic you would not find trouble mastering it.

Instead of becoming a criminal mastermind you could become a mindful person using time wisely to maximize your spiritual potential increasing your odds of friendship with Allah. Truly aren't' you ashamed to believe in Allah's Arabic book the Quran and then meet Allah without having learned Arabic or sincerely trying to do so with all your abilities? Or if you believe the devils who tell you that's you are incapable of fluently learning the language Allah sent his prophetic teachings in, what is your problem with learning the language of silence? Truly Allah's Messenger taught us to speak that which is good or remain silent. Arabic is not an absolute requirement for salvation, but speaking good in whatever language you know or being silent is a requirement for safety. While you may be a rare quality person who could pass life's tests without Arabic with high ranking, you cannot get such a status without utilizing silence as if your life and afterlife depend on it. So please be quiet! If you were wise, you would have nothing to do with that which doesn't benefit your afterlife. While if you weren't stupid you would refrain from all that harms your afterlife. Regardless of whether you are wise or just "not stupid" the believer doesn't get involved with matters that do not concern them. That means living a life actively avoiding everything that doesn't concern the improvement of your soul and your afterlife.

The Jewish Samiri who sinned in the time of Moses had as his punishment to tell people not to touch him, as a form of self-quarantine from his wicked sinfulness. Today we live with people worse than Samiri who rightly should warn us to not even listen to them or look at them. And even if they don't have the courtesy to warn us, we know better but look anyway or we know better and hear their evil without fear of contamination. So, if you know better why aren't you acting better? If you truly want to be a sincere friend of Allah, then when will you stop acting like one of Allah's sinful enemies?

Truly defending yourself from the temptations of evil sins is not the smartest defense. The truly smart defense is to never even be defending yourself because you never allow yourself to be in a position to need to defend. If you never play the defense game when not needed then you can't lose. But it's whenever you are playing defense that losing is always a possibility regardless of the scenario you are playing under. Even a perfect defense is risky due to defense naturally being a negative position to be in. As Allah commands not coming near zina, following the footsteps of shaitan, not taking kuffar as friends, etc. The smart person does not open the door to even see the paths to shaitan's footsteps, or look at them through the windows, or even see the door to the path, or live in a house nearby the path of Shaitan's footsteps; because the closer you get to battle then the closer defeat could be. Hence just as a sane healthy person doesn't riskily expose themselves to potential contagious diseases like COVID or other illnesses, the spiritually sane doesn't risk exposure to sinful environments and immediately flees from unplanned accidental exposure just as one flees from a pandemic plague. The wise warrior of Allah doesn't willingly expose themselves to the plots of shaitan. Because once you are fighting the plots of shaitan you are likely to lose track of the plots and fall off the straight track of the blessed path to paradise. Seeking refuge in Allah from shaitan doesn't mean supplicating with dua in prayers then playing with fire constantly fighting shaitan every moment hoping for total victory or a final winning percentage. Otherwise Prophet Muhammad would have fought in every military battle possible against kuffar. But prophets only fought when needed and wise to do so. And even then, the prophets were not undefeated in their battles. Thereby showing even when divinely guided by Allah to pick your battles with maximum wisdom, one can still suffer defeat sometimes. So how about the one who takes unnecessary risks with Kufr, Shirk, Bida and sin exposure? If we treated sin like it was as contagious and dangerous as COVID during the pandemic when the world was in isolationist quarantine before there was a vaccine, we still wouldn't be strict enough. May Allah protect all Muslims and guide them to true protection in the dunya and akhira as all those creatures whom Allah doesn't protect are doomed and accursed.

Likewise, our advisors and companionship should be chosen as you choose poison to consume. For it is better to be alone than with supportive kafirs, innovators or sinners. Sometimes it's even better to live with animals than certain humans because animals do less harm to your religion via animal behavior than kind supportive kafirs or innovators. As Allah says not to take the kuffar as supporters, helpers or friends lest you be like them. Allah knows some kafirs will profess love for us but are incapable of it due to their disbelief, even if sincerity were possible for such people whom Allah says will always harbor hidden religious hatred inside. Allah offers protection for us in his commands but many get fooled by comfortable slogans and catchphrases. So religiously comfortable support from kuffar is dangerous because it causes you to let your guard down to the devils of mankind. Crusaders learned swords don't work against Muslims and entertainment is more effective, so now the kuffar try entertaining us rather than torture to get us to join in with kufr, shirk, bida and sins. And this diabolical method works to a greater extent. Entertainment is the main kafir entryway to the heart today. Rather than come with pitchforks to exterminate Islam they come with TV remotes and the Internet world full of freedom from the safety of Islamic standards.

As the quote popularly attributed to Ali says: "it is better to listen to a wise enemy than seek counsel from a foolish friend." Since kuffar are inherent fools due to ignorance of Islam along with being enemies of Allah, prophets, and believers then friendly kafir companions are like consulting a foolish enemy. So when foolish friends are worse than wise enemies, what benefit is there in foolish enemies who try befriending you? They are in reality the most dangerous especially when they are too foolish to know or claim they are your enemies and profess to love you. Hence the sincere religious opponent of the Muslim at least claims to desire your salvation just like the dajjal/antichrist will. But the idiotic nominally religious non-Muslim "supporter of Muslims" insincerely claims to love you while believing incorrectly you are going to hell for not being a mushrik or kafir like them. In summary what goodness is there in worldly pampering from people who claim they support you in your choice to go to hell? Such as a secularist government that promotes freedom of religious choices. It would be better logistically to be at war with such people than peace because it is then less dangerous to the societal and individual religiosity because such peaceful support is in fact anti-religious. Whereas religious battles or conflict at least prioritize the afterlife for everybody. Hence Allah commands not taking kuffar as awliyya even during peace times and Hadith state the Prophet has nothing to do with Muslims who live within sight of mushrik fires. So consider how Muhammad has a bond with non-jihadi Muslims who refuse to fight in war and even flee from battlefields with the enemy, but the prophet said he has no bond with those who live within eyesight of kafir fires.

This shows us many lessons in the dangers of living with or alongside non-Muslims of any type. Meaning it is actually safer to refuse commands from a Muslim ruler to enlist in the Muslim army during wartime, which we know is impious and risks disbelief, than it is to live in comfortable peace in kafir vicinity during peacetime. I admit the advanced scholastic interpretation is better than mine. Yet if we are forbidden to see the mushrik fires from afar, then what of the Muslim spending countless hours in the glow of TV shows and internet videos produced by kuffar? Aren't the kafir

TV channels more dangerous to our deen than their cooking fires? With the advent of globalized communication it essentially turns the whole world into a spiritual melting mixing pot or warzone.

Traditionally it used to be said, the best strategy is to divide and conquer. But if we as Muslims, on a personal lifestyle level, are not divided from kuffar and kafir culture and evil as strangers in this dunya then we cannot conquer kufr, let alone the kuffar. Hence interfaith teambuilding and watering down the deen in reality is fleeing the spiritual battlefield and preventing Islamic victory. Because unity with kafir culture means not abolishing evil. Thus many try to exist in the wilderness in a wild era when the Muslim lands with national religions of Islam and Islamic laws still exist. Hence the importance of building civilization from the seeds the Salaf planted in Arab/Muslim lands takes precedence over dawah to kafirs in the jungle of the Wild West. But Allah puts his soldiers where he desires as a test. Yet every Muslim deep in kafir territory should emigrate before they go crazy or lose their deen. Because peacefully it's a spiritual warzone where people strictly upon the prophetic path get called crazy just as the prophet was in a nonsecular deeply religious land. Thus absolute strictness is the only safety net that can prevent us from falling into evil that we may never survive the dangers of.

When are you going to be a practitioner of Islam instead of just a preacher? Instead of being just a part-time preacher, you should be a full-time practitioner of Islam as well. Rather than have the Shahada be your slogan, your soul should go all in on it by living the motto until you finish your death throes. For how many times will you pass a graveyard or witness a funeral for the dead, then continue doing wrong failing to live right, after knowing you will soon be dead just like them? If you needed a good deed for every day you spent dead in the grave before the day of Judgement in order to save you from punishment in the grave, would you have enough? What if you were punished for a maximum of just one day in the grave for every bad deed you did? Would you ever stop doing bad? What kind of similitude does a sinner need to stop? How many examples of your evil need to be explained before you decide to quit? Will you stick to your repentance for God's sake!

Allah has taught you the method of sincere repentance and preferred you above billions of other creatures by giving you such knowledge of how to repent correctly. With other creatures Allah has not blessed them with knowledge of repentance because Allah does not want to forgive them, so he doesn't even bother teaching them how to ask for it. You know how to repent, but you constantly relapse into sin after repenting and are a perpetual promiser whose word is losing worth due to repetition without firm resolve. Don't despair of Allah's Mercy, but at some point in your life you have to stop abusing Allah's Mercy. You don't get a free pass to commit all the sins on earth and then just say a repentance speech and attain pardon. You must work hard on yourself, more than you do on others. You work so hard encouraging others to do good and avoid evil but you must be hardest on yourself. For if others disobey your invitations to abandon evil and embrace goodness it will not harm you in the least, even though it stings. But if you yourself continue in sin, whether it is recognized by others or not, it will seriously harm you more than it would if millions of others tried to.

You can be your best hero if you follow the prophetic guidance and your own advice to do so. Or you can be your own villain for constant criminality and a life of crime. And we didn't even touch much on doing the time for your crime, potentially for all eternity. We are just saying a little of what Allah made evident, which is a further testament that if Allah put this evidence in front of you to know, then there is a damn good reason it got to you! The destined advice reached you because the excuses are running out. Plain and simple, you are running out of excuses for living a sinful life. How many times will you sin and then say you will do better, then sin and say it again and repeat the cycle? What is stopping you from action and actually achieving goodness? The two paths of goodness and evil are clear, are they not? The problem is you have been walking the path of evil for so long, that in order to backtrack and recover your spot on the road to paradise you have to run a marathon to get back to the fork in the road where you choose the paved path to paradise. You can do succeed! You truly can do it, even though it will be painfully difficult at times for quite awhile until you get to safety in the gardens of paradise. But what you can't do at all costs is keep going further down the path leading to the hellfire. That will make everything worse. So even if you can't get through the marathon to the path to paradise escaping all your sinful footsteps of the past, at least stop making tracks progressing to the place of promised punishment. Meaning, please don't get worse. And by staying the same as you are for the rest of your life that is worse, because you are expected to improve as you grow. Sinful stagnation is a lack of growth which is sinful in itself. So you can't stay still on the path to sinfulness. Either you are getting less and less sinful or you are worse, or worse and worse; may Allah protect us all.

Just as a parent gives a baby one spoonful at a time waiting patiently for them to finish before feeding them more nutrition for their body, Allah feeds our spirituality as we are ready for it. Some creatures never open their heart for the first spoonful of prophetic Islamic guidance and doom themselves. Others reject the taste after awhile. While some of us have been on the same bite of Islam for far too long and haven't developed as we could have and should have due to our sins. Realistically that makes us spiritual babies that have not yet developed as much as we should have. That is a big problem. It wouldn't be as much of an issue if theoretically you were doing all the obligatory and voluntary goodness you could, and honestly could testify to Allah you just cannot do anything more to be a better person. But that ain't the case, is it? You haven't been doing all that you could every moment of your life. There have been times you deliberately knew you were doing wrong and you did it anyways. So you can never ever say to Allah that you did all you could and couldn't have been better. You know and Allah knows that you screwed up so many times and that you've been sinning on earth longer than others have been alive on it! You have more years of sin than others have of living. So let's get genuine about our options. It's not worth mentioning all the stuff you could've done worse, or the stuff you could've done better for that matter, because what was destined to occur has occurred. But from today onward you can stop playing games and live a strict sincere good-doer's life until death. That is not too hard, not even for you. Allah taught you right from wrong so you can start doing what is right and escaping what is wrong and learning more. There are many types of knowledge of right and wrong that Allah hasn't taught you yet because you weren't ready for it yet, to put it politely. Yet now that you are going to be acting correctly upon what you know, there's going to be a lot more time to learn more goodness because you are going to cut off the evil actions and things that lead you to get triggered to commit illegal evil in Allah's law. You have to mercilessly push yourself to be good in order to qualify for the Mercy of Allah. You may or may not forgive yourself for your crimes, that's not important, but you do need Allah to forgive you. And Allah remembers all your sins, even the ones you will forget to ask forgiveness for, because you will think Allah forgave you when you failed to properly repent. So, rather than roam around racking up more sins because you think God forgave your crimes already and you can afford more crimes on your record before the divine Court date, instead we have to be realistic and realize that Allah didn't give us a receipt stamped certificate of forgiveness for a single sin. Do you realize that? Do you understand you don't have a ticket to paradise with you to take into your grave? You do understand your sins do grant you a ticket to punishment right? So, if you are 100% sure you are a criminal awaiting your trial and you have no guarantee of the Judge forgiving you for any of your past crimes, then why are you acting otherwise? Does a criminal continue their criminal activity when they are actively seeking a full merciful pardon? Or do they put on their best performance of good behavior? As the believer is a prisoner in this world, prior to entering paradise, you truly have to act like you just got out of jail and are on parole. Realistically the Judge, Allah, knows all your crimes and is about to pronounce your sentence for eternity. Yet you are out on bail living on earth prior to your day in God's court. For some of us we would be better off imprisoned before our Court date because we are such hardened criminals that we cannot resist committing crime even though we promised the Judge before we wouldn't sin anymore. How many times have we faced death or even just begged for more time to be alive to do good to amend our evil sins and we got more life? And then we did more crime again?! So for that reason my judgement is, that it is justly deserved that you are imprisoned for the rest of your life for your sins that you perpetrated time and again. However Allah is so Merciful he has not sentenced many of us criminals to be imprisoned for life to reduce our sinfulness or punish us. But it might have been better for us if we were. Yet since we are not physically prevented from sin in solitary confinement for the rest of our life, we have a severe test and higher responsibility. Just imagine if you were imprisoned in solitary confinement and then released? Would you go about breaking the laws of the judge that released you? Well Allah didn't even waste your time with imprisoning you yet. Allah gave you extra time to enjoy and prove you were good and didn't deserve the punishment your prior crimes indicate you deserve. But you still got that Court date after you die. So in reality you are on parole now, mercifully not serving your lifetime in solitary confinement in hell; which you already deserve. As a parolee, if you have to dissociate from sinners and sinful environments in order to prevent the slightest possibility of committing crime willfully or accidentally that would result in your future imprisonment then would you do so? If you would escape future incarceration in an inferno of hellfire through such a means, then please take all the steps necessary and even those steps deemed unnecessary just to ensure your spiritual safety and Allah's pleasure. Really come to terms with the truth of this reality. You are a sinful criminal! You deserve, by virtue of your sinfulness, eternity in hell imprisoned forever; or at the very least hellfire for your remaining lifespan. Allah allows you the rest of your life on earth, on bail or parole or whatever you want to call it, but on condition you stop sinning as much and do the good that you know you should do or else you are going prison immediately upon death or upon committing crime. If we realize sin is a type of crime and death that we may never even be able to recover from, even through sincere monotheistic Islamic repentance, would we sin again? Would we come near to sin? If someone told you that if you do the sins you did in your past in the future, then they would imprison you in solitary confinement for the rest of your life, without torture, would you do those sins again? Well Allah, the most powerful and severe in punishment, has promised you extremely torturous pain in the grave until the Day of Judgement and punishment in Hellfire for eternity and punishment in your worldly life in ways you don't even perceive; if you commit sins. So what excuse do you have? What leverage can you utilize? What escape plan will save you from prison? The recipe for sincere life-long repentance that will likely lead to success in doing the rest of your Islamic duty to God fully for the rest of your life. Meaning, do your damn best! And I mean, do your damn best or you are damned. Not just for today, or this week, or this month, or this year, or this decade, or this century. You do your best every single second to avoid sin at all costs, or else you are going to eternal prison and can expect punishment throughout your life too. That's the only option you got for avoiding hellfire and maybe getting a chance at paradise if Allah blesses you. But at this point in your crime spree, you don't need to be worried about the bounties of paradise. You already bought many tickets to hellfire which you know are paid in full many times over. So before we even think about thinking about paradise, we have to get the crime spree to stop and work on building up our good reputation with Allah with good behavior at all times in all places in all circumstances following Islamic Shariah in all ways always.

This may be your last time to heed sincere advice. Don't be someone who needs to hear it more than once. Make it stick and make a difference in your life. You can make a lifelong commitment to give up the sins and learn as you go on how to make your lifestyle changes easier. Yet that step must be made. The step towards your personal perfection. The step towards you being truly the best Muslim you can be to where you can say to Allah in front of all the pious people on Judgement Day, as of this moment in time in my life I firmly resolved to be the best Muslim I possibly could be and ever since then I proved it as my lifetime from that moment on shows, so please forgive us for what preceded that moment and bless us for what followed that moment. Now is that moment and you cannot go backwards. The message has come to you. So whether you make the commitment sincerely, or not, there honestly is no alternative; for you will be testifying on Judgement Day about it regardless of what you do. I sincerely advise you for the sake of your Maker do whatever it is you need to do to give up sinfulness. No matter how long your sinful list of crimes is, there is no reason to commit any more adding to your evil ranking. Instead it is finally time that you are going to be a good person at all times forever. And yes, that includes repentance for mistakes. But from now on, the goal is to not have sins to repent for. Instead we should be repenting for choosing a lower value good deed instead of a higher value good deed that we would have performed if we possessed more knowledge of goodness.

If the only reward for doing a good deed is keeping you out of sinful trouble then it is worth doing it. And if the only punishment of sinfulness was that it wasted your time by preventing you from doing a good deed, then that is far too risky to ever sin. Yet we know the reality of sin is far worse than a mere wastage of time, because it results in obtaining a criminal record with the Divine Judge who watches us at all times and threatened us with tortuous harm for eternity for committing sin and promised us blissful reward for sincere good deeds.

As is attributed to Umar bin Khattab, "He who does not live in the way of his beliefs starts to believe in the way he lives." Therefore stop believing you are good due to the poor spirituality of your contemporaries so you become arrogantly lazy and complacent, which inevitably leads you back to sin and loss. Harshly examine yourself with a stricter criteria, stricter than your society's, stricter than your own, stricter than even the salaf whom we are hoping to follow on the pure path of prophetic instruction. You must examine yourself according to Allah's criteria and you will find yourself in need of immense Mercy for falling far short in all aspects. The good news is you have a lot to improve because you are far from perfect, so you can take many easy steps alongside moderate and major steps. Yet you do need a major attitude adjustment in your perspective to avoid the redundancy of rust upon the heart that prevents sincere striving towards spiritual improvement.

Once prophet Muhammad gathered his people by shouting loudly on Mount Safa near Mecca. The

Prophet ﷺ said: *"If I told you that the horsemen were advancing to attack you from the valley or the other side of this hill, would you believe me?"*

"Yes," they replied, bewildered at his question. "We have always found you honest." Then he said to them: *"I am here to warn you before a severe chastisement reaches you. I see the enemy charging toward you, and I want to protect you from his sword, but I fear he will strike you before I can give you warning. This is why I have cried out to you from atop this hill."*

Addressing everyone, the Prophet warned: *"O people of Quraysh, ransom yourselves from Allah and save yourselves from the Fire of Hell, for I am not the master of your gain and loss, nor can I be of any help in saving you from Allah. O Banu Ka'bin Lu'ayy, save yourselves from Hell, for I am not the master of your gain and loss. O Banu Qusayy! Save yourselves from Hell. O Banu Abdu Munaf! Save yourselves from Hell, for I am not the master of your gain and loss. O Banu Hashim! Save yourselves from Hell. O Banu Abdul Muttalib! Save yourselves from Hell, for I am not the master of your gain and loss, and cannot save you from Allah. Take from my property as much as you desire, but I have no power to save you from Allah.*

O Abbas bin Abdul Muttalib! I can be of no help to you in saving you from Allah. O Aunt of the Messenger, Safiyah bint Abdul Muttalib! I can be of no help to you in saving you from Allah. O Fatimah, daughter of the Messenger! Ask for whatever you want from my property, but save yourself from Hell. I cannot be of any help to you, and I will fulfil my obligations accordingly."

This message of dire warning from the hellfire applies to everyone. Even the disbelievers confessed they would believe and prepare themselves if Muhammad was warning of an enemy army behind the mountain. So you already know that death, your grave, and your judgement within sight of the eternal hellfire is a guaranteed reality even more dangerous to you than an enemy army. So why do you not strongly guard yourself vigilantly? Had anyone of any credibility, or even those lacking credibility, warned you of a threatening menace coming to harm you such as a robber, rapist, murderer or foreign military invasion directed at you, then you would be afraid and take precautions. Even the slightest economic turbulence has you contemplating how to position your finances to minimize potential wealth destruction. So, what are you doing to protect your soul from harm? Why are you so nonchalant? Do you think saying you believe and doing a few requirements of the true Islamic faith has pre-ordered your ticket to paradise paving your way over the sirat above hellfire, which is thinner than a hair and sharper than a sword, crossed in the darkest of darknesses only by those given light by the Almighty due to their proven sincere faith and good deeds outweighing their evil? How careful will you step when walking such a long bridge over the hellfire while the hooks and thorns harm you and your balance according to your sinfulness? Could you walk across a gymnastic balance beam or even a street curb with such high stakes? You wouldn't walk on a tightrope over an ocean calmly, but you feel ready to walk over the hellfire? If you knew the reward for success was eternal paradise and the reward for failure was eternal hellfire, how much effort would you give for your tightrope balancing? And if you were told ahead of time that all your sins will equal extra hardships in your task then would you sin as you have been? The actual matter is much more serious than that!

For the Hellfire will roar in powerful anger demanding Allah for more sinners and more! And

Allah will comply to the Hellfire's demands repeatedly multiple times adding more people to Hellfire. Allah will ask every time whether Hellfire is full. The Hellfire will hungrily request more by asking if there are any more who qualify for entry. What gives you safety? Are you brave enough to sincerely tell Allah your Judge in front of Hellfire and all others that you don't deserve to be given up to the Hellfire's request to burn you? Or is the Hellfire going to make a stronger argument based on the testimony of the earth, the angels, others you wronged and yourself? How will you get saved when you know that you are already doomed and rightly deserve to be damned in hellfire for your crimes? What makes you so special to the Almighty Allah that Allah will put his foot in the hellfire to fill it up, before sending you to Hell? Why should God put his foot in Hell for you, the daily sinner? Your only option is to sincerely repent from your sinful crimes and pursue perfection from now on. Just as Adam did. You know the serious consequences of Adam's first sin, as you suffer on earth because of it. But after Allah forgave Adam for that sin do you know of any other sin Adam did on earth? No? Well then, why are you living a life on earth more sinful than Adam when you know Adam's one sin had such devastating long-term consequences? That was one sin Adam did, which was forgiven in full by Allah. But you don't know if any one of your many sins are forgiven by Allah. So how can you relax? You not only are not stressed out, but you are so forgetful of your past you actually foolishly think you are good because you cannot remember all your evil due to doing so much. Do you think that is a sign of goodness and blessing that you have done so many sins it is impossible for you to keep count of them? No! Rather it would be a blessing if you could count them. For to be such a criminal mastermind as you are and forget your criminality is a characteristic of those whom Allah wants to punish with a powerful permanent surprise. Thus perfection for the rest of your life is the recipe to maybe balance out the scale of justice so that maybe when your life is done Allah may recognize the sincere effort to change for the better in every area of life at all times; and maybe you will have done one more good deed to outweigh a lifetime of crime or perhaps Allah may forgive the past that passed based on your future reformation. But you must start working harder and smarter according to the Sunnah to have any hope of safety when you die.

Be patiently persistent when you mess up in the process of spiritual reformation, as criminal rehabilitation doesn't happen overnight. It takes a lifetime of struggle to successfully repent. When repenting during your paroled life sentence, perform extra deeds that will outlast your lifespan. For example, sadaqah jariah will survive as goodness for you after you die. And while charity is hard for the stingy misers and requires true belief in the promise of Allah, in reality if you have a smart system then you can utilize your own wickedness against your own wickedness. For your disease of loving wealth you can set up a system that for certain sins you will pay a price in charity, that is in additional to your daily charity. Which I advise every Muslim gives daily charity just as Muhammad instructed us all to do in various ways. But if you are paying a meaningful price every time you sin, perhaps eventually you will sin less because you will fear the expensive cost and your greedy side will say you cannot afford the sin since it will know of your habit to donate every time you do taubah and sin. Surely it's not a winning system to donate due to sin, but it's less of a losing system that can ultimately improve your statistics and odds of eternal success. Don't think it's piety to be giving charity after every sin, you are supposed to be abstaining from sin while giving charity. But to get to that point from where you are now, it is an idea and discipline that can help you develop further.

Discipline in demeanor is important to develop. This is because anger that exceeds the limits or is for other than the sake of Allah is perhaps the unknown root of all sin. For the one who is satisfied with the destiny of Allah and happy with the Shariah would not even contemplate voluntary sin, unless they were angry with the destiny of Allah or Shariah's confinement of their desires/deeds to a certain extent. To be pleased with your destiny is to be pleased with a life of strict obedience to the divine law of Allah. Mistakes could happen, but to circumvent the law intentionally with sin indicates one is angry at something. Without such anger the motivation for sin would be too weak to influence one to action. For example, having a sinful lustful desire may occur. However it is only due to anger with the feelings of chastity and the impatience to lawfully fulfill that desire with a legal spouse in the legal way in an appropriate time that contributes to sinful action upon such a desire. So anger at patience upon obedience is an underlying factor influencing many sinners. Hence I say, unislamic anger is the root cause of all sins and even Islamic anger for the sake of Allah can become sinful if it is not managed and controlled well according to the Sunnah. Therefore the Prophet Muhammad advised not to get angry while emphasizing that true strength is in controlling anger. However safety lies in early prevention rather than medicine. So if one never gets angry except when and how Allah desires, then such a person has a higher rate of successfully emancipating themselves from enslavement to their emotions and the sins caused by such emotions. For anger, especially when unislamic and uncontrolled, is almost similar in destructiveness as is intoxication, or insanity, or being possessed by devil(s). Even for those genuinely oppressed, anger can lead to danger of over-retaliation that leads to the original victim becoming indebted to their abuser due to exceeding the limits of justified justice. Hence if you want safety from the route to over-retaliation leading to sin then maintain good manners even when faced with evil from others. Thus we must speak and do good or remain silent and harmless even if/when suffering harm. It is no coincidence that madness or the label of being mad is used to describe both anger and insanity, because the two are related in how anger is a disabling emotion most of the time. Anger is a weakness that leads to sin generally. What is right should be done whether angry or not, but whenever you are angry then you become vulnerable to extremely sinful transgression. The safe one regarding anger, does not get angry. While the only one I know who can protect us from anger is Allah the Creator. So I advise you make daily dua for specific protection from such a dangerous emotion and to die a blessed death as a Muslim. Don't limit yourself to seeking protection from sins only, but the causes that lead to sin as well. The rotten core of human anger is a fundamental surprise displeasure at the destiny of Allah. Whereas since acceptance of destined Qadr is a pillar of the Islamic faith, how can a true believer ever get angry at something destined to occur if they truly believe in the destiny of Allah; good and bad, sweet or bitter, surprising or predictable?

Consider as well how powerless Satan truly is, as the Quran states Iblis himself will confess his only ability was to invite us to sin and he had no authority in reality to manipulate us against our will. Meaning our willpower is stronger than Satan and his armies of jinn and humans but we forget Allah much thus we forget our enemies and fall into traps much. So we must remember Allah more to be safer in the future. Yet the death of your soul due to a thousand small cuts by Satan is no less dangerous than if you gave up voluntarily to a Satanic one cut spiritually fatal execution. So never ever underestimate the value of 1 single sin. You truly will regret sin more than any hardship of life. If you only knew the Honor of the Lord you disobey when you sin you would prefer every calamity to occur to you that is possible and even those that are impossible than to sin a single time. For in the grave your deeds will come to you to be your companion in the form of a person, either smelling well or worse than anything smelled on earth, as is reported in authentic hadith. Now imagine if your deeds companion smelled to the stench of 1 fart for every sin you did in your life, multiplied by the power of 1 fart for each additional sin. How would you survive such a stinky companion in your grave until Judgement Day, even if your own deeds companion were the only punishment you had? Also if you smelled like a fart on earth according to the power of such a mathematical calculation due to your sinfulness you would be ashamed of the people and boycotted. But have you not any shame to know Allah considers your sin more repulsive than passing gas? Have you no shame to have angels who worship Allah without sin write your sins to such a voluminous extent? Are you trying to kill the angels due to exhaustion from your efforts in evil? Are you trying to make the angelic book reports on your sinful crimes fill a large library?

Why not change the situation as you have already proven yourself capable of doing in certain ways? You do not commit every sin the divine law forbids? Why? Because you resist and are strong against certain sins. With some sins you may have had a long history doing them whether you knew they were sinful or not, and then you changed and gave them up. So why is it that you can go without committing certain sins 100% of the time, which you yourself had been habitually accustomed to ignorantly committing for a long time, but in regards to other sins you still can't quit? In reality you can but you need to plan wisely with strong effort. Truthfully if you were sincerely obedient to Allah in every aspect of life then you would not have this dilemma of partial abstentation from sin. Because the sin does not lie in the deed itself. The sinfulness of every sin is because Allah has forbidden it. If Allah forbade A and B and C deeds then if you were true in your obedience to Allah you would also abstain from all sinful deeds without distinction as to which category, major or minor, or what your personal sin preferences where. At the core of the matter, you must determine whether your heart is refraining from the other sins due to love for Allah or for your own personally acquired hate of that particular sin which is biased to that specific sin you refrain from but less powerful in regards to other sins you commit? Why is it that some sins we love to do more than we love to obey Allah? But other sins we love to obey Allah more than we would enjoy the sin? Such an attitude is a dangerous methodology of taking sins lightly due to our judgement of them instead of Allah's judgement of them. It's true that not all sins are equal in their evil but all sins are labeled as disobedience to Allah and decrease our precious spiritual faith. So treat sin and sinful opportunities and potential sins as something that is taking away your very faith which you need more than anything. Don't volunteer to eliminate your faith levels by any amount of sin at all! Your faith increases with good deeds and only should go down due to mistakes in lacking good deeds, not because we are choosing to decrease our spiritual connection with God by doing crimes. If the internet connection or phone reception is lost for many it is a calamity, so what about risking our connection with our one unique divine Creator?

As a secret mission, instead of having your secret private life be something that Allah knows is worse than what people think of you, make your secret private life be something better than what people think you are like. Imagine if people knew your sins in this life they would criticize and abandon you. Allah knows your sins and is giving you time to seek safety with him through the prophetic Sunnah and improve. If you don't improve then Allah will expose everything on Judgement Day when the criminals are tortured with justice and the repenting Muslim monotheists are paid rewards in paradise. Never give up your faithful struggle versus Satan's traps of sinfulness. Instead make Satan despair when you die upon Islamic goodness and the angels tell you have no fear while they take you to meet your Lord, prior to the interrogation in the grave you are soon to dwell in for a long time; of which decomposition will be the minimum potential harm sinners qualify to get.

The rest of this book contains knowledge about how in practice to attain a closer relationship with Allah through clinging to the safety of the Sunnah of the final prophet Muhammad. Repeatedly in the Quran Allah warns us to not come near certain things, people, places, etc. These warnings are to perfect us and our behavior making us stop short of sin by following the perfect religion. Have you never considered how Islam is the perfected religion as Allah says and wondered if perhaps it is possible to attain some definition of perfection if only you adhered to the perfect religion as best as truly possible instead of just better than those few you know? It is only when we ignore these warnings that we end up in dangerous tests where we must battle strenuously with Satan where we have a possibility of losing and then have to hasten to repent in order to try to expunge our criminal record of errors. Had we heeded the warnings and not come near what leads to sinful behavior in the first place, we never would have committed the sin that grants us a spot in the lowest of places in hell. Had we been strict in following the Sunnah in not just the obligatory but the recommended as well, by avoiding the forbidden along with what leads to the forbidden and the disliked and whatever leads to the disliked we would be living a blessed life. Yet the sad fact is many are living a sinful life praying for blessings, which is oxymoronic because blessings are not known to be obtained through sin. Yet we sin almost as though we expect to get rewarded for it. And we avoid doing good deeds as though we expect to be punished for them. Therefore we need an extreme improvement in our mentality and lifestyle when it comes to how we are living and how we think about how we are living. Allah warns us that if we do X we will get punished unless Allah forgives us which Allah may or may not do. Allah warns us not to come near to X so that we never get into a position of needing much forgiveness due to sinful crimes. So as a desperately needed reminder that will benefit the believers, I am trying to compile some of these warnings of Allah and the prophetic Muhammadean Sunnah for our era because the only safety we can get is by strict sincere consistent lifelong adherence to these warning signs that warn us of the poisonous harm these sins will have on us. For my warnings are of miniscule importance compared to Allah's warnings found in the Shariah. While the remaining text by no means comprises the entirety of Shariah law, or even all the forbidden matters, it is meant to highlight some of the major "Do NOT do" crimes we must take extra precaution against. Basically it is a collection of things to beware of which Allah and his Prophet Muhammad emphatically placed special emphasis on for us to beware of so that we do not err. There are other things we are forbidden from as well that are not mentioned in this book, but no single creature's book can comprise every prohibition for all of time and every circumstance in total detailed specificity. So consider this a small collection of reminders about major no nos. If Allah's words and his prophet's commands have no impact on you to not commit something then what will? What do you need to change? A book from Allah? The Quran is sent already. A prophet to educate you further? Muhammad conveyed the message already. The message has been received by you at this time. Some of us even memorized some of the messages. But we must constantly remember them and review and reflect because when we forget to remember Allah then we forget the enemies of Allah and the plots of the enemies ensnare us until Allah guides us back to goodness, which might not always happen, or allows us to permanently stray into dangerous crime for which we will then be painfully punished for. And that pain will be so great that one taste of it will make us forget any pleasure from all sins combined. Seriously the pain of the hellfire will be so severe that the punished will not remember any prior pleasure. They won't even know why they did the crime they are punished for because they will have forgotten all pleasure due to their eternal pain. So to avoid a such a pain we must be extremely cautious as though we were frantically drowning in the ocean trying not to drown. Since nobody on earth has reached the safety of the promised land of eternal paradise then we are all actively susceptible to drown in sin, so it's time to strictly seek our safety before we die. And whenever faced with a sinful situation remember how no enemy is more cruel to you or more oppressive to you than yourself when you fall into sin. For no enemy can ever cause Allah to be angry with you or qualify you for punishment in this life, the grave and hellfire no matter what they do. Although every time you sin you earn yourself the anger of Allah to a certain degree and you do not want the hatred of Allah in any amount under any circumstances. So save yourself and your families and your friends and your communities as much as possible from a fire prepared for the sinful who fail to repent from toxic evil deeds outlawed by Allah. Don't be a part-time enemy of Satan will being a part-time friend of Satan when convenient. Be a full-time perfectionist dealing diligently with yourself before you die.

Just as an imam during prayer should focus on the Divine King they are praying to when they turn their face to pray salat rather than the numbers of those they are praying with behind them, and as the caller of the Athan should focus on the Lord they are inviting people to worship rather than the responders to their call, we must focus on perfecting our slavery to the Universal Sovereign rather than the conditions of our life or our imagined victories during such blessed slavery. Meaning we can't afford to falter in our work attempting to worship our Lord as is factually deserved. Truly good slaves don't have time to think of their goodness due to being busy doing good work. If you ever feel you are on a level close to the pious humans like prophets or lesser friends of Allah then compare yourself to Angels to get a dose of reality if the sinful delusion of self-admiration blinds you to your many flaws in need of purification. You are nowhere close to perfect so being done striving for perfection is not something that can ever be contemplated by you. There is simply an expectation from Allah that a much more serious lifetime effort will be made by Muslims than you have been making thus far. The prophets were people whom Allah decreed disbelieving in their piety and close to perfect spiritual life causes all disbelievers to burn forever in hell. There is nobody like that on earth today who God has individually approved of at all, let alone to such a great extent. Yet imagine being a human prophet receiving revelation where you know everyone in the world during and after your time for all eternity must believe in your spiritual teachings and goodness or else they go to hellfire forever. We are already arrogant enough to qualify for hell due to pride alone, as our egos prevent healthy processing of simple positive or negative social interactions online and offline. The prophets were far more humble than we are, constantly seeking sincere repentance, exerting extreme efforts in goodness while avoiding evil, while knowing everyone else must accept their highly distinguished religious superiority. Additionally, the prophets would implement 100% of the religion as soon as they were commanded and learned of Allah's commands from Allah directly or the angels. Their obedience to Allah did not take them years of practice and struggles to implement what they learned and preached. Their submission was instantaneous and life-long, and they were humans. So what is our problem that we cannot at least refrain from the sins we know are sins? Imagine if the prophets had told Allah it would take them some time to stop sinning with certain sins they were inclined to more than others? We would not have any religion today. Furthermore to not have extreme egotistical pride in oneself as a prophet, where you know God requires others believing you are an eternally famous role model and will preserve your life story in detail for future generations to follow as a blueprint for life is a prophetic miracle in itself. In contrast we may go a day doing "just a few sins" and think we are the best to ever walk the earth. While the earth itself is pained by having us live on it and being disgusted our sinful corpse is to be contained within it until we get judged for our ungrateful existence. And for those who think "ungrateful existence" is not an accurate label for them, the month of Ramadan is a proof against you. For while fasting Ramadan you almost seem like a different person than who you are during the rest of the Hijri year. This proves you can be better when you truly want to and strive hard with super spiritual focus and motivation. Some may think because devils are less influential during Ramadan that makes all the difference, but when powerless influencers are chained and then unchained they do not increase in influence over those whom Allah guides. A sin therefore is a sign of Allah's temporary abandonment from your guidance and is usually a result of a past sin as the punishment for it, just as a future good deed is often the resulting reward for a present good deed. Hence the moment our vulnerable gift of guidance is taken for granted due to arrogance after a good deed streak we tend to get abandoned and left to ourself and go astray while thinking we were guiding ourselves and the world. Hence in reality we need constant divine guidance in addition to the constant supervision Allah has over us. No blessing is ever attained without Allah and every evil is a result of ourselves abandoning obedience to Allah until Allah guides us back to goodness by making us remember Allah. Yet why do we forget to such an extent that we commit evil in the first place? Allah knows best this is to test us and purify the ranks of our species distinguishing those blessed few who will strive for blessings and those many who will strive for other things inspite of the guidance Allah offered. The perfected religion of Islam deserves us to live a life of perfected moral worship with all the strength we can put forth every day until Allah causes our death. Being the best Allah says you can be according to Allah's knowledge of you and your circumstances, is how to seek eternal safety from Allah who is only a friend to those who accurately fear, worship and obey their one and only Lord. So instead of just simply worshipping Allah and then fearing the results from your lack of obedience to Allah, please improve your obedient adherence to the messenger's Sunnah as soon as now. May Allah bless the Muslims guiding humans and jinn to the pure Salafiyyah Islamic Sunnah of Muhammad, the final prophet of monotheism. May Allah motivate the repentant to repent as Allah deserves with true lifelong correction attaining the goal of purification which only comes from striving for perfection wherein lies safety due to Allah's facilitation. More could be said or written to stress the importance of the subject of safety seeking with the Sunnah but if one were admonished as long as the universe has existed it would not benefit the hard-hearted stubborn sinner unless Allah willed. Whereas the soft-hearted repenting sinner will benefit from a single letter if they are sincere, for Allah blesses the sincere when they encounter Islamic ilm and increases them in knowledge/practice and no amount of Islamic ilm will benefit those who are insincere. Yet at some point sincerity eventually eliminates most sinfulness from one's life or else if they persist upon a sinful life the sinners lose their sincerity. May Allah help us seek divine protection fearfully from the divine danger must fear. For nobody will ever dare tell Allah that they feared him too much or as Allah commanded us to fear.

QURANIC WARNINGS TO SEEK SAFETY WITH THE SUNNAH

Quran 2:11-13

وَإِذَا قِيلَ لَهُمْ لَا تُفْسِدُوا۟ فِى ٱلْأَرْضِ قَالُوٓا۟ إِنَّمَا نَحْنُ مُصْلِحُونَ (١١) أَلَآ إِنَّهُمْ هُمُ ٱلْمُفْسِدُونَ وَلَٰكِن لَّا يَشْعُرُونَ (١٢) وَإِذَا قِيلَ لَهُمْ ءَامِنُوا۟ كَمَآ ءَامَنَ ٱلنَّاسُ قَالُوٓا۟ أَنُؤْمِنُ كَمَآ ءَامَنَ ٱلسُّفَهَآءُ أَلَآ إِنَّهُمْ هُمُ ٱلسُّفَهَآءُ وَلَٰكِن لَّا يَعْلَمُونَ (١٣)

And when it is said to them, "Do not cause corruption on the earth," they say, "We are but reformers." (11) Unquestionably, it is they who are the corrupters, but they perceive [it] not. (12) And when it is said to them, "Believe as the people(Sahabah and Salaf) have believed," they say, "Should we believe as the foolish have believed?" Unquestionably, it is they who are the foolish, but they know [it] not. (13)

Quran 2:41-42

وَءَامِنُوا۟ بِمَآ أَنزَلْتُ مُصَدِّقًا لِّمَا مَعَكُمْ وَلَا تَكُونُوٓا۟ أَوَّلَ كَافِرٍۭ بِهِۦ وَلَا تَشْتَرُوا۟ بِـَٔايَٰتِى ثَمَنًا قَلِيلًا وَإِيَّٰىَ فَٱتَّقُونِ (٤١) وَلَا تَلْبِسُوا۟ ٱلْحَقَّ بِٱلْبَٰطِلِ وَتَكْتُمُوا۟ ٱلْحَقَّ وَأَنتُمْ تَعْلَمُونَ (٤٢)

And believe in what I have sent down confirming that which is [already] with you, and be not the first to disbelieve in it. And do not exchange My signs for a small price, and fear [only] Me. (41) And do not mix the truth with falsehood or conceal the truth while you know [it]. (42)

Quran 2:60

۞ وَإِذِ ٱسْتَسْقَىٰ مُوسَىٰ لِقَوْمِهِۦ فَقُلْنَا ٱضْرِب بِّعَصَاكَ ٱلْحَجَرَ ۖ فَٱنفَجَرَتْ مِنْهُ ٱثْنَتَا عَشْرَةَ عَيْنًا ۖ قَدْ عَلِمَ كُلُّ أُنَاسٍ مَّشْرَبَهُمْ ۖ كُلُوا۟ وَٱشْرَبُوا۟ مِن رِّزْقِ ٱللَّهِ وَلَا تَعْثَوْا۟ فِى ٱلْأَرْضِ مُفْسِدِينَ (٦٠)

And [recall] when Moses prayed for water for his people, so We said, "Strike with your staff the stone." And there gushed forth from it twelve springs, and every people knew its watering place. "Eat and drink from the provision of Allah, and do not commit abuse on the earth, spreading corruption." (60)

Quran 2:83-86

وَإِذْ أَخَذْنَا مِيثَـٰقَ بَنِىٓ إِسْرَٰٓءِيلَ لَا تَعْبُدُونَ إِلَّا ٱللَّهَ وَبِٱلْوَٰلِدَيْنِ إِحْسَانًا وَذِى ٱلْقُرْبَىٰ وَٱلْيَتَـٰمَىٰ وَٱلْمَسَـٰكِينِ وَقُولُوا۟ لِلنَّاسِ حُسْنًا وَأَقِيمُوا۟ ٱلصَّلَوٰةَ وَءَاتُوا۟ ٱلزَّكَوٰةَ ثُمَّ تَوَلَّيْتُمْ إِلَّا قَلِيلًا مِّنكُمْ وَأَنتُم مُّعْرِضُونَ (٨٣) وَإِذْ أَخَذْنَا مِيثَـٰقَكُمْ لَا تَسْفِكُونَ دِمَآءَكُمْ وَلَا تُخْرِجُونَ أَنفُسَكُم مِّن دِيَـٰرِكُمْ ثُمَّ أَقْرَرْتُمْ وَأَنتُمْ تَشْهَدُونَ (٨٤) ثُمَّ أَنتُمْ هَـٰٓؤُلَآءِ تَقْتُلُونَ أَنفُسَكُمْ وَتُخْرِجُونَ فَرِيقًا مِّنكُم مِّن دِيَـٰرِهِمْ تَظَـٰهَرُونَ عَلَيْهِم بِٱلْإِثْمِ وَٱلْعُدْوَٰنِ وَإِن يَأْتُوكُمْ أُسَـٰرَىٰ تُفَـٰدُوهُمْ وَهُوَ مُحَرَّمٌ عَلَيْكُمْ إِخْرَاجُهُمْ ۚ أَفَتُؤْمِنُونَ بِبَعْضِ ٱلْكِتَـٰبِ وَتَكْفُرُونَ بِبَعْضٍ ۚ فَمَا جَزَآءُ مَن يَفْعَلُ ذَٰلِكَ مِنكُمْ إِلَّا خِزْىٌ فِى ٱلْحَيَوٰةِ ٱلدُّنْيَا ۖ وَيَوْمَ ٱلْقِيَـٰمَةِ يُرَدُّونَ

إِلَىٰ أَشَدِّ ٱلْعَذَابِ ۗ وَمَا ٱللَّهُ بِغَٰفِلٍ عَمَّا تَعْمَلُونَ (٨٥) أُو۟لَٰٓئِكَ ٱلَّذِينَ ٱشْتَرَوُا۟ ٱلْحَيَوٰةَ ٱلدُّنْيَا بِٱلْءَاخِرَةِ ۖ فَلَا يُخَفَّفُ عَنْهُمُ ٱلْعَذَابُ وَلَا هُمْ يُنصَرُونَ (٨٦)

And [recall] when We took the covenant from the Children of Israel, [enjoining upon them], "Do not worship except Allah; and to parents do good and to relatives, orphans, and the needy. And speak to people good [words] and establish prayer and give zakah." Then you turned away, except a few of you, and you were refusing. (83) And [recall] when We took your covenant, [saying], "Do not shed each other's blood or evict one another from your homes." Then you acknowledged [this] while you were witnessing. (84) Then, you are those [same ones who are] killing one another and evicting a party of your people from their homes, cooperating against them in sin and aggression. And if they come to you as captives, you ransom them, although their eviction was forbidden to you. So do you believe in part of the Scripture and disbelieve in part? Then what is the recompense for those who do that among you except disgrace in worldly life; and on the Day of Resurrection they will be sent back to the severest of punishment. And Allah is not unaware of what you do. (85) Those are the ones who have bought the life of this world [in exchange] for the Hereafter, so the punishment will not be lightened for them, nor will they be aided. (86)

Quran 2:102-104

وَٱتَّبَعُوا۟ مَا تَتْلُوا۟ ٱلشَّيَٰطِينُ عَلَىٰ مُلْكِ سُلَيْمَٰنَ ۖ وَمَا كَفَرَ سُلَيْمَٰنُ وَلَٰكِنَّ ٱلشَّيَٰطِينَ كَفَرُوا۟ يُعَلِّمُونَ ٱلنَّاسَ ٱلسِّحْرَ وَمَآ أُنزِلَ عَلَى ٱلْمَلَكَيْنِ بِبَابِلَ هَٰرُوتَ وَمَٰرُوتَ ۚ وَمَا يُعَلِّمَانِ مِنْ أَحَدٍ حَتَّىٰ يَقُولَآ إِنَّمَا نَحْنُ فِتْنَةٌ فَلَا تَكْفُرْ ۖ فَيَتَعَلَّمُونَ مِنْهُمَا مَا يُفَرِّقُونَ بِهِۦ بَيْنَ ٱلْمَرْءِ وَزَوْجِهِۦ ۚ وَمَا هُم بِضَآرِّينَ بِهِۦ مِنْ أَحَدٍ إِلَّا بِإِذْنِ ٱللَّهِ ۚ وَيَتَعَلَّمُونَ مَا يَضُرُّهُمْ وَلَا يَنفَعُهُمْ ۚ وَلَقَدْ عَلِمُوا۟ لَمَنِ ٱشْتَرَىٰهُ مَا لَهُۥ فِى ٱلْءَاخِرَةِ مِنْ خَلَٰقٍ ۚ وَلَبِئْسَ مَا شَرَوْا۟ بِهِۦٓ أَنفُسَهُمْ ۚ لَوْ كَانُوا۟ يَعْلَمُونَ (١٠٢) وَلَوْ أَنَّهُمْ ءَامَنُوا۟ وَٱتَّقَوْا۟ لَمَثُوبَةٌ مِّنْ عِندِ ٱللَّهِ خَيْرٌ ۖ لَّوْ كَانُوا۟ يَعْلَمُونَ (١٠٣) يَٰٓأَيُّهَا ٱلَّذِينَ ءَامَنُوا۟ لَا تَقُولُوا۟ رَٰعِنَا وَقُولُوا۟ ٱنظُرْنَا وَٱسْمَعُوا۟ ۗ وَلِلْكَٰفِرِينَ عَذَابٌ أَلِيمٌ (١٠٤)

And they followed [instead] what the devils had recited during the reign of Solomon. It was not Solomon who disbelieved, but the devils disbelieved, teaching people magic and that which was revealed to the two angels at Babylon, Harut and Marut. But the two angels do not teach anyone unless they say, "We are a trial, so do not disbelieve [by practicing magic]." And [yet] they learn from them that by which they cause separation between a man and his wife. But they do not harm anyone through it except by permission of Allah. And the people learn what harms them and does not benefit them. But the Children of Israel certainly knew that whoever purchased the magic would not have in the Hereafter any share. And wretched is that for which they sold themselves, if they only knew. (102) And if they had believed and feared

Allah, then the reward from Allah would have been [far] better, if they only knew. (103) O you who have believed, say not [to Allah's Messenger], "Ra'ina" (roughly meaning "pay attention to us" in Arabic but is a derogatory phrase in Hebrew) but say, "Unthurna" (please look upon us) and listen. And for the disbelievers is a painful punishment. (104)

Quran 2:132

وَوَصَّىٰ بِهَآ إِبْرَٰهِۦمُ بَنِيهِ وَيَعْقُوبُ يَٰبَنِىَّ إِنَّ ٱللَّهَ ٱصْطَفَىٰ لَكُمُ ٱلدِّينَ فَلَا تَمُوتُنَّ إِلَّا وَأَنتُم مُّسْلِمُونَ (١٣٢)

And Abraham instructed his sons [to do the same] and [so did] Jacob, [saying], "O my sons, indeed Allah has chosen for you this religion, so do not die except while you are Muslims." (132)

Quran 2:136-137

قُولُوٓا۟ ءَامَنَّا بِٱللَّهِ وَمَآ أُنزِلَ إِلَيْنَا وَمَآ أُنزِلَ إِلَىٰٓ إِبْرَٰهِۦمَ وَإِسْمَٰعِيلَ وَإِسْحَٰقَ وَيَعْقُوبَ وَٱلْأَسْبَاطِ وَمَآ أُوتِىَ مُوسَىٰ وَعِيسَىٰ وَمَآ أُوتِىَ ٱلنَّبِيُّونَ مِن رَّبِّهِمْ لَا نُفَرِّقُ بَيْنَ أَحَدٍ مِّنْهُمْ وَنَحْنُ لَهُۥ مُسْلِمُونَ (١٣٦) فَإِنْ ءَامَنُوا۟ بِمِثْلِ مَآ ءَامَنتُم بِهِۦ فَقَدِ ٱهْتَدَوا۟ۖ وَّإِن تَوَلَّوْا۟ فَإِنَّمَا هُمْ فِى شِقَاقٍۢ ۖ فَسَيَكْفِيكَهُمُ ٱللَّهُ ۚ وَهُوَ ٱلسَّمِيعُ ٱلْعَلِيمُ (١٣٧)

Say, [O believers], "We have believed in Allah and what has been revealed to us and what has been revealed to Abraham and Ishmael and Isaac and Jacob and the

Descendants and what was given to Moses and Jesus and what was given to the prophets from their Lord. We make no distinction between any of them, and we are Muslims [in submission] to Him." (136) So if they believe in the same as you believe in, then they have been [rightly] guided; but if they turn away, they are only in dissension, and Allah will be sufficient for you against them. And He is the Hearing, the Knowing. (137)

Quran 2:147

ٱلْحَقُّ مِن رَّبِّكَ فَلَا تَكُونَنَّ مِنَ ٱلْمُمْتَرِينَ (١٤٧)

The truth is from your Lord, so never be among the doubters. (147)

Quran 2:150

وَمِنْ حَيْثُ خَرَجْتَ فَوَلِّ وَجْهَكَ شَطْرَ ٱلْمَسْجِدِ ٱلْحَرَامِ وَحَيْثُ مَا كُنتُمْ فَوَلُّواْ وُجُوهَكُمْ شَطْرَهُ لِئَلَّا يَكُونَ لِلنَّاسِ عَلَيْكُمْ حُجَّةٌ إِلَّا ٱلَّذِينَ ظَلَمُواْ مِنْهُمْ فَلَا تَخْشَوْهُمْ وَٱخْشَوْنِى وَلِأُتِمَّ نِعْمَتِى عَلَيْكُمْ وَلَعَلَّكُمْ تَهْتَدُونَ (١٥٠)

And from wherever you go out [for prayer], turn your face toward al-Masjid al-Haram. And wherever you [believers] may be, turn your faces toward it in order that the people will not have any argument against you, except for those of them who commit wrong; so fear them not but fear Me. And [it is] so I may complete My favor upon you and that you may be guided. (150)

Quran 2:152-154

فَاذْكُرُونِىٓ أَذْكُرْكُمْ وَٱشْكُرُوا۟ لِى وَلَا تَكْفُرُونِ (١٥٢) يَـٰٓأَيُّهَا ٱلَّذِينَ ءَامَنُوا۟ ٱسْتَعِينُوا۟ بِٱلصَّبْرِ وَٱلصَّلَوٰةِ إِنَّ ٱللَّهَ مَعَ ٱلصَّـٰبِرِينَ (١٥٣) وَلَا تَقُولُوا۟ لِمَن يُقْتَلُ فِى سَبِيلِ ٱللَّهِ أَمْوَٰتٌۢ بَلْ أَحْيَآءٌ وَلَـٰكِن لَّا تَشْعُرُونَ (١٥٤)

So remember Me; I will remember you. And be grateful to Me and do not deny Me. (152) O you who have believed, seek help through patience and prayer. Indeed, Allah is with the patient. (153) And do not say about those who are killed in the way of Allah, "They are dead." Rather, they are alive, but you perceive [it] not. (154)

Quran 2:167-169

وَقَالَ ٱلَّذِينَ ٱتَّبَعُوا۟ لَوْ أَنَّ لَنَا كَرَّةً فَنَتَبَرَّأَ مِنْهُمْ كَمَا تَبَرَّءُوا۟ مِنَّا كَذَٰلِكَ يُرِيهِمُ ٱللَّهُ أَعْمَـٰلَهُمْ حَسَرَٰتٍ عَلَيْهِمْ وَمَا هُم بِخَـٰرِجِينَ مِنَ ٱلنَّارِ (١٦٧) يَـٰٓأَيُّهَا ٱلنَّاسُ كُلُوا۟ مِمَّا فِى ٱلْأَرْضِ حَلَـٰلًا طَيِّبًا وَلَا تَتَّبِعُوا۟ خُطُوَٰتِ ٱلشَّيْطَـٰنِ إِنَّهُۥ لَكُمْ عَدُوٌّ مُّبِينٌ (١٦٨) إِنَّمَا يَأْمُرُكُم بِٱلسُّوٓءِ وَٱلْفَحْشَآءِ وَأَن تَقُولُوا۟ عَلَى ٱللَّهِ مَا لَا تَعْلَمُونَ

Those who followed will say, "If only we had another turn [at worldly life] so we could disassociate ourselves from them as they have disassociated themselves from us." Thus will Allah show them their deeds as regrets upon them. And they are never to emerge from the Fire. (167) O mankind, eat from whatever is on earth [that is] lawful and good and do not follow the footsteps of Satan. Indeed, he is to you a clear enemy. (168) He only orders you to evil and immorality and to say about Allah what you do not know. (169)

Quran 2:187-188

أُحِلَّ لَكُمْ لَيْلَةَ ٱلصِّيَامِ ٱلرَّفَثُ إِلَىٰ نِسَآئِكُمْ ۚ هُنَّ لِبَاسٌ لَّكُمْ وَأَنتُمْ لِبَاسٌ لَّهُنَّ ۗ عَلِمَ ٱللَّهُ أَنَّكُمْ كُنتُمْ تَخْتَانُونَ أَنفُسَكُمْ فَتَابَ عَلَيْكُمْ وَعَفَا عَنكُمْ ۖ فَٱلْـَٰٔنَ بَـٰشِرُوهُنَّ وَٱبْتَغُواْ مَا كَتَبَ ٱللَّهُ لَكُمْ ۚ وَكُلُواْ وَٱشْرَبُواْ حَتَّىٰ يَتَبَيَّنَ لَكُمُ ٱلْخَيْطُ ٱلْأَبْيَضُ مِنَ ٱلْخَيْطِ ٱلْأَسْوَدِ مِنَ ٱلْفَجْرِ ۖ ثُمَّ أَتِمُّواْ ٱلصِّيَامَ إِلَى ٱلَّيْلِ ۚ وَلَا تُبَـٰشِرُوهُنَّ وَأَنتُمْ عَـٰكِفُونَ فِى ٱلْمَسَـٰجِدِ ۗ تِلْكَ حُدُودُ ٱللَّهِ فَلَا تَقْرَبُوهَا ۗ كَذَٰلِكَ يُبَيِّنُ ٱللَّهُ ءَايَـٰتِهِۦ لِلنَّاسِ لَعَلَّهُمْ يَتَّقُونَ (١٨٧) وَلَا تَأْكُلُوٓاْ أَمْوَٰلَكُم بَيْنَكُم بِٱلْبَـٰطِلِ وَتُدْلُواْ بِهَآ إِلَى ٱلْحُكَّامِ لِتَأْكُلُواْ فَرِيقًا مِّنْ أَمْوَٰلِ ٱلنَّاسِ بِٱلْإِثْمِ وَأَنتُمْ تَعْلَمُونَ (١٨٨)

It has been made permissible for you the night preceding fasting to go to your wives [for sexual relations]. They are clothing for you and you are clothing for them. Allah knows that you used to deceive yourselves, so He accepted your repentance and forgave you. So now, have relations with them and seek that which Allah has decreed for you. And eat and drink until the white thread of dawn becomes distinct to you from the black thread [of night]. Then complete the fast until the sunset. And do not have relations with them as long as you are staying for worship in the mosques. These are the limits [set by] Allah, so do not approach them. Thus does Allah make clear His ordinances to the people that they may become righteous. (187) And do not consume one another's wealth unjustly or send it [in bribery] to the rulers in order that [they might aid] you [to] consume a portion of the wealth of the people in sin, while you know [it is unlawful]. (188)

Quran 2:109-193

وَقَٰتِلُوا۟ فِى سَبِيلِ ٱللَّهِ ٱلَّذِينَ يُقَٰتِلُونَكُمْ وَلَا تَعْتَدُوٓا۟ إِنَّ ٱللَّهَ لَا يُحِبُّ ٱلْمُعْتَدِينَ (١٩٠) وَٱقْتُلُوهُمْ حَيْثُ ثَقِفْتُمُوهُمْ وَأَخْرِجُوهُم مِّنْ حَيْثُ أَخْرَجُوكُمْ وَٱلْفِتْنَةُ أَشَدُّ مِنَ ٱلْقَتْلِ ۚ وَلَا تُقَٰتِلُوهُمْ عِندَ ٱلْمَسْجِدِ ٱلْحَرَامِ حَتَّىٰ يُقَٰتِلُوكُمْ فِيهِ ۖ فَإِن قَٰتَلُوكُمْ فَٱقْتُلُوهُمْ ۗ كَذَٰلِكَ جَزَآءُ ٱلْكَٰفِرِينَ (١٩١) فَإِنِ ٱنتَهَوْا۟ فَإِنَّ ٱللَّهَ غَفُورٌ رَّحِيمٌ (١٩٢) وَقَٰتِلُوهُمْ حَتَّىٰ لَا تَكُونَ فِتْنَةٌ وَيَكُونَ ٱلدِّينُ لِلَّهِ ۖ فَإِنِ ٱنتَهَوْا۟ فَلَا عُدْوَٰنَ إِلَّا عَلَى ٱلظَّٰلِمِينَ (١٩٣)

Fight in the way of Allah those who fight you but do not transgress. Indeed. Allah does not like transgressors. (190) And kill them wherever you overtake them and expel them from wherever they have expelled you, and fitnah is worse than killing. And do not fight them at al-Masjid al- Haram until they fight you there. But if they fight you, then kill them. Such is the recompense of the disbelievers. (191) And if they cease, then indeed, Allah is Forgiving and Merciful. (192) Fight them until there is no [more] fitnah and [until] worship is [acknowledged to be] for Allah. But if they cease, then there is to be no aggression except against the oppressors. (193)

Quran 2:195-197

وَأَنفِقُوا۟ فِى سَبِيلِ ٱللَّهِ وَلَا تُلْقُوا۟ بِأَيْدِيكُمْ إِلَى ٱلتَّهْلُكَةِ ۛ وَأَحْسِنُوٓا۟ ۛ إِنَّ ٱللَّهَ يُحِبُّ ٱلْمُحْسِنِينَ (١٩٥) وَأَتِمُّوا۟ ٱلْحَجَّ وَٱلْعُمْرَةَ لِلَّهِ ۚ فَإِنْ أُحْصِرْتُمْ فَمَا ٱسْتَيْسَرَ مِنَ

ٱلْهَدْىِ ۚ وَلَا تَحْلِقُوا۟ رُءُوسَكُمْ حَتَّىٰ يَبْلُغَ ٱلْهَدْىُ مَحِلَّهُۥ ۚ فَمَن كَانَ مِنكُم مَّرِيضًا أَوْ بِهِۦٓ أَذًى مِّن رَّأْسِهِۦ فَفِدْيَةٌ مِّن صِيَامٍ أَوْ صَدَقَةٍ أَوْ نُسُكٍ ۚ فَإِذَآ أَمِنتُمْ فَمَن تَمَتَّعَ بِٱلْعُمْرَةِ إِلَى ٱلْحَجِّ فَمَا ٱسْتَيْسَرَ مِنَ ٱلْهَدْىِ ۚ فَمَن لَّمْ يَجِدْ فَصِيَامُ ثَلَٰثَةِ أَيَّامٍ فِى ٱلْحَجِّ وَسَبْعَةٍ إِذَا رَجَعْتُمْ ۗ تِلْكَ عَشَرَةٌ كَامِلَةٌ ۗ ذَٰلِكَ لِمَن لَّمْ يَكُنْ أَهْلُهُۥ حَاضِرِى ٱلْمَسْجِدِ ٱلْحَرَامِ ۚ وَٱتَّقُوا۟ ٱللَّهَ وَٱعْلَمُوٓا۟ أَنَّ ٱللَّهَ شَدِيدُ ٱلْعِقَابِ (١٩٦) ٱلْحَجُّ أَشْهُرٌ مَّعْلُومَٰتٌ ۚ فَمَن فَرَضَ فِيهِنَّ ٱلْحَجَّ فَلَا رَفَثَ وَلَا فُسُوقَ وَلَا جِدَالَ فِى ٱلْحَجِّ ۗ وَمَا تَفْعَلُوا۟ مِنْ خَيْرٍ يَعْلَمْهُ ٱللَّهُ ۗ وَتَزَوَّدُوا۟ فَإِنَّ خَيْرَ ٱلزَّادِ ٱلتَّقْوَىٰ ۚ وَٱتَّقُونِ يَٰٓأُو۟لِى ٱلْأَلْبَٰبِ (١٩٧)

And spend in the way of Allah and do not throw [yourselves] with your [own] hands into destruction [by refraining]. And do good; indeed, Allah loves the doers of good. (195) And complete the Hajj and 'umrah for Allah. But if you are prevented, then [offer] what can be obtained with ease of sacrificial animals. And do not shave your heads until the sacrificial animal has reached its place of slaughter. And whoever among you is ill or has an ailment of the head [making shaving necessary must offer] a ransom of fasting [three days] or charity or sacrifice. And when you are secure, then whoever performs 'umrah [during the Hajj months] followed by Hajj [offers] what can be obtained with ease of sacrificial animals. And whoever cannot find [or afford such an animal] - then a fast of three days during Hajj and of seven when you have returned [home]. Those are ten complete [days]. This is for those whose family is not in the area of al-Masjid al-Haram. And fear Allah and know that Allah is severe in penalty. (196) Hajj is [during] well-known months, so whoever has made Hajj obligatory upon himself therein [by entering the state of ihram], there is [to be for him] no sexual relations and no disobedience and no disputing during Hajj. And whatever good you do - Allah knows it. And take provisions, but indeed, the best provision is fear of Allah. And fear Me, O you of understanding. (197)

Quran 2:208

يَٰٓأَيُّهَا ٱلَّذِينَ ءَامَنُوا۟ ٱدْخُلُوا۟ فِى ٱلسِّلْمِ كَآفَّةً وَلَا تَتَّبِعُوا۟ خُطُوَٰتِ ٱلشَّيْطَٰنِ إِنَّهُۥ لَكُمْ عَدُوٌّ مُّبِينٌ (٢٠٨)

O you who have believed, enter into Islam completely [and perfectly] and do not follow the footsteps of Satan. Indeed, he is to you a clear enemy. (208)

Quran 2:221-222

وَلَا تَنكِحُوا۟ ٱلْمُشْرِكَٰتِ حَتَّىٰ يُؤْمِنَّ وَلَأَمَةٌ مُّؤْمِنَةٌ خَيْرٌ مِّن مُّشْرِكَةٍ وَلَوْ أَعْجَبَتْكُمْ وَلَا تُنكِحُوا۟ ٱلْمُشْرِكِينَ حَتَّىٰ يُؤْمِنُوا۟ وَلَعَبْدٌ مُّؤْمِنٌ خَيْرٌ مِّن مُّشْرِكٍ وَلَوْ أَعْجَبَكُمْ أُو۟لَٰٓئِكَ يَدْعُونَ إِلَى ٱلنَّارِ وَٱللَّهُ يَدْعُوٓا۟ إِلَى ٱلْجَنَّةِ وَٱلْمَغْفِرَةِ بِإِذْنِهِۦ وَيُبَيِّنُ ءَايَٰتِهِۦ لِلنَّاسِ لَعَلَّهُمْ يَتَذَكَّرُونَ (٢٢١) وَيَسْـَٔلُونَكَ عَنِ ٱلْمَحِيضِ قُلْ هُوَ أَذًى فَٱعْتَزِلُوا۟ ٱلنِّسَآءَ فِى ٱلْمَحِيضِ وَلَا تَقْرَبُوهُنَّ حَتَّىٰ يَطْهُرْنَ فَإِذَا تَطَهَّرْنَ فَأْتُوهُنَّ مِنْ حَيْثُ أَمَرَكُمُ ٱللَّهُ إِنَّ ٱللَّهَ يُحِبُّ ٱلتَّوَّٰبِينَ وَيُحِبُّ ٱلْمُتَطَهِّرِينَ (٢٢٢)

And do not marry polytheistic women until they believe. And a believing slave woman is better than a polytheist, even though she might please you. And do not marry polytheistic men [to your women] until they believe. And a believing slave is better than a polytheist, even though he might please you. Those invite [you] to the Fire, but Allah invites to Paradise and to forgiveness, by His permission. And He makes clear His verses to the people that perhaps they may remember. (221) And they ask you about menstruation. Say, "It is harm, so keep away from wives during menstruation. And do not approach them until they are pure. And when they have purified themselves, then come to them from where Allah has ordained for you. Indeed, Allah loves those who are constantly repentant and loves those who purify themselves." (222)

Quran 2:224

وَلَا تَجْعَلُواْ ٱللَّهَ عُرْضَةً لِّأَيْمَٰنِكُمْ أَن تَبَرُّواْ وَتَتَّقُواْ وَتُصْلِحُواْ بَيْنَ ٱلنَّاسِۚ وَٱللَّهُ سَمِيعٌ عَلِيمٌ (٢٢٤)

And do not make [your oath by] Allah an excuse against being righteous and fearing Allah and making peace among people. And Allah is Hearing and Knowing. (224)

Quran 2:229-233

ٱلطَّلَـٰقُ مَرَّتَانِ ۖ فَإِمْسَاكٌۢ بِمَعْرُوفٍ أَوْ تَسْرِيحٌۢ بِإِحْسَـٰنٍ ۗ وَلَا يَحِلُّ لَكُمْ أَن تَأْخُذُوا۟ مِمَّآ ءَاتَيْتُمُوهُنَّ شَيْـًٔا إِلَّآ أَن يَخَافَآ أَلَّا يُقِيمَا حُدُودَ ٱللَّهِ ۖ فَإِنْ خِفْتُمْ أَلَّا يُقِيمَا حُدُودَ ٱللَّهِ فَلَا جُنَاحَ عَلَيْهِمَا فِيمَا ٱفْتَدَتْ بِهِۦ ۗ تِلْكَ حُدُودُ ٱللَّهِ فَلَا تَعْتَدُوهَا ۚ وَمَن يَتَعَدَّ حُدُودَ ٱللَّهِ فَأُو۟لَـٰٓئِكَ هُمُ ٱلظَّـٰلِمُونَ (٢٢٩) فَإِن طَلَّقَهَا فَلَا تَحِلُّ لَهُۥ مِنۢ بَعْدُ حَتَّىٰ تَنكِحَ زَوْجًا غَيْرَهُۥ ۗ فَإِن طَلَّقَهَا فَلَا جُنَاحَ عَلَيْهِمَآ أَن يَتَرَاجَعَآ إِن ظَنَّآ أَن يُقِيمَا حُدُودَ ٱللَّهِ ۗ وَتِلْكَ حُدُودُ ٱللَّهِ يُبَيِّنُهَا لِقَوْمٍ يَعْلَمُونَ (٢٣٠) وَإِذَا طَلَّقْتُمُ ٱلنِّسَآءَ فَبَلَغْنَ أَجَلَهُنَّ فَأَمْسِكُوهُنَّ بِمَعْرُوفٍ أَوْ سَرِّحُوهُنَّ بِمَعْرُوفٍ ۚ وَلَا تُمْسِكُوهُنَّ ضِرَارًا لِّتَعْتَدُوا۟ ۚ وَمَن يَفْعَلْ ذَٰلِكَ فَقَدْ ظَلَمَ نَفْسَهُۥ ۚ وَلَا تَتَّخِذُوٓا۟ ءَايَـٰتِ ٱللَّهِ هُزُوًا ۚ وَٱذْكُرُوا۟ نِعْمَتَ ٱللَّهِ عَلَيْكُمْ وَمَآ أَنزَلَ عَلَيْكُم مِّنَ ٱلْكِتَـٰبِ وَٱلْحِكْمَةِ يَعِظُكُم بِهِۦ ۚ وَٱتَّقُوا۟ ٱللَّهَ وَٱعْلَمُوٓا۟ أَنَّ ٱللَّهَ بِكُلِّ شَىْءٍ عَلِيمٌ (٢٣١) وَإِذَا طَلَّقْتُمُ ٱلنِّسَآءَ فَبَلَغْنَ أَجَلَهُنَّ فَلَا تَعْضُلُوهُنَّ أَن يَنكِحْنَ أَزْوَٰجَهُنَّ إِذَا تَرَٰضَوْا۟ بَيْنَهُم بِٱلْمَعْرُوفِ ۗ ذَٰلِكَ يُوعَظُ بِهِۦ مَن كَانَ مِنكُمْ يُؤْمِنُ بِٱللَّهِ وَٱلْيَوْمِ ٱلْـَٔاخِرِ ۗ ذَٰلِكُمْ أَزْكَىٰ لَكُمْ وَأَطْهَرُ ۗ وَٱللَّهُ يَعْلَمُ وَأَنتُمْ لَا تَعْلَمُونَ (٢٣٢) ۞ وَٱلْوَٰلِدَٰتُ يُرْضِعْنَ أَوْلَـٰدَهُنَّ حَوْلَيْنِ كَامِلَيْنِ ۖ لِمَنْ أَرَادَ أَن يُتِمَّ ٱلرَّضَاعَةَ ۚ وَعَلَى ٱلْمَوْلُودِ لَهُۥ رِزْقُهُنَّ وَكِسْوَتُهُنَّ بِٱلْمَعْرُوفِ ۚ لَا تُكَلَّفُ نَفْسٌ إِلَّا وُسْعَهَا ۚ لَا تُضَآرَّ وَٰلِدَةٌۢ بِوَلَدِهَا وَلَا مَوْلُودٌ لَّهُۥ بِوَلَدِهِۦ ۚ وَعَلَى ٱلْوَارِثِ مِثْلُ ذَٰلِكَ ۗ فَإِنْ أَرَادَا فِصَالًا عَن تَرَاضٍ مِّنْهُمَا وَتَشَاوُرٍ فَلَا جُنَاحَ عَلَيْهِمَا ۗ وَإِنْ أَرَدتُّمْ أَن تَسْتَرْضِعُوٓا۟ أَوْلَـٰدَكُمْ فَلَا جُنَاحَ عَلَيْكُمْ إِذَا سَلَّمْتُم مَّآ ءَاتَيْتُم بِٱلْمَعْرُوفِ ۗ وَٱتَّقُوا۟ ٱللَّهَ وَٱعْلَمُوٓا۟ أَنَّ ٱللَّهَ بِمَا تَعْمَلُونَ بَصِيرٌ (٢٣٣)

Divorce is twice. Then, either keep [her] in an acceptable manner or release [her] with good treatment. And it is not lawful for you to take anything of what you have given them unless both fear that they will not be able to keep [within] the limits of Allah. But if you fear that they will not keep [within] the limits of Allah, then there is no blame upon either of them concerning that by which she ransoms herself. These are the limits of Allah, so do not transgress them. And whoever transgresses the limits of Allah - it is those who are the wrongdoers. (229) And if he has divorced her [for the third time], then she is not lawful to him afterward until [after] she marries a husband other than him. And if the latter husband divorces her [or dies], there is no blame upon the woman and her former husband for returning to each other if they think that they can keep [within] the limits of Allah. These are the limits of Allah, which He makes clear to a people who know. (230) And when you divorce women and they have [nearly] fulfilled their term, either retain them according to acceptable terms or release them according to acceptable terms, and do not keep them, intending harm, to transgress [against them]. And whoever does that has certainly wronged himself. And do not take the verses of Allah in jest. And remember the favor of Allah upon you and what has been revealed to you of the Book and wisdom by which He instructs you. And fear Allah and know that Allah is Knowing of all things. (231) And when you divorce women and they have fulfilled their term, do not prevent them from remarrying their [former] husbands if they agree among themselves on an acceptable basis. That is instructed to whoever of you believes in Allah and the Last Day. That is better for you and purer, and Allah knows and you know not. (232) Mothers may breastfeed their children two complete years for whoever wishes to complete the nursing [period]. Upon the father is the mothers' provision and their clothing according to what is acceptable. No person is charged with more than his capacity. No mother should be harmed through her child, and no father through his child. And upon the [father's] heir is [a duty] like that [of the father]. And if they both desire weaning through mutual consent from both of them and consultation, there is no blame upon either of them. And if you wish to have your children nursed by a substitute, there is no blame upon you as long as you give payment according to what is acceptable. And fear Allah and know that Allah is Seeing of what you do. (233)

Quran 2:235-237

وَلَا جُنَاحَ عَلَيْكُمْ فِيمَا عَرَّضْتُم بِهِۦ مِنْ خِطْبَةِ ٱلنِّسَآءِ أَوْ أَكْنَنتُمْ فِىٓ أَنفُسِكُمْ ۚ عَلِمَ ٱللَّهُ أَنَّكُمْ سَتَذْكُرُونَهُنَّ وَلَـٰكِن لَّا تُوَاعِدُوهُنَّ سِرًّا إِلَّآ أَن تَقُولُوا۟ قَوْلًا مَّعْرُوفًا ۚ وَلَا تَعْزِمُوا۟ عُقْدَةَ ٱلنِّكَاحِ حَتَّىٰ يَبْلُغَ ٱلْكِتَـٰبُ أَجَلَهُۥ ۚ وَٱعْلَمُوٓا۟ أَنَّ ٱللَّهَ يَعْلَمُ مَا فِىٓ أَنفُسِكُمْ فَٱحْذَرُوهُ ۚ وَٱعْلَمُوٓا۟ أَنَّ ٱللَّهَ غَفُورٌ حَلِيمٌ (٢٣٥) لَّا جُنَاحَ عَلَيْكُمْ إِن طَلَّقْتُمُ ٱلنِّسَآءَ مَا لَمْ تَمَسُّوهُنَّ أَوْ تَفْرِضُوا۟ لَهُنَّ فَرِيضَةً ۚ وَمَتِّعُوهُنَّ عَلَى ٱلْمُوسِعِ قَدَرُهُۥ وَعَلَى ٱلْمُقْتِرِ قَدَرُهُۥ مَتَـٰعًۢا بِٱلْمَعْرُوفِ ۖ حَقًّا عَلَى ٱلْمُحْسِنِينَ (٢٣٦) وَإِن طَلَّقْتُمُوهُنَّ مِن قَبْلِ أَن تَمَسُّوهُنَّ وَقَدْ فَرَضْتُمْ لَهُنَّ فَرِيضَةً فَنِصْفُ مَا فَرَضْتُمْ إِلَّآ أَن يَعْفُونَ أَوْ يَعْفُوَا۟ ٱلَّذِى بِيَدِهِۦ عُقْدَةُ ٱلنِّكَاحِ

وَأَن تَعْفُوٓاْ أَقْرَبُ لِلتَّقْوَىٰ وَلَا تَنسَوُاْ ٱلْفَضْلَ بَيْنَكُمْ إِنَّ ٱللَّهَ بِمَا تَعْمَلُونَ بَصِيرٌ (٢٣٧)

There is no blame upon you for that to which you [indirectly] allude concerning a proposal to women or for what you conceal within yourselves. Allah knows that you will have them in mind. But do not promise them secretly except for saying a proper saying. And do not determine to undertake a marriage contract until the decreed period reaches its end. And know that Allah knows what is within yourselves, so beware of Him. And know that Allah is Forgiving and Forbearing.
(235) There is no blame upon you if you divorce women you have not touched nor specified for them an obligation. But give them [a gift of] compensation - the wealthy according to his capability and the poor according to his capability - a provision according to what is acceptable, a duty upon the doers of good.
(236) And if you divorce them before you have touched them and you have already specified for them an obligation, then [give] half of what you specified - unless they forego the right or the one in whose hand is the marriage contract foregoes it. And to forego it is nearer to righteousness. And do not forget graciousness between you. Indeed Allah, of whatever you do, is Seeing. (237)

Quran 2:256

لَا إِكْرَاهَ فِى ٱلدِّينِ ۖ قَد تَّبَيَّنَ ٱلرُّشْدُ مِنَ ٱلْغَىِّ ۚ فَمَن يَكْفُرْ بِٱلطَّٰغُوتِ وَيُؤْمِنۢ بِٱللَّهِ فَقَدِ ٱسْتَمْسَكَ بِٱلْعُرْوَةِ ٱلْوُثْقَىٰ لَا ٱنفِصَامَ لَهَا ۗ وَٱللَّهُ سَمِيعٌ عَلِيمٌ (٢٥٦)

There shall be no compulsion in [acceptance of] the religion. The right course has become clear from the wrong. So whoever disbelieves in Taghut and believes in Allah has grasped the most trustworthy handhold with no break in it. And Allah is Hearing and Knowing. (256)

Quran 2:261-264

مَّثَلُ ٱلَّذِينَ يُنفِقُونَ أَمْوَٰلَهُمْ فِى سَبِيلِ ٱللَّهِ كَمَثَلِ حَبَّةٍ أَنۢبَتَتْ سَبْعَ سَنَابِلَ فِى كُلِّ سُنۢبُلَةٍ مِّا۟ئَةُ حَبَّةٍ ۗ وَٱللَّهُ يُضَٰعِفُ لِمَن يَشَآءُ ۗ وَٱللَّهُ وَٰسِعٌ عَلِيمٌ (٢٦١) ٱلَّذِينَ يُنفِقُونَ أَمْوَٰلَهُمْ فِى سَبِيلِ ٱللَّهِ ثُمَّ لَا يُتْبِعُونَ مَآ أَنفَقُوا۟ مَنًّا وَلَآ أَذًى ۙ لَّهُمْ أَجْرُهُمْ عِندَ رَبِّهِمْ وَلَا خَوْفٌ عَلَيْهِمْ وَلَا هُمْ يَحْزَنُونَ (٢٦٢) قَوْلٌ مَّعْرُوفٌ وَمَغْفِرَةٌ خَيْرٌ مِّن صَدَقَةٍ يَتْبَعُهَآ أَذًى ۗ وَٱللَّهُ غَنِىٌّ حَلِيمٌ (٢٦٣) يَٰٓأَيُّهَا ٱلَّذِينَ ءَامَنُوا۟ لَا تُبْطِلُوا۟ صَدَقَٰتِكُم بِٱلْمَنِّ وَٱلْأَذَىٰ كَٱلَّذِى يُنفِقُ مَالَهُۥ رِئَآءَ ٱلنَّاسِ وَلَا يُؤْمِنُ بِٱللَّهِ وَٱلْيَوْمِ ٱلْءَاخِرِ ۖ فَمَثَلُهُۥ كَمَثَلِ صَفْوَانٍ عَلَيْهِ تُرَابٌ فَأَصَابَهُۥ وَابِلٌ فَتَرَكَهُۥ صَلْدًا ۖ لَّا يَقْدِرُونَ عَلَىٰ شَىْءٍ مِّمَّا كَسَبُوا۟ ۗ وَٱللَّهُ لَا يَهْدِى ٱلْقَوْمَ ٱلْكَٰفِرِينَ (٢٦٤)

The example of those who spend their wealth in the way of Allah is like a seed [of grain] which grows seven spikes; in each spike is a hundred grains. And Allah multiplies [His reward] for whom He wills. And Allah is all-Encompassing and Knowing. (261) Those who spend their wealth in the way of Allah and then do not follow up what they have spent with reminders [of it] or [other] injury will have their reward with their Lord, and there will be no fear concerning them, nor will they grieve. (262) Kind speech and forgiveness are better than charity followed by injury. And Allah is Free of need and Forbearing. (263) O you who have believed, do not invalidate your charities with reminders or injury as does one who spends his wealth [only] to be seen by the people and does not believe in Allah and the Last Day. His example is like that of a [large] smooth stone upon which is dust and is hit by a downpour that leaves it bare. They are unable [to keep] anything of what they have earned. And Allah does not guide the disbelieving people. (264)

Quran 2:267

يَـٰٓأَيُّهَا ٱلَّذِينَ ءَامَنُوٓاْ أَنفِقُواْ مِن طَيِّبَـٰتِ مَا كَسَبْتُمْ وَمِمَّآ أَخْرَجْنَا لَكُم مِّنَ ٱلْأَرْضِ ۖ وَلَا تَيَمَّمُواْ ٱلْخَبِيثَ مِنْهُ تُنفِقُونَ وَلَسْتُم بِـَٔاخِذِيهِ إِلَّآ أَن تُغْمِضُواْ فِيهِ ۚ وَٱعْلَمُوٓاْ أَنَّ ٱللَّهَ غَنِىٌّ حَمِيدٌ (٢٦٧)

O you who have believed, spend from the good things which you have earned and from that which We have produced for you from the earth. And do not aim toward the defective therefrom, spending [from that] while you would not take it [yourself] except with closed eyes. And know that Allah is Free of need and Praiseworthy. (267)

Quran 2:275-279

ٱلَّذِينَ يَأْكُلُونَ ٱلرِّبَوٰا۟ لَا يَقُومُونَ إِلَّا كَمَا يَقُومُ ٱلَّذِى يَتَخَبَّطُهُ ٱلشَّيْطَٰنُ مِنَ ٱلْمَسِّ ۚ ذَٰلِكَ بِأَنَّهُمْ قَالُوٓا۟ إِنَّمَا ٱلْبَيْعُ مِثْلُ ٱلرِّبَوٰا۟ ۗ وَأَحَلَّ ٱللَّهُ ٱلْبَيْعَ وَحَرَّمَ ٱلرِّبَوٰا۟ ۚ فَمَن جَآءَهُۥ مَوْعِظَةٌ مِّن رَّبِّهِۦ فَٱنتَهَىٰ فَلَهُۥ مَا سَلَفَ وَأَمْرُهُۥٓ إِلَى ٱللَّهِ ۖ وَمَنْ عَادَ فَأُو۟لَٰٓئِكَ أَصْحَٰبُ ٱلنَّارِ ۖ هُمْ فِيهَا خَٰلِدُونَ (٢٧٥) يَمْحَقُ ٱللَّهُ ٱلرِّبَوٰا۟ وَيُرْبِى ٱلصَّدَقَٰتِ ۗ وَٱللَّهُ لَا يُحِبُّ كُلَّ كَفَّارٍ أَثِيمٍ (٢٧٦) إِنَّ ٱلَّذِينَ ءَامَنُوا۟ وَعَمِلُوا۟ ٱلصَّٰلِحَٰتِ وَأَقَامُوا۟ ٱلصَّلَوٰةَ وَءَاتَوُا۟ ٱلزَّكَوٰةَ لَهُمْ أَجْرُهُمْ عِندَ رَبِّهِمْ وَلَا خَوْفٌ عَلَيْهِمْ وَلَا هُمْ يَحْزَنُونَ (٢٧٧) يَٰٓأَيُّهَا ٱلَّذِينَ ءَامَنُوا۟ ٱتَّقُوا۟ ٱللَّهَ وَذَرُوا۟ مَا بَقِىَ مِنَ ٱلرِّبَوٰٓا۟ إِن كُنتُم مُّؤْمِنِينَ (٢٧٨) فَإِن لَّمْ تَفْعَلُوا۟ فَأْذَنُوا۟ بِحَرْبٍ مِّنَ ٱللَّهِ وَرَسُولِهِۦ ۖ وَإِن تُبْتُمْ فَلَكُمْ رُءُوسُ أَمْوَٰلِكُمْ لَا تَظْلِمُونَ وَلَا تُظْلَمُونَ (٢٧٩)

Those who consume interest cannot stand [on the Day of Resurrection] except as one stands who is being beaten by Satan into insanity. That is because they say, "Trade is [just] like interest." But Allah has permitted trade and has forbidden interest. So whoever has received an admonition from his Lord and desists may have what is past, and his affair rests with Allah. But whoever returns to [dealing in interest or usury] - those are the companions of the Fire; they will abide eternally therein. (275) Allah destroys interest and gives increase for charities. And Allah does not like every sinning disbeliever. (276) Indeed, those who believe and do righteous deeds and establish prayer and give zakah will have their reward with their Lord, and there will be no fear concerning them, nor will they grieve. (277) O you who have believed, fear Allah and give up what remains [due to you] of interest, if you should be believers. (278) And if you do not, then be informed of a war [against you] from Allah and His Messenger. But if you repent, you may have your principal - [thus] you do no wrong, nor are you wronged. (279)

Quran 2:282-283

يَـٰٓأَيُّهَا ٱلَّذِينَ ءَامَنُوٓاْ إِذَا تَدَايَنتُم بِدَيْنٍ إِلَىٰٓ أَجَلٍ مُّسَمًّى فَٱكْتُبُوهُ ۚ وَلْيَكْتُب بَّيْنَكُمْ كَاتِبٌۢ بِٱلْعَدْلِ ۚ وَلَا يَأْبَ كَاتِبٌ أَن يَكْتُبَ كَمَا عَلَّمَهُ ٱللَّهُ ۚ فَلْيَكْتُبْ وَلْيُمْلِلِ ٱلَّذِى عَلَيْهِ ٱلْحَقُّ وَلْيَتَّقِ ٱللَّهَ رَبَّهُ ۥ وَلَا يَبْخَسْ مِنْهُ شَيْـًٔا ۚ فَإِن كَانَ ٱلَّذِى عَلَيْهِ ٱلْحَقُّ سَفِيهًا أَوْ ضَعِيفًا أَوْ لَا يَسْتَطِيعُ أَن يُمِلَّ هُوَ فَلْيُمْلِلْ وَلِيُّهُ ۥ بِٱلْعَدْلِ ۚ وَٱسْتَشْهِدُواْ شَهِيدَيْنِ مِن رِّجَالِكُمْ ۖ فَإِن لَّمْ يَكُونَا رَجُلَيْنِ فَرَجُلٌ وَٱمْرَأَتَانِ مِمَّن تَرْضَوْنَ مِنَ ٱلشُّهَدَآءِ أَن تَضِلَّ إِحْدَىٰهُمَا فَتُذَكِّرَ إِحْدَىٰهُمَا ٱلْأُخْرَىٰ ۚ وَلَا يَأْبَ ٱلشُّهَدَآءُ إِذَا مَا دُعُواْ ۚ وَلَا تَسْـَٔمُوٓاْ أَن تَكْتُبُوهُ صَغِيرًا أَوْ كَبِيرًا إِلَىٰٓ أَجَلِهِ ۦ ۚ ذَٰلِكُمْ أَقْسَطُ عِندَ ٱللَّهِ وَأَقْوَمُ لِلشَّهَـٰدَةِ وَأَدْنَىٰٓ أَلَّا تَرْتَابُوٓاْ ۖ إِلَّآ أَن تَكُونَ تِجَـٰرَةً حَاضِرَةً تُدِيرُونَهَا بَيْنَكُمْ فَلَيْسَ عَلَيْكُمْ جُنَاحٌ أَلَّا تَكْتُبُوهَا ۗ وَأَشْهِدُوٓاْ إِذَا تَبَايَعْتُمْ ۚ وَلَا يُضَآرَّ كَاتِبٌ وَلَا شَهِيدٌ ۚ وَإِن تَفْعَلُواْ فَإِنَّهُ ۥ فُسُوقٌۢ بِكُمْ ۗ وَٱتَّقُواْ ٱللَّهَ ۖ وَيُعَلِّمُكُمُ ٱللَّهُ ۗ وَٱللَّهُ بِكُلِّ شَىْءٍ عَلِيمٌ (٢٨٢) ۞ وَإِن كُنتُمْ عَلَىٰ سَفَرٍ وَلَمْ تَجِدُواْ كَاتِبًا فَرِهَـٰنٌ مَّقْبُوضَةٌ ۖ فَإِنْ أَمِنَ بَعْضُكُم بَعْضًا فَلْيُؤَدِّ ٱلَّذِى ٱؤْتُمِنَ أَمَـٰنَتَهُ ۥ وَلْيَتَّقِ ٱللَّهَ رَبَّهُ ۥ ۗ وَلَا تَكْتُمُواْ ٱلشَّهَـٰدَةَ ۚ وَمَن يَكْتُمْهَا فَإِنَّهُۥٓ ءَاثِمٌ قَلْبُهُ ۥ ۗ وَٱللَّهُ بِمَا تَعْمَلُونَ عَلِيمٌ (٢٨٣)

O you who have believed, when you contract a debt for a specified term, write it down. And let a scribe write [it] between you in justice. Let no scribe refuse to write as Allah has taught him. So let him write and let the one who has the obligation dictate. And let him fear Allah, his Lord, and not leave anything out of it. But if the one who has the obligation is of limited understanding or weak or unable to dictate himself, then let his guardian dictate in justice. And bring to witness two witnesses from among your men. And if there are not two men [available], then a man and two women from those whom you accept as witnesses - so that if one of the women errs, then the other can remind her. And let not the witnesses refuse when they are called upon. And do not be [too] weary to write it, whether it is small or large, for its [specified] term. That is more just in the sight of Allah and stronger as evidence and more likely to prevent doubt between you, except when it is an immediate transaction which you conduct among yourselves. For [then] there is no blame upon you if you do not write it. And take witnesses when you conclude a contract. Let no scribe be harmed or any witness. For if you do so, indeed, it is [grave] disobedience in you. And fear Allah. And Allah teaches you. And Allah is Knowing of all things. (282) And if you are on a journey and cannot find a scribe, then a security deposit [should be] taken. And if one of you entrusts another, then let him who is entrusted discharge his trust [faithfully] and let him fear Allah, his Lord. And do not conceal testimony, for whoever conceals it - his heart is indeed sinful, and Allah is Knowing of what you do. (283)

Quran 2:285

ءَامَنَ ٱلرَّسُولُ بِمَآ أُنزِلَ إِلَيْهِ مِن رَّبِّهِۦ وَٱلْمُؤْمِنُونَ ۚ كُلٌّ ءَامَنَ بِٱللَّهِ وَمَلَـٰٓئِكَتِهِۦ وَكُتُبِهِۦ وَرُسُلِهِۦ لَا نُفَرِّقُ بَيْنَ أَحَدٍ مِّن رُّسُلِهِۦ ۚ وَقَالُوا۟ سَمِعْنَا وَأَطَعْنَا ۖ غُفْرَانَكَ رَبَّنَا وَإِلَيْكَ ٱلْمَصِيرُ (٢٨٥)

The Messenger has believed in what was revealed to him from his Lord, and [so have] the believers. All of them have believed in Allah and His angels and His books and His messengers, [saying], "We make no distinction between any of His messengers." And they say, "We hear and we obey. [We seek] Your forgiveness, our Lord, and to You is the [final] destination." (285)

Quran 3:28

لَّا يَتَّخِذِ ٱلْمُؤْمِنُونَ ٱلْكَـٰفِرِينَ أَوْلِيَآءَ مِن دُونِ ٱلْمُؤْمِنِينَ ۖ وَمَن يَفْعَلْ ذَٰلِكَ فَلَيْسَ مِنَ ٱللَّهِ فِى شَىْءٍ إِلَّآ أَن تَتَّقُوا۟ مِنْهُمْ تُقَىٰةً ۗ وَيُحَذِّرُكُمُ ٱللَّهُ نَفْسَهُۥ ۗ وَإِلَى ٱللَّهِ ٱلْمَصِيرُ (٢٨)

Let not believers take disbelievers as allies rather than believers. And whoever [of you] does that has nothing with Allah, except when taking precaution against them in prudence. And Allah warns you of Himself, and to Allah is the [final] destination. (28)

Quran 3:79-80

مَا كَانَ لِبَشَرٍ أَن يُؤْتِيَهُ ٱللَّهُ ٱلْكِتَٰبَ وَٱلْحُكْمَ وَٱلنُّبُوَّةَ ثُمَّ يَقُولَ لِلنَّاسِ كُونُوا۟ عِبَادًا لِّى مِن دُونِ ٱللَّهِ وَلَٰكِن كُونُوا۟ رَبَّٰنِيِّۦنَ بِمَا كُنتُمْ تُعَلِّمُونَ ٱلْكِتَٰبَ وَبِمَا كُنتُمْ تَدْرُسُونَ (٧٩) وَلَا يَأْمُرَكُمْ أَن تَتَّخِذُوا۟ ٱلْمَلَٰٓئِكَةَ وَٱلنَّبِيِّۦنَ أَرْبَابًا ۗ أَيَأْمُرُكُم بِٱلْكُفْرِ بَعْدَ إِذْ أَنتُم مُّسْلِمُونَ (٨٠)

It is not for a human [prophet] that Allah should give him the Scripture and authority and prophethood and then he would say to the people, "Be servants to me rather than Allah," but [instead, he would say], "Be pious scholars of the Lord because of what you have taught of the Scripture and because of what you have studied." (79) Nor could he order you to take the angels and prophets as lords. Would he order you to disbelief after you had been Muslims? (80)

Quran 3:102-105

يَٰٓأَيُّهَا ٱلَّذِينَ ءَامَنُوا۟ ٱتَّقُوا۟ ٱللَّهَ حَقَّ تُقَاتِهِۦ وَلَا تَمُوتُنَّ إِلَّا وَأَنتُم مُّسْلِمُونَ (١٠٢) وَٱعْتَصِمُوا۟ بِحَبْلِ ٱللَّهِ جَمِيعًا وَلَا تَفَرَّقُوا۟ ۚ وَٱذْكُرُوا۟ نِعْمَتَ ٱللَّهِ عَلَيْكُمْ إِذْ كُنتُمْ أَعْدَآءً فَأَلَّفَ بَيْنَ قُلُوبِكُمْ فَأَصْبَحْتُم بِنِعْمَتِهِۦٓ إِخْوَٰنًا وَكُنتُمْ عَلَىٰ شَفَا حُفْرَةٍ مِّنَ ٱلنَّارِ فَأَنقَذَكُم مِّنْهَا ۗ كَذَٰلِكَ يُبَيِّنُ ٱللَّهُ لَكُمْ ءَايَٰتِهِۦ لَعَلَّكُمْ تَهْتَدُونَ (١٠٣) وَلْتَكُن مِّنكُمْ أُمَّةٌ يَدْعُونَ إِلَى ٱلْخَيْرِ وَيَأْمُرُونَ بِٱلْمَعْرُوفِ وَيَنْهَوْنَ عَنِ ٱلْمُنكَرِ ۚ وَأُو۟لَٰٓئِكَ هُمُ ٱلْمُفْلِحُونَ (١٠٤) وَلَا تَكُونُوا۟ كَٱلَّذِينَ تَفَرَّقُوا۟ وَٱخْتَلَفُوا۟ مِنۢ بَعْدِ مَا جَآءَهُمُ ٱلْبَيِّنَٰتُ ۚ وَأُو۟لَٰٓئِكَ لَهُمْ عَذَابٌ عَظِيمٌ (١٠٥)

O you who have believed, fear Allah as He should be feared and do not die except as Muslims [in submission to Him]. (102) And hold firmly to the rope of Allah all together and do not become divided. And remember the favor of Allah upon you - when you were enemies and He brought your hearts together and you became, by His favor, brothers. And you were on the edge of a pit of the Fire, and He saved you from it. Thus does Allah make clear to you His verses that you may be guided. (103) And let there be [arising] from you a nation inviting to [all that is] good, enjoining what is right and forbidding what is wrong, and those will be the successful. (104) And do not be like the ones who became divided and differed after the clear proofs had come to them. And those will have a great punishment. (105)

Quran 3:130-135

يَـٰٓأَيُّهَا ٱلَّذِينَ ءَامَنُوا۟ لَا تَأْكُلُوا۟ ٱلرِّبَوٰٓا۟ أَضْعَـٰفًا مُّضَـٰعَفَةً ۖ وَٱتَّقُوا۟ ٱللَّهَ لَعَلَّكُمْ تُفْلِحُونَ (١٣٠) وَٱتَّقُوا۟ ٱلنَّارَ ٱلَّتِىٓ أُعِدَّتْ لِلْكَـٰفِرِينَ (١٣١) وَأَطِيعُوا۟ ٱللَّهَ وَٱلرَّسُولَ لَعَلَّكُمْ تُرْحَمُونَ (١٣٢) ۞ وَسَارِعُوٓا۟ إِلَىٰ مَغْفِرَةٍ مِّن رَّبِّكُمْ وَجَنَّةٍ عَرْضُهَا ٱلسَّمَـٰوَٰتُ وَٱلْأَرْضُ أُعِدَّتْ لِلْمُتَّقِينَ (١٣٣) ٱلَّذِينَ يُنفِقُونَ فِى ٱلسَّرَّآءِ وَٱلضَّرَّآءِ وَٱلْكَـٰظِمِينَ ٱلْغَيْظَ وَٱلْعَافِينَ عَنِ ٱلنَّاسِ ۗ وَٱللَّهُ يُحِبُّ ٱلْمُحْسِنِينَ (١٣٤) وَٱلَّذِينَ إِذَا فَعَلُوا۟ فَـٰحِشَةً أَوْ ظَلَمُوٓا۟ أَنفُسَهُمْ ذَكَرُوا۟ ٱللَّهَ فَٱسْتَغْفَرُوا۟ لِذُنُوبِهِمْ وَمَن يَغْفِرُ ٱلذُّنُوبَ إِلَّا ٱللَّهُ وَلَمْ يُصِرُّوا۟ عَلَىٰ مَا فَعَلُوا۟ وَهُمْ يَعْلَمُونَ (١٣٥)

O you who have believed, do not consume usury, doubled and multiplied, but fear Allah that you may be successful. (130) And fear the Fire, which has been prepared for the disbelievers. (131) And obey Allah and the Messenger that you may obtain mercy. (132) And hasten to forgiveness from your Lord and a garden as wide as the heavens and earth, prepared for the righteous (133) Who spend [in the cause of Allah] during ease and hardship and who restrain anger and who pardon the people - and Allah loves the doers of good; (134) And those who, when they commit an immorality or wrong themselves [by transgression], remember Allah and seek forgiveness for their sins - and who can forgive sins except Allah? - and [who] do not persist in what they have done while they know. (135)

Quran 3:138-142

هَٰذَا بَيَانٌ لِّلنَّاسِ وَهُدًى وَمَوْعِظَةٌ لِّلْمُتَّقِينَ (١٣٨) وَلَا تَهِنُوا۟ وَلَا تَحْزَنُوا۟ وَأَنتُمُ ٱلْأَعْلَوْنَ إِن كُنتُم مُّؤْمِنِينَ (١٣٩) إِن يَمْسَسْكُمْ قَرْحٌ فَقَدْ مَسَّ ٱلْقَوْمَ قَرْحٌ مِّثْلُهُۥ ۚ وَتِلْكَ ٱلْأَيَّامُ نُدَاوِلُهَا بَيْنَ ٱلنَّاسِ وَلِيَعْلَمَ ٱللَّهُ ٱلَّذِينَ ءَامَنُوا۟ وَيَتَّخِذَ مِنكُمْ شُهَدَآءَ ۗ وَٱللَّهُ لَا يُحِبُّ ٱلظَّٰلِمِينَ (١٤٠) وَلِيُمَحِّصَ ٱللَّهُ ٱلَّذِينَ ءَامَنُوا۟ وَيَمْحَقَ ٱلْكَٰفِرِينَ (١٤١) أَمْ حَسِبْتُمْ أَن تَدْخُلُوا۟ ٱلْجَنَّةَ وَلَمَّا يَعْلَمِ ٱللَّهُ ٱلَّذِينَ جَٰهَدُوا۟ مِنكُمْ وَيَعْلَمَ ٱلصَّٰبِرِينَ (١٤٢)

This [Qur'an] is a clear statement to [all] the people and a guidance and instruction for those conscious of Allah. (138) So do not weaken and do not grieve, and you will be superior if you are [true] believers. (139) If a wound should touch you - there has already touched the [opposing] people a wound similar to it. And these days [of varying conditions] We alternate among the people so that Allah may make evident those who believe and [may] take to Himself from among you martyrs - and Allah does not like the wrongdoers - (140) And that Allah may purify the believers [through trials] and destroy the disbelievers. (141) Or do you think that you will enter Paradise while Allah has not yet made evident those of you who fight in His cause and made evident those who are steadfast? (142)

Quran 3:156

يَـٰٓأَيُّهَا ٱلَّذِينَ ءَامَنُوا۟ لَا تَكُونُوا۟ كَٱلَّذِينَ كَفَرُوا۟ وَقَالُوا۟ لِإِخْوَٰنِهِمْ إِذَا ضَرَبُوا۟ فِى ٱلْأَرْضِ أَوْ كَانُوا۟ غُزًّى لَّوْ كَانُوا۟ عِندَنَا مَا مَاتُوا۟ وَمَا قُتِلُوا۟ لِيَجْعَلَ ٱللَّهُ ذَٰلِكَ حَسْرَةً فِى قُلُوبِهِمْ ۗ وَٱللَّهُ يُحْىِۦ وَيُمِيتُ ۗ وَٱللَّهُ بِمَا تَعْمَلُونَ بَصِيرٌ (١٥٦)

O you who have believed, do not be like those who disbelieved and said about their brothers when they traveled through the land or went out to fight, "If they had been with us, they would not have died or have been killed," so Allah makes that [misconception] a regret within their hearts. And it is Allah who gives life and causes death, and Allah is Seeing of what you do. (156)

Quran 3:169-170

وَلَا تَحْسَبَنَّ ٱلَّذِينَ قُتِلُواْ فِى سَبِيلِ ٱللَّهِ أَمْوَٰتًۢا ۚ بَلْ أَحْيَآءٌ عِندَ رَبِّهِمْ يُرْزَقُونَ (١٦٩) فَرِحِينَ بِمَآ ءَاتَىٰهُمُ ٱللَّهُ مِن فَضْلِهِۦ وَيَسْتَبْشِرُونَ بِٱلَّذِينَ لَمْ يَلْحَقُواْ بِهِم مِّنْ خَلْفِهِمْ أَلَّا خَوْفٌ عَلَيْهِمْ وَلَا هُمْ يَحْزَنُونَ (١٧٠)

And never think of those who have been killed in the cause of Allah as dead. Rather, they are alive with their Lord, receiving provision, (169) Rejoicing in what Allah has bestowed upon them of His bounty, and they receive good tidings about those [to be martyred] after them who have not yet joined them - that there will be no fear concerning them, nor will they grieve. (170)

Quran 3:175-176

إِنَّمَا ذَٰلِكُمُ ٱلشَّيْطَٰنُ يُخَوِّفُ أَوْلِيَآءَهُۥ فَلَا تَخَافُوهُمْ وَخَافُونِ إِن كُنتُم مُّؤْمِنِينَ (١٧٥) وَلَا يَحْزُنكَ ٱلَّذِينَ يُسَٰرِعُونَ فِى ٱلْكُفْرِ ۚ إِنَّهُمْ لَن يَضُرُّواْ ٱللَّهَ شَيْـًٔا ۗ يُرِيدُ ٱللَّهُ أَلَّا يَجْعَلَ لَهُمْ حَظًّا فِى ٱلْءَاخِرَةِ ۖ وَلَهُمْ عَذَابٌ عَظِيمٌ (١٧٦)

That is only Satan who frightens [you] of his supporters. So fear them not, but fear Me, if you are [indeed] believers. (175) And do not be grieved, by those who hasten into disbelief. Indeed, they will never harm Allah at all. Allah intends that He should give them no share in the Hereafter, and for them is a great punishment. (176)

Quran 3:180

وَلَا يَحْسَبَنَّ ٱلَّذِينَ يَبْخَلُونَ بِمَآ ءَاتَىٰهُمُ ٱللَّهُ مِن فَضْلِهِۦ هُوَ خَيْرًا لَّهُم ۖ بَلْ هُوَ شَرٌّ لَّهُمْ ۖ سَيُطَوَّقُونَ مَا بَخِلُوا۟ بِهِۦ يَوْمَ ٱلْقِيَٰمَةِ ۗ وَلِلَّهِ مِيرَٰثُ ٱلسَّمَٰوَٰتِ وَٱلْأَرْضِ ۗ وَٱللَّهُ بِمَا تَعْمَلُونَ خَبِيرٌ (١٨٠)

And let not those who [greedily] withhold what Allah has given them of His bounty ever think that it is better for them. Rather, it is worse for them. Their necks will be encircled by what they withheld on the Day of Resurrection. And to Allah belongs the heritage of the heavens and the earth. And Allah, with what you do, is [fully] Acquainted. (180)

Quran 3:188

لَا تَحْسَبَنَّ ٱلَّذِينَ يَفْرَحُونَ بِمَآ أَتَوا۟ وَّيُحِبُّونَ أَن يُحْمَدُوا۟ بِمَا لَمْ يَفْعَلُوا۟ فَلَا تَحْسَبَنَّهُم بِمَفَازَةٍ مِّنَ ٱلْعَذَابِ ۖ وَلَهُمْ عَذَابٌ أَلِيمٌ (١٨٨)

And never think that those who rejoice in what they have perpetrated and like to be praised for what they did not do - never think them [to be] in safety from the punishment, and for them is a painful punishment. (188)

Quran 3:190-200

إِنَّ فِى خَلْقِ ٱلسَّمَٰوَٰتِ وَٱلْأَرْضِ وَٱخْتِلَٰفِ ٱلَّيْلِ وَٱلنَّهَارِ لَءَايَٰتٍ لِّأُو۟لِى ٱلْأَلْبَٰبِ (١٩٠) ٱلَّذِينَ يَذْكُرُونَ ٱللَّهَ قِيَٰمًا وَقُعُودًا وَعَلَىٰ جُنُوبِهِمْ وَيَتَفَكَّرُونَ فِى خَلْقِ ٱلسَّمَٰوَٰتِ وَٱلْأَرْضِ رَبَّنَا مَا خَلَقْتَ هَٰذَا بَٰطِلًا سُبْحَٰنَكَ فَقِنَا عَذَابَ ٱلنَّارِ (١٩١) رَبَّنَآ إِنَّكَ مَن تُدْخِلِ ٱلنَّارَ فَقَدْ أَخْزَيْتَهُۥ ۖ وَمَا لِلظَّٰلِمِينَ مِنْ أَنصَارٍ (١٩٢) رَّبَّنَآ إِنَّنَا سَمِعْنَا مُنَادِيًا يُنَادِى لِلْإِيمَٰنِ أَنْ ءَامِنُوا۟ بِرَبِّكُمْ فَـَٔامَنَّا ۚ رَبَّنَا

فَٱغْفِرْ لَنَا ذُنُوبَنَا وَكَفِّرْ عَنَّا سَيِّـَٔاتِنَا وَتَوَفَّنَا مَعَ ٱلْأَبْرَارِ (١٩٣) رَبَّنَا وَءَاتِنَا مَا وَعَدتَّنَا عَلَىٰ رُسُلِكَ وَلَا تُخْزِنَا يَوْمَ ٱلْقِيَـٰمَةِ ۗ إِنَّكَ لَا تُخْلِفُ ٱلْمِيعَادَ (١٩٤) فَٱسْتَجَابَ لَهُمْ رَبُّهُمْ أَنِّى لَا أُضِيعُ عَمَلَ عَـٰمِلٍ مِّنكُم مِّن ذَكَرٍ أَوْ أُنثَىٰ ۖ بَعْضُكُم مِّنۢ بَعْضٍ ۖ فَٱلَّذِينَ هَاجَرُوا۟ وَأُخْرِجُوا۟ مِن دِيَـٰرِهِمْ وَأُوذُوا۟ فِى سَبِيلِى وَقَـٰتَلُوا۟ وَقُتِلُوا۟ لَأُكَفِّرَنَّ عَنْهُمْ سَيِّـَٔاتِهِمْ وَلَأُدْخِلَنَّهُمْ جَنَّـٰتٍ تَجْرِى مِن تَحْتِهَا ٱلْأَنْهَـٰرُ ثَوَابًا مِّنْ عِندِ ٱللَّهِ ۗ وَٱللَّهُ عِندَهُۥ حُسْنُ ٱلثَّوَابِ (١٩٥) لَا يَغُرَّنَّكَ تَقَلُّبُ ٱلَّذِينَ كَفَرُوا۟ فِى ٱلْبِلَـٰدِ (١٩٦) مَتَـٰعٌ قَلِيلٌ ثُمَّ مَأْوَىٰهُمْ جَهَنَّمُ ۚ وَبِئْسَ ٱلْمِهَادُ (١٩٧) لَـٰكِنِ ٱلَّذِينَ ٱتَّقَوْا۟ رَبَّهُمْ لَهُمْ جَنَّـٰتٌ تَجْرِى مِن تَحْتِهَا ٱلْأَنْهَـٰرُ خَـٰلِدِينَ فِيهَا نُزُلًا مِّنْ عِندِ ٱللَّهِ ۗ وَمَا عِندَ ٱللَّهِ خَيْرٌ لِّلْأَبْرَارِ (١٩٨) وَإِنَّ مِنْ أَهْلِ ٱلْكِتَـٰبِ لَمَن يُؤْمِنُ بِٱللَّهِ وَمَا أُنزِلَ إِلَيْكُمْ وَمَا أُنزِلَ إِلَيْهِمْ خَـٰشِعِينَ لِلَّهِ لَا يَشْتَرُونَ بِـَٔايَـٰتِ ٱللَّهِ ثَمَنًا قَلِيلًا ۗ أُو۟لَـٰٓئِكَ لَهُمْ أَجْرُهُمْ عِندَ رَبِّهِمْ ۗ إِنَّ ٱللَّهَ سَرِيعُ ٱلْحِسَابِ (١٩٩) يَـٰٓأَيُّهَا ٱلَّذِينَ ءَامَنُوا۟ ٱصْبِرُوا۟ وَصَابِرُوا۟ وَرَابِطُوا۟ وَٱتَّقُوا۟ ٱللَّهَ لَعَلَّكُمْ تُفْلِحُونَ (٢٠٠)

Indeed, in the creation of the heavens and the earth and the alternation of the night and the day are signs for those of understanding. (190) Who remember Allah while standing or sitting or [lying] on their sides and give thought to the creation of the heavens and the earth, [saying], "Our Lord, You did not create this aimlessly; exalted are You [above such a thing]; then protect us from the punishment of the Fire. (191) Our Lord, indeed whoever You admit to the Fire - You have disgraced him, and for the wrongdoers there are no helpers. (192) Our Lord, indeed we have heard a caller calling to faith, [saying], 'Believe in your Lord,' and we have believed.

Our Lord, so forgive us our sins and remove from us our misdeeds and cause us to die with the righteous. (193) Our Lord, and grant us what You promised us through Your messengers and do not disgrace us on the Day of Resurrection. Indeed, You do not fail in [Your] promise." (194) And their Lord responded to them, "Never will I allow to be lost the work of [any] worker among you, whether male or female; you are of one another. So those who emigrated or were evicted from their homes or were harmed in My cause or fought or were killed - I will surely remove from them their misdeeds, and I will surely admit them to gardens beneath which rivers flow as reward from Allah, and Allah has with Him the best reward." (195) Be not deceived by the [uninhibited] movement of the disbelievers throughout the land. (196) [It is but] a small enjoyment; then their [final] refuge is Hell, and wretched is the resting place. (197) But those who feared their Lord will have gardens beneath which rivers flow, abiding eternally therein, as accommodation from Allah. And that which is with Allah is best for the righteous. (198) And indeed, among the People of the Scripture are those who believe in Allah and what was revealed to you and what was revealed to them, [being] humbly submissive to Allah. They do not exchange the verses of Allah for a small price. Those will have their reward with their Lord. Indeed, Allah is swift in account. (199) O you who have believed, persevere and endure and remain stationed and fear Allah that you may be successful. (200)

Quran 4:2-8

وَءَاتُواْ ٱلْيَتَٰمَىٰٓ أَمْوَٰلَهُمْ ۖ وَلَا تَتَبَدَّلُواْ ٱلْخَبِيثَ بِٱلطَّيِّبِ ۖ وَلَا تَأْكُلُوٓاْ أَمْوَٰلَهُمْ إِلَىٰٓ أَمْوَٰلِكُمْ ۚ إِنَّهُۥ كَانَ حُوبًا كَبِيرًا (٢) وَإِنْ خِفْتُمْ أَلَّا تُقْسِطُواْ فِى ٱلْيَتَٰمَىٰ فَٱنكِحُواْ مَا طَابَ لَكُم مِّنَ ٱلنِّسَآءِ مَثْنَىٰ وَثُلَٰثَ وَرُبَٰعَ ۖ فَإِنْ خِفْتُمْ أَلَّا تَعْدِلُواْ فَوَٰحِدَةً أَوْ مَا مَلَكَتْ أَيْمَٰنُكُمْ ۚ ذَٰلِكَ أَدْنَىٰٓ أَلَّا تَعُولُواْ (٣) وَءَاتُواْ ٱلنِّسَآءَ صَدُقَٰتِهِنَّ نِحْلَةً ۚ فَإِن طِبْنَ لَكُمْ عَن شَىْءٍ مِّنْهُ نَفْسًا فَكُلُوهُ هَنِيٓـًٔا مَّرِيٓـًٔا (٤) وَلَا تُؤْتُواْ ٱلسُّفَهَآءَ أَمْوَٰلَكُمُ ٱلَّتِى جَعَلَ ٱللَّهُ لَكُمْ قِيَٰمًا وَٱرْزُقُوهُمْ فِيهَا وَٱكْسُوهُمْ وَقُولُواْ لَهُمْ قَوْلًا مَّعْرُوفًا (٥) وَٱبْتَلُواْ ٱلْيَتَٰمَىٰ حَتَّىٰٓ إِذَا بَلَغُواْ ٱلنِّكَاحَ فَإِنْ ءَانَسْتُم مِّنْهُمْ رُشْدًا فَٱدْفَعُوٓاْ إِلَيْهِمْ أَمْوَٰلَهُمْ ۖ وَلَا تَأْكُلُوهَآ إِسْرَافًا وَبِدَارًا أَن يَكْبَرُواْ ۚ وَمَن كَانَ غَنِيًّا فَلْيَسْتَعْفِفْ ۖ وَمَن كَانَ فَقِيرًا فَلْيَأْكُلْ بِٱلْمَعْرُوفِ ۚ فَإِذَا دَفَعْتُمْ إِلَيْهِمْ أَمْوَٰلَهُمْ فَأَشْهِدُواْ عَلَيْهِمْ ۚ وَكَفَىٰ بِٱللَّهِ حَسِيبًا (٦) لِّلرِّجَالِ نَصِيبٌ مِّمَّا تَرَكَ ٱلْوَٰلِدَانِ وَٱلْأَقْرَبُونَ وَلِلنِّسَآءِ نَصِيبٌ مِّمَّا تَرَكَ ٱلْوَٰلِدَانِ وَٱلْأَقْرَبُونَ مِمَّا قَلَّ مِنْهُ أَوْ كَثُرَ ۚ نَصِيبًا مَّفْرُوضًا (٧) وَإِذَا حَضَرَ ٱلْقِسْمَةَ أُوْلُواْ ٱلْقُرْبَىٰ وَٱلْيَتَٰمَىٰ وَٱلْمَسَٰكِينُ فَٱرْزُقُوهُم مِّنْهُ وَقُولُواْ لَهُمْ قَوْلًا مَّعْرُوفًا (٨)

And give to the orphans their properties and do not substitute the defective [of your own] for the good [of theirs]. And do not consume their properties into your own. Indeed, that is ever a great sin. (2) And if you fear that you will not deal justly with the orphan girls, then marry those that please you of [other] women, two or three or four. But if you fear that you will not be just, *then [marry only] one or those your right hand possesses. That is more suitable that you may not incline [to injustice]. (3) And give the women [upon marriage] their [bridal] gifts graciously. But if they give up willingly to you anything of it, then take it in satisfaction and ease. (4) And do not give the weak-minded your property, which Allah has made a means of sustenance for you, but provide for them with it and clothe them and speak to them words of appropriate kindness. (5) And test the orphans [in their abilities] until they reach marriageable age. Then if you perceive in them sound judgement, release their property to them. And do not consume it excessively and quickly, [anticipating] that they will grow up. And whoever, [when acting as guardian], is self-sufficient should refrain [from taking a fee]; and whoever is poor - let him take according to what is acceptable. Then when you release their property to them, bring witnesses upon them. And sufficient is Allah as Accountant. (6) For men is a share of what the parents and close relatives leave, and for women is a share of what the parents and close relatives leave, be it little or much - an obligatory share. (7) And when [other] relatives and orphans and the needy are present at the [time of] division, then provide for them [something] out of the estate and speak to them words of appropriate kindness. (8)*

Quran 4:19-25

يَـٰٓأَيُّهَا ٱلَّذِينَ ءَامَنُوا۟ لَا يَحِلُّ لَكُمْ أَن تَرِثُوا۟ ٱلنِّسَآءَ كَرْهًا ۖ وَلَا تَعْضُلُوهُنَّ لِتَذْهَبُوا۟ بِبَعْضِ مَآ ءَاتَيْتُمُوهُنَّ إِلَّآ أَن يَأْتِينَ بِفَـٰحِشَةٍ مُّبَيِّنَةٍ ۚ وَعَاشِرُوهُنَّ بِٱلْمَعْرُوفِ ۚ فَإِن كَرِهْتُمُوهُنَّ فَعَسَىٰٓ أَن تَكْرَهُوا۟ شَيْـًٔا وَيَجْعَلَ ٱللَّهُ فِيهِ خَيْرًا كَثِيرًا (١٩) وَإِنْ أَرَدتُّمُ ٱسْتِبْدَالَ زَوْجٍ مَّكَانَ زَوْجٍ وَءَاتَيْتُمْ إِحْدَىٰهُنَّ قِنطَارًا فَلَا تَأْخُذُوا۟ مِنْهُ شَيْـًٔا ۚ أَتَأْخُذُونَهُۥ بُهْتَـٰنًا وَإِثْمًا مُّبِينًا (٢٠) وَكَيْفَ تَأْخُذُونَهُۥ وَقَدْ أَفْضَىٰ بَعْضُكُمْ إِلَىٰ بَعْضٍ وَأَخَذْنَ مِنكُم مِّيثَـٰقًا غَلِيظًا (٢١) وَلَا تَنكِحُوا۟ مَا نَكَحَ ءَابَآؤُكُم مِّنَ ٱلنِّسَآءِ إِلَّا مَا قَدْ سَلَفَ ۚ إِنَّهُۥ كَانَ فَـٰحِشَةً وَمَقْتًا وَسَآءَ سَبِيلًا (٢٢) حُرِّمَتْ عَلَيْكُمْ أُمَّهَـٰتُكُمْ وَبَنَاتُكُمْ وَأَخَوَٰتُكُمْ وَعَمَّـٰتُكُمْ وَخَـٰلَـٰتُكُمْ وَبَنَاتُ ٱلْأَخِ وَبَنَاتُ ٱلْأُخْتِ وَأُمَّهَـٰتُكُمُ ٱلَّـٰتِىٓ أَرْضَعْنَكُمْ وَأَخَوَٰتُكُم مِّنَ ٱلرَّضَـٰعَةِ وَأُمَّهَـٰتُ نِسَآئِكُمْ وَرَبَـٰٓئِبُكُمُ ٱلَّـٰتِى فِى حُجُورِكُم مِّن نِّسَآئِكُمُ ٱلَّـٰتِى دَخَلْتُم بِهِنَّ فَإِن لَّمْ تَكُونُوا۟ دَخَلْتُم بِهِنَّ فَلَا جُنَاحَ عَلَيْكُمْ وَحَلَـٰٓئِلُ أَبْنَآئِكُمُ ٱلَّذِينَ مِنْ أَصْلَـٰبِكُمْ وَأَن تَجْمَعُوا۟ بَيْنَ ٱلْأُخْتَيْنِ إِلَّا مَا قَدْ سَلَفَ ۗ إِنَّ ٱللَّهَ كَانَ غَفُورًا رَّحِيمًا (٢٣) ۞ وَٱلْمُحْصَنَـٰتُ مِنَ ٱلنِّسَآءِ إِلَّا مَا مَلَكَتْ أَيْمَـٰنُكُمْ ۖ كِتَـٰبَ ٱللَّهِ عَلَيْكُمْ ۚ وَأُحِلَّ لَكُم مَّا وَرَآءَ ذَٰلِكُمْ أَن تَبْتَغُوا۟ بِأَمْوَٰلِكُم مُّحْصِنِينَ غَيْرَ مُسَـٰفِحِينَ ۚ فَمَا ٱسْتَمْتَعْتُم بِهِۦ مِنْهُنَّ فَـَٔاتُوهُنَّ أُجُورَهُنَّ فَرِيضَةً ۚ وَلَا جُنَاحَ عَلَيْكُمْ فِيمَا تَرَٰضَيْتُم بِهِۦ مِنۢ بَعْدِ ٱلْفَرِيضَةِ ۚ إِنَّ ٱللَّهَ كَانَ عَلِيمًا حَكِيمًا (٢٤) وَمَن لَّمْ يَسْتَطِعْ مِنكُمْ طَوْلًا أَن يَنكِحَ ٱلْمُحْصَنَـٰتِ ٱلْمُؤْمِنَـٰتِ فَمِن مَّا مَلَكَتْ أَيْمَـٰنُكُم مِّن فَتَيَـٰتِكُمُ ٱلْمُؤْمِنَـٰتِ ۚ وَٱللَّهُ أَعْلَمُ بِإِيمَـٰنِكُم ۚ بَعْضُكُم مِّنۢ بَعْضٍ ۚ فَٱنكِحُوهُنَّ بِإِذْنِ أَهْلِهِنَّ وَءَاتُوهُنَّ أُجُورَهُنَّ بِٱلْمَعْرُوفِ مُحْصَنَـٰتٍ غَيْرَ مُسَـٰفِحَـٰتٍ وَلَا مُتَّخِذَٰتِ أَخْدَانٍ ۚ فَإِذَآ أُحْصِنَّ فَإِنْ أَتَيْنَ بِفَـٰحِشَةٍ فَعَلَيْهِنَّ نِصْفُ مَا عَلَى ٱلْمُحْصَنَـٰتِ مِنَ ٱلْعَذَابِ ۚ ذَٰلِكَ لِمَنْ خَشِىَ ٱلْعَنَتَ مِنكُمْ ۚ وَأَن تَصْبِرُوا۟ خَيْرٌ لَّكُمْ ۗ وَٱللَّهُ غَفُورٌ رَّحِيمٌ (٢٥)

O you who have believed, it is not lawful for you to inherit women by compulsion. And do not make difficulties for them in order to take [back] part of what you gave them unless they commit a clear immorality. And live with them in kindness. For if you dislike them - perhaps you dislike a thing and Allah makes therein much good. (19) But if you want to replace one wife with another and you have given one of them a great amount [in gifts], do not take [back] from it anything. Would you take it in injustice and manifest sin? (20) And how could you take it while you have gone in unto each other and they have taken from you a solemn covenant? (21) And do not marry those [women] whom your fathers married, except what has already occurred. Indeed, it was an immorality and hateful [to Allah] and was evil as a way. (22) Prohibited to you [for marriage] are your mothers, your daughters, your sisters, your father's sisters, your mother's sisters, your brother's daughters, your sister's daughters, your [milk] mothers who nursed you, your sisters through nursing, your wives' mothers, and your step-daughters under your guardianship [born] of your wives unto whom you have gone in. But if you have not gone in unto them, there is no sin upon you. And [also prohibited are] the wives of your sons who are from your [own] loins, and that you take [in marriage] two sisters simultaneously, except for what has already occurred. Indeed, Allah is ever Forgiving and Merciful. (23) And [also prohibited to you are all] married women except those your right hands possess. [This is] the decree of Allah upon you. And lawful to you are [all others] beyond these, [provided] that you seek them [in marriage] with [gifts from] your property, desiring chastity, not unlawful sexual intercourse. So for whatever you enjoy [of marriage] from them, give them their due compensation as an obligation. And there is no blame upon you for what you mutually agree to beyond the obligation. Indeed, Allah is ever Knowing and Wise. (24) And whoever among you cannot [find] the means to marry free, believing women, then [he may marry] from those whom your right hands possess of believing slave girls. And Allah is most knowing about your faith. You [believers] are of one another. So marry them with the permission of their people and give them their due compensation according to what is acceptable. [They should be] chaste, neither [of] those who commit unlawful intercourse randomly nor those who take [secret] lovers. But once they are sheltered in marriage, if they should commit adultery, then for them is half the punishment for free [unmarried] women. This [allowance] is for him among you who fears sin, but to be patient is better for you. And Allah is Forgiving and Merciful. (25)

Quran 4:29-32

يَـٰٓأَيُّهَا ٱلَّذِينَ ءَامَنُوا۟ لَا تَأْكُلُوٓا۟ أَمْوَٰلَكُم بَيْنَكُم بِٱلْبَـٰطِلِ إِلَّآ أَن تَكُونَ تِجَـٰرَةً عَن تَرَاضٍ مِّنكُمْ ۚ وَلَا تَقْتُلُوٓا۟ أَنفُسَكُمْ ۚ إِنَّ ٱللَّهَ كَانَ بِكُمْ رَحِيمًا (٢٩) وَمَن يَفْعَلْ ذَٰلِكَ عُدْوَٰنًا وَظُلْمًا فَسَوْفَ نُصْلِيهِ نَارًا ۚ وَكَانَ ذَٰلِكَ عَلَى ٱللَّهِ يَسِيرًا (٣٠) إِن تَجْتَنِبُوا۟ كَبَآئِرَ مَا تُنْهَوْنَ عَنْهُ نُكَفِّرْ عَنكُمْ سَيِّـَٔاتِكُمْ وَنُدْخِلْكُم مُّدْخَلًا كَرِيمًا (٣١) وَلَا تَتَمَنَّوْا۟ مَا فَضَّلَ ٱللَّهُ بِهِۦ بَعْضَكُمْ عَلَىٰ بَعْضٍ ۚ لِّلرِّجَالِ نَصِيبٌ مِّمَّا ٱكْتَسَبُوا۟ ۖ وَلِلنِّسَآءِ نَصِيبٌ مِّمَّا ٱكْتَسَبْنَ ۚ وَسْـَٔلُوا۟ ٱللَّهَ مِن فَضْلِهِۦٓ ۗ إِنَّ ٱللَّهَ كَانَ بِكُلِّ شَىْءٍ عَلِيمًا (٣٢)

O you who have believed, do not consume one another's wealth unjustly but only [in lawful] business by mutual consent. And do not kill yourselves [or one another]. Indeed, Allah is to you ever Merciful. (29) And whoever does that in aggression and injustice - then We will drive him into a Fire. And that, for Allah, is [always] easy. (30) If you avoid the major sins which you are forbidden, We will remove from you your lesser sins and admit you to a noble entrance [into Paradise]. (31) And do not wish for that by which Allah has made some of you exceed others. For men is a share of what they have earned, and for women is a share of what they have earned. And ask Allah of his bounty. Indeed Allah is ever, of all things, Knowing. (32)

Quran 4:43

يَـٰٓأَيُّهَا ٱلَّذِينَ ءَامَنُوا۟ لَا تَقْرَبُوا۟ ٱلصَّلَوٰةَ وَأَنتُمْ سُكَـٰرَىٰ حَتَّىٰ تَعْلَمُوا۟ مَا تَقُولُونَ وَلَا جُنُبًا إِلَّا عَابِرِى سَبِيلٍ حَتَّىٰ تَغْتَسِلُوا۟ وَإِن كُنتُم مَّرْضَىٰٓ أَوْ عَلَىٰ سَفَرٍ أَوْ جَآءَ أَحَدٌ مِّنكُم مِّنَ ٱلْغَآئِطِ أَوْ لَـٰمَسْتُمُ ٱلنِّسَآءَ فَلَمْ تَجِدُوا۟ مَآءً فَتَيَمَّمُوا۟ صَعِيدًا طَيِّبًا فَٱمْسَحُوا۟ بِوُجُوهِكُمْ وَأَيْدِيكُمْ إِنَّ ٱللَّهَ كَانَ عَفُوًّا غَفُورًا (٤٣)

O you who have believed, do not approach prayer while you are intoxicated until you know what you are saying or in a state of janabah, except those passing through [a place of prayer], until you have washed [your whole body]. And if you are ill or on a journey or one of you comes from the place of relieving himself or you have contacted women and find no water, then seek clean earth and wipe over your faces and your hands [with it]. Indeed, Allah is ever Pardoning and Forgiving. (43)

Quran 4:65

فَلَا وَرَبِّكَ لَا يُؤْمِنُونَ حَتَّىٰ يُحَكِّمُوكَ فِيمَا شَجَرَ بَيْنَهُمْ ثُمَّ لَا يَجِدُوا۟ فِىٓ أَنفُسِهِمْ حَرَجًا مِّمَّا قَضَيْتَ وَيُسَلِّمُوا۟ تَسْلِيمًا (٦٥)

But no, by your Lord, they will not [truly] believe until they make you, [O Muhammad], judge concerning that over which they dispute among themselves and then find within themselves no discomfort from what you have judged and submit in [full, willing] submission. (65)

Quran 4:92-94

وَمَا كَانَ لِمُؤْمِنٍ أَن يَقْتُلَ مُؤْمِنًا إِلَّا خَطَـًٔا ۚ وَمَن قَتَلَ مُؤْمِنًا خَطَـًٔا فَتَحْرِيرُ رَقَبَةٍ مُّؤْمِنَةٍ وَدِيَةٌ مُّسَلَّمَةٌ إِلَىٰٓ أَهْلِهِۦٓ إِلَّآ أَن يَصَّدَّقُوا۟ ۚ فَإِن كَانَ مِن قَوْمٍ عَدُوٍّ لَّكُمْ وَهُوَ مُؤْمِنٌ فَتَحْرِيرُ رَقَبَةٍ مُّؤْمِنَةٍ ۖ وَإِن كَانَ مِن قَوْمٍۭ بَيْنَكُمْ وَبَيْنَهُم مِّيثَـٰقٌ فَدِيَةٌ مُّسَلَّمَةٌ إِلَىٰٓ أَهْلِهِۦ وَتَحْرِيرُ رَقَبَةٍ مُّؤْمِنَةٍ ۖ فَمَن لَّمْ يَجِدْ فَصِيَامُ شَهْرَيْنِ مُتَتَابِعَيْنِ تَوْبَةً مِّنَ ٱللَّهِ ۗ وَكَانَ ٱللَّهُ عَلِيمًا حَكِيمًا (٩٢) وَمَن يَقْتُلْ مُؤْمِنًا مُّتَعَمِّدًا فَجَزَآؤُهُۥ جَهَنَّمُ خَـٰلِدًا فِيهَا وَغَضِبَ ٱللَّهُ عَلَيْهِ وَلَعَنَهُۥ وَأَعَدَّ لَهُۥ عَذَابًا عَظِيمًا (٩٣) يَـٰٓأَيُّهَا ٱلَّذِينَ ءَامَنُوٓا۟ إِذَا ضَرَبْتُمْ فِى سَبِيلِ ٱللَّهِ فَتَبَيَّنُوا۟ وَلَا تَقُولُوا۟ لِمَنْ أَلْقَىٰٓ إِلَيْكُمُ ٱلسَّلَـٰمَ لَسْتَ مُؤْمِنًا تَبْتَغُونَ عَرَضَ ٱلْحَيَوٰةِ ٱلدُّنْيَا فَعِندَ ٱللَّهِ مَغَانِمُ كَثِيرَةٌ ۚ كَذَٰلِكَ كُنتُم مِّن قَبْلُ فَمَنَّ ٱللَّهُ عَلَيْكُمْ فَتَبَيَّنُوٓا۟ ۚ إِنَّ ٱللَّهَ كَانَ بِمَا تَعْمَلُونَ خَبِيرًا (٩٤)

And never is it for a believer to kill a believer except by mistake. And whoever kills a believer by mistake - then the freeing of a believing slave and a compensation payment presented to the deceased's family [is required] unless they give [up their right as] charity. But if the deceased was from a people at war with you and he was a believer - then [only] the freeing of a believing slave; and if he was from a people with whom you have a treaty - then a compensation payment presented to his family and the freeing of a believing slave. And whoever does not find [one or cannot afford to buy one] - then [instead], a fast for two months consecutively, [seeking] acceptance of repentance from Allah. And Allah is ever Knowing and Wise. (92) But whoever kills a believer intentionally - his recompense is Hell, wherein he will abide eternally, and

Allah has become angry with him and has cursed him and has prepared for him a great punishment. (93) O you who have believed, when you go forth [to fight] in the cause of Allah, investigate; and do not say to one who gives you [a greeting of] peace "You are not a believer," aspiring for the goods of worldly life; for with Allah are many acquisitions. You [yourselves] were like that before; then Allah conferred His favor upon you, so investigate. Indeed Allah is ever, with what you do, Acquainted. (94)

Quran 4:104-112

وَلَا تَهِنُوا فِى ٱبْتِغَآءِ ٱلْقَوْمِ إِن تَكُونُوا۟ تَأْلَمُونَ فَإِنَّهُمْ يَأْلَمُونَ كَمَا تَأْلَمُونَ ۖ وَتَرْجُونَ مِنَ ٱللَّهِ مَا لَا يَرْجُونَ ۗ وَكَانَ ٱللَّهُ عَلِيمًا حَكِيمًا (١٠٤) إِنَّآ أَنزَلْنَآ إِلَيْكَ ٱلْكِتَـٰبَ بِٱلْحَقِّ لِتَحْكُمَ بَيْنَ ٱلنَّاسِ بِمَآ أَرَىٰكَ ٱللَّهُ ۚ وَلَا تَكُن لِّلْخَآئِنِينَ خَصِيمًا (١٠٥) وَٱسْتَغْفِرِ ٱللَّهَ ۖ إِنَّ ٱللَّهَ كَانَ غَفُورًا رَّحِيمًا (١٠٦) وَلَا تُجَـٰدِلْ عَنِ ٱلَّذِينَ يَخْتَانُونَ أَنفُسَهُمْ ۚ إِنَّ ٱللَّهَ لَا يُحِبُّ مَن كَانَ خَوَّانًا أَثِيمًا (١٠٧) يَسْتَخْفُونَ مِنَ ٱلنَّاسِ وَلَا يَسْتَخْفُونَ مِنَ ٱللَّهِ وَهُوَ مَعَهُمْ إِذْ يُبَيِّتُونَ مَا لَا يَرْضَىٰ مِنَ ٱلْقَوْلِ ۚ وَكَانَ ٱللَّهُ بِمَا يَعْمَلُونَ مُحِيطًا (١٠٨) هَـٰٓأَنتُمْ هَـٰٓؤُلَآءِ جَـٰدَلْتُمْ عَنْهُمْ فِى ٱلْحَيَوٰةِ ٱلدُّنْيَا فَمَن يُجَـٰدِلُ ٱللَّهَ عَنْهُمْ يَوْمَ ٱلْقِيَـٰمَةِ أَم مَّن يَكُونُ عَلَيْهِمْ وَكِيلًا (١٠٩) وَمَن يَعْمَلْ سُوٓءًا أَوْ يَظْلِمْ نَفْسَهُۥ ثُمَّ يَسْتَغْفِرِ ٱللَّهَ يَجِدِ ٱللَّهَ غَفُورًا رَّحِيمًا (١١٠) وَمَن يَكْسِبْ إِثْمًا فَإِنَّمَا يَكْسِبُهُۥ عَلَىٰ نَفْسِهِۦ ۚ وَكَانَ ٱللَّهُ عَلِيمًا حَكِيمًا (١١١) وَمَن يَكْسِبْ خَطِيٓـَٔةً أَوْ إِثْمًا ثُمَّ يَرْمِ بِهِۦ بَرِيٓـًٔا فَقَدِ ٱحْتَمَلَ بُهْتَـٰنًا وَإِثْمًا مُّبِينًا (١١٢)

And do not weaken in pursuit of the enemy. If you should be suffering - so are they suffering as you are suffering, but you expect from Allah that which they *expect not. And Allah is ever Knowing and Wise. (104) Indeed, We have revealed to you, [O Muhammad], the Book in truth so you may judge between the people by that which Allah has shown you. And do not be for the deceitful an advocate. (105) And seek forgiveness of Allah. Indeed, Allah is ever Forgiving and Merciful. (106) And do not argue on behalf of those who deceive themselves. Indeed, Allah loves not one who is a habitually sinful deceiver. (107) They conceal [their evil intentions and deeds] from the people, but they cannot conceal [them] from Allah, and He is with them [in His knowledge] when they spend the night in such as He does not accept of speech. And ever is Allah, of what they do, encompassing. (108) Here you are - those who argue on their behalf in [this] worldly life - but who will argue with Allah for them on the Day of Resurrection, or who will [then] be their representative? (109) And whoever does a wrong or wrongs himself but then seeks forgiveness of Allah will find Allah Forgiving and Merciful. (110) And whoever commits a sin only earns it against himself. And Allah is ever Knowing and Wise. (111) But whoever earns an offense or a sin and then blames it on an innocent [person] has taken upon himself a slander and manifest sin. (112)*

Quran 4:114-116

۞ لَا خَيْرَ فِى كَثِيرٍ مِّن نَّجْوَىٰهُمْ إِلَّا مَنْ أَمَرَ بِصَدَقَةٍ أَوْ مَعْرُوفٍ أَوْ إِصْلَٰحٍ بَيْنَ ٱلنَّاسِ ۚ وَمَن يَفْعَلْ ذَٰلِكَ ٱبْتِغَآءَ مَرْضَاتِ ٱللَّهِ فَسَوْفَ نُؤْتِيهِ أَجْرًا عَظِيمًا (١١٤) وَمَن يُشَاقِقِ ٱلرَّسُولَ مِنۢ بَعْدِ مَا تَبَيَّنَ لَهُ ٱلْهُدَىٰ وَيَتَّبِعْ غَيْرَ سَبِيلِ ٱلْمُؤْمِنِينَ نُوَلِّهِۦ مَا تَوَلَّىٰ وَنُصْلِهِۦ جَهَنَّمَ ۖ وَسَآءَتْ مَصِيرًا (١١٥) إِنَّ ٱللَّهَ لَا يَغْفِرُ أَن يُشْرَكَ بِهِۦ وَيَغْفِرُ مَا دُونَ ذَٰلِكَ لِمَن يَشَآءُ ۚ وَمَن يُشْرِكْ بِٱللَّهِ فَقَدْ ضَلَّ ضَلَٰلًۢا بَعِيدًا (١١٦)

No good is there in much of their private conversation, except for those who enjoin charity or that which is right or conciliation between people. And whoever does that seeking means to the approval of Allah - then We are going to give him a great reward. (114) And whoever opposes the Messenger after guidance has become clear to him and follows other than the way of the believers - We will give him what he has taken and drive him into Hell, and evil it is as a destination. (115) Indeed, Allah does not forgive association with Him, but He forgives what is less than that for whom He wills. And he who associates others with Allah has certainly gone far astray. (116)

Quran 4:129

وَلَن تَسْتَطِيعُوٓا۟ أَن تَعْدِلُوا۟ بَيْنَ ٱلنِّسَآءِ وَلَوْ حَرَصْتُمْ ۖ فَلَا تَمِيلُوا۟ كُلَّ ٱلْمَيْلِ فَتَذَرُوهَا كَٱلْمُعَلَّقَةِ ۚ وَإِن تُصْلِحُوا۟ وَتَتَّقُوا۟ فَإِنَّ ٱللَّهَ كَانَ غَفُورًا رَّحِيمًا (١٢٩)

And you will never be able to be equal [in feeling] between wives, even if you should strive [to do so]. So do not incline completely [toward one] and leave another hanging. And if you amend [your affairs] and fear Allah - then indeed, Allah is ever Forgiving and Merciful. (129)

Quran 4:137-148

إِنَّ ٱلَّذِينَ ءَامَنُواْ ثُمَّ كَفَرُواْ ثُمَّ ءَامَنُواْ ثُمَّ كَفَرُواْ ثُمَّ ٱزْدَادُواْ كُفْرًا لَّمْ يَكُنِ ٱللَّهُ لِيَغْفِرَ لَهُمْ وَلَا لِيَهْدِيَهُمْ سَبِيلًا (١٣٧) بَشِّرِ ٱلْمُنَٰفِقِينَ بِأَنَّ لَهُمْ عَذَابًا أَلِيمًا (١٣٨) ٱلَّذِينَ يَتَّخِذُونَ ٱلْكَٰفِرِينَ أَوْلِيَآءَ مِن دُونِ ٱلْمُؤْمِنِينَ أَيَبْتَغُونَ عِندَهُمُ ٱلْعِزَّةَ فَإِنَّ ٱلْعِزَّةَ لِلَّهِ جَمِيعًا (١٣٩) وَقَدْ نَزَّلَ عَلَيْكُمْ فِى ٱلْكِتَٰبِ أَنْ إِذَا سَمِعْتُمْ ءَايَٰتِ ٱللَّهِ يُكْفَرُ بِهَا وَيُسْتَهْزَأُ بِهَا فَلَا تَقْعُدُواْ مَعَهُمْ حَتَّىٰ يَخُوضُواْ فِى حَدِيثٍ غَيْرِهِۦٓ إِنَّكُمْ إِذًا مِّثْلُهُمْ إِنَّ ٱللَّهَ جَامِعُ ٱلْمُنَٰفِقِينَ وَٱلْكَٰفِرِينَ فِى جَهَنَّمَ جَمِيعًا (١٤٠) ٱلَّذِينَ يَتَرَبَّصُونَ بِكُمْ فَإِن كَانَ لَكُمْ فَتْحٌ مِّنَ ٱللَّهِ قَالُوٓاْ أَلَمْ نَكُن مَّعَكُمْ وَإِن كَانَ لِلْكَٰفِرِينَ نَصِيبٌ قَالُوٓاْ أَلَمْ نَسْتَحْوِذْ عَلَيْكُمْ وَنَمْنَعْكُم مِّنَ ٱلْمُؤْمِنِينَ فَٱللَّهُ يَحْكُمُ بَيْنَكُمْ يَوْمَ ٱلْقِيَٰمَةِ وَلَن يَجْعَلَ ٱللَّهُ لِلْكَٰفِرِينَ عَلَى ٱلْمُؤْمِنِينَ سَبِيلًا (١٤١) إِنَّ ٱلْمُنَٰفِقِينَ يُخَٰدِعُونَ ٱللَّهَ وَهُوَ خَٰدِعُهُمْ وَإِذَا قَامُوٓاْ إِلَى ٱلصَّلَوٰةِ قَامُواْ كُسَالَىٰ يُرَآءُونَ ٱلنَّاسَ وَلَا يَذْكُرُونَ ٱللَّهَ إِلَّا قَلِيلًا (١٤٢) مُّذَبْذَبِينَ بَيْنَ ذَٰلِكَ لَآ إِلَىٰ هَٰٓؤُلَآءِ وَلَآ إِلَىٰ هَٰٓؤُلَآءِ وَمَن يُضْلِلِ ٱللَّهُ فَلَن تَجِدَ لَهُۥ سَبِيلًا (١٤٣) يَٰٓأَيُّهَا ٱلَّذِينَ ءَامَنُواْ لَا تَتَّخِذُواْ ٱلْكَٰفِرِينَ أَوْلِيَآءَ مِن دُونِ ٱلْمُؤْمِنِينَ أَتُرِيدُونَ أَن تَجْعَلُواْ لِلَّهِ عَلَيْكُمْ سُلْطَٰنًا مُّبِينًا (١٤٤) إِنَّ ٱلْمُنَٰفِقِينَ فِى ٱلدَّرْكِ ٱلْأَسْفَلِ مِنَ ٱلنَّارِ وَلَن تَجِدَ لَهُمْ نَصِيرًا (١٤٥) إِلَّا ٱلَّذِينَ تَابُواْ وَأَصْلَحُواْ وَٱعْتَصَمُواْ بِٱللَّهِ وَأَخْلَصُواْ دِينَهُمْ لِلَّهِ فَأُوْلَٰٓئِكَ مَعَ ٱلْمُؤْمِنِينَ وَسَوْفَ يُؤْتِ ٱللَّهُ ٱلْمُؤْمِنِينَ أَجْرًا عَظِيمًا (١٤٦) مَّا يَفْعَلُ ٱللَّهُ بِعَذَابِكُمْ إِن شَكَرْتُمْ وَءَامَنتُمْ وَكَانَ ٱللَّهُ شَاكِرًا عَلِيمًا (١٤٧) ۞ لَّا يُحِبُّ ٱللَّهُ ٱلْجَهْرَ بِٱلسُّوٓءِ مِنَ ٱلْقَوْلِ إِلَّا مَن ظُلِمَ وَكَانَ ٱللَّهُ سَمِيعًا عَلِيمًا (١٤٨)

Indeed, those who have believed then disbelieved, then believed, then disbelieved, and then increased in disbelief

- never will Allah forgive them, nor will He guide them to a way. (137) Give tidings to the hypocrites that there is for them a painful punishment - (138) Those who take disbelievers as allies instead of the believers. Do they seek with them honor [through power]? But indeed, honor belongs to Allah entirely. (139) And it has already come down to you in the Book that when you hear the verses of Allah [recited], they are denied [by them] and ridiculed; so do not sit with them until they enter into another conversation. Indeed, you would then be like them. Indeed Allah will gather the hypocrites and disbelievers in Hell all together - (140) Those who wait [and watch] you. Then if you gain a victory from Allah, they say, "Were we not with you?" But if the disbelievers have a success, they say [to them], "Did we not gain the advantage over you, but we protected you from the believers?" Allah will judge between [all of] you on the Day of Resurrection, and never will Allah give the disbelievers over the believers a way [to overcome them]. (141) Indeed, the hypocrites [think to] deceive Allah, but He is deceiving them. And when they stand for prayer, they stand lazily, showing [themselves to] the people and not remembering Allah except a little, (142) Wavering between them, [belonging] neither to the believers nor to the disbelievers. And whoever Allah leaves astray - never will you find for him a way. (143) O you who have believed, do not take the disbelievers as allies instead of the believers. Do you wish to give Allah against yourselves a clear case? (144) Indeed, the hypocrites will be in the lowest depths of the Fire - and never will you find for them a helper - (145) Except for those who repent, correct themselves, hold fast to Allah, and are sincere in their religion for Allah, for those will be with the believers. And Allah is going to give the believers a great reward. (146) What would Allah do with your punishment if you are grateful and believe? And ever is Allah Appreciative and Knowing. (147) Allah does not like the public mention of evil except by one who has been wronged. And ever is Allah Hearing and Knowing. (148)

Quran 4:150-152

إِنَّ ٱلَّذِينَ يَكْفُرُونَ بِٱللَّهِ وَرُسُلِهِ وَيُرِيدُونَ أَن يُفَرِّقُوا۟ بَيْنَ ٱللَّهِ وَرُسُلِهِ وَيَقُولُونَ نُؤْمِنُ بِبَعْضٍ وَنَكْفُرُ بِبَعْضٍ وَيُرِيدُونَ أَن يَتَّخِذُوا۟ بَيْنَ ذَٰلِكَ سَبِيلًا (١٥٠) أُو۟لَٰٓئِكَ هُمُ ٱلْكَٰفِرُونَ حَقًّا وَأَعْتَدْنَا لِلْكَٰفِرِينَ عَذَابًا مُّهِينًا (١٥١) وَٱلَّذِينَ ءَامَنُوا۟ بِٱللَّهِ وَرُسُلِهِ وَلَمْ يُفَرِّقُوا۟ بَيْنَ أَحَدٍ مِّنْهُمْ أُو۟لَٰٓئِكَ سَوْفَ يُؤْتِيهِمْ أُجُورَهُمْ وَكَانَ ٱللَّهُ غَفُورًا رَّحِيمًا (١٥٢)

Indeed, those who disbelieve in Allah and His messengers and wish to discriminate between Allah and His messengers and say, "We believe in some and disbelieve in others," and wish to adopt a way in between - (150)

Those are the disbelievers, truly. And We have prepared for the disbelievers a humiliating punishment. (151) But they who believe in Allah and His messengers and do not discriminate between any of them - to those He is going to give their rewards. And ever is Allah Forgiving and Merciful. (152)

Quran 4:171-173

يَٰٓأَهْلَ ٱلْكِتَٰبِ لَا تَغْلُوا۟ فِى دِينِكُمْ وَلَا تَقُولُوا۟ عَلَى ٱللَّهِ إِلَّا ٱلْحَقَّ إِنَّمَا ٱلْمَسِيحُ عِيسَى ٱبْنُ مَرْيَمَ رَسُولُ ٱللَّهِ وَكَلِمَتُهُۥٓ أَلْقَىٰهَآ إِلَىٰ مَرْيَمَ وَرُوحٌ مِّنْهُ ۖ فَـَٔامِنُوا۟ بِٱللَّهِ وَرُسُلِهِۦ ۖ وَلَا تَقُولُوا۟ ثَلَٰثَةٌ ٱنتَهُوا۟ خَيْرًا لَّكُمْ إِنَّمَا ٱللَّهُ إِلَٰهٌ وَٰحِدٌ سُبْحَٰنَهُۥٓ أَن يَكُونَ لَهُۥ وَلَدٌ لَّهُۥ مَا فِى ٱلسَّمَٰوَٰتِ وَمَا فِى ٱلْأَرْضِ وَكَفَىٰ بِٱللَّهِ وَكِيلًا (١٧١) لَّن يَسْتَنكِفَ ٱلْمَسِيحُ أَن يَكُونَ عَبْدًا لِّلَّهِ وَلَا ٱلْمَلَٰٓئِكَةُ ٱلْمُقَرَّبُونَ وَمَن يَسْتَنكِفْ عَنْ عِبَادَتِهِۦ وَيَسْتَكْبِرْ فَسَيَحْشُرُهُمْ إِلَيْهِ جَمِيعًا (١٧٢) فَأَمَّا ٱلَّذِينَ ءَامَنُوا۟ وَعَمِلُوا۟ ٱلصَّٰلِحَٰتِ فَيُوَفِّيهِمْ أُجُورَهُمْ وَيَزِيدُهُم مِّن فَضْلِهِۦ ۖ وَأَمَّا ٱلَّذِينَ ٱسْتَنكَفُوا۟ وَٱسْتَكْبَرُوا۟ فَيُعَذِّبُهُمْ عَذَابًا أَلِيمًا وَلَا يَجِدُونَ لَهُم مِّن دُونِ ٱللَّهِ وَلِيًّا وَلَا نَصِيرًا (١٧٣)

O People of the Scripture, do not commit excess in your religion or say about Allah except the truth. The Messiah, Jesus, the son of Mary, was but a messenger of Allah and His word which He directed to Mary and a soul [created at a command] from Him. So believe in Allah and His messengers. And do not say, "Three"; desist - it is better for you. Indeed, Allah is but one God. Exalted is He above having a son. To Him belongs whatever is in the heavens and whatever is on the earth. And sufficient is Allah as Disposer of affairs. (171) Never would the Messiah disdain to be a servant of Allah, nor would the angels near [to Him]. And whoever disdains His worship and is arrogant - He will gather them to Himself all together. (172) And as for those who believed and did righteous deeds, He will give them in full their rewards and grant them extra from His bounty. But as for those who disdained and were arrogant, He will punish them with a painful punishment, and they will not find for themselves besides Allah any protector or helper. (173)

Quran 5:1-3

يَـٰٓأَيُّهَا ٱلَّذِينَ ءَامَنُوٓا۟ أَوْفُوا۟ بِٱلْعُقُودِ ۚ أُحِلَّتْ لَكُم بَهِيمَةُ ٱلْأَنْعَـٰمِ إِلَّا مَا يُتْلَىٰ عَلَيْكُمْ غَيْرَ مُحِلِّى ٱلصَّيْدِ وَأَنتُمْ حُرُمٌ ۗ إِنَّ ٱللَّهَ يَحْكُمُ مَا يُرِيدُ (١) يَـٰٓأَيُّهَا ٱلَّذِينَ ءَامَنُوا۟ لَا تُحِلُّوا۟ شَعَـٰٓئِرَ ٱللَّهِ وَلَا ٱلشَّهْرَ ٱلْحَرَامَ وَلَا ٱلْهَدْىَ وَلَا ٱلْقَلَـٰٓئِدَ وَلَآ ءَآمِّينَ ٱلْبَيْتَ ٱلْحَرَامَ يَبْتَغُونَ فَضْلًا مِّن رَّبِّهِمْ وَرِضْوَٰنًا ۚ وَإِذَا حَلَلْتُمْ فَٱصْطَادُوا۟ ۚ وَلَا يَجْرِمَنَّكُمْ شَنَـَٔانُ قَوْمٍ أَن صَدُّوكُمْ عَنِ ٱلْمَسْجِدِ ٱلْحَرَامِ أَن تَعْتَدُوا۟ ۘ وَتَعَاوَنُوا۟ عَلَى ٱلْبِرِّ وَٱلتَّقْوَىٰ ۖ وَلَا تَعَاوَنُوا۟ عَلَى ٱلْإِثْمِ وَٱلْعُدْوَٰنِ ۚ وَٱتَّقُوا۟ ٱللَّهَ ۖ إِنَّ ٱللَّهَ شَدِيدُ ٱلْعِقَابِ (٢) حُرِّمَتْ عَلَيْكُمُ ٱلْمَيْتَةُ وَٱلدَّمُ وَلَحْمُ ٱلْخِنزِيرِ وَمَآ أُهِلَّ لِغَيْرِ ٱللَّهِ بِهِۦ وَٱلْمُنْخَنِقَةُ وَٱلْمَوْقُوذَةُ وَٱلْمُتَرَدِّيَةُ وَٱلنَّطِيحَةُ وَمَآ أَكَلَ ٱلسَّبُعُ إِلَّا مَا ذَكَّيْتُمْ وَمَا ذُبِحَ عَلَى ٱلنُّصُبِ وَأَن تَسْتَقْسِمُوا۟ بِٱلْأَزْلَـٰمِ ۚ ذَٰلِكُمْ فِسْقٌ ۗ ٱلْيَوْمَ يَئِسَ ٱلَّذِينَ كَفَرُوا۟ مِن دِينِكُمْ فَلَا تَخْشَوْهُمْ وَٱخْشَوْنِ ۚ ٱلْيَوْمَ أَكْمَلْتُ لَكُمْ دِينَكُمْ وَأَتْمَمْتُ عَلَيْكُمْ نِعْمَتِى وَرَضِيتُ لَكُمُ ٱلْإِسْلَـٰمَ دِينًا ۚ فَمَنِ ٱضْطُرَّ فِى مَخْمَصَةٍ غَيْرَ مُتَجَانِفٍ لِّإِثْمٍ ۙ فَإِنَّ ٱللَّهَ غَفُورٌ رَّحِيمٌ (٣)

O you who have believed, fulfill [all] contracts. Lawful for you are the animals of grazing livestock except for that which is recited to you [in this Qur'an] - hunting not being permitted while you are in the state of ihram. Indeed, Allah ordains what He intends. (1) O you who have believed, do not violate the rites of Allah or [the sanctity of] the sacred month or [neglect the marking of] the sacrificial animals and garlanding [them] or [violate the safety of] those coming to the Sacred House seeking bounty from their Lord and [His] approval. But when you come out of ihram, then [you may] hunt. And do not let the hatred of a people for having obstructed you from al-Masjid al-Haram lead you to transgress. And cooperate in righteousness and piety, but do not cooperate in sin and aggression. And fear Allah; indeed, Allah is severe in penalty. (2) Prohibited to you are dead animals, blood, the flesh of swine, and that which has been dedicated to other than Allah, and [those animals] killed by strangling or by a violent blow or by a headlong fall or by the goring of horns, and those from which a wild animal has eaten, except what you [are able to] slaughter [before its death], and those which are sacrificed on stone altars, and [prohibited is] that you seek decision through divining arrows. That is grave disobedience. This day those who disbelieve have despaired of [defeating] your religion; so fear them not, but fear Me. This day I have perfected for you your religion and completed My favor upon you and have approved for you Islam as religion. But whoever is forced by severe hunger with no inclination to sin - then indeed, Allah is Forgiving and Merciful. (3)

Quran 5:8

يَـٰٓأَيُّهَا ٱلَّذِينَ ءَامَنُوا۟ كُونُوا۟ قَوَّٰمِينَ لِلَّهِ شُهَدَآءَ بِٱلْقِسْطِ ۖ وَلَا يَجْرِمَنَّكُمْ شَنَـَٔانُ قَوْمٍ عَلَىٰٓ أَلَّا تَعْدِلُوا۟ ۚ ٱعْدِلُوا۟ هُوَ أَقْرَبُ لِلتَّقْوَىٰ ۖ وَٱتَّقُوا۟ ٱللَّهَ ۚ إِنَّ ٱللَّهَ خَبِيرٌۢ بِمَا تَعْمَلُونَ (٨)

O you who have believed, be persistently standing firm for Allah, witnesses in justice, and do not let the hatred of a people prevent you from being just. Be just; that is nearer to righteousness. And fear Allah; indeed, Allah is Acquainted with what you do. (8)

Quran 5:44-57

إِنَّآ أَنزَلْنَا ٱلتَّوْرَىٰةَ فِيهَا هُدًى وَنُورٌ ۚ يَحْكُمُ بِهَا ٱلنَّبِيُّونَ ٱلَّذِينَ أَسْلَمُوا۟ لِلَّذِينَ هَادُوا۟ وَٱلرَّبَّـٰنِيُّونَ وَٱلْأَحْبَارُ بِمَا ٱسْتُحْفِظُوا۟ مِن كِتَـٰبِ ٱللَّهِ وَكَانُوا۟ عَلَيْهِ شُهَدَآءَ ۚ فَلَا تَخْشَوُا۟ ٱلنَّاسَ وَٱخْشَوْنِ وَلَا تَشْتَرُوا۟ بِـَٔايَـٰتِى ثَمَنًا قَلِيلًا ۚ وَمَن لَّمْ يَحْكُم بِمَآ أَنزَلَ ٱللَّهُ فَأُو۟لَـٰٓئِكَ هُمُ ٱلْكَـٰفِرُونَ (٤٤) وَكَتَبْنَا عَلَيْهِمْ فِيهَآ أَنَّ ٱلنَّفْسَ بِٱلنَّفْسِ وَٱلْعَيْنَ بِٱلْعَيْنِ وَٱلْأَنفَ بِٱلْأَنفِ وَٱلْأُذُنَ بِٱلْأُذُنِ وَٱلسِّنَّ بِٱلسِّنِّ وَٱلْجُرُوحَ قِصَاصٌ ۚ فَمَن تَصَدَّقَ بِهِۦ فَهُوَ كَفَّارَةٌ لَّهُۥ ۚ وَمَن لَّمْ يَحْكُم بِمَآ أَنزَلَ ٱللَّهُ فَأُو۟لَـٰٓئِكَ هُمُ ٱلظَّـٰلِمُونَ (٤٥) وَقَفَّيْنَا عَلَىٰٓ ءَاثَـٰرِهِم بِعِيسَى ٱبْنِ مَرْيَمَ مُصَدِّقًا لِّمَا بَيْنَ يَدَيْهِ مِنَ ٱلتَّوْرَىٰةِ ۖ وَءَاتَيْنَـٰهُ ٱلْإِنجِيلَ فِيهِ هُدًى وَنُورٌ وَمُصَدِّقًا لِّمَا بَيْنَ يَدَيْهِ مِنَ

ٱلتَّوْرَىٰةِ وَهُدًى وَمَوْعِظَةٌ لِّلْمُتَّقِينَ (٤٦) وَلْيَحْكُمْ أَهْلُ ٱلْإِنجِيلِ بِمَا أَنزَلَ ٱللَّهُ فِيهِ ۚ وَمَن لَّمْ يَحْكُم بِمَا أَنزَلَ ٱللَّهُ فَأُو۟لَـٰٓئِكَ هُمُ ٱلْفَـٰسِقُونَ (٤٧) وَأَنزَلْنَآ إِلَيْكَ ٱلْكِتَـٰبَ بِٱلْحَقِّ مُصَدِّقًا لِّمَا بَيْنَ يَدَيْهِ مِنَ ٱلْكِتَـٰبِ وَمُهَيْمِنًا عَلَيْهِ ۖ فَٱحْكُم بَيْنَهُم بِمَآ أَنزَلَ ٱللَّهُ ۖ وَلَا تَتَّبِعْ أَهْوَآءَهُمْ عَمَّا جَآءَكَ مِنَ ٱلْحَقِّ ۚ لِكُلٍّ جَعَلْنَا مِنكُمْ شِرْعَةً وَمِنْهَاجًا ۚ وَلَوْ شَآءَ ٱللَّهُ لَجَعَلَكُمْ أُمَّةً وَٰحِدَةً وَلَـٰكِن لِّيَبْلُوَكُمْ فِى مَآ ءَاتَىٰكُمْ ۖ فَٱسْتَبِقُوا۟ ٱلْخَيْرَٰتِ ۚ إِلَى ٱللَّهِ مَرْجِعُكُمْ جَمِيعًا فَيُنَبِّئُكُم بِمَا كُنتُمْ فِيهِ تَخْتَلِفُونَ (٤٨) وَأَنِ ٱحْكُم بَيْنَهُم بِمَآ أَنزَلَ ٱللَّهُ وَلَا تَتَّبِعْ أَهْوَآءَهُمْ وَٱحْذَرْهُمْ أَن يَفْتِنُوكَ عَنۢ بَعْضِ مَآ أَنزَلَ ٱللَّهُ إِلَيْكَ ۖ فَإِن تَوَلَّوْا۟ فَٱعْلَمْ أَنَّمَا يُرِيدُ ٱللَّهُ أَن يُصِيبَهُم بِبَعْضِ ذُنُوبِهِمْ ۗ وَإِنَّ كَثِيرًا مِّنَ ٱلنَّاسِ لَفَـٰسِقُونَ (٤٩) أَفَحُكْمَ ٱلْجَـٰهِلِيَّةِ يَبْغُونَ ۚ وَمَنْ أَحْسَنُ مِنَ ٱللَّهِ حُكْمًا لِّقَوْمٍ يُوقِنُونَ (٥٠) ۞ يَـٰٓأَيُّهَا ٱلَّذِينَ ءَامَنُوا۟ لَا تَتَّخِذُوا۟ ٱلْيَهُودَ وَٱلنَّصَـٰرَىٰٓ أَوْلِيَآءَ ۘ بَعْضُهُمْ أَوْلِيَآءُ بَعْضٍ ۚ وَمَن يَتَوَلَّهُم مِّنكُمْ فَإِنَّهُۥ مِنْهُمْ ۗ إِنَّ ٱللَّهَ لَا يَهْدِى ٱلْقَوْمَ ٱلظَّـٰلِمِينَ (٥١) فَتَرَى ٱلَّذِينَ فِى قُلُوبِهِم مَّرَضٌ يُسَـٰرِعُونَ فِيهِمْ يَقُولُونَ نَخْشَىٰٓ أَن تُصِيبَنَا دَآئِرَةٌ ۚ فَعَسَى ٱللَّهُ أَن يَأْتِىَ بِٱلْفَتْحِ أَوْ أَمْرٍ مِّنْ عِندِهِۦ فَيُصْبِحُوا۟ عَلَىٰ مَآ أَسَرُّوا۟ فِىٓ أَنفُسِهِمْ نَـٰدِمِينَ (٥٢) وَيَقُولُ ٱلَّذِينَ ءَامَنُوٓا۟ أَهَـٰٓؤُلَآءِ ٱلَّذِينَ أَقْسَمُوا۟ بِٱللَّهِ جَهْدَ أَيْمَـٰنِهِمْ ۙ إِنَّهُمْ لَمَعَكُمْ ۚ حَبِطَتْ أَعْمَـٰلُهُمْ فَأَصْبَحُوا۟ خَـٰسِرِينَ (٥٣) يَـٰٓأَيُّهَا ٱلَّذِينَ ءَامَنُوا۟ مَن يَرْتَدَّ مِنكُمْ عَن دِينِهِۦ فَسَوْفَ يَأْتِى ٱللَّهُ بِقَوْمٍ يُحِبُّهُمْ وَيُحِبُّونَهُۥٓ أَذِلَّةٍ عَلَى ٱلْمُؤْمِنِينَ أَعِزَّةٍ عَلَى ٱلْكَـٰفِرِينَ يُجَـٰهِدُونَ فِى سَبِيلِ ٱللَّهِ وَلَا يَخَافُونَ لَوْمَةَ لَآئِمٍ ۚ ذَٰلِكَ فَضْلُ ٱللَّهِ يُؤْتِيهِ مَن يَشَآءُ ۚ وَٱللَّهُ وَٰسِعٌ عَلِيمٌ (٥٤) إِنَّمَا وَلِيُّكُمُ ٱللَّهُ وَرَسُولُهُۥ وَٱلَّذِينَ ءَامَنُوا۟ ٱلَّذِينَ يُقِيمُونَ ٱلصَّلَوٰةَ وَيُؤْتُونَ ٱلزَّكَوٰةَ وَهُمْ رَٰكِعُونَ (٥٥) وَمَن يَتَوَلَّ ٱللَّهَ وَرَسُولَهُۥ وَٱلَّذِينَ ءَامَنُوا۟ فَإِنَّ حِزْبَ ٱللَّهِ هُمُ ٱلْغَـٰلِبُونَ (٥٦) يَـٰٓأَيُّهَا ٱلَّذِينَ ءَامَنُوا۟ لَا تَتَّخِذُوا۟ ٱلَّذِينَ ٱتَّخَذُوا۟ دِينَكُمْ هُزُوًا وَلَعِبًا مِّنَ ٱلَّذِينَ أُوتُوا۟ ٱلْكِتَـٰبَ مِن قَبْلِكُمْ وَٱلْكُفَّارَ أَوْلِيَآءَ ۚ وَٱتَّقُوا۟ ٱللَّهَ إِن كُنتُم مُّؤْمِنِينَ (٥٧)

Indeed, We sent down the Torah, in which was guidance and light. The prophets who submitted [to Allah] judged by it for the Jews, as did the rabbis and scholars by that with which they were entrusted of the Scripture of Allah, and they were witnesses thereto. So do not fear the people but fear Me, and do not exchange My verses for a small price. And whoever does not judge by what Allah has revealed - then it is those who are the disbelievers. (44) And We ordained for them therein a life for a life, an eye for an eye, a nose for a nose, an ear for an ear, a tooth for a tooth, and for wounds is legal retribution. But whoever gives [up his right as] charity, it is an expiation for him. And whoever does not judge by what Allah has revealed - then it is those who are the wrongdoers. (45) And We sent, following in their footsteps, Jesus, the son of Mary, confirming that which came before him in the Torah; and We gave him the Injeel, in which was guidance and light and confirming that which preceded it of the Torah as guidance and instruction for the righteous. (46) And let the People of the Injeel judge by what Allah has revealed therein. And whoever does not judge by what Allah has revealed - then it is those who are the defiantly disobedient. (47) And We have revealed to you, [O Muhammad], the Book in truth, confirming that which preceded it of the Scripture and as a criterion over it. So judge between them by what Allah has revealed and do not follow their inclinations away from what has come to you of the truth. To each of you We prescribed a law and a method. Had Allah willed, He would have made you one nation [united in religion], but [He intended] to test you in what He has given you; so race to [all that is] good. To Allah is your return all together, and He will [then] inform you concerning that over which you used to differ. (48) And judge, [O Muhammad], between them by what Allah has revealed and do not follow their inclinations and beware of them, lest they tempt you away from some of what Allah has revealed to you. And if they turn away - then know that Allah only intends to afflict them with some of their [own] sins. And indeed, many among the people are defiantly disobedient. (49) Then is it the judgement of [the time of] ignorance they desire? But who is better than Allah in judgement for a people who are certain [in faith]. (50) O you who have believed, do not take the Jews and the Christians as allies. They are [in fact] allies of one another. And whoever is an ally to them among you - then indeed, he is [one] of them. Indeed, Allah guides not the wrongdoing people. (51) So you see those in whose hearts is disease hastening into [association with] them, saying, "We are afraid a misfortune may strike us." But perhaps Allah will bring conquest or a decision from Him, and they will become, over what they have been concealing within themselves, regretful. (52) And those who believe will say, "Are these the ones who swore by Allah their strongest oaths that indeed they were with you?" Their deeds have become worthless, and they have become losers. (53) O you who have believed, whoever of you should revert from his religion - Allah will bring forth [in place of them] a people He will love and who will love Him [who are] humble toward the believers, powerful against the disbelievers; they strive in the cause of Allah and do not fear the blame of a critic. That is the favor of Allah; He bestows it upon whom He wills. And Allah is all-Encompassing and Knowing. (54) Your ally is none but Allah and [therefore] His Messenger and those who have believed - those who establish prayer and give zakah, and they bow [in worship]. (55) And whoever is an ally of Allah and His Messenger and those who have believed - indeed, the party of Allah - they will be the predominant. (56) O you who have believed, take not those who have taken your religion in ridicule and amusement among the ones who were given the Scripture before you nor the disbelievers as allies. And fear Allah, if you should [truly] be believers. (57)

Quran 5:68

قُلْ يَٰٓأَهْلَ ٱلْكِتَٰبِ لَسْتُمْ عَلَىٰ شَىْءٍ حَتَّىٰ تُقِيمُوا۟ ٱلتَّوْرَىٰةَ وَٱلْإِنجِيلَ وَمَآ أُنزِلَ إِلَيْكُم مِّن رَّبِّكُمْ ۗ وَلَيَزِيدَنَّ كَثِيرًا مِّنْهُم مَّآ أُنزِلَ إِلَيْكَ مِن رَّبِّكَ طُغْيَٰنًا وَكُفْرًا ۖ فَلَا تَأْسَ عَلَى ٱلْقَوْمِ ٱلْكَٰفِرِينَ (٦٨)

Say, "O People of the Scripture, you are [standing] on nothing until you uphold [the law of] the Torah, the Gospel, and what has been revealed to you from your Lord." And that which has been revealed to you from your Lord will surely increase many of them in transgression and disbelief. So do not grieve over the disbelieving people. (68)

Quran 5:81

وَلَوْ كَانُوا۟ يُؤْمِنُونَ بِٱللَّهِ وَٱلنَّبِىِّ وَمَآ أُنزِلَ إِلَيْهِ مَا ٱتَّخَذُوهُمْ أَوْلِيَآءَ وَلَٰكِنَّ كَثِيرًا مِّنْهُمْ فَٰسِقُونَ (٨١)

And if they had believed in Allah and the Prophet and in what was revealed to him, they would not have taken them as allies; but many of them are defiantly disobedient. (81)

Quran 5:87-96

يَٰٓأَيُّهَا ٱلَّذِينَ ءَامَنُوا۟ لَا تُحَرِّمُوا۟ طَيِّبَٰتِ مَآ أَحَلَّ ٱللَّهُ لَكُمْ وَلَا تَعْتَدُوٓا۟ إِنَّ ٱللَّهَ لَا يُحِبُّ ٱلْمُعْتَدِينَ (٨٧) وَكُلُوا۟ مِمَّا رَزَقَكُمُ ٱللَّهُ حَلَٰلًا طَيِّبًا ۚ وَٱتَّقُوا۟ ٱللَّهَ ٱلَّذِىٓ أَنتُم بِهِۦ مُؤْمِنُونَ (٨٨) لَا يُؤَاخِذُكُمُ ٱللَّهُ بِٱللَّغْوِ فِىٓ أَيْمَٰنِكُمْ وَلَٰكِن يُؤَاخِذُكُم بِمَا عَقَّدتُّمُ ٱلْأَيْمَٰنَ ۖ فَكَفَّٰرَتُهُۥٓ إِطْعَامُ عَشَرَةِ مَسَٰكِينَ مِنْ أَوْسَطِ مَا تُطْعِمُونَ أَهْلِيكُمْ أَوْ كِسْوَتُهُمْ أَوْ تَحْرِيرُ رَقَبَةٍ ۖ فَمَن لَّمْ يَجِدْ فَصِيَامُ ثَلَٰثَةِ أَيَّامٍ ۚ ذَٰلِكَ كَفَّٰرَةُ أَيْمَٰنِكُمْ إِذَا حَلَفْتُمْ ۚ وَٱحْفَظُوٓا۟ أَيْمَٰنَكُمْ ۚ كَذَٰلِكَ يُبَيِّنُ ٱللَّهُ لَكُمْ ءَايَٰتِهِۦ لَعَلَّكُمْ تَشْكُرُونَ (٨٩) يَٰٓأَيُّهَا ٱلَّذِينَ ءَامَنُوٓا۟ إِنَّمَا ٱلْخَمْرُ وَٱلْمَيْسِرُ وَٱلْأَنصَابُ وَٱلْأَزْلَٰمُ رِجْسٌ مِّنْ عَمَلِ ٱلشَّيْطَٰنِ فَٱجْتَنِبُوهُ لَعَلَّكُمْ تُفْلِحُونَ (٩٠) إِنَّمَا يُرِيدُ ٱلشَّيْطَٰنُ أَن يُوقِعَ بَيْنَكُمُ ٱلْعَدَٰوَةَ وَٱلْبَغْضَآءَ فِى ٱلْخَمْرِ وَٱلْمَيْسِرِ وَيَصُدَّكُمْ عَن ذِكْرِ ٱللَّهِ وَعَنِ

ٱلصَّلَوٰةِۚ فَهَلْ أَنتُم مُّنتَهُونَ (٩١) وَأَطِيعُوا۟ ٱللَّهَ وَأَطِيعُوا۟ ٱلرَّسُولَ وَٱحْذَرُوا۟ۚ فَإِن تَوَلَّيْتُمْ فَٱعْلَمُوٓا۟ أَنَّمَا عَلَىٰ رَسُولِنَا ٱلْبَلَٰغُ ٱلْمُبِينُ (٩٢) لَيْسَ عَلَى ٱلَّذِينَ ءَامَنُوا۟ وَعَمِلُوا۟ ٱلصَّٰلِحَٰتِ جُنَاحٌ فِيمَا طَعِمُوٓا۟ إِذَا مَا ٱتَّقَوا۟ وَّءَامَنُوا۟ وَعَمِلُوا۟ ٱلصَّٰلِحَٰتِ ثُمَّ ٱتَّقَوا۟ وَّءَامَنُوا۟ ثُمَّ ٱتَّقَوا۟ وَّأَحْسَنُوا۟ۗ وَٱللَّهُ يُحِبُّ ٱلْمُحْسِنِينَ (٩٣) يَٰٓأَيُّهَا ٱلَّذِينَ ءَامَنُوا۟ لَيَبْلُوَنَّكُمُ ٱللَّهُ بِشَىْءٍ مِّنَ ٱلصَّيْدِ تَنَالُهُۥٓ أَيْدِيكُمْ وَرِمَاحُكُمْ لِيَعْلَمَ ٱللَّهُ مَن يَخَافُهُۥ بِٱلْغَيْبِۚ فَمَنِ ٱعْتَدَىٰ بَعْدَ ذَٰلِكَ فَلَهُۥ عَذَابٌ أَلِيمٌ (٩٤) يَٰٓأَيُّهَا ٱلَّذِينَ ءَامَنُوا۟ لَا تَقْتُلُوا۟ ٱلصَّيْدَ وَأَنتُمْ حُرُمٌۚ وَمَن قَتَلَهُۥ مِنكُم مُّتَعَمِّدًا فَجَزَآءٌ مِّثْلُ مَا قَتَلَ مِنَ ٱلنَّعَمِ يَحْكُمُ بِهِۦ ذَوَا عَدْلٍ مِّنكُمْ هَدْيًۢا بَٰلِغَ ٱلْكَعْبَةِ أَوْ كَفَّٰرَةٌ طَعَامُ مَسَٰكِينَ أَوْ عَدْلُ ذَٰلِكَ صِيَامًا لِّيَذُوقَ وَبَالَ أَمْرِهِۦۗ عَفَا ٱللَّهُ عَمَّا سَلَفَۚ وَمَنْ عَادَ فَيَنتَقِمُ ٱللَّهُ مِنْهُۗ وَٱللَّهُ عَزِيزٌ ذُو ٱنتِقَامٍ (٩٥) أُحِلَّ لَكُمْ صَيْدُ ٱلْبَحْرِ وَطَعَامُهُۥ مَتَٰعًا لَّكُمْ وَلِلسَّيَّارَةِۖ وَحُرِّمَ عَلَيْكُمْ صَيْدُ ٱلْبَرِّ مَا دُمْتُمْ حُرُمًاۗ وَٱتَّقُوا۟ ٱللَّهَ ٱلَّذِىٓ إِلَيْهِ تُحْشَرُونَ (٩٦)

O you who have believed, do not prohibit the good things which Allah has made lawful to you and do not transgress. Indeed, Allah does not like transgressors. (87) And eat of what Allah has provided for you [which is] lawful and good. And fear Allah, in whom you are believers. (88) Allah will not impose blame upon you for what is meaningless in your oaths, but He will impose blame upon you for [breaking] what you intended of oaths. So its expiation is the feeding of ten needy people from the average of that which you feed your [own] families or clothing them or the freeing of a slave. But whoever cannot find [or afford it] - then a fast of three days [is required]. That is the expiation for oaths when you have sworn. But guard your oaths. Thus does Allah make clear to you His verses that you may be grateful. (89) O you who have believed, indeed, intoxicants, gambling, [sacrificing on] stone alters [to other than Allah], and divining arrows are but defilement from the work of Satan, so avoid it that you may be successful. (90) Satan only wants to cause between you animosity and hatred through intoxicants and gambling and to avert you from the remembrance of Allah and from prayer. So will you not desist? (91) And obey Allah and obey the Messenger and beware. And if you turn away - then know that upon Our Messenger is only [the responsibility for] clear notification. (92) There is not upon those who believe and do righteousness [any] blame concerning what they have eaten [in the past] if they [now] fear Allah and believe and do righteous deeds, and then fear Allah and believe, and then fear Allah and do good; and Allah loves the doers of good. (93) O you who have believed, Allah will surely test you through something of the game that your hands and spears [can] reach, that Allah may make evident those who fear Him unseen. And whoever transgresses after that - for him is a painful punishment. (94) O you who have believed, do not kill game while you are in the state of ihram. And whoever of you kills it intentionally - the penalty is an *equivalent from sacrificial animals to what he killed, as judged by two just men among you as an offering [to Allah] delivered to the Ka'bah, or an expiation: the feeding of needy people or the equivalent of that in fasting, that he may taste the consequence of his deed. Allah has pardoned what is past; but whoever returns [to violation], then Allah will take retribution from him. And Allah is Exalted in Might and Owner of Retribution. (95) Lawful to you is game from the sea and its food as provision for you and the travelers, but forbidden to you is game from the land as long as you are in the state of ihram. And fear Allah to whom you will be gathered. (96)*

Quran 6:19

قُلْ أَيُّ شَيْءٍ أَكْبَرُ شَهَٰدَةً ۖ قُلِ ٱللَّهُ ۖ شَهِيدٌۢ بَيْنِى وَبَيْنَكُمْ ۚ وَأُوحِىَ إِلَىَّ هَٰذَا ٱلْقُرْءَانُ لِأُنذِرَكُم بِهِۦ وَمَنۢ بَلَغَ ۚ أَئِنَّكُمْ لَتَشْهَدُونَ أَنَّ مَعَ ٱللَّهِ ءَالِهَةً أُخْرَىٰ ۚ قُل لَّآ أَشْهَدُ ۚ قُلْ إِنَّمَا هُوَ إِلَٰهٌ وَٰحِدٌ وَإِنَّنِى بَرِىٓءٌ مِّمَّا تُشْرِكُونَ (١٩)

Say, "What thing is greatest in testimony?" Say, "Allah is witness between me and you. And this Qur'an was revealed to me that I may warn you thereby and whomever it reaches. Do you [truly] testify that with Allah there are other deities?" Say, "I will not testify [with you]." Say, "Indeed, He is but one God, and indeed, I am free of what you associate [with Him]." (19)

Quran 6:52

وَلَا تَطْرُدِ ٱلَّذِينَ يَدْعُونَ رَبَّهُم بِٱلْغَدَوٰةِ وَٱلْعَشِىِّ يُرِيدُونَ وَجْهَهُ ۖ مَا عَلَيْكَ مِنْ حِسَابِهِم مِّن شَىْءٍ وَمَا مِنْ حِسَابِكَ عَلَيْهِم مِّن شَىْءٍ فَتَطْرُدَهُمْ فَتَكُونَ مِنَ ٱلظَّٰلِمِينَ (٥٢)

And do not send away those who call upon their Lord morning and afternoon, seeking His countenance. Not upon you is anything of their account and not upon them is anything of your account. So were you to send them away, you would [then] be of the wrongdoers. (52)

Quran 6:56-57

قُلْ إِنِّى نُهِيتُ أَنْ أَعْبُدَ ٱلَّذِينَ تَدْعُونَ مِن دُونِ ٱللَّهِ ۚ قُل لَّا أَتَّبِعُ أَهْوَاءَكُمْ ۙ قَدْ ضَلَلْتُ إِذًا وَمَا أَنَا۠ مِنَ ٱلْمُهْتَدِينَ (٥٦) قُلْ إِنِّى عَلَىٰ بَيِّنَةٍ مِّن رَّبِّى وَكَذَّبْتُم بِهِۦ ۚ مَا عِندِى مَا تَسْتَعْجِلُونَ بِهِۦٓ ۚ إِنِ ٱلْحُكْمُ إِلَّا لِلَّهِ ۖ يَقُصُّ ٱلْحَقَّ ۖ وَهُوَ خَيْرُ ٱلْفَٰصِلِينَ (٥٧)

Say, "Indeed, I have been forbidden to worship those you invoke besides Allah." Say, "I will not follow your desires, for I would then have gone astray, and I would not be of the [rightly] guided." (56) Say, "Indeed, I am on clear evidence from my Lord, and you have denied it. I do not have that for which you are impatient. The decision is only for Allah. He relates the truth, and He is the best of deciders." (57)

Quran 6:68-70

وَإِذَا رَأَيْتَ ٱلَّذِينَ يَخُوضُونَ فِىٓ ءَايَٰتِنَا فَأَعْرِضْ عَنْهُمْ حَتَّىٰ يَخُوضُوا۟ فِى حَدِيثٍ غَيْرِهِۦ ۚ وَإِمَّا يُنسِيَنَّكَ ٱلشَّيْطَٰنُ فَلَا تَقْعُدْ بَعْدَ ٱلذِّكْرَىٰ مَعَ ٱلْقَوْمِ ٱلظَّٰلِمِينَ (٦٨) وَمَا عَلَى ٱلَّذِينَ يَتَّقُونَ مِنْ حِسَابِهِم مِّن شَىْءٍ وَلَٰكِن ذِكْرَىٰ لَعَلَّهُمْ يَتَّقُونَ (٦٩) وَذَرِ ٱلَّذِينَ ٱتَّخَذُوا۟ دِينَهُمْ لَعِبًا وَلَهْوًا وَغَرَّتْهُمُ ٱلْحَيَوٰةُ ٱلدُّنْيَا ۚ وَذَكِّرْ بِهِۦٓ أَن تُبْسَلَ نَفْسٌۢ بِمَا كَسَبَتْ لَيْسَ لَهَا مِن دُونِ ٱللَّهِ وَلِىٌّ وَلَا شَفِيعٌ وَإِن تَعْدِلْ كُلَّ عَدْلٍ لَّا يُؤْخَذْ مِنْهَآ ۗ أُو۟لَٰٓئِكَ ٱلَّذِينَ أُبْسِلُوا۟ بِمَا كَسَبُوا۟ ۖ لَهُمْ شَرَابٌ مِّنْ حَمِيمٍ وَعَذَابٌ أَلِيمٌۢ بِمَا كَانُوا۟ يَكْفُرُونَ (٧٠)

And when you see those who engage in [offensive] discourse concerning Our verses, then turn away from them until they enter into another conversation. And if Satan should cause you to forget, then do not remain after the reminder with the wrongdoing people. (68) And those who fear Allah are not held accountable for the disbelievers at all, but [only for] a reminder - that perhaps they will fear Him. (69) And leave those who take their religion as amusement and diversion and whom the worldly life has deluded. But remind with the Qur'an, lest a soul be given up to destruction for what it earned; it will have other than Allah no protector and no intercessor. And if it should offer every compensation, it would not be taken from it. Those are the ones who are given to destruction for what they have earned. For them will be a drink of scalding water and a painful punishment because they used to disbelieve. (70)

Quran 6:80-83

وَحَاجَّهُۥ قَوْمُهُۥ ۚ قَالَ أَتُحَٰٓجُّوٓنِّى فِى ٱللَّهِ وَقَدْ هَدَىٰنِ ۚ وَلَآ أَخَافُ مَا تُشْرِكُونَ بِهِۦٓ إِلَّآ أَن يَشَآءَ رَبِّى شَيْـًٔا ۗ وَسِعَ رَبِّى كُلَّ شَىْءٍ عِلْمًا ۗ أَفَلَا تَتَذَكَّرُونَ (٨٠) وَكَيْفَ أَخَافُ مَآ أَشْرَكْتُمْ وَلَا تَخَافُونَ أَنَّكُمْ أَشْرَكْتُم بِٱللَّهِ مَا لَمْ يُنَزِّلْ بِهِۦ عَلَيْكُمْ سُلْطَٰنًا ۚ فَأَىُّ ٱلْفَرِيقَيْنِ أَحَقُّ بِٱلْأَمْنِ ۖ إِن كُنتُمْ تَعْلَمُونَ (٨١) ٱلَّذِينَ ءَامَنُوا۟ وَلَمْ يَلْبِسُوٓا۟ إِيمَٰنَهُم بِظُلْمٍ أُو۟لَٰٓئِكَ لَهُمُ ٱلْأَمْنُ وَهُم مُّهْتَدُونَ (٨٢) وَتِلْكَ حُجَّتُنَآ ءَاتَيْنَٰهَآ إِبْرَٰهِيمَ عَلَىٰ قَوْمِهِۦ ۚ نَرْفَعُ دَرَجَٰتٍ مَّن نَّشَآءُ ۗ إِنَّ رَبَّكَ حَكِيمٌ عَلِيمٌ (٨٣)

And his people argued with him. He said, "Do you argue with me concerning Allah while He has guided me? And I fear not what you associate with Him [and will not be harmed] unless my Lord should will something. My Lord encompasses all things in knowledge; then will you not remember? (80) And how should I fear what you associate while you do not fear that you have associated with Allah that for which He has not sent down to you any authority? So which of the two parties has more right to security, if you should know? (81) They who believe and do not mix their belief with injustice - those will have security, and they are [rightly] guided. (82) And that was Our [conclusive] argument which We gave Abraham against his people. We raise by degrees whom We will. Indeed, your Lord is Wise and Knowing. (83)

Quran 6:90

أُو۟لَـٰٓئِكَ ٱلَّذِينَ هَدَى ٱللَّهُ فَبِهُدَىٰهُمُ ٱقْتَدِهْ قُل لَّآ أَسْـَٔلُكُمْ عَلَيْهِ أَجْرًا إِنْ هُوَ إِلَّا ذِكْرَىٰ لِلْعَـٰلَمِينَ (٩٠)

Those are the ones whom Allah has guided, so from their guidance take an example. Say, "I ask of you for this message no payment. It is not but a reminder for the worlds." (90)

Quran 6:108

وَلَا تَسُبُّوا۟ ٱلَّذِينَ يَدْعُونَ مِن دُونِ ٱللَّهِ فَيَسُبُّوا۟ ٱللَّهَ عَدْوًۢا بِغَيْرِ عِلْمٍ ۗ كَذَٰلِكَ زَيَّنَّا لِكُلِّ أُمَّةٍ عَمَلَهُمْ ثُمَّ إِلَىٰ رَبِّهِم مَّرْجِعُهُمْ فَيُنَبِّئُهُم بِمَا كَانُوا۟ يَعْمَلُونَ (١٠٨)

And do not insult those they invoke other than Allah, lest they insult Allah in enmity without knowledge. Thus We have made pleasing to every community their deeds. Then to their Lord is their return, and He will inform them about what they used to do. (108)

Quran 6:114-121

أَفَغَيْرَ ٱللَّهِ أَبْتَغِى حَكَمًا وَهُوَ ٱلَّذِىٓ أَنزَلَ إِلَيْكُمُ ٱلْكِتَـٰبَ مُفَصَّلًا ۚ وَٱلَّذِينَ ءَاتَيْنَـٰهُمُ ٱلْكِتَـٰبَ يَعْلَمُونَ أَنَّهُۥ مُنَزَّلٌ مِّن رَّبِّكَ بِٱلْحَقِّ ۖ فَلَا تَكُونَنَّ مِنَ ٱلْمُمْتَرِينَ (١١٤) وَتَمَّتْ كَلِمَتُ رَبِّكَ صِدْقًا وَعَدْلًا ۚ لَّا مُبَدِّلَ لِكَلِمَـٰتِهِۦ ۚ وَهُوَ ٱلسَّمِيعُ ٱلْعَلِيمُ (١١٥) وَإِن تُطِعْ أَكْثَرَ مَن فِى ٱلْأَرْضِ يُضِلُّوكَ عَن سَبِيلِ ٱللَّهِ ۚ إِن يَتَّبِعُونَ إِلَّا ٱلظَّنَّ وَإِنْ هُمْ إِلَّا يَخْرُصُونَ (١١٦) إِنَّ رَبَّكَ هُوَ أَعْلَمُ مَن يَضِلُّ عَن سَبِيلِهِۦ ۖ وَهُوَ أَعْلَمُ بِٱلْمُهْتَدِينَ (١١٧) فَكُلُوا۟ مِمَّا ذُكِرَ ٱسْمُ ٱللَّهِ عَلَيْهِ إِن كُنتُم بِـَٔايَـٰتِهِۦ مُؤْمِنِينَ (١١٨) وَمَا لَكُمْ أَلَّا تَأْكُلُوا۟ مِمَّا ذُكِرَ ٱسْمُ ٱللَّهِ عَلَيْهِ وَقَدْ فَصَّلَ لَكُم مَّا حَرَّمَ عَلَيْكُمْ إِلَّا مَا ٱضْطُرِرْتُمْ إِلَيْهِ ۗ وَإِنَّ كَثِيرًا لَّيُضِلُّونَ بِأَهْوَآئِهِم

بِغَيْرِ عِلْمٍ ۗ إِنَّ رَبَّكَ هُوَ أَعْلَمُ بِالْمُعْتَدِينَ (١١٩) وَذَرُوا ظَاهِرَ الْإِثْمِ وَبَاطِنَهُ ۚ إِنَّ الَّذِينَ يَكْسِبُونَ الْإِثْمَ سَيُجْزَوْنَ بِمَا كَانُوا يَقْتَرِفُونَ (١٢٠) وَلَا تَأْكُلُوا مِمَّا لَمْ يُذْكَرِ اسْمُ اللَّهِ عَلَيْهِ وَإِنَّهُ لَفِسْقٌ ۗ وَإِنَّ الشَّيَاطِينَ لَيُوحُونَ إِلَىٰ أَوْلِيَائِهِمْ لِيُجَادِلُوكُمْ ۖ وَإِنْ أَطَعْتُمُوهُمْ إِنَّكُمْ لَمُشْرِكُونَ (١٢١)

[Say], "Then is it other than Allah I should seek as judge while it is He who has revealed to you the Book explained in detail?" And those to whom We [previously] gave the Scripture know that it is sent down from your Lord in truth, so never be among the doubters. (114) And the word of your Lord has been fulfilled in truth and in justice. None can alter His words, and He is the Hearing, the Knowing. (115) And if you obey most of those upon the earth, they will mislead you from the way of Allah. They follow not except assumption, and they are not but falsifying. (116) Indeed, your Lord is most knowing of who strays from His way, and He is most knowing of the [rightly] guided. (117) So eat of that [meat] upon which the name of Allah has been mentioned, if you are believers in His verses. (118) And why should you not eat of that upon which the name of Allah has been mentioned while He has explained in detail to you what He has forbidden you, excepting that to which you are compelled. And indeed do many lead [others] astray through their [own] inclinations without knowledge. Indeed, your Lord - He is most knowing of the transgressors. (119) And leave what is apparent of sin and what is concealed thereof. Indeed, those who earn [blame for] sin will be recompensed for that which they used to commit. (120) And do not eat of that upon which the name of Allah has not been mentioned, for indeed, it is grave disobedience. And indeed do the devils inspire their allies [among men] to dispute with you. And if you were to obey them, indeed, you would be associators [of others with Him]. (121)

Quran 6:141-142

۞ وَهُوَ ٱلَّذِىٓ أَنشَأَ جَنَّـٰتٍ مَّعْرُوشَـٰتٍ وَغَيْرَ مَعْرُوشَـٰتٍ وَٱلنَّخْلَ وَٱلزَّرْعَ مُخْتَلِفًا أُكُلُهُۥ وَٱلزَّيْتُونَ وَٱلرُّمَّانَ مُتَشَـٰبِهًا وَغَيْرَ مُتَشَـٰبِهٍ ۚ كُلُوا۟ مِن ثَمَرِهِۦٓ إِذَآ أَثْمَرَ وَءَاتُوا۟ حَقَّهُۥ يَوْمَ حَصَادِهِۦ ۖ وَلَا تُسْرِفُوٓا۟ ۚ إِنَّهُۥ لَا يُحِبُّ ٱلْمُسْرِفِينَ (١٤١) وَمِنَ ٱلْأَنْعَـٰمِ حَمُولَةً وَفَرْشًا ۚ كُلُوا۟ مِمَّا رَزَقَكُمُ ٱللَّهُ وَلَا تَتَّبِعُوا۟ خُطُوَٰتِ ٱلشَّيْطَـٰنِ ۚ إِنَّهُۥ لَكُمْ عَدُوٌّ مُّبِينٌ (١٤٢)

And He it is who causes gardens to grow, [both] trellised and untrellised, and palm trees and crops of different [kinds of] food and olives and pomegranates, similar and dissimilar. Eat of [each of] its fruit when it yields and give its due [zakah] on the day of its harvest. And be not excessive. Indeed, He does not like those who commit excess. (141) And of the grazing livestock are carriers [of burdens] and those [too] small. Eat of what Allah has provided for you and do not follow the footsteps of Satan. Indeed, he is to you a clear enemy. (142)

Quran 6:150-153

قُلْ هَلُمَّ شُهَدَآءَكُمُ ٱلَّذِينَ يَشْهَدُونَ أَنَّ ٱللَّهَ حَرَّمَ هَٰذَا ۖ فَإِن شَهِدُوا۟ فَلَا تَشْهَدْ مَعَهُمْ ۚ وَلَا تَتَّبِعْ أَهْوَآءَ ٱلَّذِينَ كَذَّبُوا۟ بِـَٔايَٰتِنَا وَٱلَّذِينَ لَا يُؤْمِنُونَ بِٱلْءَاخِرَةِ وَهُم بِرَبِّهِمْ يَعْدِلُونَ (١٥٠) ۞ قُلْ تَعَالَوْا۟ أَتْلُ مَا حَرَّمَ رَبُّكُمْ عَلَيْكُمْ ۖ أَلَّا تُشْرِكُوا۟ بِهِۦ شَيْـًٔا ۖ وَبِٱلْوَٰلِدَيْنِ إِحْسَٰنًا ۖ وَلَا تَقْتُلُوٓا۟ أَوْلَٰدَكُم مِّنْ إِمْلَٰقٍ ۖ نَّحْنُ نَرْزُقُكُمْ وَإِيَّاهُمْ ۖ وَلَا تَقْرَبُوا۟ ٱلْفَوَٰحِشَ مَا ظَهَرَ مِنْهَا وَمَا بَطَنَ ۖ وَلَا تَقْتُلُوا۟ ٱلنَّفْسَ ٱلَّتِى حَرَّمَ ٱللَّهُ إِلَّا بِٱلْحَقِّ ۚ ذَٰلِكُمْ وَصَّىٰكُم بِهِۦ لَعَلَّكُمْ تَعْقِلُونَ (١٥١) وَلَا تَقْرَبُوا۟ مَالَ ٱلْيَتِيمِ إِلَّا بِٱلَّتِى هِىَ أَحْسَنُ حَتَّىٰ يَبْلُغَ أَشُدَّهُۥ ۖ وَأَوْفُوا۟ ٱلْكَيْلَ وَٱلْمِيزَانَ بِٱلْقِسْطِ ۖ لَا نُكَلِّفُ نَفْسًا إِلَّا وُسْعَهَا ۖ وَإِذَا قُلْتُمْ فَٱعْدِلُوا۟ وَلَوْ كَانَ ذَا قُرْبَىٰ ۖ وَبِعَهْدِ ٱللَّهِ أَوْفُوا۟ ۚ ذَٰلِكُمْ وَصَّىٰكُم بِهِۦ لَعَلَّكُمْ تَذَكَّرُونَ (١٥٢) وَأَنَّ هَٰذَا صِرَٰطِى مُسْتَقِيمًا فَٱتَّبِعُوهُ ۖ وَلَا تَتَّبِعُوا۟ ٱلسُّبُلَ فَتَفَرَّقَ بِكُمْ عَن سَبِيلِهِۦ ۚ ذَٰلِكُمْ وَصَّىٰكُم بِهِۦ لَعَلَّكُمْ تَتَّقُونَ (١٥٣)

Say, [O Muhammad], "Bring forward your witnesses who will testify that Allah has prohibited this." And if they testify, do not testify with them. And do not follow the desires of those who deny Our verses and those who do not believe in the Hereafter, while they equate [others] with their Lord. (150) Say, "Come, I will recite what your Lord has prohibited to you. [He commands] that you not associate anything with Him, and to parents, good treatment, and do not kill your children out of poverty; We will provide for you and them. And do not approach immoralities - what is apparent of them and

what is concealed. And do not kill the soul which Allah has forbidden [to be killed] except by [legal] right. This has He instructed you that you may use reason."
(151) And do not approach the orphan's property except in a way that is best until he reaches maturity. And give full measure and weight in justice. We do not charge any soul except [with that within] its capacity. And when you testify, be just, even if [it concerns] a near relative. And the covenant of Allah fulfill. This has He instructed you that you may remember. (152) And, [moreover], this is My path, which is straight, so follow it; and do not follow [other] ways, for you will be separated from His way. This has He instructed you that you may become righteous. (153)

Quran 7:2-3

كِتَـٰبٌ أُنزِلَ إِلَيْكَ فَلَا يَكُن فِى صَدْرِكَ حَرَجٌ مِّنْهُ لِتُنذِرَ بِهِۦ وَذِكْرَىٰ لِلْمُؤْمِنِينَ (٢) ٱتَّبِعُواْ مَآ أُنزِلَ إِلَيْكُم مِّن رَّبِّكُمْ وَلَا تَتَّبِعُواْ مِن دُونِهِۦٓ أَوْلِيَآءَ قَلِيلاً مَّا تَذَكَّرُونَ (٣)

[This is] a Book revealed to you, [O Muhammad] - so let there not be in your breast distress therefrom - that you may warn thereby and as a reminder to the believers. (2) Follow, [O mankind], what has been revealed to you from your Lord and do not follow other than Him any allies. Little do you remember. (3)

Quran 7:27

يَٰبَنِىٓ ءَادَمَ لَا يَفْتِنَنَّكُمُ ٱلشَّيْطَٰنُ كَمَآ أَخْرَجَ أَبَوَيْكُم مِّنَ ٱلْجَنَّةِ يَنزِعُ عَنْهُمَا لِبَاسَهُمَا لِيُرِيَهُمَا سَوْءَٰتِهِمَآ إِنَّهُۥ يَرَىٰكُمْ هُوَ وَقَبِيلُهُۥ مِنْ حَيْثُ لَا تَرَوْنَهُمْ إِنَّا جَعَلْنَا ٱلشَّيَٰطِينَ أَوْلِيَآءَ لِلَّذِينَ لَا يُؤْمِنُونَ (٢٧)

O children of Adam, let not Satan tempt you as he removed your parents from Paradise, stripping them of their clothing to show them their private parts. Indeed, he sees you, he and his tribe, from where you do not see them. Indeed, We have made the devils allies to those who do not believe. (27)

Quran 7:31

۞ يَٰبَنِىٓ ءَادَمَ خُذُوا۟ زِينَتَكُمْ عِندَ كُلِّ مَسْجِدٍ وَكُلُوا۟ وَٱشْرَبُوا۟ وَلَا تُسْرِفُوٓا۟ إِنَّهُۥ لَا يُحِبُّ ٱلْمُسْرِفِينَ (٣١)

O children of Adam, take your adornment at every masjid, and eat and drink, but be not excessive. Indeed, He likes not those who commit excess. (31)

Quran 7:74

وَٱذْكُرُوٓا۟ إِذْ جَعَلَكُمْ خُلَفَآءَ مِنۢ بَعْدِ عَادٍ وَبَوَّأَكُمْ فِى ٱلْأَرْضِ تَتَّخِذُونَ مِن سُهُولِهَا قُصُورًا وَتَنْحِتُونَ ٱلْجِبَالَ بُيُوتًا فَٱذْكُرُوٓا۟ ءَالَآءَ ٱللَّهِ وَلَا تَعْثَوْا۟ فِى ٱلْأَرْضِ مُفْسِدِينَ (٧٤)

And remember when He made you successors after the 'Aad and settled you in the land, [and] you take for yourselves palaces from its plains and carve from the mountains, homes. Then remember the favors of Allah and do not commit abuse on the earth, spreading corruption." (74)

Quran 7:85-86

وَإِلَىٰ مَدْيَنَ أَخَاهُمْ شُعَيْبًا ۗ قَالَ يَٰقَوْمِ ٱعْبُدُوا۟ ٱللَّهَ مَا لَكُم مِّنْ إِلَٰهٍ غَيْرُهُۥ ۖ قَدْ جَآءَتْكُم بَيِّنَةٌ مِّن رَّبِّكُمْ ۖ فَأَوْفُوا۟ ٱلْكَيْلَ وَٱلْمِيزَانَ وَلَا تَبْخَسُوا۟ ٱلنَّاسَ أَشْيَآءَهُمْ وَلَا تُفْسِدُوا۟ فِى ٱلْأَرْضِ بَعْدَ إِصْلَٰحِهَا ۚ ذَٰلِكُمْ خَيْرٌ لَّكُمْ إِن كُنتُم مُّؤْمِنِينَ (٨٥) وَلَا تَقْعُدُوا۟ بِكُلِّ صِرَٰطٍ تُوعِدُونَ وَتَصُدُّونَ عَن سَبِيلِ ٱللَّهِ مَنْ ءَامَنَ بِهِۦ وَتَبْغُونَهَا عِوَجًا ۚ وَٱذْكُرُوٓا۟ إِذْ كُنتُمْ قَلِيلًا فَكَثَّرَكُمْ ۖ وَٱنظُرُوا۟ كَيْفَ كَانَ عَٰقِبَةُ ٱلْمُفْسِدِينَ (٨٦)

And to [the people of] Madyan [We sent] their brother Shu'ayb. He said, "O my people, worship Allah; you have no deity other than Him. There has come to you clear evidence from your Lord. So fulfill the measure and weight and do not deprive people of their due and cause not corruption upon the earth after its reformation. That is better for you, if you should be believers. (85) And do not sit on every path, threatening and averting from the way of Allah those who believe in Him, seeking to make it [seem] deviant. And remember when you were few and He increased you. And see how was the end of the corrupters. (86)

Quran 7:180

وَلِلَّهِ ٱلْأَسْمَاءُ ٱلْحُسْنَىٰ فَٱدْعُوهُ بِهَا ۖ وَذَرُوا۟ ٱلَّذِينَ يُلْحِدُونَ فِىٓ أَسْمَٰٓئِهِۦ ۚ سَيُجْزَوْنَ مَا كَانُوا۟ يَعْمَلُونَ (١٨٠)

And to Allah belong the best names, so invoke Him by them. And leave [the company of] those who practice deviation concerning His names. They will be recompensed for what they have been doing. (180)

Quran 7:204-206

وَإِذَا قُرِئَ ٱلْقُرْءَانُ فَٱسْتَمِعُوا۟ لَهُۥ وَأَنصِتُوا۟ لَعَلَّكُمْ تُرْحَمُونَ (٢٠٤) وَٱذْكُر رَّبَّكَ فِى نَفْسِكَ تَضَرُّعًا وَخِيفَةً وَدُونَ ٱلْجَهْرِ مِنَ ٱلْقَوْلِ بِٱلْغُدُوِّ وَٱلْءَاصَالِ وَلَا تَكُن مِّنَ ٱلْغَٰفِلِينَ (٢٠٥) إِنَّ ٱلَّذِينَ عِندَ رَبِّكَ لَا يَسْتَكْبِرُونَ عَنْ عِبَادَتِهِۦ وَيُسَبِّحُونَهُۥ وَلَهُۥ يَسْجُدُونَ ۩ (٢٠٦)

So when the Qur'an is recited, then listen to it and pay attention that you may receive mercy. (204) And remember your Lord within yourself in humility and in fear without being apparent in speech - in the mornings and the evenings. And do not be among the heedless. (205) Indeed, those who are near your Lord are not prevented by arrogance from His worship, and they exalt Him, and to Him they prostrate. (206)

Quran 8:20

يَٰٓأَيُّهَا ٱلَّذِينَ ءَامَنُوٓا۟ أَطِيعُوا۟ ٱللَّهَ وَرَسُولَهُۥ وَلَا تَوَلَّوْا۟ عَنْهُ وَأَنتُمْ تَسْمَعُونَ (٢٠)

O you who have believed, obey Allah and His Messenger and do not turn from him while you hear [his order]. (20)

Quran 8:27

يَـٰٓأَيُّهَا ٱلَّذِينَ ءَامَنُوا۟ لَا تَخُونُوا۟ ٱللَّهَ وَٱلرَّسُولَ وَتَخُونُوٓا۟ أَمَـٰنَـٰتِكُمْ وَأَنتُمْ تَعْلَمُونَ (٢٧)

O you who have believed, do not betray Allah and the Messenger or betray your trusts while you know [the consequence]. (27)

Quran 8:46-47

وَأَطِيعُوا۟ ٱللَّهَ وَرَسُولَهُۥ وَلَا تَنَـٰزَعُوا۟ فَتَفْشَلُوا۟ وَتَذْهَبَ رِيحُكُمْ ۖ وَٱصْبِرُوٓا۟ ۚ إِنَّ ٱللَّهَ مَعَ ٱلصَّـٰبِرِينَ (٤٦) وَلَا تَكُونُوا۟ كَٱلَّذِينَ خَرَجُوا۟ مِن دِيَـٰرِهِم بَطَرًا وَرِئَآءَ ٱلنَّاسِ وَيَصُدُّونَ عَن سَبِيلِ ٱللَّهِ ۚ وَٱللَّهُ بِمَا يَعْمَلُونَ مُحِيطٌ (٤٧)

And obey Allah and His Messenger, and do not dispute and [thus] lose courage and [then] your strength would depart; and be patient. Indeed, Allah is with the patient. (46) And do not be like those who came forth from their homes insolently and to be seen by people and avert [them] from the way of Allah. And Allah is encompassing of what they do. (47)

Quran 9:28

يَـٰٓأَيُّهَا ٱلَّذِينَ ءَامَنُوٓا۟ إِنَّمَا ٱلْمُشْرِكُونَ نَجَسٌ فَلَا يَقْرَبُوا۟ ٱلْمَسْجِدَ ٱلْحَرَامَ بَعْدَ عَامِهِمْ هَـٰذَا ۚ وَإِنْ خِفْتُمْ عَيْلَةً فَسَوْفَ يُغْنِيكُمُ ٱللَّهُ مِن فَضْلِهِۦٓ إِن شَآءَ ۚ إِنَّ ٱللَّهَ عَلِيمٌ حَكِيمٌ (٢٨)

O you who have believed, indeed the polytheists are unclean, so let them not approach al-Masjid al-Haram after this, their [final] year. And if you fear privation, Allah will enrich you from His bounty if He wills. Indeed, Allah is Knowing and Wise. (28)

Quran 9:36

إِنَّ عِدَّةَ ٱلشُّهُورِ عِندَ ٱللَّهِ ٱثْنَا عَشَرَ شَهْرًا فِى كِتَٰبِ ٱللَّهِ يَوْمَ خَلَقَ ٱلسَّمَٰوَٰتِ وَٱلْأَرْضَ مِنْهَآ أَرْبَعَةٌ حُرُمٌ ذَٰلِكَ ٱلدِّينُ ٱلْقَيِّمُ فَلَا تَظْلِمُوا۟ فِيهِنَّ أَنفُسَكُمْ وَقَٰتِلُوا۟ ٱلْمُشْرِكِينَ كَآفَّةً كَمَا يُقَٰتِلُونَكُمْ كَآفَّةً وَٱعْلَمُوٓا۟ أَنَّ ٱللَّهَ مَعَ ٱلْمُتَّقِينَ (٣٦)

Indeed, the number of months with Allah is twelve [lunar] months in the register of Allah [from] the day He created the heavens and the earth; of these, four are sacred. That is the correct religion, so do not wrong yourselves during them. And fight against the disbelievers collectively as they fight against you collectively. And know that Allah is with the righteous [who fear Him]. (36)

Quran 9:40-41

إِلَّا تَنصُرُوهُ فَقَدْ نَصَرَهُ ٱللَّهُ إِذْ أَخْرَجَهُ ٱلَّذِينَ كَفَرُوا۟ ثَانِىَ ٱثْنَيْنِ إِذْ هُمَا فِى ٱلْغَارِ إِذْ يَقُولُ لِصَٰحِبِهِ لَا تَحْزَنْ إِنَّ ٱللَّهَ مَعَنَا فَأَنزَلَ ٱللَّهُ سَكِينَتَهُۥ عَلَيْهِ وَأَيَّدَهُۥ بِجُنُودٍ لَّمْ تَرَوْهَا وَجَعَلَ كَلِمَةَ ٱلَّذِينَ كَفَرُوا۟ ٱلسُّفْلَىٰ وَكَلِمَةُ ٱللَّهِ هِىَ ٱلْعُلْيَا وَٱللَّهُ عَزِيزٌ حَكِيمٌ (٤٠) ٱنفِرُوا۟ خِفَافًا وَثِقَالًا وَجَٰهِدُوا۟ بِأَمْوَٰلِكُمْ وَأَنفُسِكُمْ فِى سَبِيلِ ٱللَّهِ ذَٰلِكُمْ خَيْرٌ لَّكُمْ إِن كُنتُمْ تَعْلَمُونَ (٤١)

If you do not aid the Prophet - Allah has already aided him when those who disbelieved had driven him out [of Makkah] as one of two, when they were in the cave and he said to his companion, "Do not grieve; indeed Allah is with us." And Allah sent down his tranquillity upon him and supported him with angels you did not see and made the word of those who disbelieved the lowest, while the word of Allah - that is the highest. And Allah is Exalted in Might and Wise. (40) Go forth, whether light or heavy, and strive with your wealth and your lives in the cause of Allah. That is better for you, if you only knew. (41)

Quran 9:44-46

لَا يَسْتَأْذِنُكَ ٱلَّذِينَ يُؤْمِنُونَ بِٱللَّهِ وَٱلْيَوْمِ ٱلْأَخِرِ أَن يُجَٰهِدُوا۟ بِأَمْوَٰلِهِمْ وَأَنفُسِهِمْ ۗ وَٱللَّهُ عَلِيمٌۢ بِٱلْمُتَّقِينَ (٤٤) إِنَّمَا يَسْتَأْذِنُكَ ٱلَّذِينَ لَا يُؤْمِنُونَ بِٱللَّهِ وَٱلْيَوْمِ ٱلْأَخِرِ وَٱرْتَابَتْ قُلُوبُهُمْ فَهُمْ فِى رَيْبِهِمْ يَتَرَدَّدُونَ (٤٥) ۞ وَلَوْ أَرَادُوا۟ ٱلْخُرُوجَ لَأَعَدُّوا۟ لَهُۥ عُدَّةً وَلَٰكِن كَرِهَ ٱللَّهُ ٱنۢبِعَاثَهُمْ فَثَبَّطَهُمْ وَقِيلَ ٱقْعُدُوا۟ مَعَ ٱلْقَٰعِدِينَ (٤٦)

Those who believe in Allah and the Last Day would not ask permission of you to be excused from striving with their wealth and their lives. And Allah is Knowing of those who fear Him. (44) Only those would ask permission of you who do not believe in Allah and the Last Day and whose hearts have doubted, and they, in their doubt, are hesitating. (45) And if they had intended to go forth, they would have prepared for it [some] preparation. But Allah disliked their being sent, so He kept them back, and they were told, "Remain [behind] with those who remain." (46)

Quran 9:55

فَلَا تُعْجِبْكَ أَمْوَالُهُمْ وَلَا أَوْلَادُهُمْ إِنَّمَا يُرِيدُ ٱللَّهُ لِيُعَذِّبَهُم بِهَا فِى ٱلْحَيَوٰةِ ٱلدُّنْيَا وَتَزْهَقَ أَنفُسُهُمْ وَهُمْ كَافِرُونَ (٥٥)

So let not their wealth or their children impress you. Allah only intends to punish them through them in worldly life and that their souls should depart [at death] while they are disbelievers. (55)

Quran 9:84-85

وَلَا تُصَلِّ عَلَىٰ أَحَدٍ مِّنْهُم مَّاتَ أَبَدًا وَلَا تَقُمْ عَلَىٰ قَبْرِهِ إِنَّهُمْ كَفَرُوا بِٱللَّهِ وَرَسُولِهِ وَمَاتُوا وَهُمْ فَاسِقُونَ (٨٤) وَلَا تُعْجِبْكَ أَمْوَالُهُمْ وَأَوْلَادُهُمْ إِنَّمَا يُرِيدُ ٱللَّهُ أَن يُعَذِّبَهُم بِهَا فِى ٱلدُّنْيَا وَتَزْهَقَ أَنفُسُهُمْ وَهُمْ كَافِرُونَ (٨٥)

And do not pray [the funeral prayer, O Muhammad], over any of them who has died - ever - or stand at his grave. Indeed, they disbelieved in Allah and His Messenger and died while they were defiantly disobedient. (84) And let not their wealth and their children impress you. Allah only intends to punish them through them in this world and that their souls should depart [at death] while they are disbelievers. (85)

Quran 9:107-108

وَٱلَّذِينَ ٱتَّخَذُواْ مَسْجِدًا ضِرَارًا وَكُفْرًا وَتَفْرِيقًۢا بَيْنَ ٱلْمُؤْمِنِينَ وَإِرْصَادًا لِّمَنْ حَارَبَ ٱللَّهَ وَرَسُولَهُۥ مِن قَبْلُ ۚ وَلَيَحْلِفُنَّ إِنْ أَرَدْنَآ إِلَّا ٱلْحُسْنَىٰ ۖ وَٱللَّهُ يَشْهَدُ إِنَّهُمْ لَكَٰذِبُونَ (١٠٧) لَا تَقُمْ فِيهِ أَبَدًا ۚ لَّمَسْجِدٌ أُسِّسَ عَلَى ٱلتَّقْوَىٰ مِنْ أَوَّلِ يَوْمٍ أَحَقُّ أَن تَقُومَ فِيهِ ۚ فِيهِ رِجَالٌ يُحِبُّونَ أَن يَتَطَهَّرُواْ ۚ وَٱللَّهُ يُحِبُّ ٱلْمُطَّهِّرِينَ (١٠٨)

And [there are] those [hypocrites] who took for themselves a mosque for causing harm and disbelief and division among the believers and as a station for whoever had warred against Allah and His Messenger before. And they will surely swear, "We intended only the best." And Allah testifies that indeed they are liars. (107) Do not stand [for prayer] within it - ever. A mosque founded on righteousness from the first day is more worthy for you to stand in. Within it are men who love to purify themselves; and Allah loves those who purify themselves. (108)

Quran 9:113-115

مَا كَانَ لِلنَّبِيِّ وَٱلَّذِينَ ءَامَنُوٓاْ أَن يَسْتَغْفِرُواْ لِلْمُشْرِكِينَ وَلَوْ كَانُوٓاْ أُوْلِى قُرْبَىٰ مِنۢ بَعْدِ مَا تَبَيَّنَ لَهُمْ أَنَّهُمْ أَصْحَٰبُ ٱلْجَحِيمِ (١١٣) وَمَا كَانَ ٱسْتِغْفَارُ إِبْرَٰهِيمَ لِأَبِيهِ إِلَّا عَن مَّوْعِدَةٍ وَعَدَهَآ إِيَّاهُ فَلَمَّا تَبَيَّنَ لَهُۥٓ أَنَّهُۥ عَدُوٌّ لِّلَّهِ تَبَرَّأَ مِنْهُ ۚ إِنَّ إِبْرَٰهِيمَ لَأَوَّٰهٌ حَلِيمٌ (١١٤) وَمَا كَانَ ٱللَّهُ لِيُضِلَّ قَوْمًۢا بَعْدَ إِذْ هَدَىٰهُمْ حَتَّىٰ يُبَيِّنَ لَهُم مَّا يَتَّقُونَ ۚ إِنَّ ٱللَّهَ بِكُلِّ شَىْءٍ عَلِيمٌ (١١٥)

It is not for the Prophet and those who have believed to ask forgiveness for the polytheists, even if they were relatives, after it has become clear to them that they are companions of Hellfire. (113) And the request of forgiveness of Abraham for his father was only because of a promise he had made to him. But when it became apparent to Abraham that his father was an enemy to Allah, he disassociated himself from him. Indeed was Abraham compassionate and patient. (114) And Allah would not let a people stray after He has guided them until He makes clear to them what they should avoid. Indeed, Allah is Knowing of all things. (115)

Quran 9:120-123

مَا كَانَ لِأَهْلِ ٱلْمَدِينَةِ وَمَنْ حَوْلَهُم مِّنَ ٱلْأَعْرَابِ أَن يَتَخَلَّفُوا۟ عَن رَّسُولِ ٱللَّهِ وَلَا يَرْغَبُوا۟ بِأَنفُسِهِمْ عَن نَّفْسِهِۦ ۚ ذَٰلِكَ بِأَنَّهُمْ لَا يُصِيبُهُمْ ظَمَأٌ وَلَا نَصَبٌ وَلَا مَخْمَصَةٌ فِى سَبِيلِ ٱللَّهِ وَلَا يَطَـُٔونَ مَوْطِئًا يَغِيظُ ٱلْكُفَّارَ وَلَا يَنَالُونَ مِنْ عَدُوٍّ نَّيْلًا إِلَّا كُتِبَ لَهُم بِهِۦ عَمَلٌ صَـٰلِحٌ ۚ إِنَّ ٱللَّهَ لَا يُضِيعُ أَجْرَ ٱلْمُحْسِنِينَ (١٢٠) وَلَا يُنفِقُونَ نَفَقَةً صَغِيرَةً وَلَا كَبِيرَةً وَلَا يَقْطَعُونَ وَادِيًا إِلَّا كُتِبَ لَهُمْ لِيَجْزِيَهُمُ ٱللَّهُ أَحْسَنَ مَا كَانُوا۟ يَعْمَلُونَ (١٢١) ۞ وَمَا كَانَ ٱلْمُؤْمِنُونَ لِيَنفِرُوا۟ كَآفَّةً ۚ فَلَوْلَا نَفَرَ مِن كُلِّ فِرْقَةٍ مِّنْهُمْ طَآئِفَةٌ لِّيَتَفَقَّهُوا۟ فِى ٱلدِّينِ وَلِيُنذِرُوا۟ قَوْمَهُمْ إِذَا رَجَعُوٓا۟ إِلَيْهِمْ لَعَلَّهُمْ يَحْذَرُونَ (١٢٢) يَـٰٓأَيُّهَا ٱلَّذِينَ ءَامَنُوا۟ قَـٰتِلُوا۟ ٱلَّذِينَ يَلُونَكُم مِّنَ ٱلْكُفَّارِ وَلْيَجِدُوا۟ فِيكُمْ غِلْظَةً ۚ وَٱعْلَمُوٓا۟ أَنَّ ٱللَّهَ مَعَ ٱلْمُتَّقِينَ (١٢٣)

It was not [proper] for the people of Madinah and those surrounding them of the bedouins that they remain behind after [the departure of] the Messenger of Allah or that they prefer themselves over his self. That is because they are not afflicted by thirst or fatigue or hunger in the cause of Allah, nor do they tread on any ground that enrages the disbelievers, nor do they inflict upon an enemy any infliction but that is registered for them as a righteous deed. Indeed, Allah does not allow to be lost the reward of the doers of good. (120) Nor do they spend an expenditure, small or large, or cross a valley but that it is registered for them that Allah may reward them for the best of what they were doing. (121) And it is not for the believers to go forth [to battle] all at once. For there should separate from every division of them a group [remaining] to obtain understanding in the religion and warn their people when they return to them that they might be cautious. (122) O you who have believed, fight those adjacent to you of the disbelievers and let them find in you harshness. And know that Allah is with the righteous. (123)

Quran 10:15

وَإِذَا تُتْلَىٰ عَلَيْهِمْ ءَايَاتُنَا بَيِّنَاتٍ ۙ قَالَ ٱلَّذِينَ لَا يَرْجُونَ لِقَآءَنَا ٱئْتِ بِقُرْءَانٍ غَيْرِ هَٰذَآ أَوْ بَدِّلْهُ ۚ قُلْ مَا يَكُونُ لِىٓ أَنْ أُبَدِّلَهُۥ مِن تِلْقَآئِ نَفْسِىٓ ۖ إِنْ أَتَّبِعُ إِلَّا مَا يُوحَىٰٓ إِلَىَّ ۖ إِنِّىٓ أَخَافُ إِنْ عَصَيْتُ رَبِّى عَذَابَ يَوْمٍ عَظِيمٍ (١٥)

And when Our verses are recited to them as clear evidences, those who do not expect the meeting with Us say, "Bring us a Qur'an other than this or change it." Say, [O Muhammad], "It is not for me to change it on my own accord. I only follow what is revealed to me. Indeed I fear, if I should disobey my Lord, the punishment of a tremendous Day." (15)

Quran 10:65

وَلَا يَحْزُنكَ قَوْلُهُمْ إِنَّ ٱلْعِزَّةَ لِلَّهِ جَمِيعًا هُوَ ٱلسَّمِيعُ ٱلْعَلِيمُ (٦٥)

And let not their speech grieve you. Indeed, honor [due to power] belongs to Allah entirely. He is the Hearing, the Knowing. (65)

Quran 10:71-72

۞ وَٱتْلُ عَلَيْهِمْ نَبَأَ نُوحٍ إِذْ قَالَ لِقَوْمِهِۦ يَٰقَوْمِ إِن كَانَ كَبُرَ عَلَيْكُم مَّقَامِى وَتَذْكِيرِى بِـَٔايَٰتِ ٱللَّهِ فَعَلَى ٱللَّهِ تَوَكَّلْتُ فَأَجْمِعُوٓا۟ أَمْرَكُمْ وَشُرَكَآءَكُمْ ثُمَّ لَا يَكُنْ أَمْرُكُمْ عَلَيْكُمْ غُمَّةً ثُمَّ ٱقْضُوٓا۟ إِلَىَّ وَلَا تُنظِرُونِ (٧١) فَإِن تَوَلَّيْتُمْ فَمَا سَأَلْتُكُم مِّنْ أَجْرٍ إِنْ أَجْرِىَ إِلَّا عَلَى ٱللَّهِ وَأُمِرْتُ أَنْ أَكُونَ مِنَ ٱلْمُسْلِمِينَ (٧٢)

And recite to them the news of Noah, when he said to his people, "O my people, if my residence and my reminding of the signs of Allah has become burdensome upon you - then I have relied upon Allah. So resolve upon your plan and [call upon] your associates. Then let not your plan be obscure to you. Then carry it out upon me and do not give me respite. (71) And if you turn away [from my advice] then no payment have I asked of you. My reward is only from Allah, and I have been commanded to be of the Muslims." (72)

Quran 10:88-89

وَقَالَ مُوسَىٰ رَبَّنَآ إِنَّكَ ءَاتَيْتَ فِرْعَوْنَ وَمَلَأَهُۥ زِينَةً وَأَمْوَٰلًا فِى ٱلْحَيَوٰةِ ٱلدُّنْيَا رَبَّنَا لِيُضِلُّوا۟ عَن سَبِيلِكَ ۖ رَبَّنَا ٱطْمِسْ عَلَىٰٓ أَمْوَٰلِهِمْ وَٱشْدُدْ عَلَىٰ قُلُوبِهِمْ فَلَا يُؤْمِنُوا۟ حَتَّىٰ يَرَوُا۟ ٱلْعَذَابَ ٱلْأَلِيمَ (٨٨) قَالَ قَدْ أُجِيبَت دَّعْوَتُكُمَا فَٱسْتَقِيمَا وَلَا تَتَّبِعَآنِّ سَبِيلَ ٱلَّذِينَ لَا يَعْلَمُونَ (٨٩)

And Moses said, "Our Lord, indeed You have given Pharaoh and his establishment splendor and wealth in the worldly life, our Lord, that they may lead [men] astray from Your way. Our Lord, obliterate their wealth and harden their hearts so that they will not believe until they see the painful punishment." (88) [Allah] said, "Your supplication has been answered." So remain on a right course and follow not the way of those who do not know." (89)

Quran 10:94-95

فَإِن كُنتَ فِى شَكٍّ مِّمَّآ أَنزَلْنَآ إِلَيْكَ فَسْـَٔلِ ٱلَّذِينَ يَقْرَءُونَ ٱلْكِتَـٰبَ مِن قَبْلِكَ ۚ لَقَدْ جَآءَكَ ٱلْحَقُّ مِن رَّبِّكَ فَلَا تَكُونَنَّ مِنَ ٱلْمُمْتَرِينَ (٩٤) وَلَا تَكُونَنَّ مِنَ ٱلَّذِينَ كَذَّبُوا۟ بِـَٔايَـٰتِ ٱللَّهِ فَتَكُونَ مِنَ ٱلْخَـٰسِرِينَ (٩٥)

So if you are in doubt, [O Muhammad], about that which We have revealed to you, then ask those who have been reading the Scripture before you. The truth has certainly come to you from your Lord, so never be among the doubters. (94) And never be of those who deny the signs of Allah and [thus] be among the losers. (95)

Quran 10:104-106

قُلْ يَٰٓأَيُّهَا ٱلنَّاسُ إِن كُنتُمْ فِى شَكٍّ مِّن دِينِى فَلَآ أَعْبُدُ ٱلَّذِينَ تَعْبُدُونَ مِن دُونِ ٱللَّهِ وَلَٰكِنْ أَعْبُدُ ٱللَّهَ ٱلَّذِى يَتَوَفَّىٰكُمْ ۖ وَأُمِرْتُ أَنْ أَكُونَ مِنَ ٱلْمُؤْمِنِينَ (١٠٤) وَأَنْ أَقِمْ وَجْهَكَ لِلدِّينِ حَنِيفًا وَلَا تَكُونَنَّ مِنَ ٱلْمُشْرِكِينَ (١٠٥) وَلَا تَدْعُ مِن دُونِ ٱللَّهِ مَا لَا يَنفَعُكَ وَلَا يَضُرُّكَ ۖ فَإِن فَعَلْتَ فَإِنَّكَ إِذًا مِّنَ ٱلظَّٰلِمِينَ (١٠٦)

Say, [O Muhammad], "O people, if you are in doubt as to my religion - then I do not worship those which you worship besides Allah; but I worship Allah, who causes your death. And I have been commanded to be of the believers (104) And [commanded], 'Direct your face toward the religion, inclining to truth, and never be of those who associate others with Allah; (105) And do not invoke besides Allah that which neither benefits you nor harms you, for if you did, then indeed you would be of the wrongdoers.'" (106)

Quran 11:1-2

الٓرۚ كِتَٰبٌ أُحْكِمَتْ ءَايَٰتُهُۥ ثُمَّ فُصِّلَتْ مِن لَّدُنْ حَكِيمٍ خَبِيرٍ (١) أَلَّا تَعْبُدُوٓا۟ إِلَّا ٱللَّهَ إِنَّنِى لَكُم مِّنْهُ نَذِيرٌ وَبَشِيرٌ (٢)

Alif, Lam, Ra. [This is] a Book whose verses are perfected and then presented in detail from [one who is] Wise and Acquainted. (1) [Through a messenger, saying], "Do not worship except Allah. Indeed, I am to you from Him a warner and a bringer of good tidings," (2)

Quran 11:28-31

قَالَ يَٰقَوْمِ أَرَءَيْتُمْ إِن كُنتُ عَلَىٰ بَيِّنَةٍ مِّن رَّبِّى وَءَاتَىٰنِى رَحْمَةً مِّنْ عِندِهِۦ فَعُمِّيَتْ عَلَيْكُمْ أَنُلْزِمُكُمُوهَا وَأَنتُمْ لَهَا كَٰرِهُونَ (٢٨) وَيَٰقَوْمِ لَآ أَسْـَٔلُكُمْ عَلَيْهِ مَالًا ۖ إِنْ أَجْرِىَ إِلَّا عَلَى ٱللَّهِ ۚ وَمَآ أَنَا۠ بِطَارِدِ ٱلَّذِينَ ءَامَنُوٓا۟ ۚ إِنَّهُم مُّلَٰقُوا۟ رَبِّهِمْ وَلَٰكِنِّىٓ أَرَىٰكُمْ قَوْمًا تَجْهَلُونَ (٢٩) وَيَٰقَوْمِ مَن يَنصُرُنِى مِنَ ٱللَّهِ إِن طَرَدتُّهُمْ ۚ أَفَلَا تَذَكَّرُونَ (٣٠) وَلَآ أَقُولُ لَكُمْ عِندِى خَزَآئِنُ ٱللَّهِ وَلَآ أَعْلَمُ ٱلْغَيْبَ وَلَآ أَقُولُ إِنِّى مَلَكٌ وَلَآ أَقُولُ لِلَّذِينَ تَزْدَرِىٓ أَعْيُنُكُمْ لَن يُؤْتِيَهُمُ ٱللَّهُ خَيْرًا ۖ ٱللَّهُ أَعْلَمُ بِمَا فِىٓ أَنفُسِهِمْ ۖ إِنِّىٓ إِذًا لَّمِنَ ٱلظَّٰلِمِينَ (٣١)

He said, "O my people have you considered: if I should be upon clear evidence from my Lord while He has given me mercy from Himself but it has been made unapparent to you, should we force it upon you while you are averse to it? (28) And O my people, I ask not of you for it any wealth. My reward is not but from Allah. And I am not one to drive away those who have believed. Indeed, they will meet their Lord, but I see that you are a people behaving ignorantly. (29) And O my people, who would protect me from Allah if I drove them away? Then will you not be reminded? (30) And I do not tell you that I have the depositories [containing the provision] of Allah or that I know the unseen, nor do I tell you that I am an angel, nor do I say of those upon whom your eyes look down that Allah will never grant them any good. Allah is most knowing of what is within their souls. Indeed, I would then be among the wrongdoers." (31)

Quran 11:50-52

وَإِلَىٰ عَادٍ أَخَاهُمْ هُودًا ۚ قَالَ يَٰقَوْمِ ٱعْبُدُوا۟ ٱللَّهَ مَا لَكُم مِّنْ إِلَٰهٍ غَيْرُهُۥ ۖ إِنْ أَنتُمْ إِلَّا مُفْتَرُونَ (٥٠) يَٰقَوْمِ لَا أَسْـَٔلُكُمْ عَلَيْهِ أَجْرًا ۖ إِنْ أَجْرِىَ إِلَّا عَلَى ٱلَّذِى فَطَرَنِىٓ ۚ أَفَلَا تَعْقِلُونَ (٥١) وَيَٰقَوْمِ ٱسْتَغْفِرُوا۟ رَبَّكُمْ ثُمَّ تُوبُوٓا۟ إِلَيْهِ يُرْسِلِ ٱلسَّمَآءَ عَلَيْكُم مِّدْرَارًا وَيَزِدْكُمْ قُوَّةً إِلَىٰ قُوَّتِكُمْ وَلَا تَتَوَلَّوْا۟ مُجْرِمِينَ (٥٢)

And to 'Aad [We sent] their brother Hud. He said, "O my people, worship Allah; you have no deity other than Him. You are not but inventors [of falsehood]. (50) O my people, I do not ask you for it any reward. My reward is only from the one who created me. Then will you not reason? (51) And O my people, ask forgiveness of your Lord and then repent to Him. He will send [rain from] the sky upon you in showers and increase you in strength [added] to your strength. And do not turn away, [being] criminals." (52)

Quran 11:84-85

۞ وَإِلَىٰ مَدْيَنَ أَخَاهُمْ شُعَيْبًا ۚ قَالَ يَٰقَوْمِ ٱعْبُدُوا۟ ٱللَّهَ مَا لَكُم مِّنْ إِلَٰهٍ غَيْرُهُۥ ۖ وَلَا تَنقُصُوا۟ ٱلْمِكْيَالَ وَٱلْمِيزَانَ ۚ إِنِّىٓ أَرَىٰكُم بِخَيْرٍ وَإِنِّىٓ أَخَافُ عَلَيْكُمْ عَذَابَ يَوْمٍ مُّحِيطٍ (٨٤) وَيَٰقَوْمِ أَوْفُوا۟ ٱلْمِكْيَالَ وَٱلْمِيزَانَ بِٱلْقِسْطِ ۖ وَلَا تَبْخَسُوا۟ ٱلنَّاسَ أَشْيَآءَهُمْ وَلَا تَعْثَوْا۟ فِى ٱلْأَرْضِ مُفْسِدِينَ (٨٥)

And to Madyan [We sent] their brother Shu'ayb. He said, "O my people, worship Allah; you have no deity other than Him. And do not decrease from the measure and the scale. Indeed, I see you in prosperity, but indeed, I fear for you the punishment of an all-encompassing Day. (84) And O my people, give full measure and weight in justice and do not deprive the people of their due and do not commit abuse on the earth, spreading corruption. (85)

Quran 11:12-13

فَٱسْتَقِمْ كَمَآ أُمِرْتَ وَمَن تَابَ مَعَكَ وَلَا تَطْغَوْا۟ ۚ إِنَّهُۥ بِمَا تَعْمَلُونَ بَصِيرٌ (١١٢) وَلَا تَرْكَنُوٓا۟ إِلَى ٱلَّذِينَ ظَلَمُوا۟ فَتَمَسَّكُمُ ٱلنَّارُ وَمَا لَكُم مِّن دُونِ ٱللَّهِ مِنْ أَوْلِيَآءَ ثُمَّ لَا تُنصَرُونَ (١١٣)

So remain on a right course as you have been commanded, [you] and those who have turned back with you [to Allah], and do not transgress. Indeed, He is Seeing of what you do. (112) And do not incline toward those who do wrong, lest you be touched by the Fire, and you would not have other than Allah any protectors; then you would not be helped. (113)

Quran 13:19-25

أَفَمَن يَعْلَمُ أَنَّمَا أُنزِلَ إِلَيْكَ مِن رَّبِّكَ ٱلْحَقُّ كَمَنْ هُوَ أَعْمَىٰٓ ۚ إِنَّمَا يَتَذَكَّرُ أُو۟لُوا۟ ٱلْأَلْبَٰبِ (١٩) ٱلَّذِينَ يُوفُونَ بِعَهْدِ ٱللَّهِ وَلَا يَنقُضُونَ ٱلْمِيثَٰقَ (٢٠) وَٱلَّذِينَ يَصِلُونَ مَآ أَمَرَ ٱللَّهُ بِهِۦٓ أَن يُوصَلَ وَيَخْشَوْنَ رَبَّهُمْ وَيَخَافُونَ سُوٓءَ ٱلْحِسَابِ (٢١) وَٱلَّذِينَ صَبَرُوا۟ ٱبْتِغَآءَ وَجْهِ رَبِّهِمْ وَأَقَامُوا۟ ٱلصَّلَوٰةَ وَأَنفَقُوا۟ مِمَّا رَزَقْنَٰهُمْ سِرًّا وَعَلَانِيَةً وَيَدْرَءُونَ بِٱلْحَسَنَةِ ٱلسَّيِّئَةَ أُو۟لَٰٓئِكَ لَهُمْ عُقْبَى ٱلدَّارِ (٢٢) جَنَّٰتُ عَدْنٍ يَدْخُلُونَهَا وَمَن صَلَحَ مِنْ ءَابَآئِهِمْ وَأَزْوَٰجِهِمْ وَذُرِّيَّٰتِهِمْ ۖ وَٱلْمَلَٰٓئِكَةُ يَدْخُلُونَ عَلَيْهِم مِّن كُلِّ بَابٍ (٢٣) سَلَٰمٌ عَلَيْكُم بِمَا صَبَرْتُمْ ۚ فَنِعْمَ عُقْبَى ٱلدَّارِ (٢٤) وَٱلَّذِينَ يَنقُضُونَ عَهْدَ ٱللَّهِ مِنۢ بَعْدِ مِيثَٰقِهِۦ وَيَقْطَعُونَ مَآ أَمَرَ ٱللَّهُ بِهِۦٓ أَن يُوصَلَ وَيُفْسِدُونَ فِى ٱلْأَرْضِ ۙ أُو۟لَٰٓئِكَ لَهُمُ ٱللَّعْنَةُ وَلَهُمْ سُوٓءُ ٱلدَّارِ (٢٥)

Then is he who knows that what has been revealed to you from your Lord is the truth like one who is blind? They will only be reminded who are people of understanding - (19) Those who fulfill the covenant of Allah and do not break the contract, (20) And those who join that which Allah has ordered to be joined and fear their Lord and are afraid of the evil of [their] account, (21) And those who are patient, seeking the countenance of their Lord, and establish prayer and spend from what We have provided for them secretly and publicly and prevent evil with good - those will have the good consequence of [this] home - (22) Gardens of perpetual residence; they will enter them with whoever were righteous among their fathers, their spouses and their descendants. And the angels will enter upon them from every gate, [saying], (23) "Peace be upon you for what you patiently endured. And excellent is the final home." (24) But those who break the covenant of Allah after contracting it and sever that which Allah has ordered to be joined and spread corruption on earth - for them is the curse, and they will have the worst home. (25)

Quran 14:22

وَقَالَ ٱلشَّيْطَٰنُ لَمَّا قُضِىَ ٱلْأَمْرُ إِنَّ ٱللَّهَ وَعَدَكُمْ وَعْدَ ٱلْحَقِّ وَوَعَدتُّكُمْ فَأَخْلَفْتُكُمْ ۖ وَمَا كَانَ لِىَ عَلَيْكُم مِّن سُلْطَٰنٍ إِلَّآ أَن دَعَوْتُكُمْ فَٱسْتَجَبْتُمْ لِى ۖ فَلَا تَلُومُونِى وَلُومُوٓا۟ أَنفُسَكُم ۖ مَّآ أَنَا۠ بِمُصْرِخِكُمْ وَمَآ أَنتُم بِمُصْرِخِىَّ ۖ إِنِّى كَفَرْتُ بِمَآ أَشْرَكْتُمُونِ مِن قَبْلُ ۗ إِنَّ ٱلظَّٰلِمِينَ لَهُمْ عَذَابٌ أَلِيمٌ (٢٢)

And Satan will say when the matter has been concluded, "Indeed, Allah had promised you the promise of truth. And I promised you, but I betrayed you. But I had no authority over you except that I invited you, and you responded to me. So do not blame me; but blame yourselves. I cannot be called to your aid, nor can you be called to my aid. Indeed, I deny your association of me [with Allah] before. Indeed, for the wrongdoers is a painful punishment." (22)

Quran 14:47

فَلَا تَحْسَبَنَّ ٱللَّهَ مُخْلِفَ وَعْدِهِۦ رُسُلَهُۥٓ ۗ إِنَّ ٱللَّهَ عَزِيزٌ ذُو ٱنتِقَامٍ (٤٧)

So never think that Allah will fail in His promise to His messengers. Indeed, Allah is Exalted in Might and Owner of Retribution. (47)

Quran 15:87-94

وَلَقَدْ ءَاتَيْنَٰكَ سَبْعًا مِّنَ ٱلْمَثَانِى وَٱلْقُرْءَانَ ٱلْعَظِيمَ (٨٧) لَا تَمُدَّنَّ عَيْنَيْكَ إِلَىٰ مَا مَتَّعْنَا بِهِۦٓ أَزْوَٰجًا مِّنْهُمْ وَلَا تَحْزَنْ عَلَيْهِمْ وَٱخْفِضْ جَنَاحَكَ لِلْمُؤْمِنِينَ (٨٨) وَقُلْ إِنِّىٓ أَنَا ٱلنَّذِيرُ ٱلْمُبِينُ (٨٩) كَمَآ أَنزَلْنَا عَلَى ٱلْمُقْتَسِمِينَ (٩٠) ٱلَّذِينَ جَعَلُوا۟ ٱلْقُرْءَانَ عِضِينَ (٩١) فَوَرَبِّكَ لَنَسْـَٔلَنَّهُمْ أَجْمَعِينَ (٩٢) عَمَّا كَانُوا۟ يَعْمَلُونَ (٩٣) فَٱصْدَعْ بِمَا تُؤْمَرُ وَأَعْرِضْ عَنِ ٱلْمُشْرِكِينَ (٩٤)

And We have certainly given you, [O Muhammad], seven of the often repeated [verses] and the great Qur'an. (87) Do not extend your eyes toward that by which We have given enjoyment to [certain] categories of the disbelievers, and do not grieve over them. And lower your wing to the believers (88) And say, "Indeed, I am the clear warner" - (89) Just as We had revealed [scriptures] to the separators (90) Who have made the Qur'an into portions. (91) So by your Lord, We will surely question them all (92) About what they used to do. (93) Then declare what you are commanded and turn away from the polytheists. (94)

Quran 16:1

أَتَىٰٓ أَمْرُ ٱللَّهِ فَلَا تَسْتَعْجِلُوهُ ۚ سُبْحَٰنَهُۥ وَتَعَٰلَىٰ عَمَّا يُشْرِكُونَ (١)

The command of Allah is coming, so be not impatient for it. Exalted is He and high above what they associate with Him. (1)

Quran 16:51-54

۞ وَقَالَ ٱللَّهُ لَا تَتَّخِذُوٓا۟ إِلَٰهَيْنِ ٱثْنَيْنِ ۖ إِنَّمَا هُوَ إِلَٰهٌ وَٰحِدٌ ۖ فَإِيَّٰىَ فَٱرْهَبُونِ (٥١) وَلَهُۥ مَا فِى ٱلسَّمَٰوَٰتِ وَٱلْأَرْضِ وَلَهُ ٱلدِّينُ وَاصِبًا ۚ أَفَغَيْرَ ٱللَّهِ تَتَّقُونَ (٥٢) وَمَا بِكُم مِّن نِّعْمَةٍ فَمِنَ ٱللَّهِ ۖ ثُمَّ إِذَا مَسَّكُمُ ٱلضُّرُّ فَإِلَيْهِ تَجْـَٔرُونَ (٥٣) ثُمَّ إِذَا كَشَفَ ٱلضُّرَّ عَنكُمْ إِذَا فَرِيقٌ مِّنكُم بِرَبِّهِمْ يُشْرِكُونَ (٥٤)

And Allah has said, "Do not take for yourselves two deities. He is but one God, so fear only Me." (51) And to Him belongs whatever is in the heavens and the earth, and to Him is [due] worship constantly. Then is it other than Allah that you fear? (52) And whatever you have of favor - it is from Allah. Then when adversity touches you, to Him you cry for help. (53) Then when He removes the adversity from you, at once a party of you associates others with their Lord (54)

Quran 16:74

فَلَا تَضْرِبُوا۟ لِلَّهِ ٱلْأَمْثَالَ ۚ إِنَّ ٱللَّهَ يَعْلَمُ وَأَنتُمْ لَا تَعْلَمُونَ (٧٤)

So do not assert similarities to Allah. Indeed, Allah knows and you do not know. (74)

Quran 16:90-100

۞ إِنَّ ٱللَّهَ يَأْمُرُ بِٱلْعَدْلِ وَٱلْإِحْسَانِ وَإِيتَآئِ ذِى ٱلْقُرْبَىٰ وَيَنْهَىٰ عَنِ ٱلْفَحْشَآءِ وَٱلْمُنكَرِ وَٱلْبَغْىِ يَعِظُكُمْ لَعَلَّكُمْ تَذَكَّرُونَ (٩٠) وَأَوْفُوا۟ بِعَهْدِ ٱللَّهِ إِذَا عَـٰهَدتُّمْ وَلَا تَنقُضُوا۟ ٱلْأَيْمَـٰنَ بَعْدَ تَوْكِيدِهَا وَقَدْ جَعَلْتُمُ ٱللَّهَ عَلَيْكُمْ كَفِيلًا إِنَّ ٱللَّهَ يَعْلَمُ مَا تَفْعَلُونَ (٩١) وَلَا تَكُونُوا۟ كَٱلَّتِى نَقَضَتْ غَزْلَهَا مِنۢ بَعْدِ قُوَّةٍ أَنكَـٰثًا تَتَّخِذُونَ أَيْمَـٰنَكُمْ دَخَلًۢا بَيْنَكُمْ أَن تَكُونَ أُمَّةٌ هِىَ أَرْبَىٰ مِنْ أُمَّةٍ إِنَّمَا يَبْلُوكُمُ ٱللَّهُ بِهِۦ وَلَيُبَيِّنَنَّ لَكُمْ يَوْمَ ٱلْقِيَـٰمَةِ مَا كُنتُمْ فِيهِ تَخْتَلِفُونَ (٩٢) وَلَوْ شَآءَ ٱللَّهُ لَجَعَلَكُمْ أُمَّةً وَٰحِدَةً وَلَـٰكِن يُضِلُّ مَن يَشَآءُ وَيَهْدِى مَن يَشَآءُ وَلَتُسْـَٔلُنَّ عَمَّا كُنتُمْ تَعْمَلُونَ (٩٣) وَلَا تَتَّخِذُوٓا۟ أَيْمَـٰنَكُمْ دَخَلًۢا بَيْنَكُمْ فَتَزِلَّ قَدَمٌۢ بَعْدَ ثُبُوتِهَا وَتَذُوقُوا۟ ٱلسُّوٓءَ بِمَا صَدَدتُّمْ عَن سَبِيلِ ٱللَّهِ وَلَكُمْ عَذَابٌ عَظِيمٌ (٩٤) وَلَا تَشْتَرُوا۟ بِعَهْدِ ٱللَّهِ ثَمَنًا قَلِيلًا إِنَّمَا عِندَ ٱللَّهِ هُوَ خَيْرٌ لَّكُمْ إِن كُنتُمْ تَعْلَمُونَ (٩٥) مَا عِندَكُمْ يَنفَدُ وَمَا عِندَ ٱللَّهِ بَاقٍ وَلَنَجْزِيَنَّ ٱلَّذِينَ صَبَرُوٓا۟ أَجْرَهُم بِأَحْسَنِ مَا كَانُوا۟ يَعْمَلُونَ (٩٦) مَنْ عَمِلَ صَـٰلِحًا مِّن ذَكَرٍ أَوْ أُنثَىٰ وَهُوَ مُؤْمِنٌ فَلَنُحْيِيَنَّهُۥ حَيَوٰةً طَيِّبَةً وَلَنَجْزِيَنَّهُمْ أَجْرَهُم بِأَحْسَنِ مَا كَانُوا۟ يَعْمَلُونَ (٩٧) فَإِذَا قَرَأْتَ ٱلْقُرْءَانَ فَٱسْتَعِذْ بِٱللَّهِ مِنَ ٱلشَّيْطَـٰنِ ٱلرَّجِيمِ (٩٨) إِنَّهُۥ لَيْسَ لَهُۥ سُلْطَـٰنٌ عَلَى ٱلَّذِينَ ءَامَنُوا۟ وَعَلَىٰ رَبِّهِمْ يَتَوَكَّلُونَ (٩٩) إِنَّمَا سُلْطَـٰنُهُۥ عَلَى ٱلَّذِينَ يَتَوَلَّوْنَهُۥ وَٱلَّذِينَ هُم بِهِۦ مُشْرِكُونَ (١٠٠)

Indeed, Allah orders justice and good conduct and giving to relatives and forbids immorality and bad conduct and oppression. He admonishes you that perhaps you will be reminded. (90) And fulfill the covenant of Allah when you have taken it, [O believers], and do not break oaths after their confirmation while you have made Allah, over you, a witness. Indeed, Allah knows what you do. (91) And do not be like she who untwisted her spun thread after it was strong [by] taking your oaths as [means of] deceit between you because one community is more *plentiful [in number or wealth] than another community. Allah only tries you thereby. And He will surely make clear to you on the Day of Resurrection that over which you used to differ. (92) And if Allah had willed, He could have made you [of] one religion, but He causes to stray whom He wills and guides whom He wills. And you will surely be questioned about what you used to do. (93) And do not take your oaths as [means of] deceit between you, lest a foot slip after it was [once] firm, and you would taste evil [in this world] for what [people] you diverted from the way of Allah, and you would have [in the Hereafter] a great punishment. (94) And do not exchange the covenant of Allah for a small price. Indeed, what is with Allah is best for you, if only you could know. (95) Whatever you have will end, but what Allah has is lasting. And We will surely give those who were patient their reward according to the best of what they used to do. (96) Whoever does righteousness, whether male or female, while he is a believer - We will surely cause him to live a good life, and We will surely give them their reward [in the Hereafter] according to the best of what they used to do. (97) So when you recite the Qur'an, [first] seek refuge in Allah from Satan, the expelled [from His mercy]. (98) Indeed, there is for him no authority over those who have believed and rely upon their Lord.*

(99) His authority is only over those who take him as an ally and those who through him associate others with Allah. (100)

Quran 16:116

وَلَا تَقُولُوا لِمَا تَصِفُ أَلْسِنَتُكُمُ ٱلْكَذِبَ هَٰذَا حَلَٰلٌ وَهَٰذَا حَرَامٌ لِّتَفْتَرُوا عَلَى ٱللَّهِ ٱلْكَذِبَ ۚ إِنَّ ٱلَّذِينَ يَفْتَرُونَ عَلَى ٱللَّهِ ٱلْكَذِبَ لَا يُفْلِحُونَ (١١٦)

And do not say about what your tongues assert of untruth, "This is lawful and this is unlawful," to invent falsehood about Allah. Indeed, those who invent falsehood about Allah will not succeed. (116)

Quran 16:120-123

إِنَّ إِبْرَٰهِيمَ كَانَ أُمَّةً قَانِتًا لِّلَّهِ حَنِيفًا وَلَمْ يَكُ مِنَ ٱلْمُشْرِكِينَ (١٢٠) شَاكِرًا لِّأَنْعُمِهِ ۚ ٱجْتَبَىٰهُ وَهَدَىٰهُ إِلَىٰ صِرَٰطٍ مُّسْتَقِيمٍ (١٢١) وَءَاتَيْنَٰهُ فِى ٱلدُّنْيَا حَسَنَةً ۖ وَإِنَّهُۥ فِى ٱلْءَاخِرَةِ لَمِنَ ٱلصَّٰلِحِينَ (١٢٢) ثُمَّ أَوْحَيْنَآ إِلَيْكَ أَنِ ٱتَّبِعْ مِلَّةَ إِبْرَٰهِيمَ حَنِيفًا ۖ وَمَا كَانَ مِنَ ٱلْمُشْرِكِينَ (١٢٣)

Indeed, Abraham was a [comprehensive] leader, devoutly obedient to Allah, inclining toward truth, and he was not of those who associate others with Allah. (120) [He was] grateful for His favors. Allah chose him and guided him to a straight path. (121) And We gave him good in this world, and indeed, in the Hereafter he will be among the righteous. (122) Then We revealed to you, [O Muhammad], to follow the religion of Abraham, *inclining toward truth; and he was not of those who associate with Allah. (123)*

Quran 16:127

وَٱصْبِرْ وَمَا صَبْرُكَ إِلَّا بِٱللَّهِ ۚ وَلَا تَحْزَنْ عَلَيْهِمْ وَلَا تَكُ فِى ضَيْقٍ مِّمَّا يَمْكُرُونَ (١٢٧)

And be patient, [O Muhammad], and your patience is not but through Allah. And do not grieve over them and do not be in distress over what they conspire. (127)

Quran 17:22-39

لَّا تَجْعَلْ مَعَ ٱللَّهِ إِلَٰهًا ءَاخَرَ فَتَقْعُدَ مَذْمُومًا مَّخْذُولًا (٢٢) ۞ وَقَضَىٰ رَبُّكَ أَلَّا تَعْبُدُوٓا۟ إِلَّآ إِيَّاهُ وَبِٱلْوَٰلِدَيْنِ إِحْسَٰنًا ۚ إِمَّا يَبْلُغَنَّ عِندَكَ ٱلْكِبَرَ أَحَدُهُمَآ أَوْ كِلَاهُمَا فَلَا تَقُل لَّهُمَآ أُفٍّ وَلَا تَنْهَرْهُمَا وَقُل لَّهُمَا قَوْلًا كَرِيمًا (٢٣) وَٱخْفِضْ لَهُمَا جَنَاحَ ٱلذُّلِّ مِنَ ٱلرَّحْمَةِ وَقُل رَّبِّ ٱرْحَمْهُمَا كَمَا رَبَّيَانِى صَغِيرًا (٢٤) رَّبُّكُمْ أَعْلَمُ بِمَا فِى نُفُوسِكُمْ ۚ إِن تَكُونُوا۟ صَٰلِحِينَ فَإِنَّهُۥ كَانَ لِلْأَوَّٰبِينَ غَفُورًا (٢٥) وَءَاتِ ذَا ٱلْقُرْبَىٰ حَقَّهُۥ وَٱلْمِسْكِينَ وَٱبْنَ ٱلسَّبِيلِ وَلَا تُبَذِّرْ تَبْذِيرًا (٢٦) إِنَّ ٱلْمُبَذِّرِينَ كَانُوٓا۟ إِخْوَٰنَ ٱلشَّيَٰطِينِ ۖ وَكَانَ ٱلشَّيْطَٰنُ لِرَبِّهِۦ كَفُورًا (٢٧) وَإِمَّا تُعْرِضَنَّ عَنْهُمُ ٱبْتِغَآءَ رَحْمَةٍ مِّن رَّبِّكَ تَرْجُوهَا فَقُل لَّهُمْ قَوْلًا مَّيْسُورًا (٢٨) وَلَا تَجْعَلْ يَدَكَ مَغْلُولَةً إِلَىٰ عُنُقِكَ وَلَا تَبْسُطْهَا كُلَّ ٱلْبَسْطِ فَتَقْعُدَ مَلُومًا مَّحْسُورًا (٢٩) إِنَّ رَبَّكَ يَبْسُطُ ٱلرِّزْقَ لِمَن يَشَآءُ وَيَقْدِرُ ۚ إِنَّهُۥ كَانَ بِعِبَادِهِۦ خَبِيرًۢا بَصِيرًا (٣٠) وَلَا تَقْتُلُوٓا۟ أَوْلَٰدَكُمْ خَشْيَةَ إِمْلَٰقٍ ۖ نَّحْنُ نَرْزُقُهُمْ وَإِيَّاكُمْ ۚ إِنَّ قَتْلَهُمْ كَانَ خِطْـًٔا كَبِيرًا (٣١) وَلَا تَقْرَبُوا۟ ٱلزِّنَىٰٓ ۖ إِنَّهُۥ كَانَ فَٰحِشَةً وَسَآءَ سَبِيلًا (٣٢) وَلَا تَقْتُلُوا۟ ٱلنَّفْسَ ٱلَّتِى حَرَّمَ ٱللَّهُ إِلَّا بِٱلْحَقِّ ۗ وَمَن قُتِلَ مَظْلُومًا فَقَدْ جَعَلْنَا لِوَلِيِّهِۦ سُلْطَٰنًا فَلَا يُسْرِف فِّى ٱلْقَتْلِ ۖ إِنَّهُۥ كَانَ مَنصُورًا (٣٣) وَلَا تَقْرَبُوا۟ مَالَ ٱلْيَتِيمِ إِلَّا بِٱلَّتِى هِىَ أَحْسَنُ حَتَّىٰ يَبْلُغَ أَشُدَّهُۥ ۚ وَأَوْفُوا۟

بِٱلْعَهْدِۚ إِنَّ ٱلْعَهْدَ كَانَ مَسْـُٔولًا (٣٤) وَأَوْفُوا۟ ٱلْكَيْلَ إِذَا كِلْتُمْ وَزِنُوا۟ بِٱلْقِسْطَاسِ ٱلْمُسْتَقِيمِۚ ذَٰلِكَ خَيْرٌ وَأَحْسَنُ تَأْوِيلًا (٣٥) وَلَا تَقْفُ مَا لَيْسَ لَكَ بِهِۦ عِلْمٌۚ إِنَّ ٱلسَّمْعَ وَٱلْبَصَرَ وَٱلْفُؤَادَ كُلُّ أُو۟لَٰٓئِكَ كَانَ عَنْهُ مَسْـُٔولًا (٣٦) وَلَا تَمْشِ فِى ٱلْأَرْضِ مَرَحًاۖ إِنَّكَ لَن تَخْرِقَ ٱلْأَرْضَ وَلَن تَبْلُغَ ٱلْجِبَالَ طُولًا (٣٧) كُلُّ ذَٰلِكَ كَانَ سَيِّئُهُۥ عِندَ رَبِّكَ مَكْرُوهًا (٣٨) ذَٰلِكَ مِمَّآ أَوْحَىٰٓ إِلَيْكَ رَبُّكَ مِنَ ٱلْحِكْمَةِۗ وَلَا تَجْعَلْ مَعَ ٱللَّهِ إِلَٰهًا ءَاخَرَ فَتُلْقَىٰ فِى جَهَنَّمَ مَلُومًا مَّدْحُورًا (٣٩)

Do not make [as equal] with Allah another deity and [thereby] become censured and forsaken. (22) And your Lord has decreed that you not worship except Him, and to parents, good treatment. Whether one or both of them reach old age [while] with you, say not to them [so much as], "uff," and do not repel them but speak to them a noble word. (23) And lower to them the wing of humility out of mercy and say, "My Lord, have mercy upon them as they brought me up [when I was] small." (24) Your Lord is most knowing of what is within yourselves. If you should be righteous [in intention] - then indeed He is ever, to the often returning [to Him], Forgiving. (25) And give the relative his right, and [also] the poor and the traveler, and do not spend wastefully. (26) Indeed, the wasteful are brothers of the devils, and ever has Satan been to his Lord ungrateful. (27) And if you [must] turn away from the needy awaiting mercy from your Lord which you expect, then speak to them a gentle word. (28) And do not make your hand [as] chained to your neck or *extend it completely and [thereby] become blamed and insolvent. (29) Indeed, your Lord extends provision for whom He wills and restricts [it]. Indeed He is ever, concerning His servants, Acquainted and Seeing. (30) And do not kill your children for fear of poverty. We provide for them and for you. Indeed, their killing is ever a great sin. (31) And do not approach unlawful sexual intercourse. Indeed, it is ever an immorality and is evil as a way. (32) And do not kill the soul which Allah has forbidden, except by right. And whoever is killed unjustly - We have given his heir authority, but let him not exceed limits in [the matter of] taking life. Indeed, he has been supported [by the law]. (33) And do not approach the property of an orphan, except in the way that is best, until he reaches maturity. And fulfill [every] commitment. Indeed, the commitment is ever [that about which one will be] questioned. (34) And give full measure when you measure, and weigh with an even balance. That is the best [way] and best in result. (35) And do not pursue that of which you have no knowledge. Indeed, the hearing, the sight and the heart - about all those [one] will be questioned. (36) And do not walk upon the earth exultantly. Indeed, you will never tear the earth [apart], and you will never reach the mountains in height. (37) All that - its evil is ever, in the sight of your*

Lord, detested. (38) That is from what your Lord has revealed to you, [O Muhammad], of wisdom. And, [O mankind], do not make [as equal] with Allah another deity, lest you be thrown into Hell, blamed and banished. (39)

Quran 18:14-15

وَرَبَطْنَا عَلَىٰ قُلُوبِهِمْ إِذْ قَامُوا۟ فَقَالُوا۟ رَبُّنَا رَبُّ ٱلسَّمَـٰوَٰتِ وَٱلْأَرْضِ لَن نَّدْعُوَا۟ مِن دُونِهِۦٓ إِلَـٰهًا ۖ لَّقَدْ قُلْنَآ إِذًۭا شَطَطًا (١٤) هَـٰٓؤُلَآءِ قَوْمُنَا ٱتَّخَذُوا۟ مِن دُونِهِۦٓ ءَالِهَةً ۖ لَّوْلَا يَأْتُونَ عَلَيْهِم بِسُلْطَـٰنٍۭ بَيِّنٍۢ ۖ فَمَنْ أَظْلَمُ مِمَّنِ ٱفْتَرَىٰ عَلَى ٱللَّهِ كَذِبًۭا (١٥)

And We made firm their hearts when they stood up and said, "Our Lord is the Lord of the heavens and the earth. Never will we invoke besides Him any deity. We would have certainly spoken, then, an excessive transgression. (14) These, our people, have taken besides Him deities. Why do they not bring for [worship of] them a clear authority? And who is more unjust than one who invents about Allah a lie?" (15)

Quran 18:22-24

سَيَقُولُونَ ثَلَـٰثَةٌۭ رَّابِعُهُمْ كَلْبُهُمْ وَيَقُولُونَ خَمْسَةٌۭ سَادِسُهُمْ كَلْبُهُمْ رَجْمًۢا بِٱلْغَيْبِ ۖ وَيَقُولُونَ سَبْعَةٌۭ وَثَامِنُهُمْ كَلْبُهُمْ ۚ قُل رَّبِّىٓ أَعْلَمُ بِعِدَّتِهِم مَّا يَعْلَمُهُمْ إِلَّا قَلِيلٌۭ ۗ فَلَا تُمَارِ فِيهِمْ إِلَّا مِرَآءًۭ ظَـٰهِرًۭا وَلَا تَسْتَفْتِ فِيهِم مِّنْهُمْ أَحَدًۭا (٢٢) وَلَا تَقُولَنَّ لِشَا۟يْءٍ إِنِّى فَاعِلٌۭ ذَٰلِكَ غَدًا (٢٣) إِلَّآ أَن يَشَآءَ ٱللَّهُ ۚ وَٱذْكُر رَّبَّكَ إِذَا نَسِيتَ وَقُلْ عَسَىٰٓ أَن يَهْدِيَنِ رَبِّى لِأَقْرَبَ مِنْ هَـٰذَا رَشَدًۭا (٢٤)

They will say there were three, the fourth of them being their dog; and they will say there were five, the sixth of them being their dog - guessing at the unseen; and they will say there were seven, and the eighth of them was their dog. Say, [O Muhammad], "My Lord is most knowing of their number. None knows them except a few. So do not argue about them except with an obvious argument and do not inquire about them among [the speculators] from anyone." (22) And never say of anything, "Indeed, I will do that tomorrow," (23) Except [when adding], "If Allah wills." And remember your Lord when you forget [it] and say, "Perhaps my Lord will guide me to what is nearer than this to right conduct." (24)

Quran 18:28

وَٱصْبِرْ نَفْسَكَ مَعَ ٱلَّذِينَ يَدْعُونَ رَبَّهُم بِٱلْغَدَوٰةِ وَٱلْعَشِىِّ يُرِيدُونَ وَجْهَهُۥ ۖ وَلَا تَعْدُ عَيْنَاكَ عَنْهُمْ تُرِيدُ زِينَةَ ٱلْحَيَوٰةِ ٱلدُّنْيَا ۖ وَلَا تُطِعْ مَنْ أَغْفَلْنَا قَلْبَهُۥ عَن ذِكْرِنَا وَٱتَّبَعَ هَوَىٰهُ وَكَانَ أَمْرُهُۥ فُرُطًا (٢٨)

And keep yourself patient [by being] with those who call upon their Lord in the morning and the evening, seeking His countenance. And let not your eyes pass beyond them, desiring adornments of the worldly life, and do not obey one whose heart We have made heedless of Our remembrance and who follows his desire and whose affair is ever [in] neglect. (28)

Quran 18:110

قُلْ إِنَّمَآ أَنَا۠ بَشَرٌ مِّثْلُكُمْ يُوحَىٰٓ إِلَىَّ أَنَّمَآ إِلَٰهُكُمْ إِلَٰهٌ وَٰحِدٌ ۖ فَمَن كَانَ يَرْجُوا۟ لِقَآءَ رَبِّهِۦ فَلْيَعْمَلْ عَمَلًا صَٰلِحًا وَلَا يُشْرِكْ بِعِبَادَةِ رَبِّهِۦٓ أَحَدًۢا (١١٠)

Say, "I am only a man like you, to whom has been revealed that your god is one God. So whoever would hope for the meeting with his Lord - let him do righteous work and not associate in the worship of his Lord anyone." (110)

Quran 19:83-84

أَلَمْ تَرَ أَنَّآ أَرْسَلْنَا ٱلشَّيَٰطِينَ عَلَى ٱلْكَٰفِرِينَ تَؤُزُّهُمْ أَزًّا (٨٣) فَلَا تَعْجَلْ عَلَيْهِمْ ۖ إِنَّمَا نَعُدُّ لَهُمْ عَدًّا (٨٤)

Do you not see that We have sent the devils upon the disbelievers, inciting them to [evil] with [constant] incitement? (83) So be not impatient over them. We only count out to them a [limited] number. (84)

Quran 20:14-16

إِنَّنِىٓ أَنَا ٱللَّهُ لَآ إِلَٰهَ إِلَّآ أَنَا۠ فَٱعْبُدْنِى وَأَقِمِ ٱلصَّلَوٰةَ لِذِكْرِىٓ (١٤) إِنَّ ٱلسَّاعَةَ ءَاتِيَةٌ أَكَادُ أُخْفِيهَا لِتُجْزَىٰ كُلُّ نَفْسٍۭ بِمَا تَسْعَىٰ (١٥) فَلَا يَصُدَّنَّكَ عَنْهَا مَن لَّا يُؤْمِنُ بِهَا وَٱتَّبَعَ هَوَىٰهُ فَتَرْدَىٰ (١٦)

Indeed, I am Allah. There is no deity except Me, so worship Me and establish prayer for My remembrance. (14) Indeed, the Hour is coming - I almost conceal it - so that every soul may be recompensed according to that for which it strives. (15) So do not let one avert you from it who does not believe in it and follows his desire, for you [then] would perish. (16)

Quran 20:42-46

اذْهَبْ أَنتَ وَأَخُوكَ بِـَٔايَـٰتِى وَلَا تَنِيَا فِى ذِكْرِى (٤٢) اذْهَبَآ إِلَىٰ فِرْعَوْنَ إِنَّهُۥ طَغَىٰ (٤٣) فَقُولَا لَهُۥ قَوْلًا لَّيِّنًا لَّعَلَّهُۥ يَتَذَكَّرُ أَوْ يَخْشَىٰ (٤٤) قَالَا رَبَّنَآ إِنَّنَا نَخَافُ أَن يَفْرُطَ عَلَيْنَآ أَوْ أَن يَطْغَىٰ (٤٥) قَالَ لَا تَخَافَآ إِنَّنِى مَعَكُمَآ أَسْمَعُ وَأَرَىٰ (٤٦)

Go, you and your brother, with My signs and do not slacken in My remembrance. (42) Go, both of you, to Pharaoh. Indeed, he has transgressed. (43) And speak to him with gentle speech that perhaps he may be reminded or fear [Allah]." (44) They said, "Our Lord, indeed we are afraid that he will hasten [punishment] against us or that he will transgress." (45) [Allah] said, "Fear not. Indeed, I am with you both; I hear and I see. (46)

Quran 20:61

قَالَ لَهُم مُّوسَىٰ وَيْلَكُمْ لَا تَفْتَرُواْ عَلَى ٱللَّهِ كَذِبًا فَيُسْحِتَكُم بِعَذَابٍ وَقَدْ خَابَ مَنِ ٱفْتَرَىٰ (٦١)

Moses said to the magicians summoned by Pharaoh, "Woe to you! Do not invent a lie against Allah or He will exterminate you with a punishment; and he has failed who invents [such falsehood]." (61)

Quran 20:68-69

قُلْنَا لَا تَخَفْ إِنَّكَ أَنتَ ٱلْأَعْلَىٰ (٦٨) وَأَلْقِ مَا فِى يَمِينِكَ تَلْقَفْ مَا صَنَعُوٓا۟ۖ إِنَّمَا صَنَعُوا۟ كَيْدُ سَٰحِرٍۖ وَلَا يُفْلِحُ ٱلسَّاحِرُ حَيْثُ أَتَىٰ (٦٩)

Allah said, "Fear not. Indeed, it is you who are superior. (68) And throw what is in your right hand; it will swallow up what they have crafted. What they have crafted is but the trick of a magician, and the magician will not succeed wherever he is." (69)

Quran 20:113-114

وَكَذَٰلِكَ أَنزَلْنَٰهُ قُرْءَانًا عَرَبِيًّا وَصَرَّفْنَا فِيهِ مِنَ ٱلْوَعِيدِ لَعَلَّهُمْ يَتَّقُونَ أَوْ يُحْدِثُ لَهُمْ ذِكْرًا (١١٣) فَتَعَٰلَى ٱللَّهُ ٱلْمَلِكُ ٱلْحَقُّۗ وَلَا تَعْجَلْ بِٱلْقُرْءَانِ مِن قَبْلِ أَن يُقْضَىٰٓ إِلَيْكَ وَحْيُهُۥۖ وَقُل رَّبِّ زِدْنِى عِلْمًا (١١٤)

And thus We have sent it down as an Arabic Qur'an and have diversified therein the warnings that perhaps they will avoid [sin] or it would cause them remembrance. (113) So high [above all] is Allah, the Sovereign, the Truth. And, [O Muhammad], do not hasten with [recitation of] the Qur'an before its revelation is completed to you, and say, "My Lord, increase me in knowledge." (114)

Quran 20:117

فَقُلْنَا يَـٰٓـَادَمُ إِنَّ هَـٰذَا عَدُوٌّ لَّكَ وَلِزَوْجِكَ فَلَا يُخْرِجَنَّكُمَا مِنَ ٱلْجَنَّةِ فَتَشْقَىٰٓ (١١٧)

So We said, "O Adam, indeed this is an enemy to you and to your wife. Then let him not remove you from Paradise so you would suffer. (117)

Quran 20:131-132

وَلَا تَمُدَّنَّ عَيْنَيْكَ إِلَىٰ مَا مَتَّعْنَا بِهِۦٓ أَزْوَٰجًا مِّنْهُمْ زَهْرَةَ ٱلْحَيَوٰةِ ٱلدُّنْيَا لِنَفْتِنَهُمْ فِيهِ وَرِزْقُ رَبِّكَ خَيْرٌ وَأَبْقَىٰ (١٣١) وَأْمُرْ أَهْلَكَ بِٱلصَّلَوٰةِ وَٱصْطَبِرْ عَلَيْهَا لَا نَسْـَٔلُكَ رِزْقًا نَّحْنُ نَرْزُقُكَ وَٱلْعَـٰقِبَةُ لِلتَّقْوَىٰ (١٣٢)

And do not extend your eyes toward that by which We have given enjoyment to [some] categories of them, [its being but] the splendor of worldly life by which We test them. And the provision of your Lord is better and more enduring. (131) And enjoin prayer upon your family [and people] and be steadfast therein. We ask you not for provision; We provide for you, and the [best] outcome is for [those of] righteousness. (132)

Quran 22:26-31

وَإِذْ بَوَّأْنَا لِإِبْرَاهِيمَ مَكَانَ ٱلْبَيْتِ أَن لَّا تُشْرِكْ بِى شَيْـًٔا وَطَهِّرْ بَيْتِىَ لِلطَّآئِفِينَ وَٱلْقَآئِمِينَ وَٱلرُّكَّعِ ٱلسُّجُودِ (٢٦) وَأَذِّن فِى ٱلنَّاسِ بِٱلْحَجِّ يَأْتُوكَ رِجَالًا وَعَلَىٰ كُلِّ ضَامِرٍ يَأْتِينَ مِن كُلِّ فَجٍّ عَمِيقٍ (٢٧) لِّيَشْهَدُوا۟ مَنَٰفِعَ لَهُمْ وَيَذْكُرُوا۟ ٱسْمَ ٱللَّهِ فِىٓ أَيَّامٍ مَّعْلُومَٰتٍ عَلَىٰ مَا رَزَقَهُم مِّنۢ بَهِيمَةِ ٱلْأَنْعَٰمِ ۖ فَكُلُوا۟ مِنْهَا وَأَطْعِمُوا۟ ٱلْبَآئِسَ ٱلْفَقِيرَ (٢٨) ثُمَّ لْيَقْضُوا۟ تَفَثَهُمْ وَلْيُوفُوا۟ نُذُورَهُمْ وَلْيَطَّوَّفُوا۟ بِٱلْبَيْتِ ٱلْعَتِيقِ (٢٩) ذَٰلِكَ وَمَن يُعَظِّمْ حُرُمَٰتِ ٱللَّهِ فَهُوَ خَيْرٌ لَّهُۥ عِندَ رَبِّهِۦ ۗ وَأُحِلَّتْ لَكُمُ ٱلْأَنْعَٰمُ إِلَّا مَا يُتْلَىٰ عَلَيْكُمْ ۖ فَٱجْتَنِبُوا۟ ٱلرِّجْسَ مِنَ ٱلْأَوْثَٰنِ وَٱجْتَنِبُوا۟ قَوْلَ ٱلزُّورِ (٣٠) حُنَفَآءَ لِلَّهِ غَيْرَ مُشْرِكِينَ بِهِۦ ۚ وَمَن يُشْرِكْ بِٱللَّهِ فَكَأَنَّمَا خَرَّ مِنَ ٱلسَّمَآءِ فَتَخْطَفُهُ ٱلطَّيْرُ أَوْ تَهْوِى بِهِ ٱلرِّيحُ فِى مَكَانٍ سَحِيقٍ (٣١)

And [mention, O Muhammad], when We designated for Abraham the site of the House, [saying], "Do not associate anything with Me and purify My House for those who perform Tawaf and those who stand [in prayer] and those who bow and prostrate. (26) And proclaim to the people the Hajj [pilgrimage]; they will come to you on foot and on every lean camel; they will come from every distant pass - (27) That they may witness benefits for themselves and mention the name of Allah on known days over what He has provided for them of [sacrificial] animals. So eat of them and feed the miserable and poor. (28) Then let them end their untidiness and fulfill their vows and perform Tawaf around the ancient House." (29) That [has been commanded], and whoever honors the sacred ordinances of Allah - it is best for him in the sight of his Lord. And permitted to you are the grazing livestock, except what is recited to you. So avoid the uncleanliness of idols and avoid false statement, (30) Inclining [only] to Allah, not associating [anything] with Him. And he who associates with Allah - it is as though he had fallen from the sky and was snatched by the birds or the wind carried him down into a remote place. (31)

Quran 22:67-69

لِكُلِّ أُمَّةٍ جَعَلْنَا مَنسَكًا هُمْ نَاسِكُوهُ ۖ فَلَا يُنَزِعُنَّكَ فِى ٱلْأَمْرِ ۚ وَٱدْعُ إِلَىٰ رَبِّكَ ۖ إِنَّكَ لَعَلَىٰ هُدًى مُّسْتَقِيمٍ (٦٧) وَإِن جَٰدَلُوكَ فَقُلِ ٱللَّهُ أَعْلَمُ بِمَا تَعْمَلُونَ (٦٨) ٱللَّهُ يَحْكُمُ بَيْنَكُمْ يَوْمَ ٱلْقِيَٰمَةِ فِيمَا كُنتُمْ فِيهِ تَخْتَلِفُونَ (٦٩)

For every religion We have appointed rites which they perform. So, [O Muhammad], let the disbelievers not contend with you over the matter but invite them to your Lord. Indeed, you are upon straight guidance. (67) And if they dispute with you, then say, "Allah is most knowing of what you do. (68) Allah will judge between you on the Day of Resurrection concerning that over which you used to differ." (69)

Quran 23:1-7

قَدْ أَفْلَحَ ٱلْمُؤْمِنُونَ (١) ٱلَّذِينَ هُمْ فِى صَلَاتِهِمْ خَٰشِعُونَ (٢) وَٱلَّذِينَ هُمْ عَنِ ٱللَّغْوِ مُعْرِضُونَ (٣) وَٱلَّذِينَ هُمْ لِلزَّكَوٰةِ فَٰعِلُونَ (٤) وَٱلَّذِينَ هُمْ لِفُرُوجِهِمْ

حَفِظُونَ (٥) إِلَّا عَلَىٰ أَزْوَٰجِهِمْ أَوْ مَا مَلَكَتْ أَيْمَـٰنُهُمْ فَإِنَّهُمْ غَيْرُ مَلُومِينَ (٦) فَمَنِ ٱبْتَغَىٰ وَرَآءَ ذَٰلِكَ فَأُو۟لَـٰٓئِكَ هُمُ ٱلْعَادُونَ (٧)

Certainly will the believers have succeeded: (1) They who are during their prayer humbly submissive (2) And they who turn away from ill speech (3) And they who are observant of zakah (4) And they who guard their private parts (5) Except from their wives or those their right hands possess, for indeed, they will not be blamed - (6) But whoever seeks beyond that, then those are the transgressors - (7)

Quran 23:32

فَأَرْسَلْنَا فِيهِمْ رَسُولًا مِّنْهُمْ أَنِ ٱعْبُدُوا۟ ٱللَّهَ مَا لَكُم مِّنْ إِلَـٰهٍ غَيْرُهُ ۖ أَفَلَا تَتَّقُونَ (٣٢)

And We sent among them a messenger from themselves, [saying], "Worship Allah; you have no deity other than Him; then will you not fear Him?" (32)

Quran 24:1-11

سُورَةٌ أَنزَلْنَـٰهَا وَفَرَضْنَـٰهَا وَأَنزَلْنَا فِيهَآ ءَايَـٰتٍۭ بَيِّنَـٰتٍ لَّعَلَّكُمْ تَذَكَّرُونَ (١) ٱلزَّانِيَةُ وَٱلزَّانِى فَٱجْلِدُوا۟ كُلَّ وَٰحِدٍ مِّنْهُمَا مِا۟ئَةَ جَلْدَةٍ ۖ وَلَا تَأْخُذْكُم بِهِمَا رَأْفَةٌ فِى دِينِ ٱللَّهِ إِن كُنتُمْ تُؤْمِنُونَ بِٱللَّهِ وَٱلْيَوْمِ ٱلْـَٔاخِرِ ۖ وَلْيَشْهَدْ عَذَابَهُمَا طَآئِفَةٌ مِّنَ ٱلْمُؤْمِنِينَ (٢) ٱلزَّانِى لَا يَنكِحُ إِلَّا زَانِيَةً أَوْ مُشْرِكَةً وَٱلزَّانِيَةُ لَا يَنكِحُهَآ إِلَّا زَانٍ أَوْ مُشْرِكٌ ۚ وَحُرِّمَ ذَٰلِكَ عَلَى ٱلْمُؤْمِنِينَ (٣) وَٱلَّذِينَ يَرْمُونَ ٱلْمُحْصَنَـٰتِ ثُمَّ لَمْ يَأْتُوا۟ بِأَرْبَعَةِ شُهَدَآءَ فَٱجْلِدُوهُمْ ثَمَـٰنِينَ جَلْدَةً وَلَا تَقْبَلُوا۟ لَهُمْ شَهَـٰدَةً أَبَدًا ۚ

وَأُوْلَٰٓئِكَ هُمُ ٱلْفَٰسِقُونَ (٤) إِلَّا ٱلَّذِينَ تَابُوا۟ مِنۢ بَعْدِ ذَٰلِكَ وَأَصْلَحُوا۟ فَإِنَّ ٱللَّهَ غَفُورٌ رَّحِيمٌ (٥) وَٱلَّذِينَ يَرْمُونَ أَزْوَٰجَهُمْ وَلَمْ يَكُن لَّهُمْ شُهَدَآءُ إِلَّآ أَنفُسُهُمْ فَشَهَٰدَةُ أَحَدِهِمْ أَرْبَعُ شَهَٰدَٰتٍۭ بِٱللَّهِ ۙ إِنَّهُۥ لَمِنَ ٱلصَّٰدِقِينَ (٦) وَٱلْخَٰمِسَةُ أَنَّ لَعْنَتَ ٱللَّهِ عَلَيْهِ إِن كَانَ مِنَ ٱلْكَٰذِبِينَ (٧) وَيَدْرَؤُا۟ عَنْهَا ٱلْعَذَابَ أَن تَشْهَدَ أَرْبَعَ شَهَٰدَٰتٍۭ بِٱللَّهِ ۙ إِنَّهُۥ لَمِنَ ٱلْكَٰذِبِينَ (٨) وَٱلْخَٰمِسَةَ أَنَّ غَضَبَ ٱللَّهِ عَلَيْهَآ إِن كَانَ مِنَ ٱلصَّٰدِقِينَ (٩) وَلَوْلَا فَضْلُ ٱللَّهِ عَلَيْكُمْ وَرَحْمَتُهُۥ وَأَنَّ ٱللَّهَ تَوَّابٌ حَكِيمٌ (١٠) إِنَّ ٱلَّذِينَ جَآءُو بِٱلْإِفْكِ عُصْبَةٌ مِّنكُمْ ۚ لَا تَحْسَبُوهُ شَرًّا لَّكُم ۖ بَلْ هُوَ خَيْرٌ لَّكُمْ ۚ لِكُلِّ ٱمْرِئٍ مِّنْهُم مَّا ٱكْتَسَبَ مِنَ ٱلْإِثْمِ ۚ وَٱلَّذِى تَوَلَّىٰ كِبْرَهُۥ مِنْهُمْ لَهُۥ عَذَابٌ عَظِيمٌ (١١)

[This is] a surah which We have sent down and made [that within it] obligatory and revealed therein verses of clear evidence that you might remember. (1) The [unmarried] woman or [unmarried] man found guilty of sexual intercourse - lash each one of them with a hundred lashes, and do not be taken by pity for them in the religion of Allah, if you should believe in Allah and the Last Day. And let a group of the believers witness their punishment. (2) The fornicator does not marry except a [female] fornicator or polytheist, and none marries her except a fornicator or a polytheist, and that has been made unlawful to the believers. (3) And those who accuse chaste women and then do not produce four witnesses - lash them with eighty lashes and do not accept from them testimony ever after. And those are the defiantly disobedient, (4) Except for those who repent thereafter and reform, for indeed, Allah is Forgiving and Merciful. (5) And those who accuse their wives [of adultery] and have no witnesses except themselves - then the witness of one of them [shall be] four testimonies [swearing] by Allah that indeed, he is of the truthful. (6) And the fifth [oath will be] that the curse of Allah be upon him if he should be among the liars. (7) But it will prevent punishment from her if she gives four testimonies [swearing] by Allah that indeed, he is of the liars. (8) And the fifth [oath will be] that the wrath of Allah be upon her if he was of the truthful. (9) And if not for the favor of Allah upon you and His mercy... and because Allah is Accepting of repentance and Wise. (10) Indeed, those who came with falsehood are a group among you. Do not think it bad for you; rather it is good for you. For every person among them is what [punishment] he has earned from the sin, and he who took upon himself the greater portion thereof - for him is a great punishment. (11)

Quran 24:21-22

يَٰٓأَيُّهَا ٱلَّذِينَ ءَامَنُواْ لَا تَتَّبِعُواْ خُطُوَٰتِ ٱلشَّيْطَٰنِ وَمَن يَتَّبِعْ خُطُوَٰتِ ٱلشَّيْطَٰنِ فَإِنَّهُۥ يَأْمُرُ بِٱلْفَحْشَآءِ وَٱلْمُنكَرِ وَلَوْلَا فَضْلُ ٱللَّهِ عَلَيْكُمْ وَرَحْمَتُهُۥ مَا زَكَىٰ مِنكُم مِّنْ أَحَدٍ أَبَدًا وَلَٰكِنَّ ٱللَّهَ يُزَكِّى مَن يَشَآءُ وَٱللَّهُ سَمِيعٌ عَلِيمٌ (٢١) وَلَا يَأْتَلِ أُوْلُواْ ٱلْفَضْلِ مِنكُمْ وَٱلسَّعَةِ أَن يُؤْتُوٓاْ أُوْلِى ٱلْقُرْبَىٰ وَٱلْمَسَٰكِينَ

وَٱلْمُهَٰجِرِينَ فِى سَبِيلِ ٱللَّهِ وَلْيَعْفُوا۟ وَلْيَصْفَحُوٓا۟ أَلَا تُحِبُّونَ أَن يَغْفِرَ ٱللَّهُ لَكُمْ وَٱللَّهُ غَفُورٌ رَّحِيمٌ (٢٢)

O you who have believed, do not follow the footsteps of Satan. And whoever follows the footsteps of Satan - indeed, he enjoins immorality and wrongdoing. And if not for the favor of Allah upon you and His mercy, not one of you would have been pure, ever, but Allah purifies whom He wills, and Allah is Hearing and Knowing. (21) And let not those of virtue among you and wealth swear not to give [aid] to their relatives and the needy and the emigrants for the cause of Allah, and let them pardon and overlook. Would you not like that Allah should forgive you? And Allah is Forgiving and Merciful. (22)

Quran 24:27-34

يَٰٓأَيُّهَا ٱلَّذِينَ ءَامَنُوا۟ لَا تَدْخُلُوا۟ بُيُوتًا غَيْرَ بُيُوتِكُمْ حَتَّىٰ تَسْتَأْنِسُوا۟ وَتُسَلِّمُوا۟ عَلَىٰٓ أَهْلِهَاۚ ذَٰلِكُمْ خَيْرٌ لَّكُمْ لَعَلَّكُمْ تَذَكَّرُونَ (٢٧) فَإِن لَّمْ تَجِدُوا۟ فِيهَآ أَحَدًا فَلَا تَدْخُلُوهَا حَتَّىٰ يُؤْذَنَ لَكُمْۖ وَإِن قِيلَ لَكُمُ ٱرْجِعُوا۟ فَٱرْجِعُوا۟ۖ هُوَ أَزْكَىٰ لَكُمْۚ وَٱللَّهُ بِمَا تَعْمَلُونَ عَلِيمٌ (٢٨) لَّيْسَ عَلَيْكُمْ جُنَاحٌ أَن تَدْخُلُوا۟ بُيُوتًا غَيْرَ مَسْكُونَةٍ فِيهَا مَتَٰعٌ لَّكُمْۚ وَٱللَّهُ يَعْلَمُ مَا تُبْدُونَ وَمَا تَكْتُمُونَ (٢٩) قُل لِّلْمُؤْمِنِينَ يَغُضُّوا۟ مِنْ أَبْصَٰرِهِمْ وَيَحْفَظُوا۟ فُرُوجَهُمْۚ ذَٰلِكَ أَزْكَىٰ لَهُمْۗ إِنَّ ٱللَّهَ خَبِيرٌۢ بِمَا يَصْنَعُونَ (٣٠) وَقُل لِّلْمُؤْمِنَٰتِ يَغْضُضْنَ مِنْ أَبْصَٰرِهِنَّ وَيَحْفَظْنَ فُرُوجَهُنَّ وَلَا يُبْدِينَ زِينَتَهُنَّ إِلَّا مَا ظَهَرَ مِنْهَاۖ وَلْيَضْرِبْنَ بِخُمُرِهِنَّ عَلَىٰ جُيُوبِهِنَّۖ وَلَا يُبْدِينَ زِينَتَهُنَّ إِلَّا لِبُعُولَتِهِنَّ أَوْ ءَابَآئِهِنَّ أَوْ ءَابَآءِ بُعُولَتِهِنَّ أَوْ أَبْنَآئِهِنَّ أَوْ أَبْنَآءِ بُعُولَتِهِنَّ أَوْ إِخْوَٰنِهِنَّ أَوْ بَنِىٓ إِخْوَٰنِهِنَّ أَوْ بَنِىٓ أَخَوَٰتِهِنَّ أَوْ نِسَآئِهِنَّ أَوْ مَا مَلَكَتْ أَيْمَٰنُهُنَّ أَوِ ٱلتَّٰبِعِينَ غَيْرِ أُو۟لِى ٱلْإِرْبَةِ مِنَ ٱلرِّجَالِ أَوِ ٱلطِّفْلِ ٱلَّذِينَ لَمْ

يَظْهَرُواْ عَلَىٰ عَوْرَٰتِ ٱلنِّسَآءِ ۖ وَلَا يَضْرِبْنَ بِأَرْجُلِهِنَّ لِيُعْلَمَ مَا يُخْفِينَ مِن زِينَتِهِنَّ ۚ وَتُوبُوٓاْ إِلَى ٱللَّهِ جَمِيعًا أَيُّهَ ٱلْمُؤْمِنُونَ لَعَلَّكُمْ تُفْلِحُونَ (٣١) وَأَنكِحُواْ ٱلْأَيَٰمَىٰ مِنكُمْ وَٱلصَّٰلِحِينَ مِنْ عِبَادِكُمْ وَإِمَآئِكُمْ ۚ إِن يَكُونُواْ فُقَرَآءَ يُغْنِهِمُ ٱللَّهُ مِن فَضْلِهِۦ ۗ وَٱللَّهُ وَٰسِعٌ عَلِيمٌ (٣٢) وَلْيَسْتَعْفِفِ ٱلَّذِينَ لَا يَجِدُونَ نِكَاحًا حَتَّىٰ يُغْنِيَهُمُ ٱللَّهُ مِن فَضْلِهِۦ ۗ وَٱلَّذِينَ يَبْتَغُونَ ٱلْكِتَٰبَ مِمَّا مَلَكَتْ أَيْمَٰنُكُمْ فَكَاتِبُوهُمْ إِنْ عَلِمْتُمْ فِيهِمْ خَيْرًا ۖ وَءَاتُوهُم مِّن مَّالِ ٱللَّهِ ٱلَّذِىٓ ءَاتَىٰكُمْ ۚ وَلَا تُكْرِهُواْ فَتَيَٰتِكُمْ عَلَى ٱلْبِغَآءِ إِنْ أَرَدْنَ تَحَصُّنًا لِّتَبْتَغُواْ عَرَضَ ٱلْحَيَوٰةِ ٱلدُّنْيَا ۚ وَمَن يُكْرِههُّنَّ فَإِنَّ ٱللَّهَ مِنۢ بَعْدِ إِكْرَٰهِهِنَّ غَفُورٌ رَّحِيمٌ (٣٣) وَلَقَدْ أَنزَلْنَآ إِلَيْكُمْ ءَايَٰتٍ مُّبَيِّنَٰتٍ وَمَثَلًا مِّنَ ٱلَّذِينَ خَلَوْاْ مِن قَبْلِكُمْ وَمَوْعِظَةً لِّلْمُتَّقِينَ (٣٤)

O you who have believed, do not enter houses other than your own houses until you ascertain welcome and greet their inhabitants. That is best for you; perhaps you will be reminded. (27) And if you do not find anyone therein, do not enter them until permission has been given you. And if it is said to you, "Go back," then go back; it is purer for you. And Allah is Knowing of what you do. (28) There is no blame upon you for entering houses not inhabited in which there is convenience for you. And Allah knows what you reveal and what you conceal. (29) Tell the believing men to reduce [some] of their vision and guard their private parts. That is purer for them. Indeed, Allah is Acquainted with what they do. (30) And tell the believing women to reduce [some] of their vision and guard their private parts and not expose their adornment except that which [necessarily] appears *thereof and to wrap [a portion of] their headcovers over their chests and not expose their adornment except to their husbands, their fathers, their husbands' fathers, their sons, their husbands' sons, their brothers, their brothers' sons, their sisters' sons, their women, that which their right hands possess, or those male attendants having no physical desire, or children who are not yet aware of the private aspects of women. And let them not stamp their feet to make known what they conceal of their adornment. And turn to Allah in repentance, all of you, O believers, that you might succeed. (31) And marry the unmarried among you and the righteous among your male slaves and female slaves. If they should be poor, Allah will enrich them from His bounty, and Allah is all-Encompassing and Knowing. (32) But let them who find not [the means for] marriage abstain [from sexual relations] until Allah enriches them from His bounty. And those who seek a contract [for eventual emancipation] from among whom your right hands possess - then make a contract with them if you know there is within them goodness and give them from the wealth of Allah which He has given you. And do not compel your slave girls to prostitution, if they desire chastity, to seek [thereby] the temporary interests of worldly life. And if someone should compel them, then* indeed, Allah is [to them], after their compulsion, Forgiving and Merciful. (33) And We have certainly sent down to you distinct verses and examples from those who passed on before you and an admonition for those who fear Allah. (34)

Quran 24:53-59

۞ وَأَقْسَمُوا۟ بِٱللَّهِ جَهْدَ أَيْمَٰنِهِمْ لَئِنْ أَمَرْتَهُمْ لَيَخْرُجُنَّ ۖ قُل لَّا تُقْسِمُوا۟ ۖ طَاعَةٌ مَّعْرُوفَةٌ ۚ إِنَّ ٱللَّهَ خَبِيرٌۢ بِمَا تَعْمَلُونَ (٥٣) قُلْ أَطِيعُوا۟ ٱللَّهَ وَأَطِيعُوا۟ ٱلرَّسُولَ ۖ فَإِن تَوَلَّوْا۟ فَإِنَّمَا عَلَيْهِ مَا حُمِّلَ وَعَلَيْكُم مَّا حُمِّلْتُمْ ۖ وَإِن تُطِيعُوهُ تَهْتَدُوا۟ ۚ وَمَا عَلَى ٱلرَّسُولِ إِلَّا ٱلْبَلَٰغُ ٱلْمُبِينُ (٥٤) وَعَدَ ٱللَّهُ ٱلَّذِينَ ءَامَنُوا۟ مِنكُمْ وَعَمِلُوا۟ ٱلصَّٰلِحَٰتِ لَيَسْتَخْلِفَنَّهُمْ فِى ٱلْأَرْضِ كَمَا ٱسْتَخْلَفَ ٱلَّذِينَ مِن قَبْلِهِمْ وَلَيُمَكِّنَنَّ لَهُمْ دِينَهُمُ ٱلَّذِى ٱرْتَضَىٰ لَهُمْ وَلَيُبَدِّلَنَّهُم مِّنۢ بَعْدِ خَوْفِهِمْ أَمْنًا ۚ يَعْبُدُونَنِى لَا يُشْرِكُونَ بِى شَيْـًٔا ۚ وَمَن كَفَرَ بَعْدَ ذَٰلِكَ فَأُو۟لَٰٓئِكَ هُمُ ٱلْفَٰسِقُونَ (٥٥) وَأَقِيمُوا۟ ٱلصَّلَوٰةَ وَءَاتُوا۟ ٱلزَّكَوٰةَ وَأَطِيعُوا۟ ٱلرَّسُولَ لَعَلَّكُمْ تُرْحَمُونَ (٥٦) لَا تَحْسَبَنَّ ٱلَّذِينَ كَفَرُوا۟ مُعْجِزِينَ فِى ٱلْأَرْضِ ۚ وَمَأْوَىٰهُمُ ٱلنَّارُ ۖ وَلَبِئْسَ ٱلْمَصِيرُ (٥٧) يَٰٓأَيُّهَا ٱلَّذِينَ ءَامَنُوا۟ لِيَسْتَـْٔذِنكُمُ ٱلَّذِينَ مَلَكَتْ أَيْمَٰنُكُمْ وَٱلَّذِينَ لَمْ يَبْلُغُوا۟ ٱلْحُلُمَ مِنكُمْ ثَلَٰثَ مَرَّٰتٍ ۚ مِّن قَبْلِ صَلَوٰةِ ٱلْفَجْرِ وَحِينَ تَضَعُونَ ثِيَابَكُم مِّنَ ٱلظَّهِيرَةِ وَمِنۢ بَعْدِ صَلَوٰةِ ٱلْعِشَآءِ ۚ ثَلَٰثُ عَوْرَٰتٍ لَّكُمْ ۚ لَيْسَ عَلَيْكُمْ وَلَا عَلَيْهِمْ جُنَاحٌۢ بَعْدَهُنَّ ۚ طَوَّٰفُونَ عَلَيْكُم بَعْضُكُمْ عَلَىٰ بَعْضٍ ۚ كَذَٰلِكَ يُبَيِّنُ ٱللَّهُ لَكُمُ ٱلْـَٔايَٰتِ ۗ وَٱللَّهُ عَلِيمٌ حَكِيمٌ (٥٨) وَإِذَا بَلَغَ ٱلْأَطْفَٰلُ مِنكُمُ ٱلْحُلُمَ فَلْيَسْتَـْٔذِنُوا۟ كَمَا ٱسْتَـْٔذَنَ ٱلَّذِينَ مِن قَبْلِهِمْ ۚ كَذَٰلِكَ يُبَيِّنُ ٱللَّهُ لَكُمْ ءَايَٰتِهِ ۗ وَٱللَّهُ عَلِيمٌ حَكِيمٌ (٥٩)

And they swear by Allah their strongest oaths that if you ordered them, they would go forth [in Allah's cause]. Say, "Do not swear. [Such] obedience is known. Indeed, Allah is Acquainted with that which you do." (53) Say,

"Obey Allah and obey the Messenger; but if you turn away - then upon him is only that [duty] with which he has been charged, and upon you is that with which you have been charged. And if you obey him, you will be [rightly] guided. And there is not upon the Messenger except the [responsibility for] clear notification." (54) Allah has promised those who have believed among you and done righteous deeds that He will surely grant them succession [to authority] upon the earth just as He granted it to those before them and that He will surely establish for them [therein] their religion which He has preferred for them and that He will surely substitute for them, after their fear, security, [for] they worship Me, not associating anything with Me. But whoever disbelieves after that - then those are the defiantly disobedient. (55) And establish prayer and give zakah and obey the Messenger - that you may receive mercy. (56) Never think that the disbelievers are causing failure [to Allah] upon the earth. Their refuge will be the Fire - and how wretched the destination. (57) O you who have believed, let those whom your right hands possess and those who have not [yet] reached puberty among you ask permission of you [before entering] at three times: before the dawn prayer and when you put aside your clothing [for rest] at noon and after the night prayer. [These are] three times of

privacy for you. There is no blame upon you nor upon them beyond these [periods], for they continually circulate among you - some of you, among others. Thus does Allah make clear to you the verses; and Allah is Knowing and Wise. (58) And when the children among you reach puberty, let them ask permission [at all times] as those before them have done. Thus does Allah make clear to you His verses; and Allah is Knowing and Wise. (59)

Quran 24:62-63

إِنَّمَا ٱلْمُؤْمِنُونَ ٱلَّذِينَ ءَامَنُوا۟ بِٱللَّهِ وَرَسُولِهِۦ وَإِذَا كَانُوا۟ مَعَهُۥ عَلَىٰٓ أَمْرٍ جَامِعٍ لَّمْ يَذْهَبُوا۟ حَتَّىٰ يَسْتَـْٔذِنُوهُ إِنَّ ٱلَّذِينَ يَسْتَـْٔذِنُونَكَ أُو۟لَـٰٓئِكَ ٱلَّذِينَ يُؤْمِنُونَ بِٱللَّهِ وَرَسُولِهِۦ فَإِذَا ٱسْتَـْٔذَنُوكَ لِبَعْضِ شَأْنِهِمْ فَأْذَن لِّمَن شِئْتَ مِنْهُمْ وَٱسْتَغْفِرْ لَهُمُ ٱللَّهَ إِنَّ ٱللَّهَ غَفُورٌ رَّحِيمٌ (٦٢) لَّا تَجْعَلُوا۟ دُعَآءَ ٱلرَّسُولِ بَيْنَكُمْ كَدُعَآءِ بَعْضِكُم بَعْضًا قَدْ يَعْلَمُ ٱللَّهُ ٱلَّذِينَ يَتَسَلَّلُونَ مِنكُمْ لِوَاذًا فَلْيَحْذَرِ ٱلَّذِينَ يُخَالِفُونَ عَنْ أَمْرِهِۦٓ أَن تُصِيبَهُمْ فِتْنَةٌ أَوْ يُصِيبَهُمْ عَذَابٌ أَلِيمٌ (٦٣)

The believers are only those who believe in Allah and His Messenger and, when they are [meeting] with him for a matter of common interest, do not depart until they have asked his permission. Indeed, those who ask your permission, [O Muhammad] - those are the ones who believe in Allah and His Messenger. So when they ask your permission for something of their affairs, then give permission to whom you will among them and ask forgiveness for them of Allah. Indeed, Allah is Forgiving and Merciful. (62) Do not make [your] calling of the Messenger among yourselves as the call of one of you to another. Already Allah knows those of you who slip away, concealed by others. So let those beware who dissent from the Prophet's order, lest fitnah strike them or a painful punishment. (63)

Quran 25:52

فَلَا تُطِعِ ٱلْكَٰفِرِينَ وَجَٰهِدْهُم بِهِۦ جِهَادًا كَبِيرًا (٥٢)

So do not obey the disbelievers, and strive against them with the Qur'an a great striving. (52)

Quran 25:63-73

وَعِبَادُ ٱلرَّحْمَٰنِ ٱلَّذِينَ يَمْشُونَ عَلَى ٱلْأَرْضِ هَوْنًا وَإِذَا خَاطَبَهُمُ ٱلْجَٰهِلُونَ قَالُوا۟ سَلَٰمًا (٦٣) وَٱلَّذِينَ يَبِيتُونَ لِرَبِّهِمْ سُجَّدًا وَقِيَٰمًا (٦٤) وَٱلَّذِينَ يَقُولُونَ رَبَّنَا ٱصْرِفْ عَنَّا عَذَابَ جَهَنَّمَ إِنَّ عَذَابَهَا كَانَ غَرَامًا (٦٥) إِنَّهَا سَآءَتْ مُسْتَقَرًّا وَمُقَامًا (٦٦) وَٱلَّذِينَ إِذَآ أَنفَقُوا۟ لَمْ يُسْرِفُوا۟ وَلَمْ يَقْتُرُوا۟ وَكَانَ بَيْنَ ذَٰلِكَ قَوَامًا (٦٧) وَٱلَّذِينَ لَا يَدْعُونَ مَعَ ٱللَّهِ إِلَٰهًا ءَاخَرَ وَلَا يَقْتُلُونَ ٱلنَّفْسَ ٱلَّتِى حَرَّمَ ٱللَّهُ إِلَّا بِٱلْحَقِّ وَلَا يَزْنُونَ وَمَن يَفْعَلْ ذَٰلِكَ يَلْقَ أَثَامًا (٦٨) يُضَٰعَفْ لَهُ ٱلْعَذَابُ يَوْمَ ٱلْقِيَٰمَةِ وَيَخْلُدْ فِيهِۦ مُهَانًا (٦٩) إِلَّا مَن تَابَ وَءَامَنَ وَعَمِلَ عَمَلًا صَٰلِحًا فَأُو۟لَٰٓئِكَ يُبَدِّلُ ٱللَّهُ سَيِّـَٔاتِهِمْ حَسَنَٰتٍ وَكَانَ ٱللَّهُ غَفُورًا رَّحِيمًا (٧٠) وَمَن تَابَ وَعَمِلَ صَٰلِحًا فَإِنَّهُۥ يَتُوبُ إِلَى ٱللَّهِ مَتَابًا (٧١) وَٱلَّذِينَ لَا يَشْهَدُونَ ٱلزُّورَ وَإِذَا مَرُّوا۟ بِٱللَّغْوِ مَرُّوا۟ كِرَامًا (٧٢) وَٱلَّذِينَ إِذَا ذُكِّرُوا۟ بِـَٔايَٰتِ رَبِّهِمْ لَمْ يَخِرُّوا۟ عَلَيْهَا صُمًّا وَعُمْيَانًا (٧٣)

And the servants of the Most Merciful are those who walk upon the earth easily, and when the ignorant address them [harshly], they say [words of] peace, (63) And those who spend [part of] the night to their Lord prostrating and standing [in prayer] (64) And those who say, "Our Lord, avert from us the punishment of Hell. Indeed, its punishment is ever adhering; (65) Indeed, it is evil as a settlement and residence." (66) And [they are] those who, when they spend, do so not excessively or sparingly but are ever, between that, [justly] moderate (67) And those who do not invoke with Allah another deity or kill the soul which Allah has forbidden [to be killed], except by right, and do not commit unlawful sexual intercourse. And whoever should do that will meet a penalty. (68) Multiplied for him is the punishment on the Day of Resurrection, and he will abide therein humiliated - (69) Except for those who repent, believe and do righteous work. For them Allah will replace their evil deeds with good. And ever is Allah Forgiving and Merciful. (70) And he who repents and does righteousness does indeed turn to Allah with [accepted] repentance. (71) And [they are] those who do not testify to falsehood, and when they pass near ill speech, they pass by with dignity. (72) And those who, when reminded of the verses of their Lord, do not fall upon them deaf and blind. (73)

Quran 26:109

وَمَآ أَسْـَٔلُكُمْ عَلَيْهِ مِنْ أَجْرٍ ۖ إِنْ أَجْرِىَ إِلَّا عَلَىٰ رَبِّ ٱلْعَٰلَمِينَ (١٠٩)

(Noah said) And I do not ask you for it any payment. My payment is only from the Lord of the worlds. (109)

Quran 26:114

وَمَآ أَنَا۠ بِطَارِدِ ٱلْمُؤْمِنِينَ (١١٤)

And I am not one to drive away the believers. (114)

Quran 26:127

وَمَآ أَسْـَٔلُكُمْ عَلَيْهِ مِنْ أَجْرٍ ۖ إِنْ أَجْرِىَ إِلَّا عَلَىٰ رَبِّ ٱلْعَٰلَمِينَ (١٢٧)

(Hud said) And I do not ask you for it any payment. My payment is only from the Lord of the worlds. (127)

Quran 26:145

وَمَآ أَسْـَٔلُكُمْ عَلَيْهِ مِنْ أَجْرٍ ۖ إِنْ أَجْرِىَ إِلَّا عَلَىٰ رَبِّ ٱلْعَٰلَمِينَ (١٤٥)

(Salih said) And I do not ask you for it any payment. My payment is only from the Lord of the worlds. (145)

Quran 26:151-152

وَلَا تُطِيعُوٓا۟ أَمْرَ ٱلْمُسْرِفِينَ (١٥١) ٱلَّذِينَ يُفْسِدُونَ فِى ٱلْأَرْضِ وَلَا يُصْلِحُونَ (١٥٢)

And do not obey the order of the transgressors, (151) Who cause corruption in the land and do not amend." (152)

Quran 26:164

وَمَا أَسْـَٔلُكُمْ عَلَيْهِ مِنْ أَجْرٍۖ إِنْ أَجْرِىَ إِلَّا عَلَىٰ رَبِّ ٱلْعَٰلَمِينَ (١٦٤)

(Lot said) And I do not ask you for it any payment. My payment is only from the Lord of the worlds. (164)

Quran 26:179-184

فَٱتَّقُوا۟ ٱللَّهَ وَأَطِيعُونِ (١٧٩) وَمَآ أَسْـَٔلُكُمْ عَلَيْهِ مِنْ أَجْرٍۖ إِنْ أَجْرِىَ إِلَّا عَلَىٰ رَبِّ ٱلْعَٰلَمِينَ (١٨٠) ۞ أَوْفُوا۟ ٱلْكَيْلَ وَلَا تَكُونُوا۟ مِنَ ٱلْمُخْسِرِينَ (١٨١) وَزِنُوا۟ بِٱلْقِسْطَاسِ ٱلْمُسْتَقِيمِ (١٨٢) وَلَا تَبْخَسُوا۟ ٱلنَّاسَ أَشْيَآءَهُمْ وَلَا تَعْثَوْا۟ فِى ٱلْأَرْضِ مُفْسِدِينَ (١٨٣) وَٱتَّقُوا۟ ٱلَّذِى خَلَقَكُمْ وَٱلْجِبِلَّةَ ٱلْأَوَّلِينَ (١٨٤)

(Shuayb said) So fear Allah and obey me. (179) And I do not ask you for it any payment. My payment is only from the Lord of the worlds. (180) Give full measure and do not be of those who cause loss. (181) And weigh with an even balance. (182) And do not deprive people of their due and do not commit abuse on earth, spreading corruption. (183) And fear He who created you and the former creation." (184)

Quran 26:213

فَلَا تَدْعُ مَعَ ٱللَّهِ إِلَٰهًا ءَاخَرَ فَتَكُونَ مِنَ ٱلْمُعَذَّبِينَ (٢١٣)

So do not invoke with Allah another deity and [thus] be among the punished. (213)

Quran 27:70

وَلَا تَحْزَنْ عَلَيْهِمْ وَلَا تَكُن فِى ضَيْقٍ مِّمَّا يَمْكُرُونَ (٧٠)

And grieve not over them or be in distress from what they conspire. (70)

Quran 28:17

قَالَ رَبِّ بِمَآ أَنْعَمْتَ عَلَىَّ فَلَنْ أَكُونَ ظَهِيرًا لِّلْمُجْرِمِينَ (١٧)

He said, "My Lord, for the favor You bestowed upon me, I will never be an assistant to the criminals." (17)

Quran 28:76-77

إِنَّ قَٰرُونَ كَانَ مِن قَوْمِ مُوسَىٰ فَبَغَىٰ عَلَيْهِمْ ۖ وَءَاتَيْنَٰهُ مِنَ ٱلْكُنُوزِ مَآ إِنَّ مَفَاتِحَهُۥ لَتَنُوٓأُ بِٱلْعُصْبَةِ أُو۟لِى ٱلْقُوَّةِ إِذْ قَالَ لَهُۥ قَوْمُهُۥ لَا تَفْرَحْ ۖ إِنَّ ٱللَّهَ لَا يُحِبُّ ٱلْفَرِحِينَ (٧٦) وَٱبْتَغِ فِيمَآ ءَاتَىٰكَ ٱللَّهُ ٱلدَّارَ ٱلْءَاخِرَةَ ۖ وَلَا تَنسَ نَصِيبَكَ مِنَ ٱلدُّنْيَا ۖ وَأَحْسِن كَمَآ أَحْسَنَ ٱللَّهُ إِلَيْكَ ۖ وَلَا تَبْغِ ٱلْفَسَادَ فِى ٱلْأَرْضِ ۖ إِنَّ ٱللَّهَ لَا يُحِبُّ ٱلْمُفْسِدِينَ (٧٧)

Indeed, Qarun was from the people of Moses, but he tyrannized them. And We gave him of treasures whose keys would burden a band of strong men; thereupon his people said to him, "Do not exult. Indeed, Allah does not like the exultant. (76) But seek, through that which Allah has given you, the home of the Hereafter; and [yet], do not forget your share of the world. And do good as Allah has done good to you. And desire not corruption in the land. Indeed, Allah does not like corrupters." (77)

Quran 28:83

تِلْكَ ٱلدَّارُ ٱلْأَخِرَةُ نَجْعَلُهَا لِلَّذِينَ لَا يُرِيدُونَ عُلُوًّا فِى ٱلْأَرْضِ وَلَا فَسَادًا ۚ وَٱلْعَـٰقِبَةُ لِلْمُتَّقِينَ (٨٣)

That home of the Hereafter We assign to those who do not desire exaltedness upon the earth or corruption. And the [best] outcome is for the righteous. (83)

Quran 28:86-88

وَمَا كُنتَ تَرْجُوٓا۟ أَن يُلْقَىٰٓ إِلَيْكَ ٱلْكِتَـٰبُ إِلَّا رَحْمَةً مِّن رَّبِّكَ ۖ فَلَا تَكُونَنَّ ظَهِيرًا لِّلْكَـٰفِرِينَ (٨٦) وَلَا يَصُدُّنَّكَ عَنْ ءَايَـٰتِ ٱللَّهِ بَعْدَ إِذْ أُنزِلَتْ إِلَيْكَ ۖ وَٱدْعُ إِلَىٰ رَبِّكَ ۖ وَلَا تَكُونَنَّ مِنَ ٱلْمُشْرِكِينَ (٨٧) وَلَا تَدْعُ مَعَ ٱللَّهِ إِلَـٰهًا ءَاخَرَ ۘ لَآ إِلَـٰهَ إِلَّا هُوَ ۚ كُلُّ شَىْءٍ هَالِكٌ إِلَّا وَجْهَهُۥ ۚ لَهُ ٱلْحُكْمُ وَإِلَيْهِ تُرْجَعُونَ (٨٨)

And you were not expecting that the Book would be conveyed to you, but [it is] a mercy from your Lord. So do not be an assistant to the disbelievers. (86) And never let them avert you from the verses of Allah after they have been revealed to you. And invite [people] to your Lord. And never be of those who associate others with Allah. (87) And do not invoke with Allah another deity. There is no deity except Him. Everything will be destroyed except His Face. His is the judgement, and to Him you will be returned. (88)

Quran 29:8

وَوَصَّيْنَا ٱلْإِنسَـٰنَ بِوَٰلِدَيْهِ حُسْنًا ۖ وَإِن جَـٰهَدَاكَ لِتُشْرِكَ بِى مَا لَيْسَ لَكَ بِهِۦ عِلْمٌ فَلَا تُطِعْهُمَآ ۚ إِلَىَّ مَرْجِعُكُمْ فَأُنَبِّئُكُم بِمَا كُنتُمْ تَعْمَلُونَ (٨)

And We have enjoined upon man goodness to parents. But if they endeavor to make you associate with Me that of which you have no knowledge, do not obey them. To Me is your return, and I will inform you about what you used to do. (8)

Quran 29:33-34

وَلَمَّآ أَن جَآءَتْ رُسُلُنَا لُوطًا سِىٓءَ بِهِمْ وَضَاقَ بِهِمْ ذَرْعًا وَقَالُوا۟ لَا تَخَفْ وَلَا تَحْزَنْ ۖ إِنَّا مُنَجُّوكَ وَأَهْلَكَ إِلَّا ٱمْرَأَتَكَ كَانَتْ مِنَ ٱلْغَـٰبِرِينَ (٣٣) إِنَّا مُنزِلُونَ عَلَىٰٓ أَهْلِ هَـٰذِهِ ٱلْقَرْيَةِ رِجْزًا مِّنَ ٱلسَّمَآءِ بِمَا كَانُوا۟ يَفْسُقُونَ (٣٤)

And when Our messengers came to Lot, he was distressed for them and felt for them great discomfort. They said, "Fear not, nor grieve. Indeed, we will save you and your family, except your wife; she is to be of those who remain behind. (33) Indeed, we will bring down on the people of this city punishment from the sky because they have been defiantly disobedient." (34)

Quran 29:36

وَإِلَىٰ مَدْيَنَ أَخَاهُمْ شُعَيْبًا فَقَالَ يَـٰقَوْمِ ٱعْبُدُوا۟ ٱللَّهَ وَٱرْجُوا۟ ٱلْيَوْمَ ٱلْـَٔاخِرَ وَلَا تَعْثَوْا۟ فِى ٱلْأَرْضِ مُفْسِدِينَ (٣٦)

And to Madyan [We sent] their brother Shu'ayb, and he said, "O my people, worship Allah and expect the Last Day and do not commit abuse on the earth, spreading corruption." (36)

Quran 29:45-46

ٱتْلُ مَآ أُوحِىَ إِلَيْكَ مِنَ ٱلْكِتَـٰبِ وَأَقِمِ ٱلصَّلَوٰةَ إِنَّ ٱلصَّلَوٰةَ تَنْهَىٰ عَنِ ٱلْفَحْشَآءِ وَٱلْمُنكَرِ وَلَذِكْرُ ٱللَّهِ أَكْبَرُ وَٱللَّهُ يَعْلَمُ مَا تَصْنَعُونَ (٤٥) وَلَا تُجَـٰدِلُوٓا۟ أَهْلَ ٱلْكِتَـٰبِ إِلَّا بِٱلَّتِى هِىَ أَحْسَنُ إِلَّا ٱلَّذِينَ ظَلَمُوا۟ مِنْهُمْ وَقُولُوٓا۟ ءَامَنَّا بِٱلَّذِىٓ أُنزِلَ إِلَيْنَا وَأُنزِلَ إِلَيْكُمْ وَإِلَـٰهُنَا وَإِلَـٰهُكُمْ وَٰحِدٌ وَنَحْنُ لَهُۥ مُسْلِمُونَ (٤٦)

Recite, [O Muhammad], what has been revealed to you of the Book and establish prayer. Indeed, prayer prohibits immorality and wrongdoing, and the remembrance of Allah is greater. And Allah knows that which you do. (45) And do not argue with the People of the Scripture except in a way that is best, except for those who commit injustice among them, and say, "We believe in that which has been revealed to us and revealed to you. And our God and your God is one; and we are Muslims [in submission] to Him." (46)

Quran 30:30-32

فَأَقِمْ وَجْهَكَ لِلدِّينِ حَنِيفًا ۚ فِطْرَتَ اللَّهِ الَّتِي فَطَرَ النَّاسَ عَلَيْهَا ۚ لَا تَبْدِيلَ لِخَلْقِ اللَّهِ ۚ ذَٰلِكَ الدِّينُ الْقَيِّمُ وَلَٰكِنَّ أَكْثَرَ النَّاسِ لَا يَعْلَمُونَ (٣٠) مُنِيبِينَ إِلَيْهِ وَاتَّقُوهُ وَأَقِيمُوا الصَّلَاةَ وَلَا تَكُونُوا مِنَ الْمُشْرِكِينَ (٣١) مِنَ الَّذِينَ فَرَّقُوا دِينَهُمْ وَكَانُوا شِيَعًا ۖ كُلُّ حِزْبٍ بِمَا لَدَيْهِمْ فَرِحُونَ (٣٢)

So direct your face toward the religion, inclining to truth. [Adhere to] the fitrah of Allah upon which He has created [all] people. No change should there be in the creation of Allah. That is the correct religion, but most of the people do not know. (30) [Adhere to it], turning in repentance to Him, and fear Him and establish prayer and do not be of those who associate others with Allah (31) [Or] of those who have divided their religion and become sects, every faction rejoicing in what it has. (32)

Quran 30:60

فَاصْبِرْ إِنَّ وَعْدَ اللَّهِ حَقٌّ ۖ وَلَا يَسْتَخِفَّنَّكَ الَّذِينَ لَا يُوقِنُونَ (٦٠)

So be patient. Indeed, the promise of Allah is truth. And let them not disquiet you who are not certain [in faith]. (60)

Quran 31:13

وَإِذْ قَالَ لُقْمَانُ لِابْنِهِ وَهُوَ يَعِظُهُ يَا بُنَيَّ لَا تُشْرِكْ بِاللَّهِ ۖ إِنَّ الشِّرْكَ لَظُلْمٌ عَظِيمٌ (١٣)

And [mention, O Muhammad], when Luqman said to his son while he was instructing him, "O my son, do not associate [anything] with Allah. Indeed, association [with him] is great injustice." (13)

Quran 31:15

وَإِن جَٰهَدَاكَ عَلَىٰٓ أَن تُشْرِكَ بِى مَا لَيْسَ لَكَ بِهِۦ عِلْمٌ فَلَا تُطِعْهُمَا ۖ وَصَاحِبْهُمَا فِى ٱلدُّنْيَا مَعْرُوفًا ۖ وَٱتَّبِعْ سَبِيلَ مَنْ أَنَابَ إِلَىَّ ۚ ثُمَّ إِلَىَّ مَرْجِعُكُمْ فَأُنَبِّئُكُم بِمَا كُنتُمْ تَعْمَلُونَ (١٥)

But if they endeavor to make you associate with Me that of which you have no knowledge, do not obey them but accompany them in [this] world with appropriate kindness and follow the way of those who turn back to Me [in repentance]. Then to Me will be your return, and I will inform you about what you used to do. (15)

Quran 31:17-19

يَٰبُنَىَّ أَقِمِ ٱلصَّلَوٰةَ وَأْمُرْ بِٱلْمَعْرُوفِ وَٱنْهَ عَنِ ٱلْمُنكَرِ وَٱصْبِرْ عَلَىٰ مَآ أَصَابَكَ ۖ إِنَّ ذَٰلِكَ مِنْ عَزْمِ ٱلْأُمُورِ (١٧) وَلَا تُصَعِّرْ خَدَّكَ لِلنَّاسِ وَلَا تَمْشِ فِى ٱلْأَرْضِ مَرَحًا ۖ إِنَّ ٱللَّهَ لَا يُحِبُّ كُلَّ مُخْتَالٍ فَخُورٍ (١٨) وَٱقْصِدْ فِى مَشْيِكَ وَٱغْضُضْ مِن صَوْتِكَ ۚ إِنَّ أَنكَرَ ٱلْأَصْوَٰتِ لَصَوْتُ ٱلْحَمِيرِ (١٩)

(Luqman said) O my son, establish prayer, enjoin what is right, forbid what is wrong, and be patient over what befalls you. Indeed, [all] that is of the matters [requiring] determination. (17) And do not turn your cheek [in contempt] toward people and do not walk through the earth exultantly. Indeed, Allah does not like everyone self-deluded and boastful. (18) And be moderate in your pace and lower your voice; indeed, the most disagreeable of sounds is the voice of donkeys." (19)

Quran 31:23

وَمَن كَفَرَ فَلَا يَحْزُنكَ كُفْرُهُ ۚ إِلَيْنَا مَرْجِعُهُمْ فَنُنَبِّئُهُم بِمَا عَمِلُوٓا۟ ۚ إِنَّ ٱللَّهَ عَلِيمٌۢ بِذَاتِ ٱلصُّدُورِ (٢٣)

And whoever has disbelieved - let not his disbelief grieve you. To Us is their return, and We will inform them of what they did. Indeed, Allah is Knowing of that within the breasts. (23)

Quran 31:33

يَٰٓأَيُّهَا ٱلنَّاسُ ٱتَّقُوا۟ رَبَّكُمْ وَٱخْشَوْا۟ يَوْمًا لَّا يَجْزِى وَالِدٌ عَن وَلَدِهِۦ وَلَا مَوْلُودٌ هُوَ جَازٍ عَن وَالِدِهِۦ شَيْـًٔا ۚ إِنَّ وَعْدَ ٱللَّهِ حَقٌّ ۖ فَلَا تَغُرَّنَّكُمُ ٱلْحَيَوٰةُ ٱلدُّنْيَا وَلَا يَغُرَّنَّكُم بِٱللَّهِ ٱلْغَرُورُ (٣٣)

O mankind, fear your Lord and fear a Day when no father will avail his son, nor will a son avail his father at all. Indeed, the promise of Allah is truth, so let not the worldly life delude you and be not deceived about Allah by the Deceiver. (33)

Quran 32:1-5

يَٰٓأَيُّهَا ٱلنَّبِىُّ ٱتَّقِ ٱللَّهَ وَلَا تُطِعِ ٱلْكَٰفِرِينَ وَٱلْمُنَٰفِقِينَ ۗ إِنَّ ٱللَّهَ كَانَ عَلِيمًا حَكِيمًا (١) وَٱتَّبِعْ مَا يُوحَىٰٓ إِلَيْكَ مِن رَّبِّكَ ۚ إِنَّ ٱللَّهَ كَانَ بِمَا تَعْمَلُونَ خَبِيرًا

(٢) وَتَوَكَّلْ عَلَى ٱللَّهِ وَكَفَىٰ بِٱللَّهِ وَكِيلًا (٣) مَّا جَعَلَ ٱللَّهُ لِرَجُلٍ مِّن قَلْبَيْنِ فِى جَوْفِهِ ۚ وَمَا جَعَلَ أَزْوَٰجَكُمُ ٱلَّـٰٓـِٔى تُظَـٰهِرُونَ مِنْهُنَّ أُمَّهَـٰتِكُمْ ۚ وَمَا جَعَلَ أَدْعِيَآءَكُمْ أَبْنَآءَكُمْ ۚ ذَٰلِكُمْ قَوْلُكُم بِأَفْوَٰهِكُمْ ۖ وَٱللَّهُ يَقُولُ ٱلْحَقَّ وَهُوَ يَهْدِى ٱلسَّبِيلَ (٤) ٱدْعُوهُمْ لِـَٔابَآئِهِمْ هُوَ أَقْسَطُ عِندَ ٱللَّهِ ۚ فَإِن لَّمْ تَعْلَمُوٓا۟ ءَابَآءَهُمْ فَإِخْوَٰنُكُمْ فِى ٱلدِّينِ وَمَوَٰلِيكُمْ ۚ وَلَيْسَ عَلَيْكُمْ جُنَاحٌ فِيمَآ أَخْطَأْتُم بِهِۦ وَلَـٰكِن مَّا تَعَمَّدَتْ قُلُوبُكُمْ ۚ وَكَانَ ٱللَّهُ غَفُورًا رَّحِيمًا (٥)

O Prophet, fear Allah and do not obey the disbelievers and the hypocrites. Indeed, Allah is ever Knowing and Wise. (1) And follow that which is revealed to you from your Lord. Indeed Allah is ever, with what you do, Acquainted. (2) And rely upon Allah; and sufficient is Allah as Disposer of affairs. (3) Allah has not made for a man two hearts in his interior. And He has not made your wives whom you declare unlawful your mothers. And he has not made your adopted sons your [true] sons. That is [merely] your saying by your mouths, but Allah says the truth, and He guides to the [right] way. (4) Call them by [the names of] their fathers; it is more just in the sight of Allah. But if you do not know their fathers - then they are [still] your brothers in religion and those entrusted to you. And there is no blame upon you for that in which you have erred but [only for] what your hearts intended. And ever is Allah Forgiving and Merciful. (5)

Quran 33:15-16

وَلَقَدْ كَانُوا۟ عَٰهَدُوا۟ ٱللَّهَ مِن قَبْلُ لَا يُوَلُّونَ ٱلْأَدْبَٰرَ ۚ وَكَانَ عَهْدُ ٱللَّهِ مَسْـُٔولًا (١٥) قُل لَّن يَنفَعَكُمُ ٱلْفِرَارُ إِن فَرَرْتُم مِّنَ ٱلْمَوْتِ أَوِ ٱلْقَتْلِ وَإِذًا لَّا تُمَتَّعُونَ إِلَّا قَلِيلًا (١٦)

And they had already promised Allah before not to turn their backs and flee. And ever is the promise to Allah [that about which one will be] questioned. (15) Say, [O Muhammad], "Never will fleeing benefit you if you should flee from death or killing; and then [if you did], you would not be given enjoyment [of life] except for a little." (16)

Quran 33:32-33

يَٰنِسَآءَ ٱلنَّبِىِّ لَسْتُنَّ كَأَحَدٍ مِّنَ ٱلنِّسَآءِ ۚ إِنِ ٱتَّقَيْتُنَّ فَلَا تَخْضَعْنَ بِٱلْقَوْلِ فَيَطْمَعَ ٱلَّذِى فِى قَلْبِهِۦ مَرَضٌ وَقُلْنَ قَوْلًا مَّعْرُوفًا (٣٢) وَقَرْنَ فِى بُيُوتِكُنَّ وَلَا تَبَرَّجْنَ تَبَرُّجَ ٱلْجَٰهِلِيَّةِ ٱلْأُولَىٰ ۖ وَأَقِمْنَ ٱلصَّلَوٰةَ وَءَاتِينَ ٱلزَّكَوٰةَ وَأَطِعْنَ ٱللَّهَ وَرَسُولَهُۥٓ ۚ إِنَّمَا يُرِيدُ ٱللَّهُ لِيُذْهِبَ عَنكُمُ ٱلرِّجْسَ أَهْلَ ٱلْبَيْتِ وَيُطَهِّرَكُمْ تَطْهِيرًا (٣٣)

O wives of the Prophet, you are not like anyone among women. If you fear Allah, then do not be soft in speech [to men], lest he in whose heart is disease should covet, but speak with appropriate speech. (32) And abide in your houses and do not display yourselves as [was] the display of the former times of ignorance. And establish prayer and give zakah and obey Allah and His Messenger. Allah intends only to remove from you the impurity [of sin], O people of the [Prophet's] household, and to purify you with [extensive] purification. (33)

Quran 33:36-40

وَمَا كَانَ لِمُؤْمِنٍ وَلَا مُؤْمِنَةٍ إِذَا قَضَى ٱللَّهُ وَرَسُولُهُۥٓ أَمْرًا أَن يَكُونَ لَهُمُ ٱلْخِيَرَةُ مِنْ أَمْرِهِمْ ۗ وَمَن يَعْصِ ٱللَّهَ وَرَسُولَهُۥ فَقَدْ ضَلَّ ضَلَٰلًا مُّبِينًا (٣٦) وَإِذْ تَقُولُ لِلَّذِىٓ أَنْعَمَ ٱللَّهُ عَلَيْهِ وَأَنْعَمْتَ عَلَيْهِ أَمْسِكْ عَلَيْكَ زَوْجَكَ وَٱتَّقِ ٱللَّهَ وَتُخْفِى فِى نَفْسِكَ مَا ٱللَّهُ مُبْدِيهِ وَتَخْشَى ٱلنَّاسَ وَٱللَّهُ أَحَقُّ أَن تَخْشَىٰهُ ۖ فَلَمَّا قَضَىٰ زَيْدٌ مِّنْهَا وَطَرًا زَوَّجْنَٰكَهَا لِكَىْ لَا يَكُونَ عَلَى ٱلْمُؤْمِنِينَ حَرَجٌ فِىٓ أَزْوَٰجِ أَدْعِيَآئِهِمْ إِذَا قَضَوْا۟ مِنْهُنَّ وَطَرًا ۚ وَكَانَ أَمْرُ ٱللَّهِ مَفْعُولًا (٣٧) مَّا كَانَ عَلَى ٱلنَّبِىِّ مِنْ حَرَجٍ فِيمَا فَرَضَ ٱللَّهُ لَهُۥ ۖ سُنَّةَ ٱللَّهِ فِى ٱلَّذِينَ خَلَوْا۟ مِن قَبْلُ ۚ وَكَانَ أَمْرُ ٱللَّهِ قَدَرًا مَّقْدُورًا (٣٨) ٱلَّذِينَ يُبَلِّغُونَ رِسَٰلَٰتِ ٱللَّهِ وَيَخْشَوْنَهُۥ وَلَا يَخْشَوْنَ أَحَدًا إِلَّا ٱللَّهَ ۗ وَكَفَىٰ بِٱللَّهِ حَسِيبًا (٣٩) مَّا كَانَ مُحَمَّدٌ أَبَآ أَحَدٍ مِّن رِّجَالِكُمْ وَلَٰكِن رَّسُولَ ٱللَّهِ وَخَاتَمَ ٱلنَّبِيِّۦنَ ۗ وَكَانَ ٱللَّهُ بِكُلِّ شَىْءٍ عَلِيمًا (٤٠)

It is not for a believing man or a believing woman, when Allah and His Messenger have decided a matter, that they should [thereafter] have any choice about their affair. And whoever disobeys Allah and His Messenger has certainly strayed into clear error. (36) And [remember, O Muhammad], when you said to the one on whom Allah bestowed favor and you bestowed favor, "Keep your wife and fear Allah," while you concealed within yourself that which Allah is to disclose. And you feared the people, while Allah has more right that you fear Him. So when Zayd had no longer any need for her, We married her to you in order that there not be upon the believers any discomfort concerning the wives of their adopted sons when they no longer have need of them. And ever is the command of Allah accomplished. (37) There is not to be upon the Prophet any discomfort concerning that which Allah has imposed upon him. [This is] the established way of Allah with those [prophets] who have passed on before. And ever is the command of Allah a destiny decreed. (38) [Allah praises] those who convey the messages of Allah and fear Him and do not fear anyone but Allah. And sufficient is Allah as Accountant. (39) Muhammad is not the father of [any] one of your men, but [he is] the Messenger of Allah and last of the prophets. And ever is Allah, of all things, Knowing. (40)

Quran 33:48-55

وَلَا تُطِعِ ٱلْكَٰفِرِينَ وَٱلْمُنَٰفِقِينَ وَدَعْ أَذَىٰهُمْ وَتَوَكَّلْ عَلَى ٱللَّهِ وَكَفَىٰ بِٱللَّهِ وَكِيلًا (٤٨) يَٰٓأَيُّهَا ٱلَّذِينَ ءَامَنُوٓا۟ إِذَا نَكَحْتُمُ ٱلْمُؤْمِنَٰتِ ثُمَّ طَلَّقْتُمُوهُنَّ مِن قَبْلِ أَن تَمَسُّوهُنَّ فَمَا لَكُمْ عَلَيْهِنَّ مِنْ عِدَّةٍ تَعْتَدُّونَهَاۖ فَمَتِّعُوهُنَّ وَسَرِّحُوهُنَّ سَرَاحًا جَمِيلًا (٤٩) يَٰٓأَيُّهَا ٱلنَّبِىُّ إِنَّآ أَحْلَلْنَا لَكَ أَزْوَٰجَكَ ٱلَّٰتِىٓ ءَاتَيْتَ أُجُورَهُنَّ وَمَا مَلَكَتْ يَمِينُكَ مِمَّآ أَفَآءَ ٱللَّهُ عَلَيْكَ وَبَنَاتِ عَمِّكَ وَبَنَاتِ عَمَّٰتِكَ وَبَنَاتِ خَالِكَ وَبَنَاتِ خَٰلَٰتِكَ ٱلَّٰتِى هَاجَرْنَ مَعَكَ وَٱمْرَأَةً مُّؤْمِنَةً إِن وَهَبَتْ نَفْسَهَا لِلنَّبِىِّ إِنْ أَرَادَ ٱلنَّبِىُّ أَن يَسْتَنكِحَهَا خَالِصَةً لَّكَ مِن دُونِ ٱلْمُؤْمِنِينَۗ قَدْ عَلِمْنَا مَا فَرَضْنَا عَلَيْهِمْ فِىٓ أَزْوَٰجِهِمْ وَمَا مَلَكَتْ أَيْمَٰنُهُمْ لِكَيْلَا يَكُونَ عَلَيْكَ حَرَجٌۗ وَكَانَ ٱللَّهُ غَفُورًا رَّحِيمًا (٥٠) تُرْجِى مَن تَشَآءُ مِنْهُنَّ وَتُـْٔوِىٓ إِلَيْكَ مَن تَشَآءُۖ وَمَنِ ٱبْتَغَيْتَ مِمَّنْ عَزَلْتَ فَلَا جُنَاحَ عَلَيْكَۚ ذَٰلِكَ أَدْنَىٰٓ أَن تَقَرَّ أَعْيُنُهُنَّ وَلَا يَحْزَنَّ

وَيَرْضَيْنَ بِمَا ءَاتَيْتَهُنَّ كُلُّهُنَّ وَاللَّهُ يَعْلَمُ مَا فِى قُلُوبِكُمْ وَكَانَ اللَّهُ عَلِيمًا حَلِيمًا (٥١) لَا يَحِلُّ لَكَ النِّسَاءُ مِن بَعْدُ وَلَا أَن تَبَدَّلَ بِهِنَّ مِنْ أَزْوَاجٍ وَلَوْ أَعْجَبَكَ حُسْنُهُنَّ إِلَّا مَا مَلَكَتْ يَمِينُكَ وَكَانَ اللَّهُ عَلَىٰ كُلِّ شَىْءٍ رَّقِيبًا (٥٢) يَٰٓأَيُّهَا الَّذِينَ ءَامَنُوا لَا تَدْخُلُوا بُيُوتَ النَّبِىِّ إِلَّا أَن يُؤْذَنَ لَكُمْ إِلَىٰ طَعَامٍ غَيْرَ نَٰظِرِينَ إِنَىٰهُ وَلَٰكِنْ إِذَا دُعِيتُمْ فَادْخُلُوا فَإِذَا طَعِمْتُمْ فَانتَشِرُوا وَلَا مُسْتَـٔنِسِينَ لِحَدِيثٍ إِنَّ ذَٰلِكُمْ كَانَ يُؤْذِى النَّبِىَّ فَيَسْتَحْىِۦ مِنكُمْ وَاللَّهُ لَا يَسْتَحْىِۦ مِنَ الْحَقِّ وَإِذَا سَأَلْتُمُوهُنَّ مَتَٰعًا فَسْـَٔلُوهُنَّ مِن وَرَاءِ حِجَابٍ ذَٰلِكُمْ أَطْهَرُ لِقُلُوبِكُمْ وَقُلُوبِهِنَّ وَمَا كَانَ لَكُمْ أَن تُؤْذُوا رَسُولَ اللَّهِ وَلَا أَن تَنكِحُوا أَزْوَٰجَهُ مِنْ بَعْدِهِۦ أَبَدًا إِنَّ ذَٰلِكُمْ كَانَ عِندَ اللَّهِ عَظِيمًا (٥٣) إِن تُبْدُوا شَيْـًٔا أَوْ تُخْفُوهُ فَإِنَّ اللَّهَ كَانَ بِكُلِّ شَىْءٍ عَلِيمًا (٥٤) لَّا جُنَاحَ عَلَيْهِنَّ فِىٓ ءَابَآئِهِنَّ وَلَآ أَبْنَآئِهِنَّ وَلَآ إِخْوَٰنِهِنَّ وَلَآ أَبْنَآءِ إِخْوَٰنِهِنَّ وَلَآ أَبْنَآءِ أَخَوَٰتِهِنَّ وَلَا نِسَآئِهِنَّ وَلَا مَا مَلَكَتْ أَيْمَٰنُهُنَّ وَاتَّقِينَ اللَّهَ إِنَّ اللَّهَ كَانَ عَلَىٰ كُلِّ شَىْءٍ شَهِيدًا (٥٥)

And do not obey the disbelievers and the hypocrites but do not harm them, and rely upon Allah. And sufficient is Allah as Disposer of affairs. (48) O You who have believed, when you marry believing women and then divorce them before you have touched them, then there is not for you any waiting period to count concerning them. So provide for them and give them a gracious release. (49) O Prophet, indeed We have made lawful to you your wives to whom you have given their due compensation and those your right hand possesses from what Allah has returned to you [of captives] and the daughters of your paternal uncles and the daughters of your paternal aunts and the daughters of your maternal uncles and the *daughters of your maternal aunts who emigrated with you and a believing woman if she gives herself to the Prophet [and] if the Prophet wishes to marry her, [this is] only for you, excluding the [other] believers. We certainly know what We have made obligatory upon them concerning their wives and those their right hands possess, [but this is for you] in order that there will be upon you no discomfort. And ever is Allah Forgiving and Merciful. (50) You, [O Muhammad], may put aside whom you will of them or take to yourself whom you will. And any that you desire of those [wives] from whom you had [temporarily] separated - there is no blame upon you [in returning her]. That is more suitable that they should be content and not grieve and that they should be satisfied with what you have given them - all of them. And Allah knows what is in your hearts. And ever is Allah Knowing and Forbearing. (51) Not lawful to you, [O Muhammad], are [any additional] women after [this], nor [is it] for you to exchange them for [other] wives, even if their beauty were to please you, except what your right hand possesses. And ever is Allah, over all things, an Observer. (52) O you who have believed, do not enter the houses of the Prophet except when you are permitted for a meal, without awaiting its readiness. But when you are invited, then enter; and when you have eaten,* disperse without seeking to remain for conversation. Indeed, that [behavior] was troubling the Prophet, and he is shy of [dismissing] you. But Allah is not shy of the truth. And when you ask [his wives] for something, ask them from behind a partition. That is purer for your hearts and their hearts. And it is not [conceivable or lawful] for you to harm the Messenger of Allah or to marry his wives after him, ever. Indeed, that would be in the sight of Allah an enormity. (53) Whether you reveal a thing or conceal it, indeed Allah is ever, of all things, Knowing. (54) There is no blame upon women concerning their fathers or their sons or their brothers or their brothers' sons or their sisters' sons or their women or those their right hands possess. And fear Allah. Indeed Allah is ever, over all things, Witness. (55)

Quran 35:5-6

يَٰٓأَيُّهَا ٱلنَّاسُ إِنَّ وَعْدَ ٱللَّهِ حَقٌّ ۖ فَلَا تَغُرَّنَّكُمُ ٱلْحَيَوٰةُ ٱلدُّنْيَا ۖ وَلَا يَغُرَّنَّكُم بِٱللَّهِ ٱلْغَرُورُ (٥) إِنَّ ٱلشَّيْطَٰنَ لَكُمْ عَدُوٌّ فَٱتَّخِذُوهُ عَدُوًّا ۚ إِنَّمَا يَدْعُواْ حِزْبَهُۥ لِيَكُونُواْ مِنْ أَصْحَٰبِ ٱلسَّعِيرِ (٦)

O mankind, indeed the promise of Allah is truth, so let not the worldly life delude you and be not deceived about Allah by the Deceiver. (5) Indeed, Satan is an enemy to you; so take him as an enemy. He only invites his party to be among the companions of the Blaze. (6)

Quran 35:8

أَفَمَن زُيِّنَ لَهُۥ سُوٓءُ عَمَلِهِۦ فَرَءَاهُ حَسَنًۭا ۖ فَإِنَّ ٱللَّهَ يُضِلُّ مَن يَشَآءُ وَيَهْدِى مَن يَشَآءُ ۖ فَلَا تَذْهَبْ نَفْسُكَ عَلَيْهِمْ حَسَرَٰتٍ ۚ إِنَّ ٱللَّهَ عَلِيمٌۢ بِمَا يَصْنَعُونَ (٨)

Then is one to whom the evil of his deed has been made attractive so he considers it good [like one rightly guided]? For indeed, Allah sends astray whom He wills and guides whom He wills. So do not let yourself perish over them in regret. Indeed, Allah is Knowing of what they do. (8)

Quran 36:60-62

۞ أَلَمْ أَعْهَدْ إِلَيْكُمْ يَٰبَنِىٓ ءَادَمَ أَن لَّا تَعْبُدُوا۟ ٱلشَّيْطَٰنَ ۖ إِنَّهُۥ لَكُمْ عَدُوٌّۭ مُّبِينٌۭ (٦٠) وَأَنِ ٱعْبُدُونِى ۚ هَٰذَا صِرَٰطٌۭ مُّسْتَقِيمٌۭ (٦١) وَلَقَدْ أَضَلَّ مِنكُمْ جِبِلًّۭا كَثِيرًا ۖ أَفَلَمْ تَكُونُوا۟ تَعْقِلُونَ (٦٢)

Did I not enjoin upon you, O children of Adam, that you not worship Satan - [for] indeed, he is to you a clear enemy - (60) And that you worship [only] Me? This is a straight path. (61) And he had already led astray from among you much of creation, so did you not use reason? (62)

Quran 36:76

فَلَا يَحْزُنكَ قَوْلُهُمْ ۘ إِنَّا نَعْلَمُ مَا يُسِرُّونَ وَمَا يُعْلِنُونَ (٧٦)

So let not their speech grieve you. Indeed, We know what they conceal and what they declare. (76)

Quran 38:86-88

قُلْ مَا أَسْـَٔلُكُمْ عَلَيْهِ مِنْ أَجْرٍ وَمَآ أَنَا۠ مِنَ ٱلْمُتَكَلِّفِينَ (٨٦) إِنْ هُوَ إِلَّا ذِكْرٌ لِّلْعَٰلَمِينَ (٨٧) وَلَتَعْلَمُنَّ نَبَأَهُۥ بَعْدَ حِينٍۭ (٨٨)

Say, [O Muhammad], "I do not ask you for the Qur'an any payment, and I am not of the pretentious (86) It is but a reminder to the worlds. (87) And you will surely know [the truth of] its information after a time." (88)

Quran 39:17

وَٱلَّذِينَ ٱجْتَنَبُوا۟ ٱلطَّٰغُوتَ أَن يَعْبُدُوهَا وَأَنَابُوٓا۟ إِلَى ٱللَّهِ لَهُمُ ٱلْبُشْرَىٰ ۚ فَبَشِّرْ عِبَادِ (١٧)

But those who have avoided Taghut, lest they worship it, and turned back to Allah - for them are good tidings. So give good tidings to My servants (17)

Quran 39:53-58

۞ قُلْ يَٰعِبَادِىَ ٱلَّذِينَ أَسْرَفُوا۟ عَلَىٰٓ أَنفُسِهِمْ لَا تَقْنَطُوا۟ مِن رَّحْمَةِ ٱللَّهِ ۚ إِنَّ ٱللَّهَ يَغْفِرُ ٱلذُّنُوبَ جَمِيعًا ۚ إِنَّهُۥ هُوَ ٱلْغَفُورُ ٱلرَّحِيمُ (٥٣) وَأَنِيبُوٓا۟ إِلَىٰ رَبِّكُمْ وَأَسْلِمُوا۟ لَهُۥ مِن قَبْلِ أَن يَأْتِيَكُمُ ٱلْعَذَابُ ثُمَّ لَا تُنصَرُونَ (٥٤) وَٱتَّبِعُوٓا۟ أَحْسَنَ مَآ أُنزِلَ إِلَيْكُم مِّن رَّبِّكُم مِّن قَبْلِ أَن يَأْتِيَكُمُ ٱلْعَذَابُ بَغْتَةً وَأَنتُمْ لَا تَشْعُرُونَ (٥٥) أَن تَقُولَ نَفْسٌ يَٰحَسْرَتَىٰ عَلَىٰ مَا فَرَّطتُ فِى جَنۢبِ ٱللَّهِ وَإِن كُنتُ لَمِنَ

ٱلسَّٰخِرِينَ (٥٦) أَوْ تَقُولَ لَوْ أَنَّ ٱللَّهَ هَدَىٰنِى لَكُنتُ مِنَ ٱلْمُتَّقِينَ (٥٧) أَوْ تَقُولَ حِينَ تَرَى ٱلْعَذَابَ لَوْ أَنَّ لِى كَرَّةً فَأَكُونَ مِنَ ٱلْمُحْسِنِينَ (٥٨)

Say, "O My servants who have transgressed against themselves [by sinning], do not despair of the mercy of Allah. Indeed, Allah forgives all sins. Indeed, it is He who is the Forgiving, the Merciful." (53) And return [in repentance] to your Lord and submit to Him before the punishment comes upon you; then you will not be helped. (54) And follow the best of what was revealed to you from your Lord before the punishment comes upon you suddenly while you do not perceive, (55) Lest a soul should say, "Oh [how great is] my regret over what I neglected in regard to Allah and that I was among the mockers." (56) Or [lest] it say, "If only Allah had guided me, I would have been among the righteous." (57) Or [lest] it say when it sees the punishment, "If only I had another turn so I could be among the doers of good." (58)

Quran 39:65-66

وَلَقَدْ أُوحِىَ إِلَيْكَ وَإِلَى ٱلَّذِينَ مِن قَبْلِكَ لَئِنْ أَشْرَكْتَ لَيَحْبَطَنَّ عَمَلُكَ وَلَتَكُونَنَّ مِنَ ٱلْخَٰسِرِينَ (٦٥) بَلِ ٱللَّهَ فَٱعْبُدْ وَكُن مِّنَ ٱلشَّٰكِرِينَ (٦٦)

And it was already revealed to you and to those before you that if you should associate [anything] with Allah, your work would surely become worthless, and you would surely be among the losers." (65) Rather, worship [only] Allah and be among the grateful. (66)

Quran 40:2-4

تَنزِيلُ ٱلْكِتَـٰبِ مِنَ ٱللَّهِ ٱلْعَزِيزِ ٱلْعَلِيمِ (٢) غَافِرِ ٱلذَّنۢبِ وَقَابِلِ ٱلتَّوْبِ شَدِيدِ ٱلْعِقَابِ ذِى ٱلطَّوْلِ لَآ إِلَـٰهَ إِلَّا هُوَ إِلَيْهِ ٱلْمَصِيرُ (٣) مَا يُجَـٰدِلُ فِىٓ ءَايَـٰتِ ٱللَّهِ إِلَّا ٱلَّذِينَ كَفَرُوا۟ فَلَا يَغْرُرْكَ تَقَلُّبُهُمْ فِى ٱلْبِلَـٰدِ (٤)

The revelation of the Book is from Allah, the Exalted in Might, the Knowing. (2) The forgiver of sin, acceptor of repentance, severe in punishment, owner of abundance. There is no deity except Him; to Him is the destination. (3) No one disputes concerning the signs of Allah except those who disbelieve, so be not deceived by their [uninhibited] movement throughout the land. (4)

Quran 41:36-37

وَإِمَّا يَنزَغَنَّكَ مِنَ ٱلشَّيْطَـٰنِ نَزْغٌ فَٱسْتَعِذْ بِٱللَّهِ إِنَّهُۥ هُوَ ٱلسَّمِيعُ ٱلْعَلِيمُ (٣٦) وَمِنْ ءَايَـٰتِهِ ٱلَّيْلُ وَٱلنَّهَارُ وَٱلشَّمْسُ وَٱلْقَمَرُ لَا تَسْجُدُوا۟ لِلشَّمْسِ وَلَا لِلْقَمَرِ وَٱسْجُدُوا۟ لِلَّهِ ٱلَّذِى خَلَقَهُنَّ إِن كُنتُمْ إِيَّاهُ تَعْبُدُونَ (٣٧)

And if there comes to you from Satan an evil suggestion, then seek refuge in Allah. Indeed, He is the Hearing, the Knowing. (36) And of His signs are the night and day and the sun and moon. Do not prostrate to the sun or to the moon, but prostate to Allah, who created them, if it should be Him that you worship. (37)

Quran 42:15

فَلِذَٰلِكَ فَٱدْعُ ۖ وَٱسْتَقِمْ كَمَآ أُمِرْتَ ۖ وَلَا تَتَّبِعْ أَهْوَآءَهُمْ ۖ وَقُلْ ءَامَنتُ بِمَآ أَنزَلَ ٱللَّهُ مِن كِتَٰبٍ ۖ وَأُمِرْتُ لِأَعْدِلَ بَيْنَكُمُ ۖ ٱللَّهُ رَبُّنَا وَرَبُّكُمْ ۖ لَنَآ أَعْمَٰلُنَا وَلَكُمْ أَعْمَٰلُكُمْ ۖ لَا حُجَّةَ بَيْنَنَا وَبَيْنَكُمُ ۖ ٱللَّهُ يَجْمَعُ بَيْنَنَا ۖ وَإِلَيْهِ ٱلْمَصِيرُ (١٥)

So to that [religion of Allah] invite, [O Muhammad], and remain on a right course as you are commanded and do not follow their inclinations but say, "I have believed in what Allah has revealed of the Qur'an, and I have been commanded to do justice among you. Allah is our Lord and your Lord. For us are our deeds, and for you your deeds. There is no [need for] argument between us and you. Allah will bring us together, and to Him is the [final] destination." (15)

Quran 42:36-44

فَمَآ أُوتِيتُم مِّن شَىْءٍ فَمَتَٰعُ ٱلْحَيَوٰةِ ٱلدُّنْيَا ۖ وَمَا عِندَ ٱللَّهِ خَيْرٌ وَأَبْقَىٰ لِلَّذِينَ ءَامَنُوا۟ وَعَلَىٰ رَبِّهِمْ يَتَوَكَّلُونَ (٣٦) وَٱلَّذِينَ يَجْتَنِبُونَ كَبَٰٓئِرَ ٱلْإِثْمِ وَٱلْفَوَٰحِشَ وَإِذَا مَا غَضِبُوا۟ هُمْ يَغْفِرُونَ (٣٧) وَٱلَّذِينَ ٱسْتَجَابُوا۟ لِرَبِّهِمْ وَأَقَامُوا۟ ٱلصَّلَوٰةَ وَأَمْرُهُمْ شُورَىٰ بَيْنَهُمْ وَمِمَّا رَزَقْنَٰهُمْ يُنفِقُونَ (٣٨) وَٱلَّذِينَ إِذَآ أَصَابَهُمُ ٱلْبَغْىُ هُمْ يَنتَصِرُونَ (٣٩) وَجَزَٰٓؤُا۟ سَيِّئَةٍ سَيِّئَةٌ مِّثْلُهَا ۖ فَمَنْ عَفَا وَأَصْلَحَ فَأَجْرُهُۥ عَلَى ٱللَّهِ ۚ إِنَّهُۥ لَا يُحِبُّ ٱلظَّٰلِمِينَ (٤٠) وَلَمَنِ ٱنتَصَرَ بَعْدَ ظُلْمِهِۦ فَأُو۟لَٰٓئِكَ مَا عَلَيْهِم مِّن سَبِيلٍ (٤١) إِنَّمَا ٱلسَّبِيلُ عَلَى ٱلَّذِينَ يَظْلِمُونَ ٱلنَّاسَ وَيَبْغُونَ فِى ٱلْأَرْضِ بِغَيْرِ ٱلْحَقِّ ۚ أُو۟لَٰٓئِكَ لَهُمْ عَذَابٌ أَلِيمٌ (٤٢) وَلَمَن صَبَرَ وَغَفَرَ إِنَّ ذَٰلِكَ لَمِنْ عَزْمِ ٱلْأُمُورِ (٤٣) وَمَن يُضْلِلِ ٱللَّهُ فَمَا لَهُۥ مِن وَلِىٍّ مِّنۢ بَعْدِهِۦ ۗ وَتَرَى ٱلظَّٰلِمِينَ لَمَّا رَأَوُا۟ ٱلْعَذَابَ يَقُولُونَ هَلْ إِلَىٰ مَرَدٍّ مِّن سَبِيلٍ (٤٤)

So whatever thing you have been given - it is but [for] enjoyment of the worldly life. But what is with Allah is better and more lasting for those who have believed and upon their Lord rely (36) And those who avoid the major sins and immoralities, and when they are angry, they forgive, (37) And those who have responded to their lord and established prayer and whose affair is [determined by] consultation among themselves, and from what We have provided them, they spend. (38) And those who, when tyranny strikes them, they defend themselves, (39) And the retribution for an evil act is an evil one like it, but whoever pardons and makes reconciliation - his reward is [due] from Allah. Indeed, He does not like wrongdoers. (40) And whoever avenges himself after having been wronged - those have not upon them any cause [for blame]. (41) The cause is only against the ones who wrong the people and tyrannize upon the earth without right. Those will have a painful punishment. (42) And whoever is patient and forgives - indeed, that is of the matters [requiring] determination. (43) And he whom Allah sends astray - for him there is no protector beyond Him. And you will see the wrongdoers, when they see the punishment, saying, "Is there for return [to the former world] any way?" (44)

Quran 43:62

وَلَا يَصُدَّنَّكُمُ ٱلشَّيْطَانُ ۖ إِنَّهُ لَكُمْ عَدُوٌّ مُّبِينٌ (٦٢)

And never let Satan avert you. Indeed, he is to you a clear enemy. (62)

Quran 45:18-19

ثُمَّ جَعَلْنَاكَ عَلَىٰ شَرِيعَةٍ مِّنَ ٱلْأَمْرِ فَٱتَّبِعْهَا وَلَا تَتَّبِعْ أَهْوَاءَ ٱلَّذِينَ لَا يَعْلَمُونَ (١٨) إِنَّهُمْ لَن يُغْنُوا عَنكَ مِنَ ٱللَّهِ شَيْئًا ۚ وَإِنَّ ٱلظَّالِمِينَ بَعْضُهُمْ أَوْلِيَاءُ بَعْضٍ ۖ وَٱللَّهُ وَلِيُّ ٱلْمُتَّقِينَ (١٩)

Then We put you, on an ordained way concerning the matter [of religion]; so follow it and do not follow the inclinations of those who do not know. (18) Indeed, they will never avail you against Allah at all. And indeed, the wrongdoers are allies of one another; but Allah is the protector of the righteous. (19)

Quran 46:21

۞ وَٱذْكُرْ أَخَا عَادٍ إِذْ أَنذَرَ قَوْمَهُ بِٱلْأَحْقَافِ وَقَدْ خَلَتِ ٱلنُّذُرُ مِنْ بَيْنِ يَدَيْهِ وَمِنْ خَلْفِهِ أَلَّا تَعْبُدُوا إِلَّا ٱللَّهَ إِنِّي أَخَافُ عَلَيْكُمْ عَذَابَ يَوْمٍ عَظِيمٍ (٢١)

And mention, [O Muhammad], the brother of 'Aad, when he warned his people in the [region of] al-Ahqaf - and warners had already passed on before him and after him - [saying], "Do not worship except Allah. Indeed, I fear for you the punishment of a terrible day." (21)

Quran 47:19-26

فَاعْلَمْ أَنَّهُۥ لَآ إِلَٰهَ إِلَّا ٱللَّهُ وَٱسْتَغْفِرْ لِذَنۢبِكَ وَلِلْمُؤْمِنِينَ وَٱلْمُؤْمِنَٰتِ ۗ وَٱللَّهُ يَعْلَمُ مُتَقَلَّبَكُمْ وَمَثْوَىٰكُمْ (١٩) وَيَقُولُ ٱلَّذِينَ ءَامَنُوا۟ لَوْلَا نُزِّلَتْ سُورَةٌ ۖ فَإِذَآ أُنزِلَتْ سُورَةٌ مُّحْكَمَةٌ وَذُكِرَ فِيهَا ٱلْقِتَالُ ۙ رَأَيْتَ ٱلَّذِينَ فِى قُلُوبِهِم مَّرَضٌ يَنظُرُونَ إِلَيْكَ نَظَرَ ٱلْمَغْشِىِّ عَلَيْهِ مِنَ ٱلْمَوْتِ ۖ فَأَوْلَىٰ لَهُمْ (٢٠) طَاعَةٌ وَقَوْلٌ مَّعْرُوفٌ ۚ فَإِذَا عَزَمَ ٱلْأَمْرُ فَلَوْ صَدَقُوا۟ ٱللَّهَ لَكَانَ خَيْرًا لَّهُمْ (٢١) فَهَلْ عَسَيْتُمْ إِن تَوَلَّيْتُمْ أَن تُفْسِدُوا۟ فِى ٱلْأَرْضِ وَتُقَطِّعُوٓا۟ أَرْحَامَكُمْ (٢٢) أُو۟لَٰٓئِكَ ٱلَّذِينَ لَعَنَهُمُ ٱللَّهُ فَأَصَمَّهُمْ وَأَعْمَىٰٓ أَبْصَٰرَهُمْ (٢٣) أَفَلَا يَتَدَبَّرُونَ ٱلْقُرْءَانَ أَمْ عَلَىٰ قُلُوبٍ أَقْفَالُهَآ (٢٤) إِنَّ ٱلَّذِينَ ٱرْتَدُّوا۟ عَلَىٰٓ أَدْبَٰرِهِم مِّنۢ بَعْدِ مَا تَبَيَّنَ لَهُمُ ٱلْهُدَى ۙ ٱلشَّيْطَٰنُ سَوَّلَ لَهُمْ وَأَمْلَىٰ لَهُمْ (٢٥) ذَٰلِكَ بِأَنَّهُمْ قَالُوا۟ لِلَّذِينَ كَرِهُوا۟ مَا نَزَّلَ ٱللَّهُ سَنُطِيعُكُمْ فِى بَعْضِ ٱلْأَمْرِ ۖ وَٱللَّهُ يَعْلَمُ إِسْرَارَهُمْ (٢٦)

So know, [O Muhammad], that there is no deity except Allah and ask forgiveness for your sin and for the believing men and believing women. And Allah knows of your movement and your resting place. (19) Those who believe say, "Why has a surah not been sent down? But when a precise surah is revealed and fighting is mentioned therein, you see those in whose hearts is hypocrisy looking at you with a look of one overcome by death. And more appropriate for them [would have been] (20) Obedience and good words. And when the matter [of fighting] was determined, if they had been true to Allah, it would have been better for them. (21) So would you perhaps, if you turned away, cause corruption on earth and sever your [ties of] relationship? (22) Those [who do so] are the ones that Allah has cursed, so He deafened them and blinded their vision. (23) Then do they not reflect upon the Qur'an, or are there locks upon [their] hearts? (24) Indeed, those who reverted back [to disbelief] after guidance had become clear to them - Satan enticed them and prolonged hope for them. (25) That is because they said to those who disliked what Allah sent down, "We will obey you in part of the matter." And Allah knows what they conceal. (26)

Quran 47:33-35

يَٰٓأَيُّهَا ٱلَّذِينَ ءَامَنُوٓاْ أَطِيعُواْ ٱللَّهَ وَأَطِيعُواْ ٱلرَّسُولَ وَلَا تُبْطِلُوٓاْ أَعْمَٰلَكُمْ (٣٣) إِنَّ ٱلَّذِينَ كَفَرُواْ وَصَدُّواْ عَن سَبِيلِ ٱللَّهِ ثُمَّ مَاتُواْ وَهُمْ كُفَّارٌ فَلَن يَغْفِرَ ٱللَّهُ لَهُمْ (٣٤) فَلَا تَهِنُواْ وَتَدْعُوٓاْ إِلَى ٱلسَّلْمِ وَأَنتُمُ ٱلْأَعْلَوْنَ وَٱللَّهُ مَعَكُمْ وَلَن يَتِرَكُمْ أَعْمَٰلَكُمْ (٣٥)

O you who have believed, obey Allah and obey the Messenger and do not invalidate your deeds. (33) Indeed, those who disbelieved and averted [people] from the path of Allah and then died while they were disbelievers - never will Allah forgive them. (34) So do not weaken and call for peace while you are superior; and Allah is with you and will never deprive you of [the reward of] your deeds. (35)

Quran 49:1-6

يَـٰٓأَيُّهَا ٱلَّذِينَ ءَامَنُوا۟ لَا تُقَدِّمُوا۟ بَيْنَ يَدَىِ ٱللَّهِ وَرَسُولِهِۦ ۖ وَٱتَّقُوا۟ ٱللَّهَ ۚ إِنَّ ٱللَّهَ سَمِيعٌ عَلِيمٌ (١) يَـٰٓأَيُّهَا ٱلَّذِينَ ءَامَنُوا۟ لَا تَرْفَعُوٓا۟ أَصْوَٰتَكُمْ فَوْقَ صَوْتِ ٱلنَّبِىِّ وَلَا تَجْهَرُوا۟ لَهُۥ بِٱلْقَوْلِ كَجَهْرِ بَعْضِكُمْ لِبَعْضٍ أَن تَحْبَطَ أَعْمَـٰلُكُمْ وَأَنتُمْ لَا تَشْعُرُونَ (٢) إِنَّ ٱلَّذِينَ يَغُضُّونَ أَصْوَٰتَهُمْ عِندَ رَسُولِ ٱللَّهِ أُو۟لَـٰٓئِكَ ٱلَّذِينَ ٱمْتَحَنَ ٱللَّهُ قُلُوبَهُمْ لِلتَّقْوَىٰ ۚ لَهُم مَّغْفِرَةٌ وَأَجْرٌ عَظِيمٌ (٣) إِنَّ ٱلَّذِينَ يُنَادُونَكَ مِن وَرَآءِ ٱلْحُجُرَٰتِ أَكْثَرُهُمْ لَا يَعْقِلُونَ (٤) وَلَوْ أَنَّهُمْ صَبَرُوا۟ حَتَّىٰ تَخْرُجَ إِلَيْهِمْ لَكَانَ خَيْرًا لَّهُمْ ۚ وَٱللَّهُ غَفُورٌ رَّحِيمٌ (٥) يَـٰٓأَيُّهَا ٱلَّذِينَ ءَامَنُوٓا۟ إِن جَآءَكُمْ فَاسِقٌۢ بِنَبَإٍ فَتَبَيَّنُوٓا۟ أَن تُصِيبُوا۟ قَوْمًۢا بِجَهَـٰلَةٍ فَتُصْبِحُوا۟ عَلَىٰ مَا فَعَلْتُمْ نَـٰدِمِينَ (٦)

O you who have believed, do not put [yourselves] before Allah and His Messenger but fear Allah. Indeed, Allah is Hearing and Knowing. (1) O you who have believed, do not raise your voices above the voice of the Prophet or be loud to him in speech like the loudness of some of you to others, lest your deeds become worthless while you perceive not. (2) Indeed, those who lower their voices before the Messenger of Allah - they are the ones whose hearts Allah has tested for righteousness. For them is forgiveness and great reward. (3) Indeed, those who call you, [O Muhammad], from behind the chambers - most of them do not use reason. (4) And if they had been patient until you [could] come out to them, it would have been better for them. But Allah is Forgiving and Merciful. (5) O you who have believed, if there comes to you a disobedient one with information, investigate, lest you harm a people out of ignorance and become, over what you have done, regretful. (6)

Quran 49:9-12

وَإِن طَآئِفَتَانِ مِنَ ٱلْمُؤْمِنِينَ ٱقْتَتَلُوا۟ فَأَصْلِحُوا۟ بَيْنَهُمَا ۖ فَإِنۢ بَغَتْ إِحْدَىٰهُمَا عَلَى ٱلْأُخْرَىٰ فَقَـٰتِلُوا۟ ٱلَّتِى تَبْغِى حَتَّىٰ تَفِىٓءَ إِلَىٰٓ أَمْرِ ٱللَّهِ ۚ فَإِن فَآءَتْ فَأَصْلِحُوا۟ بَيْنَهُمَا بِٱلْعَدْلِ وَأَقْسِطُوٓا۟ ۖ إِنَّ ٱللَّهَ يُحِبُّ ٱلْمُقْسِطِينَ (٩) إِنَّمَا ٱلْمُؤْمِنُونَ إِخْوَةٌ فَأَصْلِحُوا۟ بَيْنَ أَخَوَيْكُمْ ۚ وَٱتَّقُوا۟ ٱللَّهَ لَعَلَّكُمْ تُرْحَمُونَ (١٠) يَـٰٓأَيُّهَا ٱلَّذِينَ ءَامَنُوا۟ لَا يَسْخَرْ قَوْمٌ مِّن قَوْمٍ عَسَىٰٓ أَن يَكُونُوا۟ خَيْرًا مِّنْهُمْ وَلَا نِسَآءٌ مِّن نِّسَآءٍ عَسَىٰٓ أَن يَكُنَّ خَيْرًا مِّنْهُنَّ ۖ وَلَا تَلْمِزُوٓا۟ أَنفُسَكُمْ وَلَا تَنَابَزُوا۟ بِٱلْأَلْقَـٰبِ ۖ بِئْسَ ٱلِٱسْمُ ٱلْفُسُوقُ بَعْدَ ٱلْإِيمَـٰنِ ۚ وَمَن لَّمْ يَتُبْ فَأُو۟لَـٰٓئِكَ هُمُ ٱلظَّـٰلِمُونَ (١١) يَـٰٓأَيُّهَا ٱلَّذِينَ ءَامَنُوا۟ ٱجْتَنِبُوا۟ كَثِيرًا مِّنَ ٱلظَّنِّ إِنَّ بَعْضَ ٱلظَّنِّ إِثْمٌ ۖ وَلَا تَجَسَّسُوا۟ وَلَا يَغْتَب بَّعْضُكُم بَعْضًا ۚ أَيُحِبُّ أَحَدُكُمْ أَن يَأْكُلَ لَحْمَ أَخِيهِ مَيْتًا فَكَرِهْتُمُوهُ ۚ وَٱتَّقُوا۟ ٱللَّهَ ۚ إِنَّ ٱللَّهَ تَوَّابٌ رَّحِيمٌ (١٢)

And if two factions among the believers should fight, then make settlement between the two. But if one of them oppresses the other, then fight against the one that oppresses until it returns to the ordinance of Allah. And if it returns, then make settlement between them in justice and act justly. Indeed, Allah loves those who act justly. (9) The believers are but brothers, so make settlement between your brothers. And fear Allah that you may receive mercy. (10) O you who have believed, let not a people ridicule [another] people; perhaps they may be better than them; nor let women ridicule [other] women; perhaps they may be better than them. And do not insult one another and do not call each other by [offensive] nicknames. Wretched is the name of disobedience after [one's] faith. And whoever does not repent - then it is those who are the wrongdoers. (11) O you who have believed, avoid much [negative] assumption. Indeed, some assumption is sin. And do not spy or backbite each other. Would one of you like to eat the flesh of his brother when dead? You would detest it. And fear Allah; indeed, Allah is Accepting of repentance and Merciful. (12)

Quran 49:17

يَمُنُّونَ عَلَيْكَ أَنْ أَسْلَمُوا ۖ قُل لَّا تَمُنُّوا عَلَىَّ إِسْلَـٰمَكُم ۖ بَلِ ٱللَّهُ يَمُنُّ عَلَيْكُمْ أَنْ هَدَىٰكُمْ لِلْإِيمَـٰنِ إِن كُنتُمْ صَـٰدِقِينَ (١٧)

They consider it a favor to you that they have accepted Islam. Say, "Do not consider your Islam a favor to me. Rather, Allah has conferred favor upon you that He has guided you to the faith, if you should be truthful." (17)

Quran 51:50-51

فَفِرُّوٓا۟ إِلَى ٱللَّهِ ۖ إِنِّى لَكُم مِّنْهُ نَذِيرٌ مُّبِينٌ (٥٠) وَلَا تَجْعَلُوا۟ مَعَ ٱللَّهِ إِلَـٰهًا ءَاخَرَ ۖ إِنِّى لَكُم مِّنْهُ نَذِيرٌ مُّبِينٌ (٥١)

So flee to Allah. Indeed, I am to you from Him a clear warner. (50) And do not make [as equal] with Allah another deity. Indeed, I am to you from Him a clear warner. (51)

Quran 51:54-59

فَتَوَلَّ عَنْهُمْ فَمَآ أَنتَ بِمَلُومٍ (٥٤) وَذَكِّرْ فَإِنَّ ٱلذِّكْرَىٰ تَنفَعُ ٱلْمُؤْمِنِينَ (٥٥) وَمَا خَلَقْتُ ٱلْجِنَّ وَٱلْإِنسَ إِلَّا لِيَعْبُدُونِ (٥٦) مَآ أُرِيدُ مِنْهُم مِّن رِّزْقٍ وَمَآ أُرِيدُ أَن يُطْعِمُونِ (٥٧) إِنَّ ٱللَّهَ هُوَ ٱلرَّزَّاقُ ذُو ٱلْقُوَّةِ ٱلْمَتِينُ (٥٨) فَإِنَّ لِلَّذِينَ ظَلَمُوا۟ ذَنُوبًا مِّثْلَ ذَنُوبِ أَصْحَٰبِهِمْ فَلَا يَسْتَعْجِلُونِ (٥٩)

So leave them, [O Muhammad], for you are not to be blamed. (54) And remind, for indeed, the reminder benefits the believers. (55) And I did not create the jinn and mankind except to worship Me. (56) I do not want from them any provision, nor do I want them to feed Me. (57) Indeed, it is Allah who is the [continual] Provider, the firm possessor of strength. (58) And indeed, for those who have wronged is a portion [of punishment] like the portion of their predecessors, so let them not impatiently urge Me. (59)

Quran 53:29-42

فَأَعْرِضْ عَن مَّن تَوَلَّىٰ عَن ذِكْرِنَا وَلَمْ يُرِدْ إِلَّا ٱلْحَيَوٰةَ ٱلدُّنْيَا (٢٩) ذَٰلِكَ مَبْلَغُهُم مِّنَ ٱلْعِلْمِ إِنَّ رَبَّكَ هُوَ أَعْلَمُ بِمَن ضَلَّ عَن سَبِيلِهِۦ وَهُوَ أَعْلَمُ بِمَنِ ٱهْتَدَىٰ (٣٠) وَلِلَّهِ مَا فِى ٱلسَّمَٰوَٰتِ وَمَا فِى ٱلْأَرْضِ لِيَجْزِىَ ٱلَّذِينَ أَسَٰٓـُٔوا۟ بِمَا عَمِلُوا۟ وَيَجْزِىَ ٱلَّذِينَ أَحْسَنُوا۟ بِٱلْحُسْنَى (٣١) ٱلَّذِينَ يَجْتَنِبُونَ كَبَٰٓئِرَ ٱلْإِثْمِ وَٱلْفَوَٰحِشَ إِلَّا ٱللَّمَمَ إِنَّ رَبَّكَ وَٰسِعُ ٱلْمَغْفِرَةِ هُوَ أَعْلَمُ بِكُمْ إِذْ أَنشَأَكُم مِّنَ ٱلْأَرْضِ وَإِذْ أَنتُمْ أَجِنَّةٌ فِى بُطُونِ أُمَّهَٰتِكُمْ فَلَا تُزَكُّوٓا۟ أَنفُسَكُمْ هُوَ أَعْلَمُ بِمَنِ

اَتَّقَىٰ (٣٢) أَفَرَءَيْتَ ٱلَّذِى تَوَلَّىٰ (٣٣) وَأَعْطَىٰ قَلِيلًا وَأَكْدَىٰ (٣٤) أَعِندَهُۥ عِلْمُ ٱلْغَيْبِ فَهُوَ يَرَىٰٓ (٣٥) أَمْ لَمْ يُنَبَّأْ بِمَا فِى صُحُفِ مُوسَىٰ (٣٦) وَإِبْرَٰهِيمَ ٱلَّذِى وَفَّىٰٓ (٣٧) أَلَّا تَزِرُ وَازِرَةٌ وِزْرَ أُخْرَىٰ (٣٨) وَأَن لَّيْسَ لِلْإِنسَٰنِ إِلَّا مَا سَعَىٰ (٣٩) وَأَنَّ سَعْيَهُۥ سَوْفَ يُرَىٰ (٤٠) ثُمَّ يُجْزَىٰهُ ٱلْجَزَآءَ ٱلْأَوْفَىٰ (٤١) وَأَنَّ إِلَىٰ رَبِّكَ ٱلْمُنتَهَىٰ (٤٢)

So turn away from whoever turns his back on Our message and desires not except the worldly life. (29) That is their sum of knowledge. Indeed, your Lord is most knowing of who strays from His way, and He is most knowing of who is guided. (30) And to Allah belongs whatever is in the heavens and whatever is in the earth - that He may recompense those who do evil with [the penalty of] what they have done and recompense those who do good with the best [reward] - (31) Those who avoid the major sins and immoralities, only [committing] slight ones. Indeed, your Lord is vast in forgiveness. He was most knowing of you when He produced you from the earth and when you were fetuses in the wombs of your mothers. So do not claim yourselves to be pure; He is most knowing of who fears Him. (32) Have you seen the one who turned away (33) And gave a little and [then] refrained? (34) Does he have knowledge of the unseen, so he sees? (35) Or has he not been informed of what was in the scriptures of Moses (36) And [of] Abraham, who fulfilled [his obligations] - (37) That no bearer of burdens will bear the burden of another (38) And that there is not for man except that [good] for which he strives (39) And that his effort is going to be seen – (40) Then he will be recompensed for it with the fullest recompense (41) And that to your Lord is the finality (42)

Quran 57:7-19

ءَامِنُوا۟ بِٱللَّهِ وَرَسُولِهِۦ وَأَنفِقُوا۟ مِمَّا جَعَلَكُم مُّسْتَخْلَفِينَ فِيهِ ۖ فَٱلَّذِينَ ءَامَنُوا۟ مِنكُمْ وَأَنفَقُوا۟ لَهُمْ أَجْرٌ كَبِيرٌ (٧) وَمَا لَكُمْ لَا تُؤْمِنُونَ بِٱللَّهِ وَٱلرَّسُولُ يَدْعُوكُمْ لِتُؤْمِنُوا۟ بِرَبِّكُمْ وَقَدْ أَخَذَ مِيثَـٰقَكُمْ إِن كُنتُم مُّؤْمِنِينَ (٨) هُوَ ٱلَّذِى يُنَزِّلُ عَلَىٰ عَبْدِهِۦٓ ءَايَـٰتٍۭ بَيِّنَـٰتٍ لِّيُخْرِجَكُم مِّنَ ٱلظُّلُمَـٰتِ إِلَى ٱلنُّورِ ۚ وَإِنَّ ٱللَّهَ بِكُمْ لَرَءُوفٌ رَّحِيمٌ (٩) وَمَا لَكُمْ أَلَّا تُنفِقُوا۟ فِى سَبِيلِ ٱللَّهِ وَلِلَّهِ مِيرَٰثُ ٱلسَّمَـٰوَٰتِ وَٱلْأَرْضِ ۚ لَا يَسْتَوِى مِنكُم مَّنْ أَنفَقَ مِن قَبْلِ ٱلْفَتْحِ وَقَـٰتَلَ ۚ أُو۟لَـٰٓئِكَ أَعْظَمُ دَرَجَةً مِّنَ ٱلَّذِينَ أَنفَقُوا۟ مِنۢ بَعْدُ وَقَـٰتَلُوا۟ ۚ وَكُلًّا وَعَدَ ٱللَّهُ ٱلْحُسْنَىٰ ۚ وَٱللَّهُ بِمَا تَعْمَلُونَ خَبِيرٌ (١٠) مَّن ذَا ٱلَّذِى يُقْرِضُ ٱللَّهَ قَرْضًا حَسَنًا فَيُضَـٰعِفَهُۥ لَهُۥ وَلَهُۥٓ أَجْرٌ كَرِيمٌ (١١) يَوْمَ تَرَى ٱلْمُؤْمِنِينَ وَٱلْمُؤْمِنَـٰتِ يَسْعَىٰ نُورُهُم بَيْنَ أَيْدِيهِمْ وَبِأَيْمَـٰنِهِم بُشْرَىٰكُمُ ٱلْيَوْمَ جَنَّـٰتٌ تَجْرِى مِن تَحْتِهَا ٱلْأَنْهَـٰرُ خَـٰلِدِينَ فِيهَا ۚ ذَٰلِكَ هُوَ ٱلْفَوْزُ ٱلْعَظِيمُ (١٢) يَوْمَ يَقُولُ ٱلْمُنَـٰفِقُونَ وَٱلْمُنَـٰفِقَـٰتُ لِلَّذِينَ ءَامَنُوا۟ ٱنظُرُونَا نَقْتَبِسْ مِن نُّورِكُمْ قِيلَ ٱرْجِعُوا۟ وَرَآءَكُمْ فَٱلْتَمِسُوا۟ نُورًا فَضُرِبَ بَيْنَهُم بِسُورٍ لَّهُۥ بَابٌۢ بَاطِنُهُۥ فِيهِ ٱلرَّحْمَةُ وَظَـٰهِرُهُۥ مِن قِبَلِهِ ٱلْعَذَابُ (١٣) يُنَادُونَهُمْ أَلَمْ نَكُن مَّعَكُمْ ۖ قَالُوا۟ بَلَىٰ وَلَـٰكِنَّكُمْ فَتَنتُمْ أَنفُسَكُمْ وَتَرَبَّصْتُمْ وَٱرْتَبْتُمْ وَغَرَّتْكُمُ ٱلْأَمَانِىُّ حَتَّىٰ جَآءَ أَمْرُ ٱللَّهِ وَغَرَّكُم بِٱللَّهِ ٱلْغَرُورُ (١٤) فَٱلْيَوْمَ لَا يُؤْخَذُ مِنكُمْ فِدْيَةٌ وَلَا مِنَ ٱلَّذِينَ كَفَرُوا۟ ۚ مَأْوَىٰكُمُ ٱلنَّارُ ۖ هِىَ مَوْلَىٰكُمْ ۖ وَبِئْسَ ٱلْمَصِيرُ (١٥) ۞ أَلَمْ يَأْنِ لِلَّذِينَ ءَامَنُوٓا۟ أَن تَخْشَعَ قُلُوبُهُمْ لِذِكْرِ ٱللَّهِ وَمَا نَزَلَ مِنَ ٱلْحَقِّ وَلَا يَكُونُوا۟ كَٱلَّذِينَ أُوتُوا۟ ٱلْكِتَـٰبَ مِن قَبْلُ فَطَالَ عَلَيْهِمُ ٱلْأَمَدُ فَقَسَتْ قُلُوبُهُمْ ۖ وَكَثِيرٌ مِّنْهُمْ فَـٰسِقُونَ

(١٦) ٱعْلَمُوٓا۟ أَنَّ ٱللَّهَ يُحْىِ ٱلْأَرْضَ بَعْدَ مَوْتِهَا ۚ قَدْ بَيَّنَّا لَكُمُ ٱلْءَايَـٰتِ لَعَلَّكُمْ تَعْقِلُونَ (١٧) إِنَّ ٱلْمُصَّدِّقِينَ وَٱلْمُصَّدِّقَـٰتِ وَأَقْرَضُوا۟ ٱللَّهَ قَرْضًا حَسَنًا يُضَـٰعَفُ لَهُمْ وَلَهُمْ أَجْرٌ كَرِيمٌ (١٨) وَٱلَّذِينَ ءَامَنُوا۟ بِٱللَّهِ وَرُسُلِهِۦٓ أُو۟لَـٰٓئِكَ هُمُ ٱلصِّدِّيقُونَ ۖ وَٱلشُّهَدَآءُ عِندَ رَبِّهِمْ لَهُمْ أَجْرُهُمْ وَنُورُهُمْ ۖ وَٱلَّذِينَ كَفَرُوا۟ وَكَذَّبُوا۟ بِـَٔايَـٰتِنَآ أُو۟لَـٰٓئِكَ أَصْحَـٰبُ ٱلْجَحِيمِ (١٩)

Believe in Allah and His Messenger and spend out of that in which He has made you successors. For those who have believed among you and spent, there will be a great reward. (7) And why do you not believe in Allah while the Messenger invites you to believe in your Lord and He has taken your covenant, if you should [truly] be believers? (8) It is He who sends down upon His Servant [Muhammad] verses of clear evidence that He may bring you out from darknesses into the light. And indeed, Allah is to you Kind and Merciful. (9) And why do you not spend in the cause of Allah while to Allah belongs the heritage of the heavens and the earth? Not equal among you are those who spent before the conquest [of Makkah] and fought [and those who did so after it]. Those are greater in degree than they who spent afterwards and fought. But to all Allah has promised the best [reward]. And Allah, with what you do, is Acquainted. (10) Who is it that would loan Allah a goodly loan so He will multiply it for him and he will have a noble reward? (11) On the Day you see the believing men and believing *women, their light proceeding before them and on their right, [it will be said], "Your good tidings today are [of] gardens beneath which rivers flow, wherein you will abide eternally." That is what is the great attainment. (12) On the [same] Day the hypocrite men and hypocrite women will say to those who believed, "Wait for us that we may acquire some of your light." It will be said, "Go back behind you and seek light." And a wall will be placed between them with a door, its interior containing mercy, but on the outside of it is torment. (13) The hypocrites will call to the believers, "Were we not with you?" They will say, "Yes, but you afflicted yourselves and awaited [misfortune for us] and doubted, and wishful thinking deluded you until there came the command of Allah. And the Deceiver deceived you concerning Allah. (14) So today no ransom will be taken from you or from those who disbelieved. Your refuge is the Fire. It is most worthy of you, and wretched is the destination. (15) Has the time not come for those who have believed that their hearts should become humbly submissive at the remembrance of Allah and what has come down of the truth? And let them not be like those who were given the Scripture before, and a long period passed over them, so their hearts hardened; and many of them are defiantly disobedient. (16) Know that Allah* gives life to the earth after its lifelessness. We have made clear to you the signs; perhaps you will understand. (17) Indeed, the men who practice charity and the women who practice charity and [they who] have loaned Allah a goodly loan - it will be multiplied for them, and they will have a noble reward. (18) And those who have believed in Allah and His messengers - those are [in the ranks of] the supporters of truth and the martyrs, with their Lord. For them is their reward and their light. But those who have disbelieved and denied Our verses - those are the companions of Hellfire. (19)

Quran 57:21-25

سَابِقُوٓا۟ إِلَىٰ مَغْفِرَةٍ مِّن رَّبِّكُمْ وَجَنَّةٍ عَرْضُهَا كَعَرْضِ ٱلسَّمَآءِ وَٱلْأَرْضِ أُعِدَّتْ لِلَّذِينَ ءَامَنُوا۟ بِٱللَّهِ وَرُسُلِهِۦ ۚ ذَٰلِكَ فَضْلُ ٱللَّهِ يُؤْتِيهِ مَن يَشَآءُ ۚ وَٱللَّهُ ذُو ٱلْفَضْلِ ٱلْعَظِيمِ (٢١) مَآ أَصَابَ مِن مُّصِيبَةٍ فِى ٱلْأَرْضِ وَلَا فِىٓ أَنفُسِكُمْ إِلَّا فِى كِتَٰبٍ مِّن قَبْلِ أَن نَّبْرَأَهَآ ۚ إِنَّ ذَٰلِكَ عَلَى ٱللَّهِ يَسِيرٌ (٢٢) لِّكَيْلَا تَأْسَوْا۟ عَلَىٰ مَا فَاتَكُمْ وَلَا تَفْرَحُوا۟ بِمَآ ءَاتَىٰكُمْ ۗ وَٱللَّهُ لَا يُحِبُّ كُلَّ مُخْتَالٍ فَخُورٍ (٢٣) ٱلَّذِينَ يَبْخَلُونَ وَيَأْمُرُونَ ٱلنَّاسَ بِٱلْبُخْلِ ۗ وَمَن يَتَوَلَّ فَإِنَّ ٱللَّهَ هُوَ ٱلْغَنِىُّ ٱلْحَمِيدُ (٢٤) لَقَدْ أَرْسَلْنَا رُسُلَنَا بِٱلْبَيِّنَٰتِ وَأَنزَلْنَا مَعَهُمُ ٱلْكِتَٰبَ وَٱلْمِيزَانَ لِيَقُومَ ٱلنَّاسُ بِٱلْقِسْطِ ۖ وَأَنزَلْنَا ٱلْحَدِيدَ فِيهِ بَأْسٌ شَدِيدٌ وَمَنَٰفِعُ لِلنَّاسِ وَلِيَعْلَمَ ٱللَّهُ مَن يَنصُرُهُۥ وَرُسُلَهُۥ بِٱلْغَيْبِ ۚ إِنَّ ٱللَّهَ قَوِىٌّ عَزِيزٌ (٢٥)

Race toward forgiveness from your Lord and a Garden whose width is like the width of the heavens and earth, prepared for those who believed in Allah and His messengers. That is the bounty of Allah which He gives to whom He wills, and Allah is the possessor of great bounty. (21) No disaster strikes upon the earth or among yourselves except that it is in a register before We bring it into being - indeed that, for Allah, is easy - (22) In order that you not despair over what has eluded you and not exult [in pride] over what He has given you. And Allah does not like everyone self-deluded and boastful - (23) [Those] who are stingy and enjoin upon people stinginess. And whoever turns away - then indeed, Allah is the Free of need, the Praiseworthy. (24) We have already sent Our messengers with clear evidences and sent down with them the Scripture and the balance that the people may maintain [their affairs] in justice. And We sent down iron, wherein is great military might and benefits for the people, and so that Allah may make evident those who support Him and His messengers unseen. Indeed, Allah is Powerful and Exalted in Might. (25)

Quran 58:7-22

أَلَمْ تَرَ أَنَّ ٱللَّهَ يَعْلَمُ مَا فِى ٱلسَّمَٰوَٰتِ وَمَا فِى ٱلْأَرْضِ ۖ مَا يَكُونُ مِن نَّجْوَىٰ ثَلَٰثَةٍ إِلَّا هُوَ رَابِعُهُمْ وَلَا خَمْسَةٍ إِلَّا هُوَ سَادِسُهُمْ وَلَآ أَدْنَىٰ مِن ذَٰلِكَ وَلَآ أَكْثَرَ إِلَّا هُوَ مَعَهُمْ أَيْنَ مَا كَانُوا۟ ۖ ثُمَّ يُنَبِّئُهُم بِمَا عَمِلُوا۟ يَوْمَ ٱلْقِيَٰمَةِ ۚ إِنَّ ٱللَّهَ بِكُلِّ شَىْءٍ عَلِيمٌ (٧) أَلَمْ تَرَ إِلَى ٱلَّذِينَ نُهُوا۟ عَنِ ٱلنَّجْوَىٰ ثُمَّ يَعُودُونَ لِمَا نُهُوا۟ عَنْهُ وَيَتَنَٰجَوْنَ بِٱلْإِثْمِ وَٱلْعُدْوَٰنِ وَمَعْصِيَتِ ٱلرَّسُولِ وَإِذَا جَآءُوكَ حَيَّوْكَ بِمَا لَمْ

يُحَيِّكَ بِهِ ٱللَّهُ وَيَقُولُونَ فِىٓ أَنفُسِهِمْ لَوْلَا يُعَذِّبُنَا ٱللَّهُ بِمَا نَقُولُ ۚ حَسْبُهُمْ جَهَنَّمُ يَصْلَوْنَهَا ۖ فَبِئْسَ ٱلْمَصِيرُ (٨) يَٰٓأَيُّهَا ٱلَّذِينَ ءَامَنُوٓا۟ إِذَا تَنَٰجَيْتُمْ فَلَا تَتَنَٰجَوْا۟ بِٱلْإِثْمِ وَٱلْعُدْوَٰنِ وَمَعْصِيَتِ ٱلرَّسُولِ وَتَنَٰجَوْا۟ بِٱلْبِرِّ وَٱلتَّقْوَىٰ ۖ وَٱتَّقُوا۟ ٱللَّهَ ٱلَّذِىٓ إِلَيْهِ تُحْشَرُونَ (٩) إِنَّمَا ٱلنَّجْوَىٰ مِنَ ٱلشَّيْطَٰنِ لِيَحْزُنَ ٱلَّذِينَ ءَامَنُوا۟ وَلَيْسَ بِضَآرِّهِمْ شَيْـًٔا إِلَّا بِإِذْنِ ٱللَّهِ ۚ وَعَلَى ٱللَّهِ فَلْيَتَوَكَّلِ ٱلْمُؤْمِنُونَ (١٠) يَٰٓأَيُّهَا ٱلَّذِينَ ءَامَنُوٓا۟ إِذَا قِيلَ لَكُمْ تَفَسَّحُوا۟ فِى ٱلْمَجَٰلِسِ فَٱفْسَحُوا۟ يَفْسَحِ ٱللَّهُ لَكُمْ ۖ وَإِذَا قِيلَ ٱنشُزُوا۟ فَٱنشُزُوا۟ يَرْفَعِ ٱللَّهُ ٱلَّذِينَ ءَامَنُوا۟ مِنكُمْ وَٱلَّذِينَ أُوتُوا۟ ٱلْعِلْمَ دَرَجَٰتٍ ۚ وَٱللَّهُ بِمَا تَعْمَلُونَ خَبِيرٌ (١١) يَٰٓأَيُّهَا ٱلَّذِينَ ءَامَنُوٓا۟ إِذَا نَٰجَيْتُمُ ٱلرَّسُولَ فَقَدِّمُوا۟ بَيْنَ يَدَىْ نَجْوَىٰكُمْ صَدَقَةً ۚ ذَٰلِكَ خَيْرٌ لَّكُمْ وَأَطْهَرُ ۚ فَإِن لَّمْ تَجِدُوا۟ فَإِنَّ ٱللَّهَ غَفُورٌ رَّحِيمٌ (١٢) ءَأَشْفَقْتُمْ أَن تُقَدِّمُوا۟ بَيْنَ يَدَىْ نَجْوَىٰكُمْ صَدَقَٰتٍ ۚ فَإِذْ لَمْ تَفْعَلُوا۟ وَتَابَ ٱللَّهُ عَلَيْكُمْ فَأَقِيمُوا۟ ٱلصَّلَوٰةَ وَءَاتُوا۟ ٱلزَّكَوٰةَ وَأَطِيعُوا۟ ٱللَّهَ وَرَسُولَهُۥ ۚ وَٱللَّهُ خَبِيرٌۢ بِمَا تَعْمَلُونَ (١٣) ۞ أَلَمْ تَرَ إِلَى ٱلَّذِينَ تَوَلَّوْا۟ قَوْمًا غَضِبَ ٱللَّهُ عَلَيْهِم مَّا هُم مِّنكُمْ وَلَا مِنْهُمْ وَيَحْلِفُونَ عَلَى ٱلْكَذِبِ وَهُمْ يَعْلَمُونَ (١٤) أَعَدَّ ٱللَّهُ لَهُمْ عَذَابًا شَدِيدًا ۖ إِنَّهُمْ سَآءَ مَا كَانُوا۟ يَعْمَلُونَ (١٥) ٱتَّخَذُوٓا۟ أَيْمَٰنَهُمْ جُنَّةً فَصَدُّوا۟ عَن سَبِيلِ ٱللَّهِ فَلَهُمْ عَذَابٌ مُّهِينٌ (١٦) لَّن تُغْنِىَ عَنْهُمْ أَمْوَٰلُهُمْ وَلَآ أَوْلَٰدُهُم مِّنَ ٱللَّهِ شَيْـًٔا ۚ أُو۟لَٰٓئِكَ أَصْحَٰبُ ٱلنَّارِ ۖ هُمْ فِيهَا خَٰلِدُونَ (١٧) يَوْمَ يَبْعَثُهُمُ ٱللَّهُ جَمِيعًا فَيَحْلِفُونَ لَهُۥ كَمَا يَحْلِفُونَ لَكُمْ ۖ وَيَحْسَبُونَ أَنَّهُمْ عَلَىٰ شَىْءٍ ۚ أَلَآ إِنَّهُمْ هُمُ ٱلْكَٰذِبُونَ (١٨) ٱسْتَحْوَذَ عَلَيْهِمُ ٱلشَّيْطَٰنُ فَأَنسَىٰهُمْ ذِكْرَ ٱللَّهِ ۚ أُو۟لَٰٓئِكَ حِزْبُ ٱلشَّيْطَٰنِ ۚ أَلَآ إِنَّ حِزْبَ ٱلشَّيْطَٰنِ هُمُ ٱلْخَٰسِرُونَ (١٩) إِنَّ ٱلَّذِينَ يُحَآدُّونَ ٱللَّهَ وَرَسُولَهُۥٓ أُو۟لَٰٓئِكَ فِى ٱلْأَذَلِّينَ (٢٠) كَتَبَ ٱللَّهُ لَأَغْلِبَنَّ أَنَا۠ وَرُسُلِىٓ ۚ إِنَّ ٱللَّهَ قَوِىٌّ عَزِيزٌ (٢١) لَّا تَجِدُ قَوْمًا يُؤْمِنُونَ بِٱللَّهِ وَٱلْيَوْمِ ٱلْءَاخِرِ يُوَآدُّونَ مَنْ حَآدَّ ٱللَّهَ وَرَسُولَهُۥ وَلَوْ كَانُوٓا۟ ءَابَآءَهُمْ أَوْ أَبْنَآءَهُمْ أَوْ إِخْوَٰنَهُمْ أَوْ عَشِيرَتَهُمْ ۚ أُو۟لَٰٓئِكَ كَتَبَ فِى قُلُوبِهِمُ ٱلْإِيمَٰنَ وَأَيَّدَهُم بِرُوحٍ مِّنْهُ ۖ وَيُدْخِلُهُمْ جَنَّٰتٍ تَجْرِى مِن تَحْتِهَا ٱلْأَنْهَٰرُ خَٰلِدِينَ فِيهَا ۚ رَضِىَ ٱللَّهُ عَنْهُمْ وَرَضُوا۟ عَنْهُ ۚ أُو۟لَٰٓئِكَ حِزْبُ ٱللَّهِ ۚ أَلَآ إِنَّ حِزْبَ ٱللَّهِ هُمُ ٱلْمُفْلِحُونَ (٢٢)

Have you not considered that Allah knows what is in the heavens and what is on the earth? There is in no private conversation three but that He is the fourth of them, nor are there five but that He is the sixth of them - and no less than that and no more except that He is with them [in knowledge] wherever they are. Then He will inform them of what they did, on the Day of Resurrection. Indeed Allah is, of all things, Knowing. (7) Have you not considered those who were forbidden from private conversation, then they return to that which they were forbidden and converse among themselves about sin and aggression and disobedience to the Messenger? And when they come to you, they greet you with that [word] by which Allah does not greet you and say among themselves, "Why does Allah not punish us for what we say?" Sufficient for them is Hell, which they will [enter to] burn, and wretched is the destination. (8) O you who have believed, when you converse privately, do not converse about sin and aggression and disobedience to the Messenger but converse about righteousness and piety. And fear Allah, to whom you will be gathered. (9) Private conversation is only from Satan that he may grieve those who have believed, but he will not harm them at all except by permission of Allah. And upon Allah let the believers rely. (10) O you who have believed, when you are told, "Space yourselves" in assemblies, then make space; Allah will make space for you. And when you are told, "Arise," then arise; Allah will raise those who have believed among you and those who were given knowledge, by degrees. And Allah is Acquainted with what you do. (11) O you who have believed, when you [wish to] privately consult the Messenger, present before your consultation a charity. That is better for you and purer. But if you find not [the means] - then indeed, Allah is Forgiving and Merciful. (12) Have you feared to present before your consultation charities? Then when you do not and Allah has forgiven you, then [at least] establish prayer and give zakah and obey Allah and His Messenger. And Allah is Acquainted with what you do. (13) Have you not considered those who make allies of a people with whom Allah has become angry? They are neither of you nor of them, and they swear to untruth while they know [they are lying]. (14) Allah has prepared for them a severe punishment. Indeed, it was evil that they were doing. (15) They took their [false] oaths as a cover, so they averted [people] from the way of Allah, and for them is a humiliating punishment. (16) Never will their wealth or their children avail them against Allah at all. Those are the companions of the Fire; they will abide therein eternally (17) On the Day Allah will resurrect them all, and they will swear to Him as they swear to you and think that they are [standing] on something. Unquestionably, it is they who are the liars. (18) Satan has overcome them and made them forget the remembrance of Allah. Those are the party of Satan. Unquestionably, the party of Satan - they will be the losers. (19) Indeed, the ones who oppose Allah and His Messenger - those will be among the most humbled. (20) Allah has written, "I will surely overcome, I and My messengers." Indeed, Allah is Powerful and Exalted in Might. (21) You will not find a people who believe in Allah and the Last Day having affection for those who oppose Allah and His Messenger, even if they were their fathers or their sons or their brothers or their kindred. Those - He has decreed within their hearts faith and supported them with spirit from Him. And We will admit them to gardens beneath which rivers flow, wherein they abide eternally. Allah is pleased with them, and they are pleased with Him - those are the party of Allah. Unquestionably, the party of Allah - they are the successful. (22)

Quran 59:18-19

يَـٰٓأَيُّهَا ٱلَّذِينَ ءَامَنُوا۟ ٱتَّقُوا۟ ٱللَّهَ وَلْتَنظُرْ نَفْسٌ مَّا قَدَّمَتْ لِغَدٍۢ ۖ وَٱتَّقُوا۟ ٱللَّهَ ۚ إِنَّ ٱللَّهَ خَبِيرٌۢ بِمَا تَعْمَلُونَ (١٨) وَلَا تَكُونُوا۟ كَٱلَّذِينَ نَسُوا۟ ٱللَّهَ فَأَنسَىٰهُمْ أَنفُسَهُمْ ۚ أُو۟لَـٰٓئِكَ هُمُ ٱلْفَـٰسِقُونَ (١٩)

O you who have believed, fear Allah. And let every soul look to what it has put forth for tomorrow - and fear Allah. Indeed, Allah is Acquainted with what you do. (18) And be not like those who forgot Allah, so He made them forget themselves. Those are the defiantly disobedient. (19)

Quran 60:1-6

يَٰٓأَيُّهَا ٱلَّذِينَ ءَامَنُوا۟ لَا تَتَّخِذُوا۟ عَدُوِّى وَعَدُوَّكُمْ أَوْلِيَآءَ تُلْقُونَ إِلَيْهِم بِٱلْمَوَدَّةِ وَقَدْ كَفَرُوا۟ بِمَا جَآءَكُم مِّنَ ٱلْحَقِّ يُخْرِجُونَ ٱلرَّسُولَ وَإِيَّاكُمْ أَن تُؤْمِنُوا۟ بِٱللَّهِ رَبِّكُمْ إِن كُنتُمْ خَرَجْتُمْ جِهَٰدًا فِى سَبِيلِى وَٱبْتِغَآءَ مَرْضَاتِى تُسِرُّونَ إِلَيْهِم بِٱلْمَوَدَّةِ وَأَنَا۠ أَعْلَمُ بِمَآ أَخْفَيْتُمْ وَمَآ أَعْلَنتُمْ وَمَن يَفْعَلْهُ مِنكُمْ فَقَدْ ضَلَّ سَوَآءَ ٱلسَّبِيلِ (١) إِن يَثْقَفُوكُمْ يَكُونُوا۟ لَكُمْ أَعْدَآءً وَيَبْسُطُوٓا۟ إِلَيْكُمْ أَيْدِيَهُمْ وَأَلْسِنَتَهُم بِٱلسُّوٓءِ وَوَدُّوا۟ لَوْ تَكْفُرُونَ (٢) لَن تَنفَعَكُمْ أَرْحَامُكُمْ وَلَآ أَوْلَٰدُكُمْ يَوْمَ ٱلْقِيَٰمَةِ يَفْصِلُ بَيْنَكُمْ وَٱللَّهُ بِمَا تَعْمَلُونَ بَصِيرٌ (٣) قَدْ كَانَتْ لَكُمْ أُسْوَةٌ حَسَنَةٌ فِىٓ إِبْرَٰهِيمَ وَٱلَّذِينَ مَعَهُۥٓ إِذْ قَالُوا۟ لِقَوْمِهِمْ إِنَّا بُرَءَٰٓؤُا۟ مِنكُمْ وَمِمَّا تَعْبُدُونَ مِن دُونِ ٱللَّهِ كَفَرْنَا بِكُمْ وَبَدَا بَيْنَنَا وَبَيْنَكُمُ ٱلْعَدَٰوَةُ وَٱلْبَغْضَآءُ أَبَدًا حَتَّىٰ تُؤْمِنُوا۟ بِٱللَّهِ وَحْدَهُۥٓ إِلَّا قَوْلَ إِبْرَٰهِيمَ لِأَبِيهِ لَأَسْتَغْفِرَنَّ لَكَ وَمَآ أَمْلِكُ لَكَ مِنَ ٱللَّهِ مِن شَىْءٍ ۖ رَّبَّنَا عَلَيْكَ تَوَكَّلْنَا وَإِلَيْكَ أَنَبْنَا وَإِلَيْكَ ٱلْمَصِيرُ (٤) رَبَّنَا لَا تَجْعَلْنَا فِتْنَةً لِّلَّذِينَ كَفَرُوا۟ وَٱغْفِرْ لَنَا رَبَّنَآ إِنَّكَ أَنتَ ٱلْعَزِيزُ ٱلْحَكِيمُ (٥) لَقَدْ كَانَ لَكُمْ فِيهِمْ أُسْوَةٌ حَسَنَةٌ لِّمَن كَانَ يَرْجُوا۟ ٱللَّهَ وَٱلْيَوْمَ ٱلْءَاخِرَ وَمَن يَتَوَلَّ فَإِنَّ ٱللَّهَ هُوَ ٱلْغَنِىُّ ٱلْحَمِيدُ (٦)

O you who have believed, do not take My enemies and your enemies as allies, extending to them affection while they have disbelieved in what came to you of the truth, having driven out the Prophet and yourselves [only] *because you believe in Allah, your Lord. If you have come out for jihad in My cause and seeking means to My approval, [take them not as friends]. You confide to them affection, but I am most knowing of what you have concealed and what you have declared. And whoever does it among you has certainly strayed from the soundness of the way. (1) If they gain dominance over you, they would be to you as enemies and extend against you their hands and their tongues with evil, and they wish you would disbelieve. (2) Never will your relatives or your children benefit you; the Day of Resurrection He will judge between you. And Allah, of what you do, is Seeing. (3) There has already been for you an excellent pattern in Abraham and those with him, when they said to their people, "Indeed, we are disassociated from you and from whatever you worship other than Allah. We have denied you, and there has appeared between us and you animosity and hatred forever until you believe in Allah alone" except for the saying of Abraham to his father, "I will surely ask forgiveness for you, but I have not [power to do] for you anything against Allah. Our Lord, upon You we have relied, and to You we have returned, and to You is the destination. (4) Our Lord, make us not [objects of] torment for the disbelievers and forgive us, our Lord. Indeed, it is You who is the Exalted in Might,* the Wise." (5) There has certainly been for you in them an excellent pattern for anyone whose hope is in Allah and the Last Day. And whoever turns away - then indeed, Allah is the Free of need, the Praiseworthy. (6)

Quran 60:10-13

يَـٰٓأَيُّهَا ٱلَّذِينَ ءَامَنُوٓاْ إِذَا جَآءَكُمُ ٱلْمُؤْمِنَـٰتُ مُهَـٰجِرَٰتٍ فَٱمْتَحِنُوهُنَّۖ ٱللَّهُ أَعْلَمُ بِإِيمَـٰنِهِنَّۖ فَإِنْ عَلِمْتُمُوهُنَّ مُؤْمِنَـٰتٍ فَلَا تَرْجِعُوهُنَّ إِلَى ٱلْكُفَّارِۖ لَا هُنَّ حِلٌّ لَّهُمْ وَلَا هُمْ يَحِلُّونَ لَهُنَّۖ وَءَاتُوهُم مَّآ أَنفَقُواْۚ وَلَا جُنَاحَ عَلَيْكُمْ أَن تَنكِحُوهُنَّ إِذَآ ءَاتَيْتُمُوهُنَّ أُجُورَهُنَّۚ وَلَا تُمْسِكُواْ بِعِصَمِ ٱلْكَوَافِرِ وَسْـَٔلُواْ مَآ أَنفَقْتُمْ وَلْيَسْـَٔلُواْ مَآ أَنفَقُواْۚ ذَٰلِكُمْ حُكْمُ ٱللَّهِۖ يَحْكُمُ بَيْنَكُمْۚ وَٱللَّهُ عَلِيمٌ حَكِيمٌ (١٠) وَإِن فَاتَكُمْ شَىْءٌ مِّنْ أَزْوَٰجِكُمْ إِلَى ٱلْكُفَّارِ فَعَاقَبْتُمْ فَـَٔاتُواْ ٱلَّذِينَ ذَهَبَتْ أَزْوَٰجُهُم مِّثْلَ مَآ أَنفَقُواْۚ وَٱتَّقُواْ ٱللَّهَ ٱلَّذِىٓ أَنتُم بِهِۦ مُؤْمِنُونَ (١١) يَـٰٓأَيُّهَا ٱلنَّبِىُّ إِذَا جَآءَكَ ٱلْمُؤْمِنَـٰتُ يُبَايِعْنَكَ عَلَىٰٓ أَن لَّا يُشْرِكْنَ بِٱللَّهِ شَيْـًٔا وَلَا يَسْرِقْنَ وَلَا يَزْنِينَ وَلَا يَقْتُلْنَ أَوْلَـٰدَهُنَّ وَلَا يَأْتِينَ بِبُهْتَـٰنٍ يَفْتَرِينَهُۥ بَيْنَ أَيْدِيهِنَّ وَأَرْجُلِهِنَّ وَلَا يَعْصِينَكَ فِى مَعْرُوفٍۙ فَبَايِعْهُنَّ وَٱسْتَغْفِرْ لَهُنَّ ٱللَّهَۚ إِنَّ ٱللَّهَ غَفُورٌ رَّحِيمٌ (١٢) يَـٰٓأَيُّهَا ٱلَّذِينَ ءَامَنُواْ لَا تَتَوَلَّوْاْ قَوْمًا غَضِبَ ٱللَّهُ عَلَيْهِمْ قَدْ يَئِسُواْ مِنَ ٱلْـَٔاخِرَةِ كَمَا يَئِسَ ٱلْكُفَّارُ مِنْ أَصْحَـٰبِ ٱلْقُبُورِ (١٣)

O you who have believed, when the believing women come to you as emigrants, examine them. Allah is most knowing as to their faith. And if you know them to be believers, then do not return them to the disbelievers; they are not lawful [wives] for them, nor are they lawful [husbands] for them. But give the disbelievers what they have spent. And there is no blame upon you if you marry them when you have given them their due compensation.

And hold not to marriage bonds with disbelieving women, but ask for what you have spent and let them ask for what they have spent. That is the judgement of Allah; He judges between you. And Allah is Knowing and Wise. (10) And if you have lost any of your wives to the disbelievers and you subsequently obtain [something], then give those whose wives have gone the equivalent of what they had spent. And fear Allah, in whom you are believers. (11) O Prophet, when the believing women come to you pledging to you that they will not associate anything with Allah, nor will they steal, nor will they commit unlawful sexual intercourse, nor will they kill their children, nor will they bring forth a slander they have invented between their arms and legs, nor will they disobey you in what is right - then accept their pledge and ask forgiveness for them of Allah. Indeed, Allah is Forgiving and Merciful. (12) O you who have believed, do not make allies of a people with whom Allah has become angry. They have despaired of [reward in] the Hereafter just as the disbelievers have despaired of [meeting] the inhabitants of the graves. (13)

Quran 61:2-3

يَـٰٓأَيُّهَا ٱلَّذِينَ ءَامَنُوا۟ لِمَ تَقُولُونَ مَا لَا تَفْعَلُونَ (٢) كَبُرَ مَقْتًا عِندَ ٱللَّهِ أَن تَقُولُوا۟ مَا لَا تَفْعَلُونَ (٣)

O you who have believed, why do you say what you do not do? (2) Great is hatred in the sight of Allah that you say what you do not do. (3)

Quran 62:9-11

يَـٰٓأَيُّهَا ٱلَّذِينَ ءَامَنُوٓا۟ إِذَا نُودِىَ لِلصَّلَوٰةِ مِن يَوْمِ ٱلْجُمُعَةِ فَٱسْعَوْا۟ إِلَىٰ ذِكْرِ ٱللَّهِ وَذَرُوا۟ ٱلْبَيْعَ ۚ ذَٰلِكُمْ خَيْرٌ لَّكُمْ إِن كُنتُمْ تَعْلَمُونَ (٩) فَإِذَا قُضِيَتِ ٱلصَّلَوٰةُ فَٱنتَشِرُوا۟ فِى ٱلْأَرْضِ وَٱبْتَغُوا۟ مِن فَضْلِ ٱللَّهِ وَٱذْكُرُوا۟ ٱللَّهَ كَثِيرًا لَّعَلَّكُمْ تُفْلِحُونَ (١٠) وَإِذَا رَأَوْا۟ تِجَـٰرَةً أَوْ لَهْوًا ٱنفَضُّوٓا۟ إِلَيْهَا وَتَرَكُوكَ قَآئِمًا ۚ قُلْ مَا عِندَ ٱللَّهِ خَيْرٌ مِّنَ ٱللَّهْوِ وَمِنَ ٱلتِّجَـٰرَةِ ۚ وَٱللَّهُ خَيْرُ ٱلرَّٰزِقِينَ (١١)

O you who have believed, when [the adhan] is called for the prayer on the day of Jumu'ah [Friday], then proceed to the remembrance of Allah and leave trade. That is better for you, if you only knew. (9) And when the prayer has been concluded, disperse within the land and seek from the bounty of Allah, and remember Allah often that you may succeed. (10) But when they saw a transaction or a diversion, [O Muhammad], they rushed to it and left you standing. Say, "What is with Allah is better than diversion and than a transaction, and Allah is the best of providers." (11)

Quran 63:1-5

إِذَا جَآءَكَ ٱلْمُنَـٰفِقُونَ قَالُوا۟ نَشْهَدُ إِنَّكَ لَرَسُولُ ٱللَّهِ ۗ وَٱللَّهُ يَعْلَمُ إِنَّكَ لَرَسُولُهُۥ وَٱللَّهُ يَشْهَدُ إِنَّ ٱلْمُنَـٰفِقِينَ لَكَـٰذِبُونَ (١) ٱتَّخَذُوٓا۟ أَيْمَـٰنَهُمْ جُنَّةً فَصَدُّوا۟ عَن سَبِيلِ ٱللَّهِ ۚ إِنَّهُمْ سَآءَ مَا كَانُوا۟ يَعْمَلُونَ (٢) ذَٰلِكَ بِأَنَّهُمْ ءَامَنُوا۟ ثُمَّ كَفَرُوا۟ فَطُبِعَ عَلَىٰ قُلُوبِهِمْ

فَهُمْ لَا يَفْقَهُونَ (٣) ۞ وَإِذَا رَأَيْتَهُمْ تُعْجِبُكَ أَجْسَامُهُمْ ۖ وَإِن يَقُولُوا تَسْمَعْ لِقَوْلِهِمْ ۖ كَأَنَّهُمْ خُشُبٌ مُّسَنَّدَةٌ ۖ يَحْسَبُونَ كُلَّ صَيْحَةٍ عَلَيْهِمْ ۚ هُمُ ٱلْعَدُوُّ فَٱحْذَرْهُمْ ۚ قَاتَلَهُمُ ٱللَّهُ ۖ أَنَّىٰ يُؤْفَكُونَ (٤) وَإِذَا قِيلَ لَهُمْ تَعَالَوْا يَسْتَغْفِرْ لَكُمْ رَسُولُ ٱللَّهِ لَوَّوْا رُءُوسَهُمْ وَرَأَيْتَهُمْ يَصُدُّونَ وَهُم مُّسْتَكْبِرُونَ (٥)

When the hypocrites come to you, [O Muhammad], they say, "We testify that you are the Messenger of Allah." And Allah knows that you are His Messenger, and Allah testifies that the hypocrites are liars. (1) They have taken their oaths as a cover, so they averted [people] from the way of Allah. Indeed, it was evil that they were doing. (2) That is because they believed, and then they disbelieved; so their hearts were sealed over, and they do not understand. (3) And when you see them, their forms please you, and if they speak, you listen to their speech. [They are] as if they were pieces of wood propped up - they think that every shout is against them. They are the enemy, so beware of them. May Allah destroy them; how are they deluded? (4) And when it is said to them, "Come, the Messenger of Allah will ask forgiveness for you," they turn their heads aside and you see them evading while they are arrogant. (5)

Quran 63:9-11

يَـٰٓأَيُّهَا ٱلَّذِينَ ءَامَنُوا لَا تُلْهِكُمْ أَمْوَٰلُكُمْ وَلَآ أَوْلَـٰدُكُمْ عَن ذِكْرِ ٱللَّهِ ۚ وَمَن يَفْعَلْ ذَٰلِكَ فَأُوْلَـٰٓئِكَ هُمُ ٱلْخَـٰسِرُونَ (٩) وَأَنفِقُوا مِن مَّا رَزَقْنَـٰكُم مِّن قَبْلِ أَن يَأْتِىَ

أَحَدَكُمُ ٱلْمَوْتُ فَيَقُولَ رَبِّ لَوْلَا أَخَّرْتَنِى إِلَىٰ أَجَلٍ قَرِيبٍ فَأَصَّدَّقَ وَأَكُن مِّنَ ٱلصَّٰلِحِينَ (١٠) وَلَن يُؤَخِّرَ ٱللَّهُ نَفْسًا إِذَا جَآءَ أَجَلُهَا ۚ وَٱللَّهُ خَبِيرٌۢ بِمَا تَعْمَلُونَ (١١)

O you who have believed, let not your wealth and your children divert you from remembrance of Allah. And whoever does that - then those are the losers. (9) And spend [in the way of Allah] from what We have provided you before death approaches one of you and he says, "My Lord, if only You would delay me for a brief term so I would give charity and be among the righteous." (10) But never will Allah delay a soul when its time has come. And Allah is Acquainted with what you do. (11)

Quran 64:12-17

وَأَطِيعُوا۟ ٱللَّهَ وَأَطِيعُوا۟ ٱلرَّسُولَ ۚ فَإِن تَوَلَّيْتُمْ فَإِنَّمَا عَلَىٰ رَسُولِنَا ٱلْبَلَٰغُ ٱلْمُبِينُ (١٢) ٱللَّهُ لَآ إِلَٰهَ إِلَّا هُوَ ۚ وَعَلَى ٱللَّهِ فَلْيَتَوَكَّلِ ٱلْمُؤْمِنُونَ (١٣) يَٰٓأَيُّهَا ٱلَّذِينَ ءَامَنُوٓا۟ إِنَّ مِنْ أَزْوَٰجِكُمْ وَأَوْلَٰدِكُمْ عَدُوًّا لَّكُمْ فَٱحْذَرُوهُمْ ۚ وَإِن تَعْفُوا۟ وَتَصْفَحُوا۟ وَتَغْفِرُوا۟ فَإِنَّ ٱللَّهَ غَفُورٌ رَّحِيمٌ (١٤) إِنَّمَآ أَمْوَٰلُكُمْ وَأَوْلَٰدُكُمْ فِتْنَةٌ ۚ وَٱللَّهُ عِندَهُۥٓ أَجْرٌ عَظِيمٌ (١٥) فَٱتَّقُوا۟ ٱللَّهَ مَا ٱسْتَطَعْتُمْ وَٱسْمَعُوا۟ وَأَطِيعُوا۟ وَأَنفِقُوا۟ خَيْرًا لِّأَنفُسِكُمْ ۗ وَمَن يُوقَ شُحَّ نَفْسِهِۦ فَأُو۟لَٰٓئِكَ هُمُ ٱلْمُفْلِحُونَ (١٦) إِن تُقْرِضُوا۟ ٱللَّهَ قَرْضًا حَسَنًا يُضَٰعِفْهُ لَكُمْ وَيَغْفِرْ لَكُمْ ۚ وَٱللَّهُ شَكُورٌ حَلِيمٌ (١٧)

And obey Allah and obey the Messenger; but if you turn away - then upon Our Messenger is only [the duty of] clear notification. (12) Allah - there is no deity except Him. And upon Allah let the believers rely. (13) O you who have believed, indeed, among your wives and your children are enemies to you, so beware of them. But if you pardon and overlook and forgive - then indeed, Allah is Forgiving and Merciful. (14) Your wealth and your children are but a trial, and Allah has with Him a great reward. (15) So fear Allah as much as you are able and listen and obey and spend [in the way of Allah]; it is better for your selves. And whoever is protected from the stinginess of his soul - it is those who will be the successful. (16) If you loan Allah a goodly loan, He will multiply it for you and forgive you. And Allah is Most Appreciative and Forbearing. (17)

Quran 65:1-7

يَٰٓأَيُّهَا ٱلنَّبِىُّ إِذَا طَلَّقْتُمُ ٱلنِّسَآءَ فَطَلِّقُوهُنَّ لِعِدَّتِهِنَّ وَأَحْصُوا۟ ٱلْعِدَّةَ ۖ وَٱتَّقُوا۟ ٱللَّهَ رَبَّكُمْ ۖ لَا تُخْرِجُوهُنَّ مِنۢ بُيُوتِهِنَّ وَلَا يَخْرُجْنَ إِلَّآ أَن يَأْتِينَ بِفَٰحِشَةٍ مُّبَيِّنَةٍ ۚ وَتِلْكَ حُدُودُ ٱللَّهِ ۚ وَمَن يَتَعَدَّ حُدُودَ ٱللَّهِ فَقَدْ ظَلَمَ نَفْسَهُۥ ۚ لَا تَدْرِى لَعَلَّ ٱللَّهَ يُحْدِثُ بَعْدَ ذَٰلِكَ أَمْرًا (١) فَإِذَا بَلَغْنَ أَجَلَهُنَّ فَأَمْسِكُوهُنَّ بِمَعْرُوفٍ أَوْ فَارِقُوهُنَّ بِمَعْرُوفٍ وَأَشْهِدُوا۟ ذَوَىْ عَدْلٍ مِّنكُمْ وَأَقِيمُوا۟ ٱلشَّهَٰدَةَ لِلَّهِ ۚ ذَٰلِكُمْ يُوعَظُ بِهِۦ مَن كَانَ يُؤْمِنُ بِٱللَّهِ وَٱلْيَوْمِ ٱلْءَاخِرِ ۚ وَمَن يَتَّقِ ٱللَّهَ يَجْعَل لَّهُۥ مَخْرَجًا (٢) وَيَرْزُقْهُ مِنْ حَيْثُ لَا يَحْتَسِبُ ۚ وَمَن يَتَوَكَّلْ عَلَى ٱللَّهِ فَهُوَ حَسْبُهُۥٓ ۚ إِنَّ ٱللَّهَ بَٰلِغُ أَمْرِهِۦ ۚ قَدْ جَعَلَ ٱللَّهُ لِكُلِّ شَىْءٍ قَدْرًا (٣) وَٱلَّٰٓـِٔى يَئِسْنَ مِنَ ٱلْمَحِيضِ مِن نِّسَآئِكُمْ إِنِ ٱرْتَبْتُمْ فَعِدَّتُهُنَّ ثَلَٰثَةُ أَشْهُرٍ وَٱلَّٰٓـِٔى لَمْ يَحِضْنَ ۚ وَأُو۟لَٰتُ ٱلْأَحْمَالِ أَجَلُهُنَّ أَن يَضَعْنَ حَمْلَهُنَّ ۚ وَمَن يَتَّقِ ٱللَّهَ يَجْعَل لَّهُۥ مِنْ أَمْرِهِۦ يُسْرًا (٤) ذَٰلِكَ أَمْرُ ٱللَّهِ أَنزَلَهُۥٓ إِلَيْكُمْ ۚ وَمَن يَتَّقِ ٱللَّهَ يُكَفِّرْ عَنْهُ سَيِّـَٔاتِهِۦ وَيُعْظِمْ لَهُۥٓ أَجْرًا (٥) أَسْكِنُوهُنَّ مِنْ حَيْثُ سَكَنتُم مِّن وُجْدِكُمْ وَلَا تُضَآرُّوهُنَّ لِتُضَيِّقُوا۟ عَلَيْهِنَّ

وَإِن كُنَّ أُوْلَٰتِ حَمْلٍ فَأَنفِقُواْ عَلَيْهِنَّ حَتَّىٰ يَضَعْنَ حَمْلَهُنَّ ۚ فَإِنْ أَرْضَعْنَ لَكُمْ فَـَٔاتُوهُنَّ أُجُورَهُنَّ ۖ وَأْتَمِرُواْ بَيْنَكُم بِمَعْرُوفٍ ۖ وَإِن تَعَاسَرْتُمْ فَسَتُرْضِعُ لَهُۥٓ أُخْرَىٰ (٦) لِيُنفِقْ ذُو سَعَةٍ مِّن سَعَتِهِۦ ۖ وَمَن قُدِرَ عَلَيْهِ رِزْقُهُۥ فَلْيُنفِقْ مِمَّآ ءَاتَىٰهُ ٱللَّهُ ۚ لَا يُكَلِّفُ ٱللَّهُ نَفْسًا إِلَّا مَآ ءَاتَىٰهَا ۚ سَيَجْعَلُ ٱللَّهُ بَعْدَ عُسْرٍ يُسْرًا (٧)

O Prophet, when you [Muslims] divorce women, divorce them for [the commencement of] their waiting period and keep count of the waiting period, and fear Allah, your Lord. Do not turn them out of their [husbands'] houses, nor should they [themselves] leave [during that period] unless they are committing a clear immorality. And those are the limits [set by] Allah. And whoever transgresses the limits of Allah has certainly wronged himself. You know not; perhaps Allah will bring about after that a [different] matter. (1) And when they have [nearly] fulfilled their term, either retain them according to acceptable terms or part with them according to acceptable terms. And bring to witness two just men from among you and establish the testimony for [the acceptance of] Allah. That is instructed to whoever should believe in Allah and the Last day. And whoever fears Allah - He will make for him a way out (2) And will provide for him from where he does not expect. And whoever relies upon Allah - then He is sufficient for him. Indeed, Allah will accomplish His purpose. Allah has already set for everything a [decreed] extent. (3) And those who no longer expect menstruation among your women - if you doubt, then their period is three months, and [also for] those who have not menstruated. And for those who are pregnant, their term is until they give birth. And whoever fears Allah - He will make for him of his matter ease. (4) That is the command of Allah, which He has sent down to you; and whoever fears Allah - He will remove for him his misdeeds and make great for him his reward. (5) Lodge them [in a section] of where you dwell out of your means and do not harm them in order to oppress them. And if they should be pregnant, then spend on them until they give birth. And if they breastfeed for you, then give them their payment and confer among yourselves in the acceptable way; but if you are in discord, then there may breastfeed for the father another woman. (6) Let a man of wealth spend from his wealth, and he whose provision is restricted - let him spend from what Allah has given him. Allah does not charge a soul except [according to] what He has given it. Allah will bring about, after hardship, ease. (7)

Quran 66:6

يَـٰٓأَيُّهَا ٱلَّذِينَ ءَامَنُوا۟ قُوٓا۟ أَنفُسَكُمْ وَأَهْلِيكُمْ نَارًا وَقُودُهَا ٱلنَّاسُ وَٱلْحِجَارَةُ عَلَيْهَا مَلَـٰٓئِكَةٌ غِلَاظٌ شِدَادٌ لَّا يَعْصُونَ ٱللَّهَ مَآ أَمَرَهُمْ وَيَفْعَلُونَ مَا يُؤْمَرُونَ (٦)

O you who have believed, protect yourselves and your families from a Fire whose fuel is people and stones, over which are [appointed] angels, harsh and severe; they do not disobey Allah in what He commands them but do what they are commanded. (6)

Quran 66:8-9

يَـٰٓأَيُّهَا ٱلَّذِينَ ءَامَنُوا۟ تُوبُوٓا۟ إِلَى ٱللَّهِ تَوْبَةً نَّصُوحًا عَسَىٰ رَبُّكُمْ أَن يُكَفِّرَ عَنكُمْ سَيِّـَٔاتِكُمْ وَيُدْخِلَكُمْ جَنَّـٰتٍ تَجْرِى مِن تَحْتِهَا ٱلْأَنْهَـٰرُ يَوْمَ لَا يُخْزِى ٱللَّهُ ٱلنَّبِىَّ وَٱلَّذِينَ ءَامَنُوا۟ مَعَهُۥ نُورُهُمْ يَسْعَىٰ بَيْنَ أَيْدِيهِمْ وَبِأَيْمَـٰنِهِمْ يَقُولُونَ رَبَّنَآ أَتْمِمْ لَنَا نُورَنَا وَٱغْفِرْ لَنَآ إِنَّكَ عَلَىٰ كُلِّ شَىْءٍ قَدِيرٌ (٨) يَـٰٓأَيُّهَا ٱلنَّبِىُّ جَـٰهِدِ ٱلْكُفَّارَ وَٱلْمُنَـٰفِقِينَ وَٱغْلُظْ عَلَيْهِمْ وَمَأْوَىٰهُمْ جَهَنَّمُ وَبِئْسَ ٱلْمَصِيرُ (٩)

O you who have believed, repent to Allah with sincere repentance. Perhaps your Lord will remove from you your misdeeds and admit you into gardens beneath which rivers flow [on] the Day when Allah will not disgrace the Prophet and those who believed with him. Their light will proceed before them and on their right; they will say, "Our Lord, perfect for us our light and forgive us. Indeed, You are over all things competent." (8) O Prophet, strive against the disbelievers and the hypocrites and be harsh upon them. And their refuge is Hell, and wretched is the destination. (9)

Quran 68:8-15

فَلَا تُطِعِ ٱلْمُكَذِّبِينَ (٨) وَدُّوا لَوْ تُدْهِنُ فَيُدْهِنُونَ (٩) وَلَا تُطِعْ كُلَّ حَلَّافٍ مَّهِينٍ (١٠) هَمَّازٍ مَّشَّاءٍ بِنَمِيمٍ (١١) مَّنَّاعٍ لِّلْخَيْرِ مُعْتَدٍ أَثِيمٍ (١٢) عُتُلٍّ بَعْدَ ذَٰلِكَ زَنِيمٍ (١٣) أَن كَانَ ذَا مَالٍ وَبَنِينَ (١٤) إِذَا تُتْلَىٰ عَلَيْهِ ءَايَٰتُنَا قَالَ أَسَٰطِيرُ ٱلْأَوَّلِينَ (١٥)

Then do not obey the deniers. (8) They wish that you would soften [in your position], so they would soften [toward you]. (9) And do not obey every worthless habitual swearer (10) [And] scorner, going about with malicious gossip – (11) A preventer of good, transgressing and sinful, (12) Cruel, moreover, and an illegitimate pretender. (13) Because he is a possessor of wealth and children, (14) When Our verses are recited to him, he says, "Legends of the former peoples." (15)

Quran 68:44-48

فَذَرْنِي وَمَن يُكَذِّبُ بِهَٰذَا ٱلْحَدِيثِ سَنَسْتَدْرِجُهُم مِّنْ حَيْثُ لَا يَعْلَمُونَ (٤٤) وَأُمْلِي لَهُمْ إِنَّ كَيْدِي مَتِينٌ (٤٥) أَمْ تَسْـَٔلُهُمْ أَجْرًا فَهُم مِّن مَّغْرَمٍ مُّثْقَلُونَ (٤٦) أَمْ عِندَهُمُ ٱلْغَيْبُ فَهُمْ يَكْتُبُونَ (٤٧) فَٱصْبِرْ لِحُكْمِ رَبِّكَ وَلَا تَكُن كَصَاحِبِ ٱلْحُوتِ إِذْ نَادَىٰ وَهُوَ مَكْظُومٌ (٤٨)

So leave Me, with [the matter of] whoever denies the Qur'an. We will progressively lead them [to punishment] from where they do not know. (44) And I will give them time. Indeed, My plan is firm. (45) Or do you ask of them a payment, so they are by debt burdened down? (46) Or have they [knowledge of] the unseen, so they write [it] down? (47) Then be patient for the decision of your Lord, and be not like the companion of the fish when he called out while he was distressed. (48)

Quran 70:23-35

ٱلَّذِينَ هُمْ عَلَىٰ صَلَاتِهِمْ دَآئِمُونَ (٢٣) وَٱلَّذِينَ فِىٓ أَمْوَٰلِهِمْ حَقٌّ مَّعْلُومٌ (٢٤) لِّلسَّآئِلِ وَٱلْمَحْرُومِ (٢٥) وَٱلَّذِينَ يُصَدِّقُونَ بِيَوْمِ ٱلدِّينِ (٢٦) وَٱلَّذِينَ هُم مِّنْ عَذَابِ رَبِّهِم مُّشْفِقُونَ (٢٧) إِنَّ عَذَابَ رَبِّهِمْ غَيْرُ مَأْمُونٍ (٢٨) وَٱلَّذِينَ هُمْ لِفُرُوجِهِمْ حَٰفِظُونَ (٢٩) إِلَّا عَلَىٰٓ أَزْوَٰجِهِمْ أَوْ مَا مَلَكَتْ أَيْمَٰنُهُمْ فَإِنَّهُمْ غَيْرُ مَلُومِينَ (٣٠) فَمَنِ ٱبْتَغَىٰ وَرَآءَ ذَٰلِكَ فَأُو۟لَٰٓئِكَ هُمُ ٱلْعَادُونَ (٣١) وَٱلَّذِينَ هُمْ لِأَمَٰنَٰتِهِمْ وَعَهْدِهِمْ رَٰعُونَ (٣٢) وَٱلَّذِينَ هُم بِشَهَٰدَٰتِهِمْ قَآئِمُونَ (٣٣) وَٱلَّذِينَ هُمْ عَلَىٰ صَلَاتِهِمْ يُحَافِظُونَ (٣٤) أُو۟لَٰٓئِكَ فِى جَنَّٰتٍ مُّكْرَمُونَ (٣٥)

Those who are constant in their prayer (23) And those within whose wealth is a known right (24) For the petitioner and the deprived - (25) And those who believe in the Day of Recompense (26) And those who are fearful of the punishment of their Lord - (27) Indeed, the punishment of their Lord is not that from which one is safe - (28) And those who guard their private parts (29) Except from their wives or those their right hands possess, for indeed, they are not to be blamed - (30) But whoever seeks beyond that, then they are the transgressors - (31) And those who are to their trusts and promises attentive (32) And those who are in their testimonies upright (33) And those who [carefully] maintain their prayer: (34) They will be in gardens, honored. (35)

Quran 70:42-44

فَذَرْهُمْ يَخُوضُوا۟ وَيَلْعَبُوا۟ حَتَّىٰ يُلَـٰقُوا۟ يَوْمَهُمُ ٱلَّذِى يُوعَدُونَ (٤٢) يَوْمَ يَخْرُجُونَ مِنَ ٱلْأَجْدَاثِ سِرَاعًۭا كَأَنَّهُمْ إِلَىٰ نُصُبٍۢ يُوفِضُونَ (٤٣) خَـٰشِعَةً أَبْصَـٰرُهُمْ تَرْهَقُهُمْ ذِلَّةٌۭ ذَٰلِكَ ٱلْيَوْمُ ٱلَّذِى كَانُوا۟ يُوعَدُونَ (٤٤)

So leave them to converse vainly and amuse themselves until they meet their Day which they are promised - (42) The Day they will emerge from the graves rapidly as if they were, toward an erected idol, hastening. (43) Their eyes humbled, humiliation will cover them. That is the Day which they had been promised. (44)

Quran 72:1-4

قُلْ أُوحِىَ إِلَىَّ أَنَّهُ ٱسْتَمَعَ نَفَرٌۭ مِّنَ ٱلْجِنِّ فَقَالُوٓا۟ إِنَّا سَمِعْنَا قُرْءَانًا عَجَبًۭا (١) يَهْدِىٓ إِلَى ٱلرُّشْدِ فَـَٔامَنَّا بِهِۦ ۖ وَلَن نُّشْرِكَ بِرَبِّنَآ أَحَدًۭا (٢) وَأَنَّهُۥ تَعَـٰلَىٰ جَدُّ رَبِّنَا مَا ٱتَّخَذَ صَـٰحِبَةًۭ وَلَا وَلَدًۭا (٣) وَأَنَّهُۥ كَانَ يَقُولُ سَفِيهُنَا عَلَى ٱللَّهِ شَطَطًۭا (٤)

Say, [O Muhammad], "It has been revealed to me that a group of the jinn listened and said, 'Indeed, we have heard an amazing Qur'an. (1) It guides to the right course, and we have believed in it. And we will never associate with our Lord anyone. (2) And [it teaches] that exalted is the nobleness of our Lord; He has not taken a wife or a son (3) And that our foolish one has been saying about Allah an excessive transgression. (4)

Quran 73:10-11

وَٱصْبِرْ عَلَىٰ مَا يَقُولُونَ وَٱهْجُرْهُمْ هَجْرًا جَمِيلًا (١٠) وَذَرْنِى وَٱلْمُكَذِّبِينَ أُو۟لِى ٱلنَّعْمَةِ وَمَهِّلْهُمْ قَلِيلًا (١١)

And be patient over what they say and avoid them with gracious avoidance. (10) And leave Me with [the matter of] the deniers, those of ease [in life], and allow them respite a little. (11)

Quran 75:16-18

لَا تُحَرِّكْ بِهِۦ لِسَانَكَ لِتَعْجَلَ بِهِۦٓ (١٦) إِنَّ عَلَيْنَا جَمْعَهُۥ وَقُرْءَانَهُۥ (١٧) فَإِذَا قَرَأْنَاهُ فَٱتَّبِعْ قُرْءَانَهُۥ (١٨)

Move not your tongue with it, [O Muhammad], to hasten with recitation of the Qur'an. (16) Indeed, upon Us is its collection [in your heart] and [to make possible] its recitation. (17) So when We have recited it [through Gabriel], then follow its recitation. (18)

Quran 76:23-26

إِنَّا نَحْنُ نَزَّلْنَا عَلَيْكَ ٱلْقُرْءَانَ تَنزِيلًا (٢٣) فَٱصْبِرْ لِحُكْمِ رَبِّكَ وَلَا تُطِعْ مِنْهُمْ ءَاثِمًا أَوْ كَفُورًا (٢٤) وَٱذْكُرِ ٱسْمَ رَبِّكَ بُكْرَةً وَأَصِيلًا (٢٥) وَمِنَ ٱلَّيْلِ فَٱسْجُدْ لَهُۥ وَسَبِّحْهُ لَيْلًا طَوِيلًا (٢٦)

Indeed, it is We who have sent down to you, [O Muhammad], the Qur'an progressively. (23) So be patient for the decision of your Lord and do not obey from among them a sinner or ungrateful [disbeliever]. (24) And mention the name of your Lord [in prayer] morning and evening (25) And during the night prostrate to Him and exalt Him a long [part of the] night. (26)

Quran 79:40-41

وَأَمَّا مَنْ خَافَ مَقَامَ رَبِّهِ وَنَهَى ٱلنَّفْسَ عَنِ ٱلْهَوَىٰ (٤٠) فَإِنَّ ٱلْجَنَّةَ هِيَ ٱلْمَأْوَىٰ (٤١)

But as for he who feared the position of his Lord and prevented the soul from [unlawful] inclination, (40) Then indeed, Paradise will be [his] refuge. (41)

Quran 92:5-12

فَأَمَّا مَنْ أَعْطَىٰ وَٱتَّقَىٰ (٥) وَصَدَّقَ بِٱلْحُسْنَىٰ (٦) فَسَنُيَسِّرُهُ لِلْيُسْرَىٰ (٧) وَأَمَّا مَنْ بَخِلَ وَٱسْتَغْنَىٰ (٨) وَكَذَّبَ بِٱلْحُسْنَىٰ (٩) فَسَنُيَسِّرُهُ لِلْعُسْرَىٰ (١٠) وَمَا يُغْنِي عَنْهُ مَالُهُ إِذَا تَرَدَّىٰ (١١) إِنَّ عَلَيْنَا لَلْهُدَىٰ (١٢)

As for he who gives and fears Allah (5) And believes in the best [reward], (6) We will ease him toward ease. (7) But as for he who withholds and considers himself free of need (8) And denies the best [reward], (9) We will ease him toward difficulty. (10) And what will his wealth avail him when he falls? (11) Indeed, [incumbent] upon Us is guidance. (12)

Quran 92:14-21

فَأَنذَرْتُكُمْ نَارًا تَلَظَّىٰ (١٤) لَا يَصْلَىٰهَا إِلَّا ٱلْأَشْقَى (١٥) ٱلَّذِى كَذَّبَ وَتَوَلَّىٰ (١٦) وَسَيُجَنَّبُهَا ٱلْأَتْقَى (١٧) ٱلَّذِى يُؤْتِى مَالَهُ يَتَزَكَّىٰ (١٨) وَمَا لِأَحَدٍ عِندَهُ مِن نِّعْمَةٍ تُجْزَىٰ (١٩) إِلَّا ٱبْتِغَاءَ وَجْهِ رَبِّهِ ٱلْأَعْلَىٰ (٢٠) وَلَسَوْفَ يَرْضَىٰ (٢١)

So I have warned you of a Fire which is blazing. (14) None will [enter to] burn therein except the most wretched one. (15) Who had denied and turned away. (16) But the righteous one will avoid it - (17) [He] who gives [from] his wealth to purify himself (18) And not [giving] for anyone who has [done him] a favor to be rewarded (19) But only seeking the countenance of his Lord, Most High. (20) And he is going to be satisfied. (21)

Quran 93:9-11

فَأَمَّا ٱلْيَتِيمَ فَلَا تَقْهَرْ (٩) وَأَمَّا ٱلسَّائِلَ فَلَا تَنْهَرْ (١٠) وَأَمَّا بِنِعْمَةِ رَبِّكَ فَحَدِّثْ (١١)

So as for the orphan, do not oppress [him]. (9) And as for the petitioner, do not repel [him]. (10) But as for the favor of your Lord, report [it]. (11)

Quran 96:9-19

أَرَءَيْتَ ٱلَّذِى يَنْهَىٰ (٩) عَبْدًا إِذَا صَلَّىٰ (١٠) أَرَءَيْتَ إِن كَانَ عَلَى ٱلْهُدَىٰ (١١) أَوْ أَمَرَ بِٱلتَّقْوَىٰ (١٢) أَرَءَيْتَ إِن كَذَّبَ وَتَوَلَّىٰ (١٣) أَلَمْ يَعْلَم بِأَنَّ ٱللَّهَ يَرَىٰ (١٤) كَلَّا لَئِن لَّمْ يَنتَهِ لَنَسْفَعًۢا بِٱلنَّاصِيَةِ (١٥) نَاصِيَةٍ كَـٰذِبَةٍ خَاطِئَةٍ (١٦) فَلْيَدْعُ نَادِيَهُۥ (١٧) سَنَدْعُ ٱلزَّبَانِيَةَ (١٨) كَلَّا لَا تُطِعْهُ وَٱسْجُدْ وَٱقْتَرِب (١٩)

Have you seen the one who forbids (9) A servant when he prays? (10) Have you seen if he is upon guidance (11) Or enjoins righteousness? (12) Have you seen if he denies and turns away - (13) Does he not know that Allah sees? (14) No! If he does not desist, We will surely drag him by the forelock - (15) A lying, sinning forelock. (16) Then let him call his associates; (17) We will call the angels of Hell. (18) No! Do not obey him. But prostrate and draw near [to Allah]. (19)

Quran 98:7-8

إِنَّ ٱلَّذِينَ ءَامَنُوا۟ وَعَمِلُوا۟ ٱلصَّـٰلِحَـٰتِ أُو۟لَـٰٓئِكَ هُمْ خَيْرُ ٱلْبَرِيَّةِ (٧) جَزَآؤُهُمْ عِندَ رَبِّهِمْ جَنَّـٰتُ عَدْنٍ تَجْرِى مِن تَحْتِهَا ٱلْأَنْهَـٰرُ خَـٰلِدِينَ فِيهَآ أَبَدًا ۖ رَّضِىَ ٱللَّهُ عَنْهُمْ وَرَضُوا۟ عَنْهُ ۚ ذَٰلِكَ لِمَنْ خَشِىَ رَبَّهُۥ (٨)

Indeed, they who have believed and done righteous deeds - those are the best of creatures. (7) Their reward with Allah will be gardens of perpetual residence beneath which rivers flow, wherein they will abide forever, Allah being pleased with them and they with Him. That is for whoever has feared his Lord. (8)

Quran 99:6-8

يَوْمَئِذٍ يَصْدُرُ ٱلنَّاسُ أَشْتَاتًا لِّيُرَوْاْ أَعْمَـٰلَهُمْ (٦) فَمَن يَعْمَلْ مِثْقَالَ ذَرَّةٍ خَيْرًا يَرَهُۥ (٧) وَمَن يَعْمَلْ مِثْقَالَ ذَرَّةٍ شَرًّا يَرَهُۥ (٨)

That Day, the people will depart separated [into categories] to be shown [the result of] their deeds. (6) So whoever does an atom's weight of good will see it, (7) And whoever does an atom's weight of evil will see it. (8)

Quran 101:6-11

فَأَمَّا مَن ثَقُلَتْ مَوَازِينُهُۥ (٦) فَهُوَ فِى عِيشَةٍ رَّاضِيَةٍ (٧) وَأَمَّا مَنْ خَفَّتْ مَوَازِينُهُۥ (٨) فَأُمُّهُۥ هَاوِيَةٌ (٩) وَمَآ أَدْرَىٰكَ مَا هِيَهْ (١٠) نَارٌ حَامِيَةٌۢ (١١)

Then as for one whose scales are heavy [with good deeds], (6) He will be in a pleasant life. (7) But as for one whose scales are light, (8) His refuge will be an abyss. (9) And what can make you know what that is? (10) It is a Fire, intensely hot. (11)

Quran 103

وَٱلْعَصْرِ (١) إِنَّ ٱلْإِنسَـٰنَ لَفِى خُسْرٍ (٢) إِلَّا ٱلَّذِينَ ءَامَنُواْ وَعَمِلُواْ ٱلصَّـٰلِحَـٰتِ وَتَوَاصَوْاْ بِٱلْحَقِّ وَتَوَاصَوْاْ بِٱلصَّبْرِ (٣)

By time, (1) Indeed, mankind is in loss, (2) Except for those who have believed and done righteous deeds and advised each other to truth and advised each other to patience. (3)

Quran 104:1

وَيْلٌ لِّكُلِّ هُمَزَةٍ لُّمَزَةٍ (١)

Woe to every scorner and mocker (1)

Quran 107:4-7

فَوَيْلٌ لِّلْمُصَلِّينَ (٤) ٱلَّذِينَ هُمْ عَن صَلَاتِهِمْ سَاهُونَ (٥) ٱلَّذِينَ هُمْ يُرَآءُونَ (٦) وَيَمْنَعُونَ ٱلْمَاعُونَ (٧)

So woe to those who pray (4) [But] who are heedless of their prayer - (5) Those who make show [of their deeds] (6) And withhold [simple] assistance. (7)

Quran 109

قُلْ يَـٰٓأَيُّهَا ٱلْكَـٰفِرُونَ (١) لَآ أَعْبُدُ مَا تَعْبُدُونَ (٢) وَلَآ أَنتُمْ عَـٰبِدُونَ مَآ أَعْبُدُ (٣) وَلَآ أَنَا۠ عَابِدٌ مَّا عَبَدتُّمْ (٤) وَلَآ أَنتُمْ عَـٰبِدُونَ مَآ أَعْبُدُ (٥) لَكُمْ دِينُكُمْ وَلِىَ دِينِ (٦)

Say, "O disbelievers, (1) I do not worship what you worship. (2) Nor are you worshippers of what I worship. (3) Nor will I be a worshipper of what you worship. (4) Nor will you be worshippers of what I worship. (5) For you is your religion, and for me is my religion." (6)

Quran 114

قُلْ أَعُوذُ بِرَبِّ ٱلنَّاسِ (١) مَلِكِ ٱلنَّاسِ (٢) إِلَـٰهِ ٱلنَّاسِ (٣) مِن شَرِّ ٱلْوَسْوَاسِ ٱلْخَنَّاسِ (٤) ٱلَّذِى يُوَسْوِسُ فِى صُدُورِ ٱلنَّاسِ (٥) مِنَ ٱلْجِنَّةِ وَٱلنَّاسِ (٦)

Say, "I seek refuge in the Lord of mankind, (1) The Sovereign of mankind. (2) The God of mankind, (3) From the evil of the retreating whisperer - (4) Who whispers [evil] into the breasts of mankind - (5) From among the jinn and mankind." (6)

HADITH ABOUT SEEKING SAFETY

It was narrated from Ubaidullah bin Abu Rafi from his father that:

The Messenger of Allah (ﷺ) said: "I do not want to find anyone of you reclining on his pillow, and when news comes to him of something that I have commanded or forbidden, he says, 'I do not know, whatever we find in the Book of Allah, we will follow."

Source: Sunan Ibn Majah 13 Grade: Sahih

Hudhaifah narrated the Messenger of Allah said:

"Do not be a people without a will of your own, saying: 'If people treat us well, we will treat them well; and if they do wrong, we will do wrong,' but accustom yourselves to do good if people do good, and do not behave unjustly if they do evil."

Source: Jami` at-Tirmidhi 2007 Grade: Hasan

Abu Hurairah said:

The Messenger of Allah (ﷺ) said, "Beware of suspicion, for suspicion is the worst of false tales. Do not look for other's faults. Do not spy on one another, and do not practise Najsh (means to offer a high price for something in order to allure another customer who is interested in the thing). Do not be jealous of one another and do not nurse enmity against one another. Do not sever ties with one another. Become the slaves of Allah, and be brothers to one another as He commanded. A Muslim is the brother of a Muslim. He should neither oppress him nor humiliate him. The piety is here! The piety is here!" While saying so he pointed towards his chest. "It is enough evil for a Muslim to look down upon his Muslim brother. All things of a Muslim are inviolable for his brother in Faith: his blood, his wealth and his honour. Verily, Allah does not look to your bodies nor to your faces but He looks to your hearts and your deeds."

Source: Riyad as-Salihin 1570 Grade: Sahih

Jabir bin Abdullah reported Allah's Messenger (ﷺ) as saying:

"Do not walk in one sandal and do not wrap the lower garment round your knees and do not eat with your left hand and do not wrap yourself completely leaving no room for the arms (to draw out) and do not place one of your feet upon the other while lying on your back."

Source: Sahih Muslim 2099d

Sulaiman bin Buraidah reported on his father's authority, The Prophet(ﷺ) said:

"Fight in the name of Allaah and in the path of Allaah and with him who disbelieves in Allaah fight and do not be treacherous and do not be dishonest about booty and do not deface (in killing) and do not kill a child."

Source: Sunan Abi Dawud 2613 Grade: Sahih

Narrated Abu Sa`id Al-Khudri:

Allah's Messenger (ﷺ) said, "Do not sell gold for gold unless equivalent in weight, and do not sell less amount for greater amount or vice versa; and do not sell silver for silver unless equivalent in weight, and do not sell less amount for greater amount or vice versa and do not sell gold or silver that is not present at the moment of exchange for gold or silver that is present.

Source: Sahih al-Bukhari 2177

It was narrated from 'Abdullah bin as-Sa'di that he came to 'Umar bin al-Khattab during his caliphate and 'Umar said to him:

Was I not told that you do work for people, then when you are given your wages you do not accept it? I said: Yes. `Umar said: Why do you do that? I said: I have horses and slaves, and I am well off. I want my work to be an act of charity towards the Muslims. 'Umar said: Do not do that, for I wanted to do the same as you want to do. The Prophet ﷺ would give me some payment and I would say: Give it to one who is more in need of it than me. One day he gave me something and I said: Give it to one who is more in need of it than me. The Prophet ﷺ said: `Take it, keep it, and give it in charity, Whatever of this wealth comes to you when you are not hoping for it or asking for it, accept it, but if it does not come to you, do not hope for it."

Source: Musnad Ahmad 100 Grade: Sahih

Jabir bin 'Abd Allah reported the Messenger of Allah (ﷺ) as saying:

"Do not invoke curse on yourselves, and do not invoke curse on your children, and do not invoke curse on your servants, and do not invoke curse on your property, lest you happen to do it at a time when Allah is asked for something and grants your request."

Source: Sunan Abi Dawud 1532 Grade: Sahih

Narrated `Abdullah bin `Umar:

Allah's Messenger (ﷺ) said, "Do not enter (the places) of these people where Allah's punishment had fallen unless *you do so weeping. If you do not weep, do not enter (the places of these people) because Allah's curse and punishment which fell upon them may fall upon you."*

Source: Sahih al-Bukhari 433

Mu'aiqib reported the Prophet (ﷺ) as saying:

"Do not remove pebbles while you are praying; if you do it out of sheer necessity, do it only once to smooth the pebbles."

Source: Sunan Abi Dawud 946 Grade: Sahih

Narrated Abu Sa`id Al-Khudri:

The Prophet (ﷺ) said, "Allah never sends a prophet or gives the Caliphate to a Caliph but that he (the prophet or the Caliph) has two groups of advisors: A group advising him to do good and exhorts him to do it, and the other group advising him to do evil and exhorts him to do it. But the protected person (against such evil advisors) is the one protected by Allah.' "

Source: Sahih al-Bukhari 7198

Anas ibn Malik heard the Messenger of Allah say:

"I have nothing to do with diversions and diversions have nothing to do with me." He meant that he does not do anything worthless."

Source: Al-Adab Al-Mufrad 785 Grade: Hasan

Ibn Abbas narrated the Messenger of Allah said:

"Do not argue with your brother, do not joke with him, and do not make a promise, only to not fulfill it."

Source: Jami` at-Tirmidhi 1995 Grade: Daif

Narrated Abu Huraira:

Allah's Messenger (ﷺ) said, "The Jews and the Christians do not dye (grey hair), so you shall do the opposite of what they do (dye your grey hair and beards).

Source: Sahih al-Bukhari 3462

Narrated Anas:

The Prophet (ﷺ) said, "Do the prostration properly and do not put your forearms flat with elbows touching the ground like a dog. And if you want to spit, do not spit in front, nor to the right for the person in prayer is speaking in private to his Lord."

Source: Sahih al-Bukhari 532

Narrated Sa'd bin Hisham:

It was narrated from Sa'd bin Hisham that he came to the Mother of the Believers, 'Aishah. He said: "I want to ask you about celibacy, what do you think about it?" She said: "Do not do that; have you not heard that Allah, the Mighty and Sublime, says: 'And indeed We sent Messengers before you, and made for them wives and offspring'? So do not be celibate."

Source: Sunan an-Nasa'i 3216 Grade: Sahih

It was narrated that Jabir bin 'Abdullah said:

"The Messenger of Allah (ﷺ) said: 'The Magians of this Ummah are those who deny the decrees of Allah. If they fall sick, do not visit them; if they die, do not attend their funerals; and if you meet them, do not greet them with Salam.'"

Source: Sunan Ibn Majah 92 Grade: Daif

Narrated Abu Qatada:

Allah's Messenger (ﷺ) said, "When you drink (water), do not breath in the vessel; and when you urinate, do not touch your penis with your right hand. And when you cleanse yourself after defecation, do not use your right hand."

Source: Sahih al-Bukhari 5630

Abu'd-Darda' said, "The Messenger of Allah recommended nine things to me:

'Do not associate anything with Allah, even if you are cut to pieces or burned. Do not abandon a prescribed prayer deliberately. Anyone who abandons it will forfeit Allah's protection. Do not drink wine – it is the key to every evil. Obey your parents. If they command you to abandon your worldly possessions, then leave them for them. Do not contend with those in power, even if you think that you are in the right. Do not run away from the army when it advances, even if you are killed while your companions run away. Spend on your wife out of your means. Do not raise a stick against your wife. Cause your family to fear Allah, the Almighty and Exalted.'"

Source: Al-Adab Al-Mufrad 18 Grade: Hasan

Musa bin Talha reported:

I and Allah's Messenger (ﷺ) happened to pass by people near the date-palm trees. He (the Prophet) said: What are these people doing? They said: They are grafting, i. e. they combine the male with the female (tree) and thus they yield more fruit. Thereupon Allah's Messenger (ﷺ) said: I do not find it to be of any use. The people were informed about it and they abandoned this practice. Allah's Messenger (ﷺ) (was later) on informed (that the yield had dwindled), whereupon he said: If there is any use of it, then they should do it, for it was just a personal opinion of mine, and do not go after my personal opinion; but when I say to you anything on behalf of Allah, then do accept it, for I do not attribute lies to Allah, the Exalted and Glorious.

Source: Sahih Muslim 2361

Narrated Abu Marthad al-Ghanawi :

The Messenger of Allah (ﷺ) as saying: Do not sit on the graves, and do not pray facing them.

Source: Sunan Abi Dawud 3229 Grade: Sahih

Narrated Ali ibn Abu Talib:

Do not be extravagant in shrouding, for I heard the Messenger of Allah (ﷺ) say: Do not be extravagant in shrouding, for it will be quickly decayed.

Source: Sunan Abi Dawud 3154 Grade: Daif

Narrated Mu'adh bin Jabal:

that the Messenger of Allah (ﷺ) said: "Do you know what Allah's right upon His slaves is?" I said: "Allah and His Messenger know best." He said: "His right upon them is that they worship Him alone and do not associate any partners with Him." He said: "And do you know what their right over Allah is if they do that?" I said: "Allah and His Messenger know best." He said: "That He will not punish them."

Source: Jami` at-Tirmidhi 2643 Grade: Sahih

It was narrated from Abu Hurairah that the Messenger of Allah said:

"Do not go out to meet the riders, and do not urge someone to cancel a sale he has already agreed upon so as to sell him your own goods, do not artificially inflate prices, and let not a town-dweller sell for a desert-dweller."

Source: Sunan an-Nasa'i 4496 Grade: Sahih

It was narrated that Hakim bin Hizam said:

"I asked the Prophet "O Messenger of Allah, a man may come to me and ask me to sell him something that I do not have. Can I sell it to him then go and buy it from the market?' He said: 'Do not sell what you do not have.'"

Source: Sunan an-Nasa'i 4613 Grade: Hasan

Narrated Jubair bin Mut'im:

that a woman came to the Messenger of Allah (ﷺ) to speak to him about something. Then he ordered her with something, and she said: "What should I do O Messenger of Allah if I do not find you?" He said: "If you do not find me, then go to Abu Bakr."

Source: Jami` at-Tirmidhi 3676 Grade: Sahih

Abu Sa'eed narrated the Messenger of Allah said:

"Do not accompany except a believer, and do not serve your food except to one with Taqwa."

Source: Jami` at-Tirmidhi 2395 Grade: Sahih

Narrated Mu'awiyah al-Qushayri:

I went to the Messenger of Allah (ﷺ) and asked him: What do you say (command) about our wives? He replied: Give them food what you have for yourself, and clothe them by which you clothe yourself, and do not beat them, and do not revile them.

Source: Sunan Abi Dawud 2144 Grade: Sahih

Narrated Abu Huraira:

The Prophet (ﷺ) said, "Leave me as I leave you, for the people who were before you were ruined because of their questions and their differences over their prophets. So, if I *forbid you to do something, then keep away from it. And if I order you to do something, then do of it as much as you can."*

Source: Sahih al-Bukhari 7288

Narrated `Aisha:

The Prophet (ﷺ) did something as it was allowed from the religious point of view but some people refrained from it. When the Prophet (ﷺ) heard of that, he, after glorifying and praising Allah, said, "Why do some people refrain from doing something which I do? By Allah, I know Allah more than they."

Source: Sahih al-Bukhari 7301

Abdullah reported that the Prophet said:

"Respond to invitations. Do not reject gifts. Do not beat Muslims."

Source: Al-Adab Al-Mufrad 157 Grade: Sahih

Abu Musa reported the Messenger of Allah (ﷺ) as saying:

Gladden people and do not scare them; make things easy and do not make them difficult.

Source: Sunan Abi Dawud 4835 Grade: Sahih

An-Nu'man ibn Bashir said that his father had carried him to the Messenger of Allah.

He said, 'Messenger of Allah, I testify to you that I have given an-Nu'man such-and-such. (It was a slave). The Prophet asked, "Have you given each of your children the same"?" "No," he replied. He said, "Then testify to someone other than me." Then the Prophet asked, "Do you not want to show equal kindness to all of them?" "Indeed I do," he replied. He said, "Then do not do it."

Source: Al-Adab Al-Mufrad 93 Grade: Sahih

Abu Huraira reported Allah's Messenger (ﷺ) said:

None of you should say to Allah (like this): O Allah, grant me mercy, if thou so likest. The supplication (of his) should (be permeated with) conviction (that it would be accepted by the Lord), for Allah is the Doer of (everything) He likes to do, and there is none to force Him (to do or not to do this or that).

Source: Sahih Muslim 2679b

Narrated Hudhaifa:

The Prophet (ﷺ) said, "Do not drink in gold or silver utensils, and do not wear clothes of silk or Dibaj, for these things are for them (unbelievers) in this world and for you in the Hereafter."

Source: Sahih al-Bukhari 5633

Narrated Saud:

The Prophet (ﷺ) said, "If you hear of an outbreak of plague in a land, do not enter it; but if the plague breaks out in a place while you are in it, do not leave that place."

Source: Sahih al-Bukhari 5728

It was narrated that Adi bin Hatim said:

"I asked the Messenger of Allah: 'I release my dog, and I find another dog with mine, and I do not know which mine, and I do not know which of them caught (the game).' He said: 'do not eat it, for you said the name of Allah over your dog, but not over any other.'"

Source: Sunan an-Nasa'i 4273 Grade: Sahih

It was narrated from Abu Qatadah that:

The Messenger of Allah said: "Do not soak Az-Zahuw and ripe dates together, and do not soak raisins and ripe dates together."

Source: Sunan an-Nasa'i 5552 Grade: Sahih

It was narrated that Jabir said:

"The Messenger of Allah (ﷺ) was ill, and we prayed behind him while he was sitting, and Abu Bakr repeated his takbirs so that the people could hear them. He turned to us and saw us standing, so he gestured to us to sit down. So we prayed behind him sitting. When he said the salam he said: 'Just now you were doing what the Persians and Romans do for their kings when they are sitting. Do not do that. Follow your Imams: If they pray standing then pray standing, and if they pray sitting then pray sitting.'"

Source: Sunan an-Nasa'i 1200 Grade: Sahih

Narrated `Abdur-Rahman bin Samura:

The Prophet (ﷺ) said, "O `Abdur-Rahman! Do not seek to be a ruler, for if you are given authority on your demand then you will be held responsible for it, but if you are given it without asking (for it), then you will be helped (by Allah) in it. If you ever take an oath to do something and later on you find that something else is better, then you should expiate your oath and do what is better."

Source: Sahih al-Bukhari 7146

It was narrated that Abu Hurairah said:

"The Messenger of Allah said: 'Do not swear by your fathers, nor by your mothers, nor by the idols. Swear only by Allah, and do not swear unless you are sincere.'"

Source: Sunan an-Nasa'i 3769 Grade: Sahih

Abu Hurairah reported that the Prophet said:

"The slave has his food and clothing. Do not burden a slave with work which he is incapable of doing."

Source: Al-Adab Al-Mufrad 192 Grade: Sahih

It was narrated from Abu Hurairah that the Messenger of Allah (ﷺ) said:

"Allah has forgiven my nation for the evil suggestions of their hearts, so long as they do not act upon it or speak of it, and for what they are forced to do."

Source: Sunan Ibn Majah 2044 Grade: Sahih

It was narrated that Asma' bint Yazid said:

"Some food was brought to the Prophet (ﷺ) and it was offered to us. We said: 'We do not have any appetite for it.' He said: 'Do not combine hunger and lies.'"

Source: Sunan Ibn Majah 3298 Grade: Hasan

It was narrated that Anas bin Malik said:

"The Messenger of Allah said: 'Do not be so close to the Mushrikin that you can benefit from the light of their fires, and do not engrave Arabic (words) on your rings.'"

Source: Sunan an-Nasa'i 5209 Grade: Daif

It was narrated that Anas said:

"The Messenger of Allah came out wearing a silver ring. He said: 'Whoever wants to make a ring like this, let him do so, but do not put the same inscription.'"

Source: Sunan an-Nasa'i 5207 Grade: Sahih

Abu Hurairah reported:

The Messenger of Allah said: Wind is the mercy of Allah. It brings mercy or punishment. Do not denounce it, but ask Allah, the exalted, for the good of it and seek the protection of Allah from its evil.

Source: Adab Mufrad 720 Grade: Sahih

Narrated Abu Hurairah:

The Prophet (ﷺ) said: Do not make your houses graves, and do not make my grave a place of festivity. But invoke blessings on me, for your blessings reach me wherever you may be.

Source: Sunan Abi Dawud 2042 Grade: Sahih

Asma' reported Allah's Messenger saying (to her):

Spend and do not calculate, (for) Allah would calculate in your case; and do not hoard, otherwise Allah would be withholding from you.

Source: Sahih Muslim 1029b

Abu Bakrah narrated that he entered the Masjid when the Prophet (ﷺ) was bowing, so he bowed outside the row. The Prophet said:

"May Allah increase you in keenness, but do not do this again."

Source: Sunan an-Nasa'I 871 Grade: Sahih

Narrated Mu'awiyah:

Abu Mijlaz said: Mu'awiyah went out to Ibn az-Zubayr and Ibn Amir. Ibn Amir got up and Ibn az-Zubayr remained sitting. Mu'awiyah said to Ibn Amir: Sit down, for I heard the Messenger of Allah (ﷺ) say:

"Let him who likes people to stand up before him prepare his place in Hell."

Source: Sunan Abi Dawud 5229 Grade: Sahih

Narrated Abu Umamah:

The Messenger of Allah (ﷺ) came out to us leaning on a stick. We stood up to show respect to him. He said: Do not stand up as foreigners do for showing respect to one another.

Source: Sunan abu Dawood 5230 Grade: Sahih

Narrated Abu Huraira:

A man said to the Prophet (ﷺ), "Advise me! "The Prophet (ﷺ) said, "Do not become angry." The man asked (the same) again and again, and the Prophet (ﷺ) said in each case, "Do not become angry."

Source: Sahih al-Bukhari 6116

Narrated Mu'awiyah al-Qushayri:

Mu'awiyah asked: Messenger of Allah, what is the right of the wife of one of us over him? He replied: That you should give her food when you eat, clothe her when you clothe yourself, do not strike her on the face, do not revile her or separate yourself from her except in the house.

Source: Sunan Abi Dawud 2142 Grade: Hasan Sahih

Narrated Abdullah:

A man got up and said, O Allah's Messenger (ﷺ)! What do you order us to wear when we assume the state of

Ihram?" The Prophet (ﷺ) replied, "Do not wear shirts, trousers, turbans, hooded cloaks or Khuffs (socks made from thick fabric or leather), but if a man has no sandals, he can wear Khuffs after cutting them short below the ankles; and do not wear clothes touched with (perfumes) of saffron or wars."

Source: Sahih al-Bukhari 5805

It was narrated that 'Aishah said:

"We went out with the Messenger of Allah (ﷺ) with no intention other than Hajj. When he was in Sarif I began menstruating. The Messenger of Allah (ﷺ) entered upon me and I was weeping. He said: 'What is the matter with you? Has you Nifas begun?' I said: 'Yes.' He said: 'This is something that Allah the Mighty and Sublime has decreed for the daughters of Adam. Do what the pilgrims do but do not perform Tawaf around the House.'"

Source: Sunan an-Nasa'i 348 Grade: Sahih

It has been reported from Sulaiman bin Buraida through his father that when the Messenger of Allah (ﷺ) appointed anyone as leader of an army or detachment he would especially exhort him to fear Allah and to be good to the Muslims who were with him. He would say:

Fight in the name of Allah and in the way of Allah. Fight against those who disbelieve in Allah. Make a holy war, do not embezzle the spoils; do not break your pledge; and do not mutilate (the dead) bodies; do not kill the children. When you meet your enemies who are polytheists, invite them to three courses of action. If they respond to any one of these, you also accept it and withhold yourself from doing them any harm. Invite them to (accept) Islam; if they respond to you, accept it from them and desist from fighting against them. Then invite them to migrate from their lands to the land of the Muhajireen and inform them that, if they do so, they shall have all the privileges and obligations of the Muhajireen. If they refuse to migrate, tell them that they will have the status of Bedouin Muslims and will be subjected to the Commands of Allah like other Muslims, but they will not get any share from the spoils of war or Fai' except when they actually fight with the Muslims (against the disbelievers). If they refuse to accept Islam, demand from them the Jizya. If they agree to pay, accept it from them and hold off your hands. If they refuse to pay the tax, seek Allah's help and fight them. When you lay siege to a fort and the besieged appeal to you for protection in the name of Allah and His Prophet, do not accord to them the guarantee of Allah and His Prophet, but accord to them your own guarantee and the guarantee of your companions for it is a lesser sin that the security given by you or your companions be disregarded than that the security granted in the name of Allah and His Prophet be violated. When you besiege a fort and the besieged want you to let them out in accordance with Allah's Command, do not let them come out in accordance with His Command, but do so at your (own) command, for you do not know whether or not you will be able to carry out Allah's behest with regard to them.

Source: Sahih Muslim 1731 A+B

It was narrated from Jabir bin `Abdullah that:

"A man passed by the Prophet while he was urinating, and greeted him by the Salam. The Messenger of Allah said to him: "If you see me in this situation, do not greet me with the Salam, for if you do that I will not respond to you."

Source: Sunan Ibn Majah 352 Grade: Hasan

Abu Hurairah reported:

One of the Prophet's Companions came upon a valley containing a rivulet of fresh water and was delighted by it. He reflected: 'I wish to withdraw from people and settle in this valley; but I won't do so without the permission of the Messenger of Allah (ﷺ).' This was mentioned to the Messenger of Allah (ﷺ) and he said (to the man), "Do not do that, for when any of you remains in Allah's way, it is better for him than performing Salat (prayer) in his house for seventy years. Do you not wish that Allah should forgive you and admit you to Paradise? Fight in Allah's way, for he who fights in Allah's Cause as long as the time between two consecutive turns of milking a she-camel, will be surely admitted to Paradise."

Source: Riyad as-Salihin 1297 Grade: Hasan

Narrated Abu Namlah al-Ansari:

When he was sitting with the Messenger of Allah (ﷺ) and a Jew was also with him, a funeral passed by him. He (the Jew) asked (Him): Muhammad, does this funeral speak? The Prophet (ﷺ) said: Allah has more knowledge. The Jew said: It speaks.

The Messenger of Allah (ﷺ) said: Whatever the people of the Book tell you, do not verify them, nor falsify them, but say: We believe in Allah and His Messenger. If it is false, do not confirm it, and if it is right, do not falsify it.

Source: Sunan Abi Dawud 3644 Grade: Daif

It was narrated that Abu Hurairah said:

"A woman who did tattoos was brought to 'Umar and he said: 'I adjure you by Allah, did any one among you hear (anything from) the Messenger of Allah?' Abu Hurairah said: "I stood up and said: 'O Commander of the Believers! I heard him (say something).' He said: 'What did you hear?' I said: 'I heard him say: Do not do tattoos and do not have tattoos done.'"

Source: Sunan an-Nasa'i 5106 Grade: Sahih

Ali said:

My prostatic fluid flowed excessively. I used to take a bath until my back cracked (because of frequent washing). I mentioned it to the prophet, or the fact was mentioned to him (by someone else). The Messenger of Allah said; Do not do so. When you find prostatic fluid, wash your penis and perform ablution as you do for your prayer(wudu), but when you have seminal emission, you should take a bath(ghusl).

Source: Sunan Abi Dawud 206 Grade: Sahih

It was narrated from Abdullah bin Amr that:

the Prophet said: "Do not marry women for their beauty for it may lead to their doom. Do not marry them for their wealth, for it may lead them to fall into sin. Rather, marry them for their religion. A black slave woman with piercings who is religious is better."

Source: Sunan Ibn Majah 1859 Grade: Daif

It was narrated that Abu Dharr said:

"The Messenger of Allah said to me: 'O Abu Dharr, I think that you are weak, and I like for you what I like for myself. Do not accept a position of Amir over two people, and do not agree to be the guardian of an orphan's property.'"

Source: Sunan an-Nasa'i 3667 Grade: Sahih

Umar bin Al-Khattab said:

I donated a horse in the way of Allah. Its new possessor did not treat it properly. I made my mind to buy it because I thought that he would sell it at a cheap price (now that it became weak and emaciated). I asked the Prophet (ﷺ) about it, whereupon he said, "Do not buy it and do not get back your charity, for one who gets back the charity is like a dog that eats its own vomit."

Source: Riyad as-Salihin 1613 Grade: Sahih

It was narrated from Jabir bin 'Abdullah that:

The Prophet said: "Do not seek knowledge in order to show off in front of the scholars, or to argue with the foolish, and do not choose the best seat in a gathering, due to it (i.e. the knowledge which you have learned) for whoever does that, the Fire, the Fire (awaits him)."

Source: Sunan Ibn Majah 254 Grade: Daif

Abu Qatadah said:

The Prophet (ﷺ) said, "Do not touch your private parts with your right hand while urinating, nor for washing or cleaning (your private parts); and do not breathe into the drinking vessel from which you drink."

Source: Riyad as-Salihin 1648 Grade: Sahih

Narrated `Abdullah bin `Umar:

Allah's Messenger (ﷺ) mentioned Ramadan and said, "Do not fast unless you see the crescent (of Ramadan), and do not give up fasting till you see the crescent (of Shawwal), but if the sky is overcast (if you cannot see it), then act on estimation (i.e. count Sha'ban as 30 days).

Source: Sahih al-Bukhari 1906

Narrated Jubayr ibn Mut'im:

The Prophet (ﷺ) said: Do not prevent anyone from going round this House (the Ka'bah) and from praying any moment he desires by day or by night. The narrator Fadl (ibn Ya'qub) said: The Messenger of Allah (ﷺ) said: Banu Abdu Munaf, do not stop anyone.

Source: Sunan Abi Dawud 1894 Grade: Sahih

Abu Huraira reported Allah's Messenger (ﷺ) said:

Do not greet the Jews and the Christians before they greet you and when you meet any one of them on the roads force him to go to the narrowest part of it.

Source: Sahih Muslim 2167a

It was narrated that Umaimah bint Ruqaiqah said:

"I came to the Prophet with some other Ansari women to give our pledge. We said: 'O Messenger of Allah, we give you our pledge that we will not associate anything with Allah, we will not steal, we will not have unlawful sexual relations, we will not utter slander, fabricating from between our hands and feet, and we will not disobey you in goodness.' He said: 'As much as you can and are able.' We said: 'Allah and His Messenger are more merciful toward us. Come, let us give you our pledge, O Messenger of Allah! The Messenger of Allah said: 'I do

not shake hands with women. Rather my word to a hundred women is like my word to one woman."

Source: Sunan an-Nasa'i 4181

Narrated Mu`adh bin Jabal:

While I was riding behind the Prophet (ﷺ) and between me and him and between me and him there was only the back of the saddle, he said, "O Mu`adh!" I replied, "Labbaik, 0 Allah's Messenger (ﷺ), and Sa`daik!" he said, "Do you know what is Allah's right upon his slave?" I said, "Allah and His Messenger know best" He said "Allah's right upon his slaves is that they should worship Him alone and not worship anything else besides Him." Then he proceeded for a while and then said, "O Mu`adh bin Jabal!" I replied, "Labbaik, O Allah's Messenger (ﷺ):, Sa`daik!' He said, "Do you know what is the right of the slaves upon Allah if they do that?" I replied, "Allah and His Messenger know best." He said, "The right of the slaves upon Allah is that He will not punish them (if they do that).

Source: Sahih al-Bukhari 5967

Narrated Abu Barzah al-Aslami:

The Prophet (ﷺ) said: O community of people, who believed by their tongue, and belief did not enter their hearts, do not back-bite Muslims, and do not search for their faults, for if anyone searches for their faults, Allah will search for his fault, and if Allah searches for the fault of anyone, He disgraces him in his house.*

Source: Sunan Abi Dawud 4880 Grade: Hasan Sahih

It was narrated that Habbah and Sawa', the two daughters of Khalid, said:

"We entered upon the Prophet (ﷺ) when he was doing something, so we helped him with it. Then he said: 'Do not despair of provision so long as your heads are still moving, for a person's mother bears him red with raw skin, then Allah provides for him.'"

Source: Sunan Ibn Majah 4165 Grade: Daif

Abu Huraira reported Allah's Messenger (ﷺ) said:

Do not revile my Companions, do not revile my Companions. By Him in Whose Hand is my life, if one amongst you would have spent as much gold as Mount Uhud it would not amount to as much as one mudd on behalf of one of them or half of it.

Source: Sahih Muslim 2540

Narrated Ibn 'Abbas:

A man wearing ihram was thrown by his she-camel and had his neck broken and he died. He was brought to the Messenger of Allah (ﷺ), and he said: Wash and shroud him, but do not cover his head and do not put any perfume on him, for he will be raised on the Day of Resurrection saying the talbiyah.

Source: Sunan Abi Dawud 3241 Grade: Sahih

Abu Hurairah reported:

A man came to the Messenger of Allah (ﷺ) and asked, "O Messenger of Allah! What shall I do if someone comes to me with the intention of taking away my property?" He replied, "Do not hand over it to him." The man asked, "What shall I do if he fights me?" The Messenger of Allah (ﷺ) said, "Then fight him." "What will be my position in the Hereafter if he has killed me?" The Messenger of Allah replied, "In that case you are a martyr." The man asked: "What if I killed him?" The Messenger of Allah replied, "He will be in the Hell-fire."

Source: Riyad as-Salihin 1357 Grade: Sahih

It was narrated from Abu Sa'eed Al-Khudri that the Messenger of Allah (ﷺ) sent 'Alqamah bin Mujazziz at the head of a detachment, and I was among them.

When he reached the battle site, or when he was partway there, a group of the army asked permission to take a different route, and he gave them permission, and appointed 'Abdullah bin Hudhafah bin Qais As-Sahmi as their leader, and I was one of those who fought alongside with him. When we were partway there, the people lit a fire to warm themselves and cook some food. 'Abdullah, who was a man who liked to joke, said:

"Do I not have the right that you should listen to me and obey?" They said: "Yes." He said: "And if I command you to do something, will you not do it?" They said: "Of course." He said: "Then I command you to jump into this fire." Some people got up and got ready to jump, and when he saw that they were about to jump, he said: "Restrain yourselves, for I was joking with you."

When we came to Al-Madinah, they mentioned that to the Prophet (ﷺ), and the Messenger of Allah (ﷺ) said: "Whoever among you commands you to do something that involves disobedience to Allah, do not obey him."

Source: Sunan Ibn Majah 2863 Grade: Hasan

It was narrated from Jabir that his father was killed on the day of Uhud. He said:

"I started to uncover his face, weeping. The people told me not to do that but the Messenger of Allah did not forbid me. My paternal aunt started to weep, and the Messenger of Allah said: 'Do not weep, for angels kept on shading him with their wings until you lifted him up.'"

Source: Sunan an-Nasa'i 1845 Grade: Sahih

Narrated Adi bin Hatim:

"I asked the Messenger of Allah (ﷺ) about hunting, so he said: 'Mention Allah's Name when you shoot your arrow. Then, if you find it dead, eat from it, unless you found that it has fallen in (some body of) water. Then do not eat it, for you do not know if the water killed it, or your arrow.'"

Source: Jami` at-Tirmidhi 1469 Grade: Sahih

It was narrated from 'Abdullah Ad-Dailami that his father Fairuz said:

"I came to the Messenger of Allah and said: 'O Messenger of Allah, we have grapevines and Allah, the Mighty and Sublime, has revealed that Khamr (wine) is forbidden, so what should we do?' He said: 'Make raisins.' I said: 'What should we do with the raisins?' He said: 'Soak them in the morning and drink them in the evening, and soak them in the evening and drink them in the morning.' I said: 'Can we leave it until it gets stronger?' He said: 'Do not put it in clay vessels, rather put it in skins, for if it stays there for a long time, it will turn into vinegar.'"

Source: Sunan an-Nasa'i 5735 Grade: Sahih

Ubadah bin As-Samit narrated:

"Allah's Messenger prayed the Subh(Fajr) prayer, and he had difficulty with the recitation. When turned (after finishing) he said: 'I think that you are reciting behind your Imam?'" He said: "We said: 'Yes, Messenger of Allah, by Allah!' He said: 'Do not do that, except for Umm Al-Kitab(Fatihah), for there is no Salat for one who does not recite it.'"

Source: Jami` at-Tirmidhi 311 Grade: Sahih

Mu'awiya bin al-Hakam as-Sulami reported:

I said: Messenger of Allah, there were things we used to do in the pre-Islamic days. We used to visit Kahins,(soothsaying fortune-tellers) whereupon he said: Don't visit Kahins. I said: We used to take omens. He said: That is a sort of personal whim of yours, so let it not prevent you (from doing a thing).

Source: Sahih Muslim 537c

Narrated Abu Sa`id:

The Prophet (ﷺ) said, "Do not prefer some prophets to others."

Source: Sahih al-Bukhari 6916

Fadala ibn 'Ubayd reported that the Prophet said:

"Do not ask about three: a man who parts company with the community, rebels the ruler and dies while he is still a rebel. Do not ask about him. Or a slave or slavegirl who runs away from his master. Or a woman whose husband is absent and who has sufficient provision and then displays her adornments to strangers and mixes freely. Do not ask about three: a man who contends with Allah regarding His cloak. His cloak is pride and His wrapper is His might. Also a man who doubts the command of Allah. And someone who despairs of Allah's mercy."

Source: Al-Adab Al-Mufrad 590 Grade: Sahih

It was narrated that 'Ali said:

The Messenger of Allah (ﷺ) sent me to Yemen. I said: O Messenger of Allah, you are sending me to people who are older than me, and I am young and do not know how to judge. He put his hand on my chest and said: `O Allah, make his tongue steadfast and guide his heart. O Ali, when two disputants sit before you, do not judge between them until you listen to the second one as you listened to the first. If you do that, the verdict will become clear to you." 'Ali said: I never got confused about any judgement after that or doubted a verdict after that.

Source: Musnad Ahmad 882 Grade: Hasan

Abu'l-Hayyaj al-Asadi told that 'Ali said to him:

Should I not send you on the same mission as Allah's Messenger (ﷺ) sent me? Do not leave an image without obliterating it, or a high grave without levelling it. This hadith has been reported by Habib with the same chain of transmitters and he said: (Do not leave) a picture without obliterating it.

Source: Sahih Muslim 969a, 969b

Salim, on the authority of his father, reported Allah's Messenger (ﷺ) as saying:

None of you should eat with his left hand and drink with that (left hand), for the Satan eats with left hand and drinks with that (hand). Nafi' has made this addition in that:" Do not take up anything with that (left hand) and do not give anything with that"

Source: Sahih Muslim 2020c

Narrated Zayd ibn Khalid:

The Prophet (ﷺ) said: Do not curse the cock, for it awakens for prayer.

Source: Sunan Abi Dawud 5101 Grade: Sahih

Aishah narrated the Messenger of Allah (ﷺ) said:

"We do not seek the help of the polytheist."

Source: Sunan Ibn Majah 2832 Grade: Sahih

It was narrated that Humran said:

Uthman was sitting in al-Maqa`id. He called for water and did wudoo', then he said: I saw the Messenger of Allah (ﷺ) doing wudoo` in this place where I am sitting then he said: "whoever does wudoo' as I have done, then gets up and prays two rak`ahs, his previous sins will be forgiven." And the Messenger of Allah (ﷺ) said: `Do not become complacent.`

Source: Musnad Ahmad 478 Grade: Sahih

Ali bin Talq narrated that a Bedouin came to the Prophet and said:

"O Messenger of Allah! A man among us would be in the desert and a small smell would come from him, (what should he do) while the water is scarce? So the Messenger of Allah said: "When one of you breaks wind then let him perform Wudu, and do not go into your women in their behinds for indeed Allah is not shy of the truth."

Source: Jami` at-Tirmidhi 1164 Grade: Hasan

Al-A`raj narrated from Abu Hurairah, saying:

"I heard him saying: 'the Messenger of Allah (ﷺ) said: "When one of you seeks his neighbor's permission to affix a wooden beam in his wall, then do not prevent him."' When Abu Hurairah narrated it, they tilted their heads, so he said: 'Why do I see that you are averse to it? By Allah! I will continue to narrate it among you.'"

Source: Jami` at-Tirmidhi 1353 Grade: Sahih

Hammam bin Munabbih said:

Abu Huraira narrated to us ahadith from Allah's Messenger (ﷺ) and out of these, one is that Allah's Messenger (ﷺ) said: None amongst you should make a request for death, and do not call for it before it comes, for when any one of you dies, he ceases (to do good) deeds and the life of a believer is not prolonged but for goodness.

Source: Sahih Muslim 2682

Abdullah ibn as-Samit said:

"I questioned my close friend Abu Dharr who said, 'I brought some water for wudu' to the Prophet. He shook his head and bit his lip. I said, "May my father and mother be your ransom, have I injured you?" "No," he replied, "but you will meet amirs or imams, who will delay the prayer until it is past its time." "So what do you command me to do?" I asked. He replied, "Pray the prayer at the proper time. If you come across them, then pray with them and do not say, 'I have already prayed, so I will not pray again.'"'"

Source: Al-Adab Al-Mufrad 954 Grade: Sahih

Abdullah bin Abu Awfa said:

"When Muadh bin Jabal came from Sham, he prostrated to the Prophet who said: 'What is this, O Muadh?' He said: 'I went to Sham and saw them prostrating to their bishops and patricians and I wanted to do that for you.' The messenger of Allah said: 'Do not do that. If I were to *command anyone to prostrate to anyone other than Allah, I would have commanded women to prostrate to their husbands. By the One in Whose Hand is the soul of Muhammad! No woman can fulfill her duty towards Allah until she fulfills her duty towards her husband. If he asks her (for intimacy) even if she is on her camel saddle, she should not refuse.'"*

Source: Sunan Ibn Majah 1853 Grade: Hasan

It was narrated from 'Umar that he said:

Allah, may He be glorified and exalted, sent Muhammad (ﷺ) with the truth, and He sent down with him the Book. One of the things that were revealed to him was the verse of stoning. The Messenger of Allah (ﷺ) stoned [adulterers] and we stoned [them] after him. Then he said: We used to recite, `Do not forsake your real father (and attribute yourself to someone else), for this is an act of kufr, if you do that, or it is an act of kufr to forsake your real father (and attribute yourself to someone else).` And the Messenger of Allah (ﷺ) said: `Do not praise me as the son of Maryam was praised; rather I am a slave, so say: His slave and His Messenger.` Perhaps Ma`mar said: `As the Christians praised the son of Maryam."

Source: Musnad Ahmad 331 Grade: Sahih

It was narrated from Jabir that the Messenger of Allah(ﷺ) said:

"Do not camp on the middle of the road, or relieve yourselves there."

Source: Sunan Ibn Majah 3772 Grade: Daif

Ibn Abbas said the Messenger of Allah (ﷺ) said:

"Do not take anything with a soul as a target."

Source: Sunan Ibn Majah 3187 Grade: Sahih

Ali narrated the Messenger of Allah (ﷺ) said:

"Do not crack your fingers during the prayer."

Source: Sunan Ibn Majah 965 Grade: Daif

Narrated `Aisha:

The Prophet (ﷺ) said, "Do not abuse the dead, for they have reached the result of what they have done."

Source: Sahih al-Bukhari 6516

Amr bin Shu'aib narrated from his father, from his grandfather, the Messenger of Allah (ﷺ) said:

"People of two different religions do not inherit from one another."

Source: Sunan Ibn Majah 2731 Grade: Sahih

Narrated Jabir:

The Prophet (ﷺ) said, "Name yourselves after me, but do not call yourselves by my Kuniya."

Source: Sahih al-Bukhari 3538

Abdallah bin 'Amr bin al-'As told of God's messenger saying to him:

"Have I not been informed, 'Abdallah, that you fast during the day and get up at night for prayer?" [Mirqat explains this as meaning all night.] When he replied that that was so, he said, "Do not do it. Fast and break your fast, get up for prayer and sleep, for you have a duty to your body, your eye, your wife, and your visitors. May he who observe a perpetual fast never fast!* Fasting three days every month is equivalent to a perpetual fast. Fast three days every month and recite the Qur'an every month." When he replied that he was able to do more than that, he said, "Observe the most excellent fast, that of David, fasting every second day, and recite the Qur'an(completely) once every seven nights, but do no more than that."

* Some hold that the meaning here is, 'He who observes a perpetual fast has not fasted.'

Source: Mishkat al-Masabih 2054 Grade: Sahih

Narrated Abdullah ibn Abbas:

The Prophet said: Do not fast one day or two days just before Ramadan except in the case of a man who has been in the habit or observing a fast (that day); and do not fast until you sight it (the moon). Then fast until you sight it. If a cloud appears on that day (29th of Ramadan) then complete the number thirty (days) and then end the fasting: a month consists of twenty-nine days.

Source: Sunan Abi Dawud 2327 Grade: Sahih

Narrated `Aisha:

Whenever Allah's Messenger (ﷺ) was given the choice of one of two matters, he would choose the easier of the two, as long as it was not sinful to do so, but if it was sinful to do so, he would not approach it. Allah's Messenger (ﷺ) never took revenge (over anybody) for his own sake but (he did) only when Allah's Legal Bindings were outraged in which case he would take revenge for Allah's Sake.

Source: Sahih al-Bukhari 3560

Narrated Abu Jurayy Jabir ibn Salim al-Hujaymi:

I saw a man whose opinion was accepted by the people, and whatever he said they submitted to it. I asked: Who is he? They said: This is the Messenger of Allah (ﷺ). I said: On you be peace, Messenger of Allah, twice. He said: Do not say "On you be peace," for "On you be peace" is a greeting for the dead, but say "Peace be upon you".

I asked: You are the Messenger of Allah? He said: I am the Messenger of Allah Whom you call when a calamity befalls you and He removes it; when you suffer from drought and you call Him, He grows food for you; and when you are in a desolate land or in a desert and your she-camel strays and you call Him, He returns it to you.

I said: Give me some advice. He said: Do not abuse anyone. He said that he did not abuse a freeman, or a slave, or a camel or a sheep thenceforth. He said: Do not look down upon any good work, and when you speak to your brother, show him a cheerful face. This is a good work. Have your lower garment halfway down your shin; if you cannot do it, have it up to the ankles. Beware of trailing the lower garment, for it is conceit and Allah does not like conceit. And if a man abuses and shames you for something which he finds in you, then do not shame him for something which you find in him; he will bear the evil consequences for it.

Source: Sunan Abi Dawud 4084 Grade: Sahih

Narrated Samurah ibn Jundub:

The Prophet (ﷺ) said: Do not invoke Allah's curse, Allah's anger, or Hell.

Source: Sunan Abi Dawud 4906 Grade: Hasan

It was narrated from Abu Hurairah that the Messenger of Allah (ﷺ) said:

"Do not sell fruits until they have ripened."'

Source: Sunan Ibn Majah 2215 Grade: Sahih

It was narrated from Ibn Abbas that the Messenger of Allah (ﷺ) said:

"Do not carry out the legal punishment in the mosque."

Source: Sunan Ibn Majah 2599 Grade: Sahih

Ibn 'Abbas narrated that the Prophet (ﷺ) said:

"Do not keep looking at those who have leprosy."

Source: Sunan Ibn Majah 3543 Grade: Hasan

Narrated Abu Huraira:

Allah's Messenger said, "Do not withhold the superfluous water in order to withhold the superfluous grass."

Source: Sahih al-Bukhari 2354

Narrated Daylam al-Himyari:

I asked the Prophet (ﷺ) and said: Messenger of Allah! We live in a cold land in which we do heavy work and we make a liquor from wheat to get strength from it for our work and to stand the cold of our country. He asked: Is it intoxicating? I replied: Yes. He said: You must avoid it. I said: The people will not abandon it. He said: If they do not abandon it, fight with them.

Source: Sunan Abi Dawud 3683 Grade: Sahih

It was narrated from Muhammad bin Az-Zubair, from his father, from a man from the inhabitants of Al-Basrah, who said:

"I accompanied 'Imran bin Husain, who said: 'I heard the Messenger of Allah say: Vows are of two types: A vow that is made to do an act of obedience to Allah; that is for Allah and must be fulfilled, and a vow that is made to do an act of disobedience to Allah; that is for Shaitan and should not be fulfilled, and its expiation is the expiation for an oath.'"

Source: Sunan an-Nasa'i 3845 Grade: Sahih

It was narrated from 'Ali bin Abu Talib that the Messenger of Allah (ﷺ) said:

"Do not delay the funeral once it is ready."

Source: Sunan Ibn Majah 1486 Grade: Sahih

It was narrated from Abu Hurairah that the Messenger of Allah (ﷺ) said:

"Do not laugh a lot, for laughing a lot deadens the heart."

Source: Sunan Ibn Majah 4193 Grade: Hasan

Narrated Salim's father:

The Prophet (ﷺ) said, "Do not keep the fire burning in your houses when you go to bed."

Source: Sahih al-Bukhari 6293

Abu 'Ubaidah said:

"I heard the Messenger of Allah say: 'Fasting is a shield, so long as you do not damage it.'"

Source: Sunan an-Nasa'i 2233 Grade: Hasan

It was narrated that Ibn 'Umar said:

"The Messenger of Allah said: 'Do not revert to disbelievers after I am gone, striking the necks of one another (killing one another). No man is to be punished for the sins of his father, or for the sins of his brother.'"

Source: Sunan an-Nasa'i 4126 Grade: Sahih

Narrated Abu Huraira:

The Prophet (ﷺ) said: "Do not wish to meet the enemy, but when you meet face) the enemy, be patient."

Source: Sahih al-Bukhari 3026

Abu Hurairah said:

"The Messenger of Allah said: '(On the Day of Resurrection) camels will come to their owner in the best state of health that they ever had (in this world) and if he did not pay what was due on them, they will trample him with their hooves. Sheep will come to their owner in the best state of health that they ever had (in this world) and if he did not pay what was due on them, they will trample him with their cloven hooves and gore him with their horns. And among their rights are that they should be milked with water in the front of them. I do not want any one of you to come on the Day of Resurrection with a groaning camel on his neck, saying , O Muhammad, and I will say: I cannot do anything for you, I conveyed the message. I do not want any one of you to come on the Day of Resurrection with a bleating sheep on his neck, saying, "O Muhammad," and I will say: "I cannot do anything for you, I conveyed the message." And on the Day of Resurrection the hoarded treasure of one of you will be a bald-headed Shujaa snake from which its owner

will flee, but it will chase him (saying), I am your hoarded treasure, and it will keep (chasing him) until he gives it his finger to swallow."'

Source: Sunan an-Nasa'i 2448 Grade: Sahih

It was narrated from 'Amr bin Shu'aib from his father, that his grandfather said:

"A man came to the Prophet (ﷺ) and said: 'I do not have anything and I have no wealth, but I have an orphan (under my care) who has wealth." He said: "Eat from the wealth of your orphan, without being extravagant or use it for trade." He (narrator) said: "And I think he said: 'Do not preserve your wealth using his instead.'"

Source: Sunan Ibn Majah 2718 Grade: Hasan

Abu Hurairah reported:

A man who had drunk wine was brought to the Prophet (ﷺ) and he asked us to beat him; some struck him with their hands, some with their garments (making a whip) and some with their sandals. When he (the drunkard) had gone, some of the people said: "May Allah disgrace you!" He (the Prophet (ﷺ)) said, "Do not say so. Do not help the devil against him".

Source: Riyad as-Salihin 243 Grade: Sahih

Narrated Anas:

"When the Prophet (ﷺ) ate, he would lick his three fingers, and he said: 'If one of you drops a piece (of food) then let him remove any harm (dirt) from it and eat it, and do not leave it for Ash-Shaitan.' And he would order us to finish (clean) the dish. And he said: 'Indeed you do not know in which part of your food is the blessing.'

Source: Jami` at-Tirmidhi 1803 Grade: Sahih

Abu Hurairah reported:

Messenger of Allah (ﷺ) said, "A strong believer is better and dearer to Allah than a weak one, and both are good. Adhere to that which is beneficial for you. Keep asking Allah for help and do not refrain from it. If you are afflicted in any way, do not say: 'If I had taken this or that step, it would have resulted into such and such,' but say only: 'Allah so determined and did as He willed.' The word 'if' opens the gates of satanic thoughts".

Source: Riyad as-Salihin 100 Grade: Sahih

Narrated Amr ibn Za'dah, Ibn Umm Maktum:

Ibn Umm Maktum asked the Prophet (ﷺ) saying: Messenger of Allah, I am a blind man, my house is far away (from the mosque), and I have a guide who does not *follow me. Is it possible that permission be granted to me for saying prayer in my house? He asked: Do you hear summons (adhan)? He said: Yes. He said: I do not find any permission for you.*

Source: Sunan Abi Dawud 552 Grade: Hasan Sahih

Narrated Ibn 'Umar:

That the Messenger of Allah (ﷺ) said: "Whoever arrogantly drags his garment, Allah will not look at him on the Day of Judgement." So Umm Salamah said: "What should the women do with their hems?" He said: "Slacken them a handspan." So she said: "Then their feet will be uncovered." He said: "Then slacken them a forearm's length and do not add to that."

Source: Jami` at-Tirmidhi 1731 Grade: Sahih

It was narrated from Anas that:

The Messenger of Allah (ﷺ) said: "Do not rest your forearms on the ground like a dog when prostrating."

Source: Sunan an-Nasa'i 1103 Grade: Sahih

Narrated Ibn `Abbas:

The Prophet (ﷺ) said, "Beware! Do not renegade as (disbelievers) after me by striking (cutting) the necks of one another."

Source: Sahih al-Bukhari 7079

It was narrated that Abdullah bin 'Ukaim said:

"The Messenger of Allah wrote to us: 'Do not make use of the skins and sinew of dead animals.'"

Source: Sunan an-Nasa'i 4250 Grade: Hasan

Abu Hudhaifah narrated – and he was one of the companions of Abdullāh bin Mas'ūd – from Aishah who said:

"I told the Prophet (ﷺ) about a man, so he said: 'I do not like to talk about a man, even if I were to get this or that (for doing so)." She said: "I said: 'O Messenger of Allah! Safiyyah is a woman who is ..." and she used her hand as if to indicate that she is short – "So he said: 'You have said a statement which, if it were mixed in with the water of the sea, it would pollute it."

Source: Jami` at-Tirmidhi 2502 Grade: Sahih

Abu Huraira reported Allah's Messenger (ﷺ) said:

"Do not curse Time, for it is Allah Who is Time."

Source: Sahih Muslim 2246e

It was narrated from Jabir bin 'Abdullah that the Messenger of Allah (ﷺ) said:

"Do not bury your dead at night unless you are forced to."

Source: Sunan Ibn Majah 1521 Grade: Daif

It was narrated that Hakim bin Hizam said:

"The Messenger of Allah said: "Do not sell food until you have bought it and taken possession of it.""

Source: Sunan an-Nasa'i 4601 Grade: Sahih

It was narrated from 'Aishah that:

The Prophet said: "Do not soak (fruits) in Ad-Dubba', An-Naqir, Al-Hantam, and every intoxicant is unlawful."

Source: Sunan an-Nasa'i 5590 Grade: Sahih

It was narrated that Ali said:

*We were with the Messenger of Allah (ﷺ) at a funeral, and he said: `Who will go to Madinah and not leave any grave without levelling it, or any image without smearing it, or any idol without breaking it?` A man stood up and said: I will. Then he felt afraid of the people of Madinah, so he sat down. `Ali said: So I went, then I* came back and said: O Messenger of Allah (ﷺ), I did not leave any grave in Madinah but I levelled it, or any image but I smeared it, or any idol but I broke it. He said: `Whoever goes back to doing any of that has disbelieved in what Allah revealed to Muhammad. O Ali, do not be a cause of division – or he said: a show-off – or a merchant, except a good merchant, for they are the ones who procrastinate in doing good deeds."

Source: Musnad Ahmad 1170 Grade: Daif

Abdullah bin Umar reported:

I heard Allah's Messenger (ﷺ) say: Don't prevent your women from going to the mosque when they seek your permission. Bilal bin Abdullah said: By Allah, we shall certainly prevent them. On this Abdullah bin Umar turned towards him and reprimanded him so harshly as I had never heard him do before. He ('Abdullah bin Umar) said: I am narrating to you that which comes from the Messenger of Allah (ﷺ) and you (have the audacity) to say: By Allah, we shall certainly prevent them?!

Source: Sahih Muslim 442b

It was narrated that Ali said:

The Messenger of Allah (ﷺ) sent me with the sacrificial animals and said: `Do not give the butcher any of it.`

Source: Musnad Ahmad 897 Grade: Sahih

Narrated Aws ibn Thabit al-Ansari:

The Messenger of Allah (ﷺ) said: Act differently from the Jews, for they do not pray in their sandals or their shoes.

Source: Sunan Abi Dawud 652 Grade: Sahih

Ibn Abbas narrated:

"The Prophet advanced the weak among his family and he said: 'Do not stone the Jamrah(during Hajj pilgrimage) until the sun has risen.'"

Source: Jami` at-Tirmidhi 893 Grade: Sahih

Aisha narrated the Messenger of Allah said:

"Do not cut off (the thief's hand) except for something worth one quarter of a Dinar or more

Source: Sunan Ibn Majah 2585 Grade: Sahih

Ibn 'Umar said:

"The Messenger of Allah (ﷺ) forbade eating two dates at once unless he asks his companions permission to do so."

Source: Sunan Ibn Majah 3331 Grade: Sahih

Abdullah bin Mas'ud narrated that :

Allah's Messenger said: "Do not perform Istinja(cleaning private parts), with dung, nor with bones. For indeed it is provisions for your brothers among the Jinn."

Source: Jami` at-Tirmidhi 18 Grade: Sahih

It was narrated from Mu'awiyah that the Messenger of Allah said:

"Do not be demanding when asking. If one of you asks me for anything and I give it reluctantly, there will be no blessing in it."

Source: Sunan an-Nasa'i 2593 Grade: Sahih

It was narrated that 'Abdullah bin 'Umar said:

"The Messenger of Allah forbade vows and said: 'They do not change anything; they are just a means of taking wealth from the miserly.'"

Source: Sunan an-Nasa'i 3802 Grade: Sahih

It was narrated that Abu Musa said:

"Some people from among the Ash'aris came to me and said: 'Go with us to the Messenger of Allah, for we have something to ask him.' So I went with them, and they said: 'O Messenger of Allah, use us to do your work.'"

Abu Musa said: "I apologized for what they said, and I told him that I did not know what they were going to ask. He believed me and excused me, and said: 'We do not appoint for our work anyone who asks for that.'"

Source: Sunan an-Nasa'i 5382 Grade: Sahih

Salama bin al-Akwa' reported Allah's Messenger having said:

He who sacrifices (animal) among you nothing should be left in his house (out of its flesh) on the morning of the third day. When it was the next year they (his Companions) said: Should we do this year as we did during the previous year? Thereupon he said: Don't do that, for that was a year when the people were hard pressed (on account of poverty). So I wanted that the (flesh) might be distributed amongst them.

Source: Sahih Muslim 1974

Abdullah bin Ukaim reported:

While we were with Hudhaifa in Mada'in he asked for water. A villager brought a drink for him in a silver vessel. He (Hudhaifa) threw it away saying: I inform you that I have already conveyed to him that he should not serve me drink in it (silver vessel) for Allah's Messenger (ﷺ) had said: Do not drink in gold and silver vessels, and do not wear brocade or silk, for these are meant for them (the non-believers) in this world, but they are meant for you in the Hereafter on the Day of Resurrection.

Source: Sahih Muslim 2067a

Abu Hurairah reported that the Prophet said:

"Do not say, 'May Allah make your face ugly.'"

Source: Al-Adab Al-Mufrad 172 Grade: Hasan

Jundub bin Sufyan narrated that:

the Prophet said: "Whoever prays the Subh(Fajr) then he is under the protection of Allah's covenant, so do not be treacherous with Allah in his covenant."

Source: Jami` at-Tirmidhi 222 Grade: Sahih

Narrated Ibn `Abbas:

The Prophet said, 'When you eat, do not wipe your hands till you have licked it, or had it licked by somebody else."

Source: Sahih al-Bukhari 5456

Narrated `Ali:

The Prophet (ﷺ) said, "Do not tell a lie against me for whoever tells a lie against me (intentionally) then he will surely enter the Hell-fire."

Source: Sahih al-Bukhari 106

Abdullah bin 'Amr narrated that:

The Messenger of Allah saw him wearing two garments dyed with safflower and he said: "This is the clothing of disbelievers; do not wear it."

Source: Sunan an-Nasa'i 5316 Grade: Sahih

Abu Hurairah narrated:

"They said: 'O Messenger of Allah! You joke with us?' He said: 'Indeed I do not say except what is true.'"

Source: Jami` at-Tirmidhi 1990 Grade: Hasan

Al-Miqdad bin Al-Aswad reported:

I said, "Tell me, O Messenger of Allah, if I meet an infidel, and we fight together, and he cuts off my hands with his sword, then hides from me behind a tree and (then) says he has submitted himself to Allah. Shall I kill him after he has said it?" He (ﷺ) replied, "Do not kill him." I submitted, "But O Messenger of Allah, he cut off one of my hands and only then he said it." Messenger of Allah then replied, "Do not kill him, for if you do so, he will be in the position in which you were before you killed him (i.e., he will be considered a Muslim and thus his life will be inviolable), and you will be in the position in which he was before he made his testimony (i.e., your life will not be inviolable, for his heirs can ask for Qisas)".

Source: Riyad as-Salihin 392 Grade: Sahih

Narrated An-Nu`man bin Bashir:

The Prophet (ﷺ) said, "The example of the person abiding by Allah's orders and limits (or the one who abides by the limits and regulations prescribed by Allah) in comparison to the one who do wrong and violate Allah's limits and orders is like the example of people drawing lots for seats in a boat. Some of them got seats in the upper part while the others in the lower part ; those in the, lower part have to pass by those in the upper one to get water, and that troubled the latter. One of them (i.e. the people in the lower part) took an ax and started making a hole in the bottom of the boat. The people of the upper part came and asked him, (saying), 'What is wrong with you?' He replied, "You have been troubled much by my (coming up to you), and I have to get water.' Now if they prevent him from doing that they will save him and themselves, but if they leave him (to do what he wants), they will destroy him and themselves."

Source: Sahih al-Bukhari 2686

Narrated Buraydah ibn al-Hasib:

The Prophet (ﷺ) said: Do not call a hypocrite sayyid (master), for if he is a sayyid, you will displease your Lord, Most High.

Source: Sunan Abi Dawud 4977 Grade: Sahih

Narrated Hudhayfah:

The Prophet (ﷺ) said: Do not say: "What Allah wills and so and so wills," but say: "What Allah wills and afterwards so and so wills.

Source: Sunan Abi Dawud 4980 Grade: Sahih

It was narrated that Ali said:

The Messenger of Allah (ﷺ) said to me: "Do not follow one glance with another; you may be allowed the first but not the second.`

Source: Musnad Ahmad 1369 Grade: Hasan

Narrated Abu Huraira:

The Prophet (ﷺ) said, "Allah forgives my followers those (evil deeds) their souls may whisper or suggest to them as long as they do not act (on it) or speak."

Source: Sahih al-Bukhari 6664

It was narrated from 'Amr bin Shu'aib, from his father, from his grandfather that :

the Prophet forbade the deal involving earnest money.

Abu 'Abdullah said: Earnest money refers to when a man buys an animal for one hundred Dinar, then he gives the seller two Dinar in advance and says: "If I do not buy the animal, then the two Dinar are yours." And it was said that it refers, and Allah knows best, to when a man buys something, and gives the seller a Dirham or less or more, and says: "If I take it (all well and good), and if I do not, then the Dirham is yours."

Source: Sunan Ibn Majah 2193 Grade: Hasan

It was narrated from Hudhaifah bin Yaman that the Messenger of Allah (ﷺ) said:

"There will be callers at the gates of Hell; whoever responds to them they throw them into it." I said: "O Messenger of Allah, describe them to us." He said: "They will be from our people, speaking our language." I said: "What do you command me to do, if I live to see that?" He said: "Adhere I main body of the Muslims and their leader. If there is no such body and no leader, then withdraw from all their groups, even if you bite onto the trunk of a tree until death finds you in that state."

Source: Sunan Ibn Majah 3979 Grade: Sahih

It was narrated that Abu Masud said:

"The Messenger of Allah(ﷺ)said: 'Let the one who has most knowledge of the Book of Allah lead the people in prayer. If they are equal in terms of knowledge of the Quran, let the one who emigrated first (lead them). If they are equal in terms of emigration, let the one who has more knowledge of the Sunnah, (lead them). If they are equal in terms of knowledge of the Sunnah, let the one who is oldest (lead them). Do not lead a man in prayer in his place of authority, and do not sit in his place of honor, unless he gives you permission.'"

Source: Sunan an-Nasa'i 780 Grade: Sahih

Narrated Isam al-Muzani:

The Messenger of Allah (ﷺ) sent us in a detachment and said (to us): If you see a mosque or hear a mu'adhdhin (calling to prayer), do not kill anyone.

Source: Sunan Abi Dawud 2635 Grade: Daif

Narrated Aisha, Ummul Mu'minin:

Something of hers was stolen, and she began to curse him (i.e. the thief). The Messenger of Allah (ﷺ) said to her: Do not lessen his sin.

Source: Sunan Abi Dawud 4909 Grade: Daif

It was narrated that Abdullah bin 'Amr said:

"The Messenger of Allah (ﷺ) said to me: 'Do not be like so-and-so; he used to pray Qiyam Al-Lail then he stopped.'"

Source: Sunan an-Nasa'I 1763 Grade: Sahih

Narrated Abu Huraira:

Allah's Messenger said, "If the prayer is started do not run for it but just walk for it calmly and pray whatever you get, and complete whatever is missed."

Source: Sahih al-Bukhari 908

It was narrated that Hamzah said:

"I asked the Messenger of Allah about fasting while traveling. He said: 'If you wish to fast then fast, and if you wish not to fast then do not fast.'"

Source: Sunan an-Nasa'i 2296 Grade: Sahih

It is narrated on the authority of Abu Huraira that the Messenger of Allah observed:

Do not detest your fathers; he who detested his father committed infidelity.

Source: Sahih Muslim 62

Narrated Abu Usayd as-Sa'idi:

The Prophet (ﷺ) said at the battle of Badr: When they come near you shoot arrows at them; and do not draw swords at them until they come near you.

Source: Sunan Abi Dawud 2664 Grade: Daif

Abu Dharr reported:

The Prophet said, "Do not belittle any good deed, even meeting your brother (Muslim) with a cheerful face".

Source: Riyad as-Salihin 121 Grade: Sahih

Narrated Aisha, Ummul Mu'minin:

Do not give up prayer at night, for the Messenger of Allah (ﷺ) would not leave it. Whenever he fell ill or lethargic, he would offer it sitting.

Source: Sunan Abi Dawud 1307 Grade: Sahih

Narrated Musa bin Talhah:

that Abu Al-Yasar said: "A woman came to me selling dates. I said to her: 'There are better dates than these in the house.' So she entered the house with me. I had an urge for her so I began kissing her. I went to Abu Bakr and mentioned that to him, so he said: 'Cover what you have done, repent, do not inform any one, and never do it *again.' So I went to 'Umar and mentioned that to him. He said: 'Cover what you have done, repent, do not inform any one, and never do it again.' Then I went to the Prophet (ﷺ) and mentioned it to him." He said: 'Is this how you take care of the wife of someone who is away fighting in Allah's cause?" Such that he had wished he had not accepted Islam until that very time, and he thought that he must be one of the people of the Fire." He said: "The Messenger of Allah (ﷺ) bowed his head for a long time, until Allah revealed to him: And perform the Salat, at the two ends of the day and in some hours of the night. Verily, the good deeds remove the evil deeds. That is a reminder for the mindful (11:114). Abu Al-Yasar said: "So I went to him and the Messenger of Allah (ﷺ) recited it for me. A companion of his said: "O Messenger of Allah! Is this specific, or is it for the people in general?" He said: "Rather it is for the people in general."*

Source: Jami` at-Tirmidhi 3115 Grade: Hasan

Narrated Al-Bara' ibn Azib:

The Messenger of Allah (ﷺ) was asked about performing ablution after eating the flesh of the camel. He replied: Perform ablution, after eating it. He was asked about performing ablution after eating meat. He replied: Do not perform ablution after eating it. He was asked about saying prayer in places where the camels lie down. He replied: Do not offer prayer in places where the camels lie down. These are the places of Satan. He was asked about saying prayer in the sheepfolds. He replied: You may offer prayer in such places; these are the places of blessing.

Source: Sunan Abi Dawud 184 Grade: Sahih

Narrated Abdullah ibn Umar:

The Prophet (ﷺ) saw a boy with part of his head shaved and part left unshaven. He forbade them to do that, saying: Shave it all or leave it all.

Source: Sunan Abi Dawud 4195 Grade: Sahih

It was narrated from 'Uqbah bin 'Amir Al-Juhani that the Messenger of Allah (ﷺ) said:

"Do not force your sick ones to eat or drink. Allah will feed them and give them to drink."

Source: Sunan Ibn Majah 3444 Grade: Daif

Narrated Abu Burda Al-Ansari:

I heard the Prophet (ﷺ) saying, "Do not flog anyone more than ten stripes except if he is involved in a crime necessitating Allah's legal Punishment."

Source: Sahih al-Bukhari 6850

It was narrated that Umar said:

"The Messenger of Allah saw me urinating while standing, and he said: 'O 'Umar, do not urinate standing up.' So I never urinated whilst standing after that."

Source: Sunan Ibn Majah 308 Grade: Daif

It was narrated that Abu Hurairah said:

"Mention of fever was made in the presence of the Messenger of Allah (ﷺ), and a man cursed it. The Prophet (ﷺ) said: 'Do not curse it, for it erases sin as fire removes filth from iron.'"

Source: Sunan Ibn Majah 3469 Grade: Sahih

Uqbah bin 'Amir narrated that:

The Messenger of Allah used to tell his wives not to wear jewelry and silk. He said: "If you want the jewelry and silk of Paradise, then do not wear them in this world."

Source: Sunan an-Nasa'i 5136 Grade: Sahih

Narrated 'Abdullah bin Abi Qatadah:

From his father, that the Messenger of Allah (ﷺ) said: "When one of you drinks, then do not breathe into the vessel."

Source: Jami` at-Tirmidhi 1889 Grade: Sahih

Tariq bin Abdullah Al-Muharibi narrated that:

the Messenger of Allah said: "When you are in Salat then do not spit on your right, but behind you or toward your left, or under your left foot."

Source: Jami` at-Tirmidhi 571 Grade: Sahih

Narrated Yazid ibn al-Aswad:

Yazid prayed along with the Messenger of Allah (ﷺ) when he was a young boy. When he (the Prophet) had prayed there were two persons (sitting) in the corner of the mosque; they did not pray (along with the Prophet). He called for them. They were brought trembling (before him). He asked: What prevented you from praying along with us? They replied: We have already prayed in our houses. He said: Do not do so. If any of you prays in his house and finds that the imam has not prayed, he should pray along with him; and that will be a supererogatory prayer for him.

Source: Sunan Abi Dawud 575 Grade: Sahih

Abu Huraira reported Allah's Messenger said:

Do not go out to meet riders to enter into transaction with them; none of you must buy in opposition to another, nor must you bid against one another; a townsman must not sell for a man from the desert, and do not tie up udders of camels and sheep, and he who buys them after that has been done has two courses open to him: after he has milked them he may keep them if he is pleased with them, or he may return them along with a bit of dates if he is displeased with them.

Source: Sahih Muslim 1515c

Abu Hurairah reported that the Messenger of Allah (ﷺ) said:

"Look at those who are beneath you and do not look at those who are above you, for it is more suitable that you should not consider as less the blessing of Allah."

Source: Sunan Ibn Majah 4142 Grade: Sahih

It was narrated from `Ubadah bin Samit that the Messenger of Allah (ﷺ) said:

"Carry out the legal punishments on relatives and strangers, and do not let the fear of blame stop you from carrying out the command of Allah."

Source: Sunan Ibn Majah 2540 Grade: Hasan

Abdullah bin Mas'ud reported:

Messenger of Allah (ﷺ) said: "Do not crave for property lest you should be absorbed in the desire of worldly life."

Source: Riyad as-Salihin 478 Grade: Hasan

Narrated Abu Huraira:

The Prophet (ﷺ) said, "Do not set out on a journey except for three Mosques i.e. Al-Masjid-Al-Haram, the Mosque of Allah's Messenger (ﷺ), and the Mosque of Al-Aqsa, (Mosque of Jerusalem)."

Source: Sahih al-Bukhari 1189

Abu Usaid reported the Messenger of Allaah(ﷺ) as saying to us at the battle of Badr when he drew up in rows.

When they come near you, shoot arrows at them, but do not use all your arrows.

Source: Sunan Abi Dawud 2663 Grade: Sahih

Ubaid bin Fairuz said:

"I said to Al-Bara bin Azib: 'Tell me of the sacrificial animals that the Messenger of Allah disliked or forbade. He said: "The Messenger of Allah gestured like this with *his hand, and my hands are shorter than the hand of the Messenger of Allah, (and he said). 'There are four that will not do as sacrifices: The animal that clearly has one bad eye: the sick animals that is obviously sick; the lame animal with an obvious lamp; and the animal that is so emaciated that it is as if there is no marrow in its bones: He said: "And I dislike that the animal should have some fault in its horns or ears." He said: "What you dislike, forget about it, and do not make it forbidden to anyone."*

Source: Sunan an-Nasa'i 4370 Grade: Sahih

It was narrated from Mughirah bin Shu'bah that the Messenger of Allah (ﷺ) said:

"O Sufyan bin Sahl, do not let your garment hang, for Allah does not like those (men) who let their garments hang below the ankles.'"

Source: Sunan Ibn Majah 3574 Grade: Hasan

Narrated `Abdullah bin `Umar:

Allah's Messenger (ﷺ) said, "Do not urge somebody to return what he has already bought (i.e. in optional sale) from another seller so as to sell him your own goods."

Source: Sahih al-Bukhari 2139

Salim bin 'Abdullah bin 'Umar said:

"I heard my father say: 'I heard 'Umar bin Khattab say: "The Messenger of Allah (ﷺ) said: 'Eat together and do not eat separately, for the blessing is in being together.'"'

Source: Sunan Ibn Majah 3287 Grade: Hasan

Narrated Ibn Masud:

We used to fight in the holy battles in the company of the Prophet (ﷺ) and we had no wives with us. So we said, "O Allah's Messenger (ﷺ)! Shall we get castrated?" The Prophet (ﷺ) forbade us to do so.

Source: Sahih al-Bukhari 5071

Narrated Abu Hurairah:

That the Messenger of Allah (ﷺ) said: "Do not walk in one sandal, either wear both sandals, or go barefoot."

Source: Jami` at-Tirmidhi 1774 Grade: Sahih

Ibn 'Umar narrated the Messenger of Allah said:

"Do not talk too much without remembrance of Allah. Indeed excessive talking without remembrance of Allah hardens the heart. And indeed the furthest of people from Allah is the harsh-hearted."

Source: Jami` at-Tirmidhi 2411 Grade: Hasan

Narrated Al-Miswar bin Makhramah:

I lifted a heavy stone. While I was walking my garment fell down. The Messenger of Allah (ﷺ) said to me: Take your garment upon you, and do not walk naked.

Source: Sunan Abi Dawud 4016 Grade: Sahih

Narrated Rafi` bin Khadij:

I said, "O Allah's Messenger (ﷺ)! We are going to face the enemy tomorrow and we do not have knives." He said, "Hurry up (in killing the animal). If the killing tool causes blood to flow out, and if Allah's Name is mentioned, eat (of the slaughtered animal). But do not slaughter with a tooth or a nail. I will tell you why: As for the tooth, it is a bone; and as for the nail, it is the knife of Ethiopians." Then we got some camels and sheep as war booty, and one of those camels ran away, whereupon a man shot it with an arrow and stopped it. Allah's Messenger (ﷺ) said, "Of these camels there are some which are as wild as wild beasts, so if one of them (runs away and) makes you tired, treat it in this manner."

Source: Sahih al-Bukhari 5509

Ibn Abbas reported that the Prophet said:

"We do not give a bad example. The one who takes back his gift is like the dog who returns to his own vomit."

Source: Al-Adab Al-Mufrad 417 Grade: Sahih

Abdullah (Ibn Masud) narrated that :

the Prophet said: "Let those among you with understanding and reason be close to me, then those after them, then those after them. And do not separate or dissention will occur among your hearts, and beware of the commotion of the markets."

Source: Jami` at-Tirmidhi 228 Grade: Sahih

Abu Sufyan reported:

Messenger of Allah (ﷺ) said, "Do not be importunate in begging. By Allah! If one of you asks me for something and I give it to him unwillingly, there is no blessing in what I give him."

Source: Riyad as-Salihin 527 Grade: Sahih

Abdullah bin Al-Harith narrated that a man from among the Companions of the Prophet said:

"I entered upon the Prophet when he was having Sahur. He said: 'It is a blessing that Allah has given to you, so do not neglect it."

Source: Sunan an-Nasa'i 2162 Grade: Sahih

Narrated Nu'aym ibn Hammar:

I heard the Messenger of Allah (ﷺ) say: Allah, the Exalted, says: Son of Adam, do not be helpless in performing four rak'ahs for Me at the beginning of the day: I will supply what you need till the end of it.

Source: Sunan Abi Dawud 1289 Grade: Sahih

Narrated Abu Huraira:

The people of the Scripture (Jews) used to recite the Torah in Hebrew and they used to explain it in Arabic to the Muslims. On that Allah's Messenger said, "Do not believe the people of the Scripture or disbelieve them, but say:-- "We believe in Allah and what is revealed to us."

Source: Sahih al-Bukhari 4485

It was narrated that Ibn 'Umar said:

"We passed by a pond and we started to lap up water from it. The Messenger of Allah (ﷺ) said: 'Do not lap up the water, rather wash your hands then drink from them, for there is no better vessel than the hand.'"

Source: Sunan Ibn Majah 3433 Grade: Daif

It was narrated that Jabir bin 'Abdullah said:

"The Messenger of Allah (ﷺ) said: 'The mother of Sulaiman bin Dawud said to Sulaiman: "O my son, do

not sleep too much at night, for sleeping too much at night will leave a man poor on the Day of Resurrection."

Source: Sunan Ibn Majah 1332 Grade: Daif

It was narrated from 'Aishah that the Messenger of Allah (ﷺ) entered upon her and there was a close relative of hers who was in the throes of death. When the Prophet (ﷺ) saw how upset she was, he said:

"Do not grieve for your relative, for that is part of his Hasanat (merits)."

Source: Sunan Ibn Majah 1451 Grade: Daif

It was narrated from Sunabih Al-Ahmasi that the Messenger of Allah (ﷺ) said:

"I shall reach the Cistern (Haud) before you, and I will boast of your great numbers before the nations, so do not fight one another after I am gone.'"

Source: Sunan Ibn Majah 3944 Grade: Sahih

Salman Al-Farisi said:

The Prophet said, "Do not, if you can help, be the first to enter the market and the last to leave it because it is an arena of Satan and the standard of Satan is set there."

Source: Riyad as-Salihin 1842 Grade: Sahih

It was narrated from Abu Hurairah that the Messenger of Allah said:

"None of you should wish for death. Either he is a doer of good, so perhaps he may do more good, or he is an evildoer but perhaps he will give up his evil ways."

Source: Sunan an-Nasa'i 1818 Grade: Sahih

Narrated Anas bin Malik:

Allah's Messenger (ﷺ) said, "Whoever prays like us and faces our Qibla and eats our slaughtered animals is a Muslim and is under Allah's and His Messenger's protection. So do not betray Allah by betraying those who are in His protection."

Source: Sahih al-Bukhari 391

Narrated Abu Huraira:

The Prophet said, "Whoever performs Hajj for Allah's pleasure and does not have sexual relations with his wife, and does not do evil or sins then he will return (after Hajj free from all sins) as if he were born anew."

Source: Sahih al-Bukhari 1521

Abu Hurairah narrated that the Messenger of Allah said:

"None of you should say: 'O Allah forgive me if You wish. O Allah have mercy on me if You wish.' Let him be firm in asking, for there is none that can compel Him to do things."

Source: Jami` at-Tirmidhi 3497 Grade: Sahih

It was narrated from 'Abdullah bin Abi Qatadah, from his father that the Prophet (ﷺ) said:

"I stand in prayer, then I hear a child crying, so I make my prayer brief, because I do not want to cause hardship for his mother."

Source: Sunan an-Nasa'i 825 Grade: Sahih

It was narrated from Abu Hurairah that :

the Messenger of Allah said: "It is necessary that you do not become hasty." It was said: "What does being hasty mean, O Messenger of Allah?" He said: "When one says: 'I supplicated to Allah but Allah did not answer me.'"

Source: Sunan Ibn Majah 3853 Grade: Sahih

It was narrated that Abu Umamah said:

"A woman came to the Prophet with two of her children, carrying one and leading the other. The Messenger of Allah said: 'They carry children and give birth to them and are compassionate. If they do not annoy their husbands, those among them who perform prayer will enter Paradise.'"

Source: Sunan Ibn Majah 2013 Grade: Daif

Abu Dharr reported Allah's Messenger (ﷺ) as saying that Allah, the Exalted and Glorious, said:

"O My servants, I have forbidden oppression for Myself and have made it forbidden amongst you, so do not oppress one another. O My servants, all of you are astray except for those I have guided, so seek guidance of Me and I shall guide you, O My servants, all of you are hungry except for those I have fed, so seek food of Me and I shall feed you. O My servants, all of you are naked except for those I have clothed, so seek clothing of Me and I shall clothe you. O My servants, you sin by night and by day, and I forgive all sins, so seek forgiveness of Me and I shall forgive you. O My servants, you will not attain harming Me so as to harm Me, and will not attain benefitting Me so as to benefit Me. O My servants, were the first of you and the last of you, the human of you and the jinn of you to be as pious as the most pious heart of

any one man of you, that would not increase My dominion in anything. O My servants, were the first of you and the last of you, the human of you and the jinn of you to be as wicked as the most wicked heart of any one man of you, that would not decrease My dominion in anything. O My servants, were the first of you and the last of you, the human of you and the jinn of you to rise up in one place and make a request of Me, and were I to give everyone what he requested, that would not decrease what I have, any more that a needle decreases the sea if put into it. O My servants, it is but your deeds that I record for you and then recompense you for. So let him who finds good, praise Allah, and let him who finds other than that blame no one but himself."

Source: Sahih Muslim 2577

Jabir bin 'Abd Allaah reported the Messenger of Allaah(ﷺ) as saying:

"Do not send out your beasts when the sun has set till the darkness of the night prevails, for the devils grope about in the dark when the sun has set till the darkness of the night prevails."

Source: Sunan Abi Dawud 2604 Grade: Sahih

It was narrated from Abu Sa'eed that the Messenger of Allah (ﷺ) stood up to deliver a sermon and one of the things that he said was:

"This world is fresh and sweet, and Allah will make your successive generations therein, so look at what you do and beware of (the temptations of) this world and beware of (the temptations of) women."

Source: Sunan Ibn Majah 4000 Grade: Sahih

Narrated `Abdur Rahman bin Abi Bakra:

Abu Bakra wrote to his son who was in Sijistan: 'Do not judge between two persons when you are angry, for I heard the Prophet (ﷺ) saying, "A judge should not judge between two persons while he is in an angry mood."

Source: Sahih al-Bukhari 7158

Sa'eed – meaning Ibn Al-Musayyab – and 'Abbad bin Tamim narrated that his uncle – 'Abdullah bin Zaid – said:

"A man who felt something during Salah complained to the Prophet (ﷺ). He said: 'Do not stop praying unless you notice a smell or hear a sound.'"

Source: Sunan an-Nasa'i 160 Grade: Sahih

It was narrated Qailah Umm Bani Anmar said:

"I came to the Messenger of Allah (ﷺ), during one of his 'Umrah at Marwah and said: 'O Messenger of Allah, I am a woman who buys and sells. When I want to buy something, I state a price less than I want to pay, then I raise it gradually until it reaches the price I want to pay. And when I want to sell something, I state a price more than I want, then I lower it until it reaches the price I want.' The Messenger of Allah (ﷺ) said: 'Do not do that, O Qailah. When you want to buy something, state the price you want, whether it is given or not. And when you want to sell something, state the price you want, whether it is given or not.'"

Source: Sunan Ibn Majah 2204 Grade: Daif

Narrated Abu Rafi':

The Prophet (ﷺ) said: Let me not find one of you reclining on his couch when he hears something regarding me which I have commanded or forbidden and saying: We do not know. What we found in Allah's Book we have followed.

Source: Sunan Abi Dawud 4605 Grade: Sahih

Abdullah ibn al-'As reported the Prophet said:

"Show mercy and you will be shown mercy. Forgive and Allah will forgive you. Woe to the vessels that catch words (i.e. the ears). Woe to those who persist and consciously continue in what they are doing."

Source: Al-Adab Al-Mufrad 380 Grade: Sahih

Narrated `Abdullah:

Allah's Messenger (ﷺ) said, "Do not wish to be like anyone, except in two cases: (1) A man whom Allah has given wealth and he spends it righteously. (2) A man whom Allah has given wisdom (knowledge of the Qur'an and the Hadith) and he acts according to it and teaches it to others."

Source: Sahih al-Bukhari 7141

Mu'awiyah bin al-Hakam al-Sulami said:

I was praying with the Messenger of Allah(ﷺ). A man in the company sneezed, and I said: May Allah have mercy on you! The people gave me disapproving looks, so I said: Woe is to me! What do you mean by looking at me? They began to strike their hand on their thighs; then I realized that they were urging me to be silent. When the Messenger of Allah (ﷺ) finished his prayer – for whom I would give my father and mother as ransom-he did not beat, scold or revile me, but said: No talk to people is *lawful in this prayer, for it consists only in glorifying Allah, declaring His greatness, and reciting the Qur'an or words to that effect said by the Messenger of Allah (ﷺ).*

I said: Messenger of Allah, we were only recently pagans, but Allah has brought Islam to us, and among us there are men who have recourse to soothsayers (kahins). He replied: Do not have recourse to them.

I said: Among us are there are men who take omens. He replied: That is something which they find, but let it not turn them away (from what they intended to do).

I said: among us there are men who draw lines. He replied: There was a prophet who drew lines; so if the line of anyone tallies with this line, that might come true.

I said: A slave-girl of mine used to tend goats before (the mountain) Uhud and al-Jawaniyyah. Once when I reached her (suddenly) I found that a wolf had taken away a goat of them. I am a human being; I feel grieved as others do. But I gave her a good knocking. This was unbearable for the Messenger of Allah (ﷺ). I asked: Should I set her free? He replied: Bring her to me. So I brought her to him. He asked (her): Where is Allah? She said: In the heaven. He said: Who am I? She replied: You are the Messenger of Allah. He said: Set her free, for she is believer.

Source: Sunan Abi Dawud 930 Grade: Sahih

It was narrated that Abdullah bin Amr said:

"*The Messenger of Allah(ﷺ) said: 'You will conquer the lands of the non-Arabs, where you will find houses called Hammamat (bathhouses). Men Should only enter them wearing a waist wrap, and do not let women enter them unless they are sick or bleeding following childbirth.'*"

Source: Sunan Ibn Majah 3748 Grade: Daif

Narrated Salman:

"*The Messenger of Allah (ﷺ) said to me: 'O Salman! Do not detest me and thereby leave your religion.' I said: 'O Messenger of Allah! How could I detest you while Allah guided us by you.' He said: 'You will detest the Arabs and thereby detest me.'*"

Source: Jami` at-Tirmidhi 3927 Grade: Daif

It has been narrated on the authority of Ibn 'Umar that the Messenger of Allah (ﷺ) said:

Do not take the Qur'an on a journey with you, for I am afraid lest it should fall into the hands of the enemy.

Ayyub (one of the narrators in the chain of transmitters) said: The enemy may seize it and may quarrel with you over it.

Source: Sahih Muslim 1869c

Narrated Ibn `Abbas:

The Prophet (ﷺ) once came out to us and said, "Some nations were displayed before me. A prophet would pass in front of me with one man, and another with two men, and another with a group of people. and another with nobody with him. Then I saw a great crowd covering the horizon and I wished that they were my followers, but it was said to me, 'This is Moses and his followers.' Then it was said to me, 'Look'' I looked and saw a big gathering with a large number of people covering the horizon. It was said, "Look this way and that way.' So I saw a big crowd covering the horizon. Then it was said to me, "These are your followers, and among them there are 70,000 who will enter Paradise without (being asked about their) accounts. " Then the people dispersed and the Prophet (ﷺ) did not tell who those 70,000 were. So the companions of the Prophet (ﷺ) started talking about that and some of them said, "As regards us, we were born in the era of heathenism, but then we believed in Allah and His Apostle . We think however, that these (70,000) are our offspring." That talk reached the Prophet (ﷺ) who said, "These (70,000) are the people who do not draw an evil omen from (birds) and do not get treated by branding themselves and do not treat with Ruqya(by seeking it from others or using forbidden methods), but put their trust (only) in their Lord." then 'Ukasha bin Muhsin got up and said, "O Allah's Messenger (ﷺ)! Am I one of those (70,000)?" The Prophet (ﷺ) said, "Yes." Then another person got up and said, "Am I one of them?" The Prophet (ﷺ) said, " 'Ukasha has anticipated you."

Source: Sahih al-Bukhari 5752

Sulaiman bin Amr bin Ahwas said:

"My father told me that he was present at the Farewell Pilgrimage with the Messenger of Allah. He praised and glorified Allah, and reminded and exhorted (the people). Then he said: 'I enjoin good treatment of women, for they are prisoners with you, and you have no right to treat them otherwise, unless they commit clear indecency. If they do that, then forsake them in their beds and hit them, but without causing injury or leaving a mark. If they obey you, then do not seek means of annoyance against them. You have rights over your women and your women have rights over you. Your rights over your women are that they are not to allow anyone whom you

dislike to tread on your bedding (furniture), nor allow anyone whom you dislike to enter your houses. And their right over you are that you should treat them kindly with regard to their clothing and food.'"

Source: Sunan Ibn Majah 1851 Grade: Sahih

It was narrated from Abu Bakr Siddiq that the Messenger of Allah (ﷺ) said:

"Whoever offers the morning prayer, he is under the protection of Allah, so do not betray Allah by betraying those who are under His protection. Whoever kills him, Allah will seek him out until He throws him on his face into Hell."

Source: Sunan Ibn Majah 3945 Grade: Sahih

It was narrated that Abu Ayyub said:

"A man came to the Prophet (ﷺ) and said: 'O Messenger of Allah, teach me but make it concise.' He said: 'When you stand to pray, pray like a man bidding farewell. Do not say anything for which you will have to apologize. And give up hope for what other people have.'"

Source: Sunan Ibn Majah 4171 Grade: Hasan

Narrated Ibn `Abbas:

The Prophet (ﷺ) said, "If somebody sees his Muslim ruler doing something he disapproves of, he should be patient, for whoever becomes separate from the Muslim group even for a span and then dies, he will die as those who died in the Pre-Islamic period of ignorance (as rebellious sinners).

Source: Sahih al-Bukhari 7143

Amr bin shu'aib said:

"My father told me, narrating from his father, from his father (and he mentioned 'Abdullah bin 'Amr) that he said: "The Messenger of Allah said: "It is not permissible to lend on the condition of a sale, or to stipulate two conditions in one transaction, or to make a profit on that which you do not possess.

Source: Sunan an-Nasa'i 4630 Grade: Sahih

Ruwaifi' bin Thabit said:

"The Messenger of Allah said: 'O Ruwaifi', you may live for a long time after me, so tell the people that whoever ties up his beard, or twists it, or hangs an amulet, or cleans himself (after relieving himself) with animal dung or bones, Muhammad has nothing to do with him.'"

Source: Sunan an-Nasa'i 5067 Grade: Sahih

Narrated Abu Umamah:

that the Messenger of Allah (ﷺ) said: "Do not sell the female singers, nor purchase them, nor teach them (to sing). And there is no good in trade in them, and their prices are unlawful. It was about the likes of this that this Ayah was revealed: 'And among mankind is he who purchases idle talk to divert from the way of Allah.'"

Source: Jami` at-Tirmidhi 3195 Grade: Daif

Anas bin Malik said the Messenger of Allah said:

"Whoever avoids lying while he is doing so falsely, a house will be built for him on the skirts of Paradise. Whoever avoids arguing while he is in the right, a house will be built for him in its midst. And whoever has good character, a house will be built for him in its heights."

Source: Jami` at-Tirmidhi 1993 Grade: Daif

It was narrated from Aishah that:

the Messenger of Allah said: "Marriage is part of my sunnah, and whoever does not follow my sunnah has nothing to do with me. Get married, for I will boast of your great numbers before the nations. Whoever has the means, let him get married, and whoever does not, then he should fast for it will diminish his desire."

Source: Sunan Ibn Majah 1846 Grade: Hasan

Aishah narrated:

"Umm Habibah bint Jahsh sought a verdict from Allah's Messenger. She said 'I suffer from persistent bleeding such that I do not become pure. Shall I give up the Salat?' He said: 'No, that is only a blood vessel. So perform Ghusl then pray.' So she would perform Ghusl for each prayer."

Source: Jami` at-Tirmidhi 129 Grade: Sahih

Humaidah bint Yasir narrated from her grandmother Yusairah - and she was one of those who emigrated - she said:

"The Messenger of Allah (ﷺ) said to us: 'Hold fast to At-Tasbih, At-Tahlil, and At-Taqdis, and count them upon the fingertips, for indeed they shall be questioned, and they will be made to speak. And do not become heedless, so that you forget about the Mercy (of Allah).'"

Source: Jami` at-Tirmidhi 3583 Grade: Hasan

Umar bin 'Ata reported that Nafi' bin Jubair sent him to Sa'ib bin Ukht Namir to ask him about something that Mu'awiyah had seen him doing in Salat (prayer). He said:

"Yes, I performed the Friday prayer along with him in the enclosure (Maqsurah), and when the Imam concluded the Salat with Taslim, I stood up in my place and performed the Sunnah prayer. When Mu'awiyah went home, he sent for me (and when I came) he said: "Never do again what you have done. When you have observed the Friday prayer, you must not start another Sunnah prayer till you have spoken to someone or have shifted your place; because the Messenger of Allah (ﷺ) ordered us not to follow up the congregational Salat with any other Salat until we have talked (to someone) or moved from the place."

Source: Riyad as-Salihin 1131 Grade: Sahih

Amr bin Shu'aib, on his father's authority, told that his grandfather reported that the Messenger of Allah (ﷺ) said:

Do not pluck out grey hair. If any believer grows a grey hair in Islam, he will have light on the Day of Resurrection. (This is Sufyan's version). Yahya's version says: Allah will record on his behalf a good deed for it, and will blot out a sin for it.

Source: Sunan Abi Dawud 4202 Grade: Hasan Sahih

It was narrated that Al-Bara bin Azib said:

"The Messenger of Allah (ﷺ) used to go between the rows from one side to another, patting our shoulders and chests and saying: 'Do not make your rows ragged or your hearts will be filled with enmity toward one another.' And he used to say: 'Allah and His angels send Salah upon the front rows.'"

Source: Sunan an-Nasa'i 811 Grade: Sahih

Amr bin Shu'aib reported on his father's authority that his grandfather said:

Messenger of Allah (ﷺ) said, "Command your children to perform Salat (prayer) when they are seven (lunar) years old, and beat them for (not offering) it when they are ten, and do not let (boys and girls) sleep together".

Source: Riyad as-Salihin 301 Grade: Hasan

It was narrated that Abu Hurairah said:

"A man came to the Prophet and said: 'O Messenger of Allah, what kind of charity brings the greatest reward?' He said: 'To give in charity when you are healthy and feeling miserly, and fearing poverty and hoping for a long life. Do not wait until the (death rattle) reaches the throat and then say: "This is for so and so," and it nearly became the property of so and so (the heirs).'"

Source: Sunan an-Nasa'i 3611 Grade: Sahih

Jabir reported Allah's Messenger (ﷺ) as saying:

There came to him (the Prophet) a desert Arab and said: I saw in a dream that I had been beheaded and I had been following it (the severed head). Allah's Messenger (ﷺ) reprimanded him saying: Do not inform about the vain sporting of devil with you during the night.

Source: Sahih Muslim 2268c

Umm Salamah narrated:

'The Messenger of Allah (ﷺ) came to see Abu Salamah when his sight had become fixed (with his eyes open, as he had already passed away). So the Prophet (ﷺ), closed his eyes and said, "When the soul is seized and leaves the body, the sight follows it.' Some of Abu Salamah's family wept and wailed, whereupon the Messenger of Allah said to them, 'Do not supplicate to Allah anything except that which is good for you (i.e. do not say anything which goes against you at that moment), because the angels (who are present at the time of death), say "Amin" (asking Allah to accept your invocation) to whatever you say." Then he said, "O Allah! Forgive Abu Salamah, raise his status among (Your) rightly guided servants, make his grave spacious, and fill it with light for him, and be his successor in taking good care of his descendants whom he has left behind (make them pious)."

Source: Bulugh al-Maram 538 Grade: Sahih

Abu Ayyub al-Ansari told that a bedouin came to the Prophet while he was travelling.

He (the Bedouin) asked, "Tell me what will bring me near to the Garden and keep me far from the Fire." He (the Prophet) replied, "Worship Allah and do not associate anything with Him, perform the prayer, pay zakat, and maintain ties of kinship."

Source: Al-Adab Al-Mufrad 49 Grade: Sahih

Ibn 'Umar reported the Messenger of Allah said:

"Anyone who seeks refuge in Allah will find refuge with Him. Anyone who asks from Allah will be receive. Anyone who does a favour should repay it. If you do not find anything, then make supplication for the doer of the favour so that he knows that you have repaid him."

Source: Al-Adab Al-Mufrad 216 Grade: Sahih

Abdur-Rahman bin Yazid narrated that:

Thawban said: "The Messenger of Allah said: 'Who will commit himself to one thing, I will guarantee him paradise?' I said: 'I will.' He said: 'Do not ask people for anything.' So Thawban would drop his whip while he was on his mount, and he would not say to anyone: 'Get that for me' rather he would dismount and grab it."

Source: Sunan Ibn Majah 1837 Grade: Sahih

Narrated Jabir bin `Abdullah:

The Prophet (ﷺ) said, "If you enter (your town) at night (after coming from a journey), do not enter upon your family till the woman whose husband was absent shaves her pubic hair and the woman with unkempt hair, combs her hair" Allah's Messenger (ﷺ) further said, "(O Jabir!) Seek to have offspring, seek to have offspring!"

Source: Sahih al-Bukhari 5246

Narrated Al-Mughira:

The Prophet (ﷺ) said, "Allah has forbidden you (1) to be undutiful to your mothers (2) to withhold (what you should give) or (3) demand (what you do not deserve), and (4) to bury your daughters alive. And Allah has disliked that (A) you talk too much about others (B), ask too many questions (in religion), or (C) waste your property."

Source: Sahih al-Bukhari 5975

Abu Hurairah said the Messenger of Allah said:

"Fasting is a protection for you, so when you are fasting, do not behave obscenely or foolishly, and if any one argues with you or abuses you, say, 'I am fasting. I am fasting.'"

Source: Muwatta Imam Malik Book 18 Hadith 690

Narrated Ibn 'Abbas:

That the Prophet (ﷺ) said: "Indeed the blessing descends to the middle of the food, so eat from its edges, and do not eat from its middle."

Source: Jami` at-Tirmidhi 1805 Grade: Hasan

It was narrated that Ibn 'Umar said:

"The Messenger of Allah delivered a Khutbah and quoted the Verse about Khamr. A man said: 'O Messenger of Allah, what do you think about Al-Mizr (beer)?' He said: 'What is beer?' He said: 'A (drink) from grains that is made in Yemen.' He said: 'Does it intoxicate?' He said: 'Yes.' He said: 'Every intoxicant is unlawful.'"

Source: Sunan an-Nasa'i 5605 Grade: Sahih

It was narrated that Harithah bin Mudarrib said:

"We came to Khabbab to visit him (when he was sick), and he said: 'I have been sick for a long time, and were it not that I heard the Messenger of Allah (ﷺ) say: "Do not wish for death," I would have wished for it.' And he said: "A person will be rewarded for all his spending, except for (what he spends) on dust," or he said, "on building."

Source: Sunan Ibn Majah 4163 Grade: Hasan

Abu Tha'labah Al-Khushani said:

The Messenger of Allah (ﷺ) said, "Allah, the Exalted, has laid down certain duties which you should not neglect, and has put certain limits which you should not transgress, and has kept silent about other matters out of mercy for you and not out of forgetfulness, so do not seek to investigate them."

Source: Riyad as-Salihin 1832 Grade: Sahih

Narrated Anas bin Malik:

"The Messenger of Allah (ﷺ) said to me: 'O my son! If you are capable of (waking up in) the morning and (ending) the evening, while there is nothing of deception in your heart for anything, then do so.' Then he said to me: 'O my son! That is from my Sunnah. Whoever revives my Sunnah then he has loved me. And whoever loved me, he shall be with me in Paradise.'"

Source: Jami` at-Tirmidhi 2678 Grade: Daif

Narrated Thawban:

The Messenger of Allah (ﷺ) said: Three things one is not allowed to do: supplicating Allah specifically for himself and ignoring others while leading people in prayer; if he did so, he deceived them; looking inside a house before taking permission: if he did so, it is as if he entered the house, saying prayer while one is feeling the call of nature until one eases oneself.

Source: Sunan Abi Dawud 90 Grade: Daif

Sufyan narrated from Amr bin Dinar that he heard Jabir bin Abdullah saying:

"We were in a battle" – Sufyan said: "They say it was the battle of Banu Mustaliq" – "A man from the Muhajirin kicked a man from the Ansar. The man from the Muhajirin said: 'O Muhajirin!' the man from the Ansar said: 'O Ansar!' The Prophet heard that and said: 'What is this evil call of Jahliyyah?' They said: 'A man from the Muhajirin kicked a man from the Ansar.' So the Prophet said: 'Leave that, for it is offensive.' Abdullah bin Ubayy bin Salul heard that and said: 'Did they really do that? By Allah! If we return to Al-Madinah indeed the more honorable will expel therefrom the meaner.'

Umar said: 'Allow me to chop off the head of this hypocrite, O Messenger of Allah!' The Prophet said: 'Leave him, I do not want the people to say that Muhammad kills his Companions.'" Someone other than Amr said: "So his son, Abdullah bin Abdullah, said: 'By Allah! You shall not return until you say that you are the mean and that the Messenger of Allah is the honorable.' So he did so."

Source: Jami` at-Tirmidhi 3315 Grade: Hasan

Ibn 'Abbas reported the Messenger of Allah said:

If anyone asks you refuge for Allah's sake give him refuge; and if anyone asks you (for something) for Allah's sake, give him.

Source: Sunan Abi Dawud 5109 Grade: Sahih

Narrated Hamzah al-Aslami:

The Messenger of Allah (ﷺ) appointed him commander over a detachment. He said: I went out along with it. He (the Prophet) said: If you find so-and-so, burn him with the fire. I then turned away, and he called me. So I returned to him, and he said: If you find so-and-so, kill him, and do not burn him, for no one punishes with fire except the Lord of the fire.

Source: Sunan Abi Dawud 2673 Grade: Sahih

Urwah bin Ruwaim Al-Lakhmi narrated that Abu Tha'labah Al-Khushani – whom he said he met and spoke with – said:

"I came to the Messenger of Allah (ﷺ) and asked him: 'O Messenger of Allah! Can we cook in the vessels of the idolaters?' He said: 'Do not cook in them.' I said: 'What if we need them and cannot find anything else?' He said: 'Wash them well, then cook and eat.'"

Source: Sunan Ibn Majah 2831 Grade: Sahih

It was narrated from Jabir bin 'Abdullah that the Messenger of Allah (ﷺ) said:

"Cover your vessels, tie your water skins, extinguish your lamps and lock your doors, for Satan does not untie a water skin, open a door or uncover a vessel. If a person cannot find anything but a stick with which to cover his vessel and mention the Name of Allah, then let him do so. And the mouse could set fire to the house with its people inside."

Source: Sunan Ibn Majah 3410 Grade: Sahih

It was narrated that Abu Sa'eed Al-Khudri said:

"A Bedouin came to the Prophet (ﷺ) to ask him to pay back a debt that he owed him, and he spoke harshly,

saying: 'I will make things difficult for you unless you repay me.' His Companions rebuked him and said: 'Woe to you, do you know who you are speaking to?' He said: 'I am only asking for my rights.' The Prophet (ﷺ) said: 'Why do you not support the one who has a right?' Then he sent word to Khawlah bint Qais, saying to her: 'If you have dates, lend them to us until our dates come, then we will pay you back.' She said: 'Yes, may my father be ransomed for you, O Messenger of Allah (ﷺ)!' So she gave him a loan, and he paid back the Bedouin and fed him. He (the Bedouin) said: 'You have paid me in full, may Allah pay you in full.' He (the Prophet (ﷺ)) said: 'Those are the best of people. May that nation not be cleansed (of sin) among whom the weak cannot get their rights without trouble.' "

Source: Sunan Ibn Majah 2426 Grade: Hasan

Narrated Safwan bin Assal:

"A Jew said to his companion: 'Accompany us to this Prophet.' So his companion said: 'Do not say: "Prophet". For if he hears you (say that) then he will be very happy.' So they went to the Messenger of Allah (ﷺ) to question him about nine clear signs. So he said to them: 'Do not associate anything with Allah, nor steal, nor commit unlawful intercourse, nor take a life which Allah has *made prohibited, except for what is required (in the law), nor hasten to damage the reputation of one of power so that he will be killed, nor practice magic, nor consume Riba(usury/interest), nor falsely accuse the chaste woman, nor turn to flee on the day of the march, and for you Jews particularly, to not violate the Sabbath.'" He said: "So they kissed his hands and his feet, and they said: 'We bear witness that you are a Prophet.' So he (ﷺ) said: 'Then what prevents you from following me?' They said: 'Because Dawud supplicated to his Lord that his offspring never be devoid of Prophets and we feared that if we follow you then the Jews will kill us.'"*

Source: Jami` at-Tirmidhi 2733 Grade: Hasan

Narrated Al-Bara' bin `Azib:

The Prophet (ﷺ) forbade us to use seven things: He forbade using gold rings, silk, Istabraq, Dibaj, red Mayathir, Al-Qassiy, and silver utensils. He ordered us to do seven other things. To pay a visit to the sick; to follow funeral processions; to say, "May Allah be merciful to you" to a sneezer if he says "Praise be to Allah"; to return greetings, to accept invitations; to help others to fulfil their oaths and to help the oppressed ones.

Source: Sahih al-Bukhari 5863

Zainab bint Umm Salama reported that a relative of Umm Habiba died. She sent for a yellow (perfume) and applied it to her forearm and said:

I, am doing it, for I have heard Allah's Messenger (ﷺ) saying: It is not permissible for a woman believing in Allah and the Hereafter to mourn beyond three days except the husband (for whom she can mourn) for four months and ten days.

Source: Sahih Muslim 1486b

Anas narrated that the Messenger of Allah said:

"O Allah! Cause me to live needy, and cause me to die needy and gather me in the group of the needy on the Day of Resurrection." 'Aishah said: "Why O Messenger of Allah?" He said: "Indeed they enter Paradise before their rich by forty autumns. O 'Aishah! Do not turn away the needy even if with a piece of date. O 'Aishah! Love the needy and be near them, for indeed Allah will make you near on the Day of Judgement."

Source: Jami` at-Tirmidhi 2352 Grade: Daif

Abu Qatada reported Allah's Messenger (ﷺ) as saying:

The good visions are from Allah and the evil dreams are from the satan. If one sees a dream which one does not like, one should spit on one's left side and seek the refuge of Allah from the satan; it will not do one any harm, and one should not disclose it to anyone and if one sees a good vision one should feel pleased but should not disclose it to anyone but whom one loves.

Source: Sahih Muslim 2261f

Narrated Umm Atiyyah al-Ansariyyah:

A woman used to perform circumcision in Medina. The Prophet (ﷺ) said to her: Do not cut severely as that is better for a woman and more desirable for a husband.

Source: Sunan Abi Dawud 5271 Grade: Sahih

Iyas ibn Abdullah ibn Abu Dhubab reported the Messenger of Allah (ﷺ) as saying:

Do not beat Allah's handmaidens, but when Umar came to the Messenger of Allah (ﷺ) and said: Women have become emboldened towards their husbands, he (the Prophet) gave permission to beat them. Then many women came round the family of the Messenger of Allah (ﷺ) complaining against their husbands. So the Messenger of Allah (ﷺ) said: Many women have gone round Muhammad's family complaining against their husbands. They (those husbands who take to beating their wives) are not the best among you.

Source: Sunan Abi Dawud 2146 Grade: Sahih

Narrated `Umar bin Al-Khattab:

During the lifetime of the Prophet (ﷺ) there was a man called `Abdullah whose nickname was Donkey, and he used to make Allah's Messenger (ﷺ) laugh. The Prophet (ﷺ) lashed him because of drinking (alcohol). And one-day he was brought to the Prophet (ﷺ) on the same charge and was lashed. On that, a man among the people said, "O Allah, curse him ! How frequently he has been brought (to the Prophet (ﷺ) on such a charge)!" The Prophet (ﷺ) said, "Do not curse him, for by Allah, I know he loves Allah and His Messenger."

Source: Sahih al-Bukhari 6780

Abu Hurairah reported:

A man said to Messenger of Allah (ﷺ): "I have relatives with whom I try to maintain good relationship but they sever relations with me; whom I treat kindly but they treat me badly, with whom I am gentle but they are rough to me." He (ﷺ) replied, "If you are as you have said, then it is as though you are feeding them hot ashes and you will not be without a supporter against them from Allah, as long as you do so."

Source: Riyad as-Salihin 647 Grade: Sahih

It was narrated from 'Amr bin Shu'aib, from his father, from his grandfather, that:

a woman from among the people of Yemen came to the Messenger of Allah with a daughter of hers, and on the daughter's hand were two thick bangles of gold. He said: "Do you pay Zakah on these? She said: "No." He said: "Would it please you if Allah were to put two bangles of fire on you on the Day of Resurrection? " So she took them off and gave them to the Messenger of Allah and said: "They are for Allah and His Messenger."

Source: Sunan an-Nasa'i 2479 Grade: Hasan

Narrated 'Abdullah bin Mughaffal:

that the Messenger of Allah (ﷺ) said: "(Fear) Allah! (Fear) Allah regarding my Companions! Do not make them objects of insults after me. Whoever loves them, it is out of love of me that he loves them. And whoever hates them, it is out of hatred for me that he hates them. And whoever harms them, he has harmed me, and whoever harms me, he has offended Allah, and whoever offends Allah, [then] he shall soon be punished."

Source: Jami` at-Tirmidhi 3862 Grade: Daif

It was narrated that Ma'din bin Abi Talhah Al-Ya'muri said:

"Abu Ad-Darda said to me: 'Where do you live?' I said: 'In a town near Hims.' Abu Ad-Darda said: 'I heard the Messenger of Allah (ﷺ) say: "There are no three people in a town or encampment among whom prayer is not established, but the Shaitan takes control of them. Therefore, stick to the congregation, for the wolf eats the sheep that strays off on its own." (One of the narrators (As Sa'ib) said: "The congregation means the congregational prayer."

Source: Sunan an-Nasa'i 847 Grade: Sahih

Abu Huraira reported Allah's Messenger (ﷺ) as saying:

All the people of my Ummah would get pardon for their sins except those who publicize them. And (it means) that a servant should do a deed during the night and tell the people in the morning that he has done so and so, whereas Allah has concealed it. And he does a deed during the day and when it is night he tells the people, whereas Allah has concealed it.

Source: Sahih Muslim 2990

Narrated `Aisha:

Allah's Messenger (ﷺ) came to me and I told him about the slave-girl (Barirah) Allah's Messenger (ﷺ) said, "Buy and manumit her, for the Wala is for the one who manumits." In the evening the Prophet (ﷺ) got up and glorified Allah as He deserved and then said, "Why do some people impose conditions which are not present in Allah's Book (Laws)? Whoever imposes such a condition as is not in Allah's Laws, then that condition is invalid even if he imposes one hundred conditions, for Allah's conditions are more binding and reliable."

Source: Sahih al-Bukhari 2155

It was narrated that Mu'adh bin Jabal said:

"I was with the Messenger of Allah (ﷺ) on a journey. One morning I drew close to him when we were on the move and said: 'O Messenger of Allah, tell me of an action that will gain me admittance to Paradise and keep me far away from Hell.' He said: 'You have asked for something great, but it is easy for the one for whom Allah makes it easy. Worship Allah and do not associate anything in worship with Him, establish prayer, pay charity, fast Ramadan, and perform Hajj to the House.' Then he said: 'Shall I not tell you of the means of goodness? Fasting is a shield, and charity extinguishes sin as water extinguishes fire, and a man's prayer in the middle of the night.' Then he recited: "Their sides forsake their beds" until he reached: "As a reward for what they used to do."[32:16-17] Then he said: 'Shall I not tell you of the head of the matter, and its pillar and pinnacle? (It is) Jihad.' Then he said: 'Shall I not tell you of the basis of all that?' I said: 'Yes.' He took hold of his tongue then said: 'Restrain this.' I said: 'O Prophet of Allah, will we be brought to account for what we say?' He said: 'May your mother not found you, O Mu'adh! Are people thrown onto their faces in Hell for anything other than the harvest of their tongues?'"

Source: Sunan Ibn Majah 3973 Grade: Hasan

Abu Sa'id Khudri reported Allah's Messenger (ﷺ) as saying:

Avoid sitting on the paths. They (the Companions) said: Allah's Messenger, we cannot help but holding our meetings (in these paths) and discuss matters (there). Thereupon Allah's Messenger (ﷺ) said: If you insist on holding meetings, then give the path its due right. They said: What are its due rights? Upon this he said: Lowering the gaze, refraining from doing harm, exchanging of greetings. commanding of good and forbidding from evil.

Source: Sahih Muslim 2121c

Narrated Ibn 'Abbas:

When the Messenger of Allah(ﷺ) sent Mu'adh to Yemen, he said to him You are going to a people who are people of the book. So call them to bear witness that there is no deity but Allah, and that I am the Messenger of Allah. If they obey you in this respect, tell them that Allah has prescribed five prayers on them every day and night. If they obey you in this regard tell them that Allah has prescribed sadaqah(zakat) on their property and returned it to their poor. If they obey you in this respect, do not take the best of their property. Beware of the curse of the oppressed, for there is no curtain between it and Allah.

Source: Sunan Abi Dawud 1584 Grade: Sahih

It was narrated that Asma' bint Yazid said:

"When Ibrahim, the son of the Messenger of Allah (ﷺ), died, the Messenger of Allah (ﷺ) wept. The one who was consoling him, either Abu Bakr or 'Umar, said to him: 'You are indeed the best of those who glorify Allah with what is due to him.' The Messenger of Allah (ﷺ) said: 'The eye weeps and the heart grieves, but we do not say anything that angers the Lord. Were it not that death is something that inevitably comes to all, and that the latter

will surely join the former, then we would have been more than we are, verily we grieve for you.'"

Source: Sunan Ibn Majah 1589 Grade: Hasan

Numan ibn Murra said the Messenger of Allah said:

"What about drunkenness, stealing and adultery?" That was before anything had been revealed about them. They said, "Allah and His Messenger know best." He said, "They are excesses and in them is a punishment. And the worst of thieves is the one who steals his prayer." They said, "How does he steal his prayer, Messenger of Allah?" He replied, "He does not do ruku or sajda properly."

Source: Muwatta Imam Malik 406

It was narrated that Abu Sa'eed Al-Khudri said:

"in the year of Tabuk, the Messenger of Allah (ﷺ) addressed the people, while leaning against his mount. He said: 'Shall I not tell you of the best of the people and the worst of the people? Among the best of the people is a man who strives in the cause of Allah on the back of his horse, or on the back of his camel, or on his own two feet, until death comes to him. And among the worst of the people, is an immoral man (Fajir) who reads the Book of

Allah but he does not refrain from doing anything bad because of it.'"

Source: Sunan an-Nasa'i 3106 Grade: Hasan

It was narrated from 'Abdullah bin Abi Qatadah that his father said:

"A man came to the Messenger of Allah (ﷺ) and said: 'O Messenger of Allah, if I am killed in the cause of Allah with patience and seeking reward, facing the enemy and not running away, do you think that Allah will forgive my sins?' The Messenger of Allah (ﷺ) said: 'Yes.' When the man turned away, the Messenger of Allah (ﷺ) called him back and said: 'What did you say?' He repeated his question, and the Messenger of Allah (ﷺ) said: 'Yes, except debt. Jibril told me.'"

Source: Sunan an-Nasa'i 3156 Grade: Sahih

Narrated Abdullah ibn Sunabihi:

Abu Muhammad fancies that witr prayer is essential. So Ubadah ibn as-Samit said: Abu Muhammad was wrong. I bear witness that I heard the Messenger of Allah (ﷺ) say: Allah, the Exalted, has made five prayers obligatory. If anyone performs ablution for them well, offers them at their (right) time, and observes perfectly their bowing and submissiveness in them, it is the guarantee of Allah that He will pardon him; if anyone does not do so, there is no guarantee for him on the part of Allah; He may pardon him if He wills, and punish him if He wills.

Source: Sunan Abi Dawud 425 Grade: Sahih

Narrated Abu Bakra:

A man praised another man in front of the Prophet (ﷺ). The Prophet (ﷺ) said to him, "Woe to you, you have cut off your companion's neck, you have cut off your companion's neck," repeating it several times and then added, "Whoever amongst you has to praise his brother should say, 'I think that he is so and so, and Allah knows exactly the truth, and I do not confirm anybody's good conduct before Allah, but I think him so and so,' if he really knows what he says about him."

Source: Sahih al-Bukhari 2662

Narrated Sulaiman bin 'Amr b. al-Ahwas:

On the authority of his mother: I saw the Messenger of Allah (ﷺ) throwing pebbles at the jamrah from the botton of wadi (valley) while he was riding (on a camel). He was uttering the takbir (Allah is most great) with each pebble. A man behind him was shading him. I asked about the man. They (the people) said: He is al-Fadl bin al-'Abbas. The people crowded. The Prophet (ﷺ) said: 'O people, do *not kill each other; when you throw pebbles at the jamrah, throw small pebbles.*

Source: Sunan Abi Dawud 1966 Grade: Hasan

Narrated Hudhaifa bin Al-Yaman:

The people used to ask Allah's Messenger (ﷺ) about the good but I used to ask him about the evil lest I should be overtaken by them. So I said, "O Allah's Messenger (ﷺ)! We were living in ignorance and in an (extremely) worst atmosphere, then Allah brought to us this good (i.e., Islam); will there be any evil after this good?" He said, "Yes." I said, 'Will there be any good after that evil?" He replied, "Yes, but it will be tainted (not pure.)'' I asked, "What will be its taint?" He replied, "(There will be) some people who will guide others not according to my tradition? You will approve of some of their deeds and disapprove of some others." I asked, "Will there be any evil after that good?" He replied, "Yes, (there will be) some people calling at the gates of the (Hell) Fire, and whoever will respond to their call, will be thrown by them into the (Hell) Fire." I said, "O Allah s Apostle! Will you describe them to us?" He said, "They will be from our own people and will speak our language." I said, "What do you order me to do if such a state should take place in my life?" He said, "Stick to the group of

Muslims and their Imam (ruler)." I said, "If there is neither a group of Muslims nor an Imam (ruler)?" He said, "Then turn away from all those sects even if you were to bite (eat) the roots of a tree till death overtakes you while you are in that state."

Source: Sahih al-Bukhari 7084

Abu Kabshah Al-Anmari narrated that the Messenger of Allah said:

"There are three things for which I swear and narrate to you about, so remember it." He said: "The wealth of a slave (of Allah) shall not be decreased by charity, no slave (of Allah) suffers injustice and is patient with it except that Allah adds to his honor; no slave (of Allah) opens up a door to begging except that Allah opens a door for him to poverty"- or a statement similar- "And I shall narrate to you a narration, so remember it." He said: "The world is only for four persons: A slave whom Allah provides with wealth and knowledge, so he has Taqwa of his Lord with it, nurtures the ties of kinship with it, and he knows that Allah has a right in it. So this is the most virtuous rank. And a slave whom Allah provides with knowledge, but He does not provide with wealth. So he has a truthful intent, saying: 'If I had wealth, then I would do the deeds of so-and-so with it.' He has his intention, so their rewards are the same. And a slave whom Allah provides with wealth, but He does not provide him with knowledge. [So he] spends his wealth rashly without knowledge, nor having Taqwa of his Lord, nor nurturing the ties of kinship, and he does not know that Allah has a right in it. So this is the most despicable rank. And a slave whom Allah does not provide with wealth nor knowledge, so he says: 'If I had wealth, then I would do the deeds of so-and-so with it.' He has his intention, so their sin is the same."

Source: Jami` at-Tirmidhi 2325 Grade: Sahih

Narrated Abdullah ibn Amr ibn al-'As:

When we were around the Messenger of Allah (ﷺ), he mentioned the period of commotion (fitnah) saying: When you see the people that their covenants have been impaired, (the fulfilling of) the guarantees becomes rare, and they become thus (intertwining his fingers). I then got up and said: What should I do at that time, may Allah make me ransom for you? He replied: Keep to your house, control your tongue, accept what you approve, abandon what you disapprove, attend to your own affairs, and leave alone the affairs of the generality.

Source: Sunan Abi Dawud 4343 Grade: Hasan Sahih

It was narrated from Busr bin Sa'eed that Zaid bin Khalid sent word to Abu Juhaim Al-Ansari to ask:

"What did you hear from the Prophet (ﷺ) about a man when he is performing prayer?" He said: "I heard the Prophet (ﷺ) saying: 'If anyone of you knew (how great is the sin involved) when he passed in front of his brother who is performing prayer, then waiting for forty'," (one of the narrators) said: "I do not know if he meant forty years, forty months, or forty days, 'would be better for him than that."

Source: Sunan Ibn Majah 945 Grade: Sahih

It was narrated that Qais bin Abu Hazim said:

"Abu Bakr stood up and praised and glorified Allah, then he said: 'O people, you recite this Verse – "O you who believe! Take care of your own selves. If you follow the (right) guidance no hurt can come to you from those who are in error."[5:105] – but I heard the Messenger of Allah (ﷺ) say: 'If people see some evil but do not change it, soon Allah will send His punishment upon them all.'"

Source: Sunan Ibn Majah 4005 Grade: Hasan

Narrated `Abdullah bin Maghaffal:

that he saw a man throwing stones with two fingers (at something) and said to him, "Do not throw stones, for Allah's Messenger (ﷺ) has forbidden throwing stones, or he used to dislike it." `Abdullah added: Throwing stones will neither hunt the game, nor kill (or hurt) an enemy, but it may break a tooth or gouge out an eye." Afterwards `Abdullah once again saw the man throwing stones. He said to him, "I tell you that Allah's Messenger (ﷺ) has forbidden or disliked the throwing the stones (in such a way), yet you are throwing stones! I shall not talk to you for such-and-such a period."

Source: Sahih al-Bukhari 5479

Narrated Abu Musa:

While we were with Allah's Messenger (ﷺ) in a holy battle, we never went up a hill or reached its peak or went down a valley but raised our voices with Takbir. Allah's Messenger (ﷺ) came close to us and said, "O people! Don't exert yourselves, for you do not call a deaf or an absent one, but you call the All-Listener, the All-Seer." The Prophet (ﷺ) then said, "O `Abdullah bin Qais! Shall I teach you a sentence which is from the treasures of Paradise? (It is): 'La haula wala quwata illa billah. (There is neither might nor power except with Allah).

Source: Sahih al-Bukhari 6610

Ata' bin Abu Rabah said:

I heard Jabir bin 'Abdullah say: "In the Year of the Conquest, while he was in Makkah the Messenger of Allah, said: 'Allah and His Messenger have forbidden the sale of wines, meat of dead animals, pigs and 'idols.' It was said to him: 'O Messenger of Allah, what do you think of the fat of dead animals, for it is used to caulk ships, it is daubed on animal skins and people use it to light their lamps?' He said: 'No, it is unlawful.' Then the Messenger of Allah said: 'May Allah curse the jews, for Allah forbade them the fat (of animals) but they rendered it, (i.e. melted it) sold it and consumed its price."'

Source: Sunan Ibn Majah 2167 Grade: Sahih

It was narrated from Zaid bin Khalid that the Prophet (ﷺ) was asked about a lost camel. :

He turned red, and he said: "What does it have to do with you? It has its feet and its water supply, it can go and drink water and eat from the trees until its owner finds it." And he was asked about lost sheep, and he said: "Take it, for it will be for you or for your brother or for the wolf." And he was asked about lost property and he said: "Remember the features of its leather bag and strap, and announce it for one year, then if someone claims it, describing it to you with those features (give it to him), otherwise incorporate it into your own wealth."

Source: Sunan Ibn Majah 2504 Grade: Sahih

It was narrated that Usamah bin Sharik said:

"I saw the Bedouins asking the Prophet (ﷺ): 'Is there any harm in such and such, is there any harm in such and such?' He said to them: 'O slaves of Allah! Allah has only made harm in that which transgresses the honor of one's brother. That is what is sinful.' They said: 'O Messenger of Allah! Is there any sin if we do not seek treatment?' He said: 'Seek treatment, O slaves of Allah! For Allah does not create any disease but He also creates with it the cure, except for old age.' They said: 'O Messenger of Allah, what is the best thing that a person may be given?' He said: 'Good manners.'"

Source: Sunan Ibn Majah 3436 Grade: Sahih

It was narrated that Muhammad bin 'Abdur-Rahman bin Abu Bakr said:

"I was sitting with Ibn 'Abbas, and a man came to him and he said: 'Where have you come from?' He said: 'From Zamzam.' He said: 'Did you drink from it as you should?' He said: 'How is that?' He said: 'When you

drink from it, turn to face the Qiblah and mention the name of Allah, drink three draughts and drink your fill of it. When you have finished, then praise Allah.' The Messenger of Allah (ﷺ) said: 'The sign (that differentiates) between us and the hypocrites is that they do not drink their fill from Zamzam."

Source: Sunan Ibn Majah 3061 Grade: Hasan

Abdullah bin Mas'ud reported:

Messenger of Allah (ﷺ) said, "Never a Prophet had been sent before me by Allah to his people but he had, among his people, (his) disciples and companions, who followed his ways and obeyed his command. Then there came after them their successors who proclaimed what they did not practise, and practised what they were not commanded to do. And (he) who strove against them with his hand is a believer; he who strove against them with his heart is a believer; and he who strove against them with his tongue is a believer ; and beyond that there is no grain of Faith".

Source: Riyad as-Salihin 185 Grade: Sahih

It was narrated from Ibn Buraidah, from his father, that the Messenger of Allah (ﷺ) said:

"The sanctity of the wives of the Mujahidin to those who stay behind is like the sanctity of their mothers. There is

no man among those who stay behind who takes on the responsibility of looking after the wife of one of the Mujahidin (and betrays him) but he (the betrayer) will be made to stand before him on the Day Resurrection and it will be said: 'O So-and-so, this is so-and-so, take whatever you want from his good deeds.'" Then the Prophet (ﷺ) turned to his Companions and said: *"What do you think: Will he leave him any of his good deeds?"*

Source: Sunan an-Nasa'i 3191 Grade: Sahih

It has been narrated on the authority of Umm Salama that the Messenger of Allah (ﷺ) said:

In the near future there will be Amirs and you will like their good deeds and dislike their bad deeds. One who sees through their bad deeds (and tries to prevent their repetition by his band or through his speech), is absolved from blame, but one who hates their bad deeds (in the heart of his heart, being unable to prevent their recurrence by his hand or his tongue), is (also) fate (so far as God's wrath is concerned). But one who approves of their bad deeds and imitates them is spiritually ruined. People asked (the Prophet): Shouldn't we fight against them? He replied: No, as long as they say their prayers.

Source: Sahih Muslim 1854a

It is narrated by Safwan bin Muhriz that Jundab bin 'Abdullah al-Bajali during the stormy days of Ibn Zubair sent a message to 'As'as bin Salama:

Gather some men of your family so that I should talk to them. He ('As'as) sent a messenger to them (to the members of his family). When they had assembled, Jundab came there with a yellow hooded cloak on him, He said: Talk what you were busy in talking. The talk went on by turns, till there came his (Jundab's) turn. He took off the hooded cloak from his head and said: I have come to you with no other intention but to narrate to you a hadith of your Apostle: Verily the Messenger of Allah (ﷺ) sent a squad of the Muslims to a tribe of the polytheists. Both the armies confronted one another. There was a man among the army of polytheists who (was so dashing that), whenever he intended to kill a man from among the Muslims, he killed him. Amongst the Muslims too was a man looking forward to (an opportunity of) his (the polytheist's) unmindfulness. He (the narrator) said: We talked that he was Usama bin Zaid. When he raised his sword, he (the soldier of the polytheists) uttered:" There is no god but Allah," but he (Usama bin Zaid) killed him. When the messenger of the glad tidings came to the Apostle (ﷺ) he asked him (about the events of the battle) and he informed him about the man (Usama) and what he had done He (the Prophet of Allah) called for him and asked him why he had killed him. He (Usama) said: Messenger of Allah, he struck the Muslims and killed such and such of them. And he even named some of them. (He continued): I attacked him and when he saw the sword he said: There is no god but Allah. The Messenger of Allah (ﷺ) said: Did you kill him? He (Usama) replied in the affirmative. He (the Prophet) remarked: What would you do with:" There is no god but Allah," when he would come (before you) on the Day of Judgment? He (Usama) said: Messenger of Allah, beg pardon for me (from your Lord). He (the Prophet) said: What would you do with:" There is no god but Allah" when he would come (before you) on the Day of Judgment? He (the Prophet) added nothing to it but kept saying: What would you do with:" There is no god but Allah," when he would come (before you) on the Day of Judgment?

Source: Sahih Muslim 97

It was narrated from Anas bin Malik that :

a man from among the Ansar came to the Prophet (ﷺ) and begged from him. He said, "Do you have anything in your house?" He said: "Yes, a blanket, part of which we cover ourselves with and part we spread beneath us, and a bowl from which we drink water." He said: "Give them to me." So he brought them to him, and the Messenger of Allah (ﷺ) took them in his hand and said, "Who will by these two things?" A man said: "I will by them for one Dirham." He said: "Who will offer more than a Dirham?" two or three times. A man said: "I will buy them for two Dirham." So he gave them to him and took the two Dirham, which he gave to the Ansari and said: "Buy food with one of them and give it to your family, and buy an axe with the other and bring it to me." So he did that, and the Messenger of Allah (ﷺ) took it and fixed a handle to it, and said: "Go and gather firewood, and I do not want to see you for fifteen days." So he went and gathered firewood and sold it, then he came back, and he had earned ten Dirham. (The Prophet (ﷺ)) said: "Buy food with some of it and clothes with some." Then he said: "This is better for you than coming with begging (appearing) as a spot on your face on the Day of Resurrection. Begging is only appropriate for one who is extremely poor or who is in severe debt, or one who must pay painful blood money."

Source: Sunan Ibn Majah 2198 Grade: Hasan

Narrated `Aisha:

The wives of the Prophet (ﷺ) used to go to Al-Manasi, a vast open place (near Baqi` at Medina) to answer the call of nature at night. `Umar used to say to the Prophet (ﷺ) "Let your wives be veiled," but Allah's Messenger did not do so. One night Sauda bint Zam`a the wife of the Prophet (ﷺ) went out at `Isha' time and she was a tall lady. `Umar addressed her and said, "I have recognized you, O Sauda." He said so, as he desired eagerly that the verses of Al-Hijab (the observing of veils by the Muslim women) may be revealed. So Allah revealed the verses of "Al-Hijab" (A complete body cover excluding the eyes).

Source: Sahih al-Bukhari 146

Bahz bin Hakim narrated from his father that his grandfather said:

"I said: 'O Messenger of Allah, with regard to our 'Awrah, what may we uncover of it and what must we conceal?' He said: 'Cover your 'Awrah, except from your wife and those whom your right hand possesses.' I said: 'O Messenger of Allah, what if the people live close together?' He said: 'If you can make sure that no one sees it, then do not let anyone see it.' I said: 'O Messenger of Allah, what if one of us is alone?' He said: 'Allah is more deserving that you should feel shy before Him than People.' "

Source: Sunan Ibn Majah 1920 Grade: Hasan

It was narrated that Ibn 'Abbas said:

"The Messenger of Allah (ﷺ) passed by two graves and said: 'These two are being punished, but they are not being punished for something that was difficult to avoid. As for this, he used not to take precautions to avoid (his body to clothes being soiled by) urine, and this one used to walk around spreading malicious gossip.' Then he called for a fresh palm-leaf stalk and split it in two, and placed one piece on each of the two graves. They said: 'O Messenger of Allah, why did you do that?' He said: 'Perhaps the torment will be reduced for them so long as this does not dry out.'"

Source: Sunan an-Nasa'i 31 Grade: Sahih

Abu Sa'id reported:

Dates were brought to Allah's Messenger (ﷺ), and he said: These dates are not like our dates, whereupon a man said: We sold two sa's of our dates (in order to get) one sa', of these (fine dates), whereupon Allah's Messenger (ﷺ) said: That is interest; so return (these dates of fine quality), and get your (inferior dates) ; then sell our dates (for money) and buy for us (with the help of money) such (fine dates).

Source: Sahih Muslim 1594b

Nafi' narrated that Ibn 'Umar said:

"The Messenger of Allah ascended the Minbar and called out with a raised voice: 'O you who accepted Islam with his tongue, while faith has not reached his heart! Do not harm the Muslims, nor revile them, nor spy on them to expose their secrets. For indeed whoever tries to expose his Muslims brother's secrets, Allah exposes his secrets wide open, even if he were in the depth of his house.'" He (Nafl') said: ' One day Ibn 'Umar looked at the House- or – the Ka'bah and said: 'What is it that is more honored than you, and whose honor is more sacred than yours! And the believer's honor is more sacred to Allah than yours.'"

Source: Jami` at-Tirmidhi 2032 Grade: Hasan

A'isha, the wife of Allah's Messenger (ﷺ), reported that the Quraish were concerned about the woman who had committed theft during the lifetime of Allah's Messenger (ﷺ), in the expedition of Victory (of Mecca). They said:

Who would speak to Allah's Messenger (ﷺ) about her? They (again) said: Who can dare do this but Usama bin Zaid, the loved one of Allah's Messenger (ﷺ)? She was *brought to Allah's Messenger (ﷺ) and Usama bin Zaid spoke about her to him (interceded on her behalf). The color of the face of Allah's Messenger (ﷺ) changed, and he said: Do you intercede in one of the prescribed punishments of Allah? He (Usama) said: 'Messenger of Allah, seek forgiveness for me.' When it was dusk. Allah's Messenger (ﷺ) stood up and gave an address. He (first) glorified Allah as He deserves, and then said: Now to our topic. This (injustice) destroyed those before you that when any one of (high) rank committed theft among them, they spared him, and when any weak one among them committed theft, they inflicted the prescribed punishment upon him. By Him in Whose Hand is my life, even if Fatima daughter of Muhammad were to commit theft, I would have cut off her hand. He (the Prophet) then commanded about that woman who had committed theft, and her hand was cut off. `A'isha said: Hers was a good repentance, and she later on married and used to come to me after that, and I conveyed her needs (and problems) to Allah's Messenger (ﷺ).*

Source: Sahih Muslim 1688b

Narrated Abu Huraira:

The Prophet (ﷺ) said, "Allah created the creations, and when He finished from His creations, Ar-Rahm i.e., the womb said, "(O Allah) at this place I seek refuge with You from all those who sever me (i.e. sever the ties of Kith and kin). Allah said, 'Yes, won't you be pleased that I will keep good relations with the one who will keep good relations with you, and I will sever the relation with the one who will sever the relations with you.' It said, 'Yes, O my Lord.' Allah said, 'Then that is for you '" Allah's Messenger (ﷺ) added. "Read (in the Qur'an) if you wish, the Statement of Allah: 'Would you then, if you were given the authority, do mischief in the land and sever your ties of kinship?' (47:22)

Source: Sahih al-Bukhari 5987

It was narrated from Abu Hurairah that :

The Messenger of Allah said: "There are seven whom Allah, the Mighty and Sublime, will shade with His shade on the Day of Resurrection, the Day when there will be no shade but His: A just ruler, a young man who grows up worshipping Allah, the Mighty and Sublime; a man who remembers Allah when he is alone and his eyes flow (with tears); a man whose heart is attached to the Masjid; two men who love each other for the sake of Allah, the Mighty and Sublime; a man who is called (to commit sin) by a woman of high status and beauty, but he says: 'I fear Allah'; and a man who gives charity and conceals it, so that his left hand does not know what his right hand is doing."

Source: Sunan an-Nasa'i 5380 Grade: Sahih

Abu Umamah bin Sahl bin Hunaif narrated that on the day of siege, 'Uthman bin 'Affan stood overlooking the people, and he said:

"I swear to you by Allah! You know that the Messenger of Allah said: 'The blood of a Muslim man is not lawful, except for one of three (cases):Illegitimate sexual relations after Ihsan (having been married), or apostasy after Islam, or taking a life without right, for which he is killed.' By Allah! I have never committed illegitimate sexual relations, not during Jahiliyyah nor during Islam, and I have not committed apostasy since I gave my pledge to the Messenger of Allah, and I have not taken a life that Allah had made unlawful. So for what do you fight me?"'

Source: Jami` at-Tirmidhi 2158 Grade: Sahih

Narrated Abdullah ibn Mas'ud:

The Messenger of Allah (ﷺ) said: The first defect that permeated Banu Isra'il was that a man (of them) met another man and said: O so-and-so, fear Allah, and abandon what you are doing, for it is not lawful for you.

He then met him the next day and that did not prevent him from eating with him, drinking with him and sitting with him. When they did so. Allah mingled their hearts with each other.

He then recited the verse: "curses were pronounced on those among the children of Isra'il who rejected Faith, by the tongue of David and of Jesus the son of Mary"...up to "wrongdoers".

He then said: By no means, I swear by Allah, you must enjoin what is good and prohibit what is evil, prevent the wrongdoer, bend him into conformity with what is right, and restrict him to what is right.

Source: Sunan Abi Dawud 4336 Grade: Daif

It was narrated from Ibn 'Umar that 'Umar bin al-Khattab addressed us in al-Jabiyah, and said:

The Messenger of Allah ﷺ stood before us as I am standing before you, and said: `I urge you to show respect to my Companions, then those who come after them, then those who come after them, then lying will become so widespread that a man will start to give testimony before he is asked to do so. Whoever among you wants to attain a spacious abode in Paradise, let him adhere to the jama'ah (main body of Muslims), for the

Shaitan is with the one who is alone, but he is further away from two. And no one of you should be alone with a woman for the Shaitan will be the third one present. The one who is pleased with his good deeds and upset by his bad deeds is a believer.

Source: Musnad Ahmad 114 Grade: Sahih

It was narrated from Zaid bin Zabyan who attributed it to Abu Dharr that:

The Prophet (ﷺ) said: "There are three whom Allah loves: A man who comes to some people and asks (to be given something) for the sake of Allah and not for the sake of their relationship, but they do not give him, so a man stayed behind and gave it to him in secret, and no one knew of his giving except Allah and the one to whom he gave it. People who travel all night until sleep becomes dearer to them than anything equated with it, so they lay down their heads (and slept), then a man among them got up and started praying to Me and beseeching Me, reciting My Verses. And a man who was on a campaign and met the enemy and they fled, but he went forward (pursuing them) until he was killed or victory was granted."

Source: Sunan an-Nasa'i 1615 Grade: Hasan

Narrated 'Ubada bin As-Samit:

Allah's Messenger (ﷺ) said to us while we were in a gathering, "Give me the oath (Pledge of allegiance for: (1) Not to join anything in worship along with Allah, (2) Not to steal, (3) Not to commit illegal sexual intercourse, (4) Not to kill your children, (5) Not to accuse an innocent person (to spread such an accusation among people), (6) Not to be disobedient (when ordered) to do good deeds. The Prophet (ﷺ) added: Whoever amongst you fulfill his pledge, his reward will be with Allah, and whoever commits any of those sins and receives the legal punishment in this world for that sin, then that punishment will be an expiation for that sin, and whoever commits any of those sins and Allah does not expose him, then it is up to Allah if He wishes He will punish him or if He wishes, He will forgive him." So we gave the Pledge for that.

Source: Sahih al-Bukhari 7213

Ahnaf bin Qais reported:

I set out with the intention of helping this person (Ali) when Abu Bakra met me. He said: Ahnaf, where do you intend to go? I said: I intend to help the cousin of Allah's Messenger (ﷺ), 'Ali. Thereupon he said to me: Ahnaf, go back, for I heard Allah's Messenger (ﷺ) as saying: When two Muslims confront one another with swords (in hand) both the slayer and the slain would be in Fire. He (Ahnaf) said: I said, or it was said: Allah's Messenger, it may be the case of one who kills. but what about the slain (why he would be put in Hell-Fire)? Thereupon he said: He also intended to kill his companion.

Source: Sahih Muslim 2888a

Narrated Sulaiman bin 'Amr bin Al-Ahwas:

"My father narrated to me that he attended the Farewell Hajj with the Messenger of Allah (ﷺ). He (ﷺ) expressed his gratitude to Allah and praised Him, and reminded and exhorted, then he said: 'Which day is most sacred? Which day is most sacred? Which day is most sacred?' He said: "So the people said: 'The day of Al-Hajj Al-Akbar O Messenger of Allah!' So he said: 'Indeed, your blood, your wealth, your honor, is as sacred for you as the sacredness of this day of yours, in this city of yours, in this month of yours. Behold! None commits a crime but against himself, none offends a father for a son, nor a son for a father. Behold! Indeed the Muslim is the brother of the Muslim, so it is not lawful for the Muslim to do anything to his brother, which is not lawful to be done to himself. Behold! All Usury from Jahiliyyah is invalid, for you is the principle of your wealth, but you are not to *wrong nor be wronged - except in the case of Usury of Al-'Abbas bin 'Abdul-Muttalib - otherwise it is all invalid. Behold! All retribution regarding cases of blood during Jahiliyyah are invalid. The first case of blood retribution invalidated among those of Jahiliyyah, is the blood of Al-Harith bin 'Abdul-Muttalib who was nursed among Banu Laith and killed by Hudhail. Behold! I order you to treat women well, for they are but like captives with you, you have no sovereignty beyond this over them, unless they manifest lewdness. If they do that, then abandon their beds, and beat them with a beating that is not painful. Then if they obey you, then there is no cause for you against them beyond that. Behold! There are rights for you upon your women, and rights for your women upon you. As for your rights upon them, then they are not to allow anyone on your bedding whom you dislike, nor to permit anyone whom you dislike in your homes. Behold! Indeed their rights upon you are that you treat them well in clothing them and feeding them.'"*

Source: Jami` at-Tirmidhi 3087 Grade: Hasan

Narrated Ali bin Al-Husain:

Safiya, the wife of the Prophet (ﷺ) told me that she went to Allah's Messenger (ﷺ) to visit him in the mosque while he was in I`tikaf in the last ten days of Ramadan.

She had a talk with him for a while, then she got up in order to return home. The Prophet (ﷺ) accompanied her. When they reached the gate of the mosque, opposite the door of Um-Salama, two Ansari men were passing by and they greeted Allah's Messenger. He told them: Do not run away! And said, "She is (my wife) Safiya bint Huyai." Both of them said, "Subhan Allah, (How dare we think of any evil) O Allah's Messenger (ﷺ)!" And they felt it. The Prophet said (to them), "Satan reaches everywhere in the human body as blood reaches in it, (everywhere in one's body). I was afraid lest Satan might insert an evil thought in your minds."

Source: Sahih al-Bukhari 2035

On the authority of Abu Dharr:

Some people from amongst the Companions of the Messenger of Allah said to the Prophet, "O Messenger of Allah, the affluent have made off with the rewards; they pray as we pray, they fast as we fast, and they give [much] in charity by virtue of their wealth."

He said, "Has not Allah made things for you to give in charity? Truly every tasbeehah [saying: 'subhan-Allah'] is a charity, and every takbeerah [saying: 'Allahu akbar'] is a charity, and every tahmeedah [saying: 'al-hamdu lillah'] is a charity, and every tahleelah [saying: 'laa ilaha ill-Allah'] is a charity. And commanding the good is a charity, and forbidding an evil is a charity, and in the bud`i [sexual act] of each one of you there is a charity."

They said, "O Messenger of Allah, when one of us fulfils his carnal desire will he have some reward for that?" He said, "Do you not see that if he were to act upon it [his desire] in an unlawful manner then he would be deserving of punishment? Likewise, if he were to act upon it in a lawful manner then he will be deserving of a reward."

Source: 40 Hadith of Nawwawi #25 Grade: Sahih

Abd Allah bin Mas'ud said:

when we (prayed and) sat up during prayer along the Messenger of Allah, we said: "Peace be to Allah before it is supplicated for His servants; peace be to so and so. "The Messenger of Allah (ﷺ) said: Do not say "Peace be to Allah ,"for Allah Himself is peace. When one of you sits(during prayer), he should say: The adoration of the tongue are due to Allah, and acts of worship and all good things. Peace be upon you, O Prophet, and Allah's mercy and His blessings. Peace be upon us and upon Allah's upright servants. When you say that, it reaches every upright servant in heavens and earth or between heavens and earth. I testify that there is no god but Allah, and I testify that Muhammad is His servant and Messenger. Then he may choose any supplication which pleases him and offer it.

Source: Sunan Abi Dawud 968 Grade: Sahih

It was narrated that Abu Ad-Darda' said:

"The Messenger of Allah (ﷺ) said: 'Whoever established Salah, pays Zakah, and dies not associating anything with Allah, he has a right from Allah the Mighty and Sublime, that He will forgive him, whether he emigrated, or died in his birthplace.' We said: 'O Messenger of Allah! Shall we not tell the people about it so that they may rejoice?' He said: 'In Paradise there are one hundred levels, (the distance) between each two of which is like (the distance) between the Heaven and the Earth; Allah has prepared them fro the Mujahidin who strive in His cause. Were it not that it would be too difficult for the believers and I cannot find mounts for them - and they do not like to stay behind if I go out (on a campaign) - I would not have stayed behind from any expedition. I wish that I could be killed then brought back to life, then killed again.'"

Source: Sunan an-Nasa'i 3132 Grade: Hasan

Jabir ibn 'Abdullah reported:

the Prophet, may Allah bless him and grant him peace, went up the minbar. When he reached the first step, he said, "Ameen". When he ascended to the second step, he said, "Amen," and when he stepped onto the third step, he said, "Ameen." They said, "Messenger of Allah, we heard you say 'Ameen' three times." He said, "When I went up the first step, Jibril, came to me and said, 'Wretched is the slave to whom Ramadan comes and when it passes from him is not forgiven.' I said, 'Ameen.' Then he said, 'Wretched is the slave who has one or both of his parents alive and they do not let him enter the Garden.' I said, 'Ameen.' Then he said, 'Wretched is a slave who does not bless you when you are mentioned in his presence,' and I said, 'Ameen.'"

Source: Al-Adab Al-Mufrad 644 Grade: Sahih

It was narrated from Abu Hurairah that a man entered the mosque and performed prayer, and the Prophet (ﷺ) was in a corner of the mosque. The man came and greeted him, and he said:

"And also upon you. Go back and repeat your prayer, for you have not prayed." So he went back and repeated his prayer, then he came and greeted the Prophet (ﷺ). He said: "And also upon you. Go back and repeat your prayer, for you have not prayed." On the third occasion,

the man said: "Teach me, O Messenger of Allah!" He said: "When you stand up to offer the prayer, perform ablution properly, then stand to face the prayer direction and say Allahu Akbar. Then recite whatever you can of Qur'an, and then bow until you can feel at ease bowing. Then stand up until you feel at ease standing, then prostrate until you feel at ease prostrating. Then raise your head until you are sitting up straight. Do that throughout your prayer."

Source: Sunan Ibn Majah 1060 Grade: Sahih

Abu Sa'eed Al-Khudri said:

"The Messenger of Allah (ﷺ) stood up and addressed the people saying: 'No, by Allah, I do not fear for you, O people, but I fear the attractions of this world that Allah brings forth for you.' A man said to him: 'O Messenger of Allah(ﷺ), does good bring forth evil?' The Messenger of Allah (ﷺ) remained silent for a while, then he said: 'What did you say?' He said: 'I said, does good bring forth evil?' The Messenger of Allah (ﷺ) said: 'Good does not bring forth anything but good, but is it really good? Everything that grows on the banks of a stream may either kill if overeaten or (at least) make the animals sick, except if an animal eats its fill of Khadir and then faces the sun, and then defecates and urinates, chews the cud

and then returns to graze again. Whoever takes wealth in a lawful manner, it will be blessed for him, but whoever takes it in an unlawful manner, his likeness is that of one who eats and is never satisfied.'"

Source: Sunan Ibn Majah 3995 Grade: Sahih

A'isha the wife of Allah's Messenger (ﷺ), reported that one day Allah's Messenger (ﷺ) came out of her (apartment) during the night and she felt jealous. Then he came and he saw me (in that agitated state of mind). He said:

A'isha, what has happened to you? Do you feel jealous? Thereupon she said: How can it be (that a woman like me) should not feel jealous in regard to a husband like you. Thereupon Allah's Messenger (ﷺ) said: It was your devil who had come to you, and she said: Allah's Messenger, is there along with me a devil? He said: Yes. I said: Is a devil attached to everyone? He said: Yes. I (Aisha) again said: Allah's Messenger, is it with you also? He said: Yes, but my Lord has helped me against him and as such I am absolutely safe from his mischief.

Source: Sahih Muslim 2815

Narrated Ibn 'Umar:

That the Prophet (ﷺ) said: "Procrastination (in paying a debt) by a rich person is oppression. So if your debt is transferred from your debtor you should agree, and do not make two sales in one sale."

Source: Jami` at-Tirmidhi 1309 Grade: Sahih

Narrated Suwaid bin Ghafala:

While I as in the company of Salman bin Rabi`a and Suhan, in one of the holy battles, I found a whip. One of them told me to drop it but I refused to do so and said that I would give it to its owner if I found him, otherwise I would utilize it. On our return we performed Hajj and on passing by Medina, I asked Ubai bin Ka`b about it. He said, "I found a bag containing a hundred Dinars in the lifetime of the Prophet (ﷺ) and took it to the Prophet (ﷺ) who said to me, 'Make public announcement about it for one year.' So, I announced it for one year and went to the Prophet (ﷺ) who said, 'Announce it publicly for another year.' So, I announced it for another year. I went to him again and he said, "Announce for another year." So I announced for still another year. I went to the Prophet (ﷺ) for the fourth time, and he said, 'Remember the amount of money, the description of its container and the string it is tied with, and if the owner comes, give it to him; otherwise, utilize it.' "

Source: Sahih al-Bukhari 2437

Narrated Al-Harith Al-Ash'ari:

that the Messenger of Allah (ﷺ) said: "Indeed Allah commanded Yahya bin Zakariyya with five commandments to abide by, and to command the Children of Isra'il to abide by them. But he was slow in doing so. So 'Eisa said: 'Indeed Allah commanded you with five commandments to abide by and to command the Children of Isra'il to abide by. Either you command them, or I shall command them.' So Yahya said: 'I fear that if you precede me in this, then the earth may swallow me, or I shall be punished.'

So he gathered the people in Jerusalem, and they filled [the Masjid] and sat upon its balconies. So he said: 'Indeed Allah has commanded me with five commandments to abide by, and to command you to abide by. The first of them is that you worship Allah and not associate anything with him. The parable of the one who associates others with Allah is that of a man who buys a servant with his own gold or silver, then he says to him: "This is my home and this is my business so take care of it and give me the profits." So he takes care of it and gives the profits to someone other than his master. Which of you would live to have a servant like that? And

Allah commands you to perform Salat, and when you perform Salat then do not turn away, for Allah is facing the face of His worshipers as long as he does not turn away. And He commands you with fasting. For indeed the parable of fasting, is that of a man in a group with a sachet containing musk. All of them enjoy its fragrance. Indeed the breath of the fasting person is more pleasant to Allah than the scent of musk. And He commands you to give charity. The parable of that, is a man captured by his enemies, tying his hands to his neck, and they come to him to beat his neck. Then he said: "I can ransom myself from you with a little or a lot" so he ransoms himself from them. And He commands you to remember Allah. For indeed the parable of that, is a man whose enemy quickly tracks him until he reaches an impermeable fortress in which he protects himself from them. This is how the worshiper is; he does not protect himself from Ash-Shaitan except by the remembrance of Allah.'"

The Prophet (ﷺ) said: "And I command you with five that Allah commanded me: Listening and obeying, Jihad, Hijrah, and the Jama'ah. For indeed whoever parts from the Jama'ah the measure of a hand-span, then he has cast off the yoke of Islam from his neck, unless he returns. And whoever calls with the call of Jahiliyyah then he is from the coals of Hell."

A man said: "O Messenger of Allah! Even if he performs Salat and fasts?" So he (ﷺ) said: "Even if he performs Salat and fasts. So call with the call that Allah named you with: Muslims, believers, worshipers of Allah."

Source: Jami` at-Tirmidhi 2863 Grade: Sahih

It was narrated that Jabir bin 'Abdullah said:

"The Messenger of Allah (ﷺ) delivered a sermon to us and said: 'O people! Repent to Allah before you die. Hasten to do good deeds before you become preoccupied (because of sickness and old age). Uphold the relationship that exists between you and your Lord by remembering Him a great deal and by giving a great deal of charity in secret and openly. (Then) you will be granted provision and Divine support, and your condition will improve. Know that Allah has enjoined Friday upon you in this place of mine, on this day, in this month, in this year, until the Day of Resurrection. Whoever abandons it, whether during my lifetime or after I am gone, whether he has a just or an unjust ruler, whether he takes it lightly or denies (that it is obligatory), may Allah cause him to lose all sense of tranquility and contentment, and may He not bless him in his affairs. Indeed, his prayer will not be valid, his Zakat will not be valid, his Hajj will not be valid, his fasting will not be valid, and his

righteous deeds will not be accepted, until he repents. Whoever repents, Allah will accept his repentance. No woman should be appointed as Imam over a man, no Bedouin should be appointed as Imam over a Muhajir, no immoral person should be appointed as Imam over a (true) believer, unless that is forced upon him and he fears his sword or whip.'"

Source: Sunan Ibn Majah 1081 Grade: Daif

Narrated 'Amr bin Shu'aib:

It was narrated from 'Amr bin Shu'aib, from his father, from his grandfather, that Marthad bin Abi Marthad Al-Ghanawi --a strong man who used to take the prisoners from Makkah to Al-Madinah-- said: "I arranged with a man to bring him (from Makkah to Al-Madinah). There was a prostitute in Makkah who was called 'Anaq, and she was his friend. She came out and saw my shadow on the wall, and said: 'Who is this? Marthad? Welcome, O Marthad, come tonight and stay at our place.' I said: 'O 'Anaq, the Messenger of Allah has forbidden adultery.' She said: 'O people of the tents, this porcupine is the one who is taking your prisoners from Makkah to Al-Madinah!' I headed toward (the mountain of) Al-Khandamah, and eight men came after me. They came and stood over my head, and they urinated, and their urine reached me, but Allah caused them not to see me. Then I went to my companion (the prisoner) and brought him to Al-Arak, where I undid his fetters. Then I came to the Messenger of Allah and said: 'O Messenger of Allah, shall I marry 'Anaq?' He remained silent and did not answer me, then the following was revealed: 'And the adulteress-fornicator, none marries her except an adulterer-fornicator or an idolater.' He called me and recited them to me and said: 'Do not marry her.'"

Source: Sunan an-Nasa'i 3228 Grade: Hasan

Salim bin 'Abdullah narrated that his father said:

"The Messenger of Allah said: "There are three at whom Allah will not look on the Day of Resurrection: The one who disobeys his parents, the woman who imitates men in her outward appearance, and the cuckold. And there are three who will not enter Paradise: The one who disobeys his parents, the drunkard, and the one who reminds people of what he has given them."'

Source: Sunan an-Nasa'i 2562 Grade: Hasan

Abu Sa'id Al-Khudri reported:

Prophet of Allah (ﷺ) said: "There was a man from among a nation before you who killed ninety-nine people and then made an inquiry about the most learned person on *the earth. He was directed to a monk. He came to him and told him that he had killed ninety-nine people and asked him if there was any chance for his repentance to be accepted. He replied in the negative and the man killed him also completing one hundred. He then asked about the most learned man in the earth. He was directed to a scholar. He told him that he had killed one hundred people and asked him if there was any chance for his repentance to be accepted. He replied in the affirmative and asked, 'Who stands between you and repentance? Go to such and such land; there (you will find) people devoted to prayer and worship of Allah, join them in worship, and do not come back to your land because it is an evil place.' So he went away and hardly had he covered half the distance when death overtook him; and there was a dispute between the angels of mercy and the angels of torment. The angels of mercy pleaded, 'This man has come with a repenting heart to Allah,' and the angels of punishment argued, 'He never did a virtuous deed in his life.' Then there appeared another angel in the form of a human being and the contending angels agreed to make him arbiter between them. He said, 'Measure the distance between the two lands. He will be considered belonging to the land to which he is nearer.' They measured and found him closer to the land (land of piety)* where he intended to go, and so the angels of mercy collected his soul".

Source: Riyad as-Salihin 20 Grade: Sahih

It was narrated that Ibn Dailami said:

"I was confused about this Divine Decree (Qadar), and I was afraid lest that adversely affect my religion and my affairs. So I went to Ubayy bin Ka'b and said: 'O Abu Mundhir! I am confused about the Divine Decree, and I fear for my religion and my affairs, so tell me something about that through which Allah may benefit me.' He said: 'If Allah were to punish the inhabitants of His heavens and of his earth, He would do so and He would not be unjust towards them. And if He were to have mercy on them, His mercy would be better for them than their own deeds. If you had the equivalent of Mount Uhud which you spent in the cause of Allah, that would not be accepted from you until you believed in the Divine Decree and you know that whatever has befallen you, could not have passed you by; and whatever has passed you by, could not have befallen you; and that if you were to die believing anything other than this, you would enter Hell. And it will not harm you to go to my brother, 'Abdullah bin Mas'ud, and ask him (about this).'

So I went to 'Abdullah and asked him, and he said something similar to what Ubayy had said, and he told me: 'It will not harm you to go to Hudhaifah.' So I went to Hudhaifah and asked him, and he said something similar to what they had said. And he told me: 'Go to Zaid bin Thabit and ask him.' So I went to Zaid bun Thabit and asked him, and he said: 'I heard the Messenger of Allah (ﷺ) say: "If Allah were to punish the inhabitants of His heavens and of His earth, he would do so and He would not be unjust towards them. And if He were to have mercy on them, His mercy would be better for them than their own deeds. If you had the equivalent of Mount Uhud which you spent in the cause of Allah, that would not be accepted from you until you believed in the Divine Decree and you know that whatever has befallen you, could not have passed you by; and whatever has passed you by, could not have befallen you; and that if you were to die believing anything other than this, you would enter Hell."*

Source: Sunan Ibn Majah 77 Grade: Sahih

Narrated `Imran bin Husain:

A man said, "O Allah's Messenger (ﷺ)! Can the people of Paradise be known (differentiated) from the people of the Fire; The Prophet (ﷺ) replied, "Yes." The man said,

"Why do people (try to) do (good) deeds?" The Prophet said, *"Everyone will do the deeds for which he has been created to do or he will do those deeds which will be made easy for him to do."* (i.e. everybody will find easy to do such deeds as will lead him to his destined place for which he has been created).

Source: Sahih al-Bukhari 6596

Narrated Sahl bin Sa`d:

Allah's Messenger (ﷺ) said, "Whoever can guarantee (the chastity of) what is between his two jaw-bones and what is between his two legs (i.e. his tongue and his private parts), I guarantee Paradise for him."

Source: Sahih al-Bukhari 6474

It was narrated that Ma`qil ibn Yassar said:

the Messenger of Allah said: "For one of you to be stabbed in the head with an iron needle is better for him than that he should touch a woman who is not permissible for him."

Source: Al-Kabir by Tabrani 486 Grade: Sahih

Narrated Abu Huraira:

Allah's Messenger (ﷺ) said, "Allah says, 'If My slave intends to do a bad deed then (O Angels) do not write it unless he does it; if he does it, then write it as it is, but if he refrains from doing it for My Sake, then write it as a good deed (in his account). (On the other hand) if he intends to do a good deed, but does not do it, then write a good deed (in his account), and if he does it, then write it for him (in his account) as 10 good deeds up to 700 times.'"

Source: Sahih al-Bukhari 7501

Abu Huraira reported:

The Messenger of Allah said, "Among the perfection of one's Islam is to leave what does not concern him."

Source: Sunan al-Tirmidhī 2679 Grade: Hasan

It is narrated on the authority of Abu Hurairah that the Messenger of Allah said:

"Faith has over seventy branches or over sixty branches, the most excellent of which is the declaration that there is no god worthy of worship but Allah, and the humblest of which is the, removal of what is injurious from the path: and modesty is a branch of faith."

Source: Sahih Muslim 35b

It was narrated from Atiyyah As-Sa'di, who was one of the Companions of the Prophet (ﷺ), that the Messenger of Allah (ﷺ) said:

"A person will not reach the status of being one of those who have piety until he refrains from doing something in which there is no sin, for fear of falling into something in which there is sin."

Source: Sunan Ibn Majah 4215 Grade: Hasan

Abdullah related the Messenger of Allah (ﷺ) said:

"He who has in his heart the weight of a mustard seed of pride shall not enter Paradise."

Source: Sahih Muslim 91c

Narrated Abu Huraira:

Allah's Messenger said, "All my followers will enter Paradise except those who refuse."

They said, "O Allah's Messenger! Who will refuse?"

He(Prophet Muhammad) said, "Whoever obeys me will enter Paradise, and whoever disobeys me is the one who refuses (to enter it)."

Source: Sahih Bukhari 7280

www.ingramcontent.com/pod-product-compliance
Lightning Source LLC
Chambersburg PA
CBHW050253010526
44107CB00003B/310